THE GEOPOLITICAL ECONOMY OF SPORT

This is the first book to define and explore the geopolitical economy of sport – the intersection of power, politics, money, and state interests that both exploit and shape elite sport around the world.

Russia's invasion of Ukraine, the global response, and the consequent ramifications for sport have put the geopolitical economy of sport front and centre in both public debate and academic thinking. Similarly, the Winter Olympics in Beijing and the FIFA World Cup in Qatar illustrate the political, economic, and geographic imperatives that shape modern sport. This book brings together studies from around the world to describe this new geopolitical economy of sport, from the way in which countries use natural resource revenues, accusations of sport washing, and the deployment of sport for soft power purposes, to the way in which sport has become a focus for industrial development. This book looks at the geopolitical economy of sport across the globe, from the Gulf States' interests in European soccer to Israel seeking to build a national competitive advantage by positioning itself as a global sports tech start-up hub, and the United States continuing to extend its economic and cultural influence through geopolitical sport activities in Africa, Latin America, and the Indian subcontinent. This book captures a pivotal moment in the history of sport and sport business.

This is essential reading for any student, researcher, practitioner, or policymaker with an interest in sport business, the politics of sport, geopolitics, soft power, diplomacy, international relations, or international political economy.

Simon Chadwick is Professor of Sport and Geopolitical Economy at Skema Business School in Paris, France, where he is also a member of its Publika think tank and Director of its Global Executive MBA in Sport. Chadwick's work combines his global interests in sport, geography, politics, and economics, meaning that his current research is focused on, for example, ownership and sponsorship in football by state-owned corporations. He has worked extensively in sport with clubs, governing bodies, commercial partners, and governments.

Paul Widdop is Senior Lecturer at the University of Manchester, UK. His research explores social and economic networks around the consumption and production of sport. He has published widely in the areas of sport and culture including articles in the *Journal of Consumer Culture, Cultural Sociology, Cultural Trends, Electoral Studies*, and the *Journal of Political Marketing*. Widdop serves on the editorial board of several academic journals and is co-founder of the Football Collective, a learned society of academics researching impacts of football on society.

Michael M. Goldman is Professor with the Sport Management Program at the University of San Francisco, USA, while also working with the Gordon Institute of Business Science in South Africa. He works with students, managers, and clients to enhance their abilities to acquire, grow, and retain profitable customers and fans.

THE GEOPOLITICAL ECONOMY OF SPORT

Power, Politics, Money, and the State

Edited by Simon Chadwick, Paul Widdop, and Michael M. Goldman

LONDON AND NEW YORK

Designed cover image: Maksym Tymchyk

First published 2023
by Routledge
4 Park Square, Milton Park, Abingdon, Oxon OX14 4RN

and by Routledge
605 Third Avenue, New York, NY 10158

Routledge is an imprint of the Taylor & Francis Group, an informa business

© 2023 selection and editorial matter, Simon Chadwick, Paul Widdop
and Michael M. Goldman; individual chapters, the contributors

The right of Simon Chadwick, Paul Widdop and Michael M. Goldman
to be identified as the authors of the editorial material, and of the
authors for their individual chapters, has been asserted in accordance
with sections 77 and 78 of the Copyright, Designs and Patents Act 1988.

All rights reserved. No part of this book may be reprinted or reproduced
or utilised in any form or by any electronic, mechanical, or other
means, now known or hereafter invented, including photocopying and
recording, or in any information storage or retrieval system, without
permission in writing from the publishers.

Trademark notice: Product or corporate names may be trademarks
or registered trademarks, and are used only for identification and
explanation without intent to infringe.

British Library Cataloguing-in-Publication Data
A catalogue record for this book is available from the British Library

Library of Congress Cataloging-in-Publication Data
Names: Chadwick, Simon, 1964- editor. | Widdop, Paul, editor. |
Goldman, Michael M., editor.
Title: The geopolitical economy of sport : power, politics, money
and the state / edited by Simon Chadwick, Paul Widdop and
Michael M. Goldman.
Description: Abingdon, Oxon ; New York, N.Y. : Routledge, 2023. |
Includes bibliographical references and index. |
Identifiers: LCCN 2022057046 | ISBN 9781032390611 (hardback) |
ISBN 9781032390598 (paperback) | ISBN 9781003348238 (ebook)
Subjects: LCSH: Sports and international relations. | Sports--Political
aspects. | Sports--Economic aspects. | Sports and state. | Nationalism
and sports. | Geopolitics.
Classification: LCC GV706.35 .G465 2023 | DDC 306.4/83--dc23/
eng/20230109
LC record available at https://lccn.loc.gov/2022057046

ISBN: 978-1-032-39061-1 (hbk)
ISBN: 978-1-032-39059-8 (pbk)
ISBN: 978-1-003-34823-8 (ebk)

DOI: 10.4324/9781003348238

Typeset in Bembo
by Deanta Global Publishing Services, Chennai, India

CONTENTS

List of Contributors	ix
1 Introduction: Towards a Geopolitical Economy of Sport *Simon Chadwick, Paul Widdop, and Michael M. Goldman*	1

PART I
Russia and Ukraine   7

2 Athletes' Early Responses to the War Against Ukraine *Leo Goretti*	9
3 Sport Sanctions Against Invasive Russia *Daryl Adair*	20
4 What Future for Putin's Sport Power? *Lukas Aubin*	29
5 Governance Dysfunction in World Sport: Issues Raised by the Conflict in Ukraine *Sergey Altukhov*	36
6 Public Remembering of Sochi 2014 at a Time of War: The Kremlin's Soft Disempowerment through Sport *Vitaly Kazakov*	42

vi Contents

7 Transnational Leagues and Their Role in Projecting Soft Power 49
Olivier Jarosz, Konstantin Kornakov, and Adam Metelski

PART II
China 65

8 The International Paralympic Committee, Beijing
2022 Winter Paralympic Games, and the Invasion of Ukraine 67
Verity Postlethwaite

9 Israel's Winter Sports Diplomacy and Beijing 2022 75
Yoav Dubinsky

10 The Global Sporting Power Elite: Eileen Gu 85
Donna Wong and Yue Meng-Lewis

11 China's Moves to Influence the Geopolitical Economy of
Sports: The Three Axe Strokes 93
Lingling Liu and Dan Zhang

12 Making of (Not Only) a Sports Superpower: The Chinese
Dream 101
Abhishek Khajuria

13 Chinese Super League: Soft Power, Investment, and
Sustainability 108
Ricardo Gúdel and Emilio Hernández

14 Doing Sports Business in China: Still a Slam Dunk? 116
Jonathan Sullivan and Tobias Ross

PART III
The Gulf and South Asia 125

15 Qatar and the 2022 FIFA World Cup: Soft Power, State
Branding, or Nation Building? 127
Kristian Coates Ulrichsen

16 Geopolitics of Sport in the MENA Region 134
Mahfoud Amara and Sara Mehanna Al-Naimi

Contents **vii**

17 Sport and Saudi Arabia: Mimetic Isomorphism, Soft Power, and Disempowerment 141
Nicholas Burton and Michael L. Naraine

18 Sport Washing and the Gulf Region: Myth or Reality? 148
Simon Chadwick and Paul Widdop

19 Geopolitics of Cricket in India 155
Mohit Anand

PART IV
Africa 163

20 Africa in the Global Football Business Complex 165
Gerard A. Akindes

21 The NBA's Partnership with Rwanda 173
Michael M. Goldman and Jeffrey W. Paller

PART V
Football 183

22 The Politics of Alternative Football: Curious Friends 185
Steve Menary

23 The Conjunctural Politics of the 2026 FIFA Men's World Cup: United 2026 191
Adam S. Beissel

24 The Attempted Reshaping of the Turkish Football Landscape under the AK Party: A Transaction Cost Economics Explanation 203
Steven H. Seggie

25 Football and the City: A Sports Place Branding Perspective of Barcelona and Manchester 210
Xavier Ginesta and Carles Viñas

26 The European Super League and Football's Privatization 217
Alexey Kirichek

viii Contents

PART VI
Motorsport

225

27 Sport Governance, Geopolitical Change, and Organizational
Resilience: The Case of *Fédération Internationale de
l'Automobile* (FIA)
Hans Erik Næss

227

28 The Geopolitics of Money Versus Morals: Location,
Location, Location of the Formula 1 Race Calendar
Tim Dewhirst

235

29 The End of Oil?: Formula One's Changing Face
Josh Rayman

242

PART VII
Peace, Diplomacy, and Society

251

30 Sport, Geo-Politics, and the Peace Process
Grant Jarvie

253

31 Sports Diplomacy in the Pacific Region and the
Sino-Australian Great Game
Stuart Murray and Tony Yang

262

32 Sports, Race, and Cosmopolitanism
J.P. Singh

271

33 Transgender Sport Bans Come for Elite Sport: Federations'
New Attempt to Define Womanhood
Sydney Bauer

277

PART VIII
Implications

285

34 What the Cases of Gazprom, the NBA, and Qatar Mean for
Sport Industry Decision-Makers
Simon Chadwick and Paul Widdop

287

Index

295

LIST OF CONTRIBUTORS

Daryl Adair is Associate Professor of Sport Management at the Business School, University of Technology Sydney, Australia. Daryl is interested in sport history, politics, and policy, with an eclectic engagement in contemporary issues as they pertain to sport and society. He is on the editorial boards of *Sport and Society*, *Journal of Sport History*, and *Performance Enhancement and Health*.

Gerard Akindes is Adjunct Faculty at Northwestern University, Qatar, and New York University, USA. In Qatar, he worked as senior insight and research manager for the Josoor Institute, a legacy programme of the FIFA World Cup Qatar 2022. He co-created an annual conference on sports in Africa (the 15th was held at Nelson Mandela University, South Africa, in June 2021). He also co-founded SportsAfrica Network, an African sports scholars and practitioners organization.

Sarah Muhanna Al-Naimi is Researcher at the Diplomatic Institute at the Ministry of Foreign Affairs, Qatar, and is a PhD student in "Gulf Studies" at Qatar University. Her academic and research vocation is to explore Qatar's foreign policy, demonstrate how non-traditional tools enabled branding Qatar's image regionally and internationally.

Sergey Altukhov is Professor and Director of the Institute of Sports Management and Law in the Higher School of Law and Administration of the NRU HSE, Russia. He is the Academics Director of the International Sport Management Master programme at this university. His main research interests deal with good governance in sport and geopolitics in sport. He is Visiting Professor at the Russian International Olympic University, a member of the Council for Professional Qualifications in Sports, and a member of the Expert Council for Physical Culture, Sports and Tourism of the Russian Parliament.

x List of Contributors

Mahfoud Amara is Associate Professor of Sport Social Sciences and Management in the Physical Education & Sport Science Department, College of Education at Qatar University, Qatar. His work focuses on sport, business, culture, politics, and society in the MENA region, and sport, cultural diversity, and Muslim communities in the West. He has been invited as speaker and expert to a number of working groups, international conferences, symposia, panels, and lecture series/webinars.

Mohit Anand is a Professor in International Business and Strategy at the EMLYON Business School, France. Dr. Anand has over 17 years of experience in industry and academia. Within the fields of International Business and Strategy, his research interests include Emerging Markets, Innovation, and BOP studies. While his focus area of study is inclined towards Microinsurance and Frugal and Reverse Innovation, more recent areas of interest also include Geopolitics in Asia, Regional Trade Blocs, and Public Policy Innovations. He has been a visiting faculty member at Shri Ram College of Commerce (SRCC), the University of Delhi, and ESCE (Paris). Previously he was Associate Professor at FORE School of Management (New Delhi) where he also headed the "Centre for Emerging Markets". Several of his papers have been published and presented in leading international journals and conferences. In 2018, he received Milliman Fellow in Microinsurance at ILO-ITC Impact Insurance Academy, Turin, Italy.

Lukas Aubin is Senior Research Fellow at the French Institute for International and Strategic Affairs (IRIS), Doctor in Slavic studies, specialist in the geopolitics of Russia and sport, and member of the Multidisciplinary Research Center (CRPM) of Paris Nanterre-University of Paris Lumières, France. His studies mainly focus on the new geopolitical issues of Russia and sport. He is also interested in the question of sovereignty within the post-Soviet space.

Sydney Bauer is a Freelance Journalist who has covered the Olympic Movement for the past decade. She began her work at Around the Rings and was based in Rio de Janeiro for the final year of preparations for the 2016 Olympics. Having covered every Olympics since London 2012, she is reporting in a freelance capacity on understanding how sporting bodies' growing political power intersects with the world at large, specifically when it relates to marginalized communities.

Adam Beissel is Assistant Professor of Sport Leadership & Management at Miami University, Ohio, USA. Adam's scholarship interrogates the geopolitical economy of sport. His primary research interests include: the economics of sport mega-events, geopolitics of sport, sport stadiums and urban development, social and economic (in)justice in college sport, sports labour markets, and global athletic migration and sport globalization. Beissel is currently working on two research projects critically examining the political economy of the 2023 FIFA Women's World Cup in Australia and New Zealand and the 2026 FIFA Men's World Cup jointly hosted by Canada, Mexico, and the United States.

List of Contributors **xi**

Nicholas Burton (PhD, Coventry University) is an Associate Professor in the Department of Sport Management at Brock University. His research explores sport business and marketing strategy, with particular interest in sponsorship management, social media marketing and user engagement, and sport's geopolitical positioning.

Timothy Dewhirst is Professor in the Department of Marketing and Consumer Studies and Senior Research Fellow in Marketing and Public Policy at the Gordon S. Lang School of Business and Economics at the University of Guelph, Canada. He has held visiting scholar positions at the University of California, San Francisco, University of Sydney, in Australia, and Hanyang University in South Korea. He is Associate Editor of the journal *Tobacco Control*, and he serves on the Editorial Review Board for the *Journal of Public Policy & Marketing*. Additionally, he served as an invited expert for the WHO with respect to Article 13 guidelines, concerning cross-border advertising, promotion, and sponsorship of the Framework Convention on Tobacco Control (FCTC).

Yoav Dubinsky is Instructor of Sports Business in the Lundquist College of Business, at the University of Oregon, USA. His research focuses on sports, nation branding, and public diplomacy. Dubinsky covered or researched four summer Olympic Games as an accredited journalist from Beijing, London, Rio de Janeiro, and Tokyo; attended the Lausanne 2020 Winter Youth Olympic Games; and lectured at the International Olympic Academy in Olympia, Greece.

Xavier Ginesta is Associate Lecturer in Media Studies and Sport Communication at the University of Vic-Central University of Catalonia (UVic-UCC), Spain. His PhD thesis is about Sport Corporate Communication in LaLiga, and he has been a research fellow of the Olympics Studies Center at the Autonomous University of Barcelona, Spain. He is currently a member of the TRACTE Research Group at the UVic-UCC, where he works on sports place branding and sport diplomacy.

Leo Goretti is Senior Fellow in the Italian Foreign Policy Programme at the Istituto Affari Internazionali (IAI), Rome, Italy, and co-editor of *The International Spectator*, the peer-reviewed English-language journal of IAI. He holds a PhD in history from the University of Reading, UK.

Ricardo Gúdel is Associate Lecturer of Business Management and International Trade at the University of Valladolid, Spain. He is also a member of the International Trade Chair and the Asian Studies Centre of the Faculty of Commerce. Gúdel is currently a PhD candidate, and his thesis focuses on studying the development and internationalization of football industries in Asia. In recent years, he has developed his professional activity in foreign trade and the sports field, working as a grassroots football coach at Real Valladolid. His research focuses mainly on overseas sports industries, and the cultural impact on business management.

xii List of Contributors

Emilio Hernández is Coordinator of the China Department of the Asian Studies Centre at the University of Valladolid, Spain, and Lecturer at the Faculty of Commerce. He has worked and researched in China for two years in the tourism and trade sectors. His research also focuses on the Chinese sports industry, outbound Chinese tourism and its economic impact, international trade with China, and intercultural relations in companies and organizations.

Olivier Jarosz has over ten years of experience in research and development activities in the European Club Association (ECA), where he was also the Head of Club Affairs and Club Management Programme Director. He was one of the architects of the UEFA Women's Champions League reform and cooperated with clubs all over the world. He has been a guest of over 200 football clubs in Europe, the United States, Asia, and the Middle East. Olivier is the author of many publications on football, concerning youth academies, women's football as well as club management and strategy.

Grant Jarvie is Professor and Chair of Sport at the University of Edinburgh, UK. He is Visiting Professor with the University of Toronto, Canada, and has held senior positions in both universities and the sports industry. He is Vice-Convener of the Iona Community and a director with Scottish Football Clubs.

Vitaly Kazakov is an ESRC Postdoctoral Fellow in the School of Arts, Languages and Cultures at the University of Manchester, UK. His research interests include media events, social media, nation projection, and soft power. Previously, he has worked as a Lecturer in Politics at the Universities of Liverpool and Manchester, Postdoctoral Research Associate at the University of Manchester, and as a journalist and communications specialist in Canada and Russia.

Abhishek Khajuria is a PhD candidate at the Centre for European Studies in the School of International Studies at Jawaharlal Nehru University, India. Apart from European politics (including electoral politics) and Indian foreign policy, he has a deep interest in sports which include the political role of sports and the economic aspects of sports and hopes to contribute to the field of geopolitical economy of sport.

Alexey Kirichek lectures in the Football Business Academy (Switzerland), European Sport Business School (Valencia), and Russian International Olympic University (Sochi, Russia). He is a member of Marketing Committee of Football Union of Russia and Consultant in the international sports projects including football grassroots events, sponsorship activations, and strategic development. His research interests include sports marketing, sport sponsorship, football management, and fan engagement.

List of Contributors **xiii**

Konstantin Kornakov is a club football expert with an analytical mind, a systematic approach to solving football's strategic challenges, and a keen interest in knowledge sharing and multidisciplinary methods, with a combined experience of almost two decades in the football industry in club operational and advisory roles.

Lingling Liu is a Sports Business Specialist with a long history of working in the sports industry on international relations, PR and communications, sponsorships, market research, and media operations in mega-events such as the Olympics and FIFA World Cup. She was a columnist for *Sport Business International*, and she recently founded Sports DAO Ltd. to bring blockchain strategy to sports projects and organizations.

Steve Menary is an author, journalist, and researcher. A regular contributor to *World Soccer* magazine and *Play the Game* for more than 15 years, he is also a CIES Havelange scholar and has lectured at the universities of East London, Southampton Solent, and Winchester and the Sport Business Centre at Birkbeck, University of London, UK.

Yue Meng-Lewis is Senior Lecturer (Associate Professor) in Digital Marketing at the Open University Business School, UK. Her research interests focus on international communication strategy, sports and digital marketing, and the esports ecosystem. Her publications have appeared in the *European Journal of Marketing, Journal of Business Research, International Journal of Human Resource Management, Information Technology & People*, as well as other international journals.

Adam Metelski is Assistant Professor at the Poznań University of Economics and Business, Poland. A former professional basketball player with experience in the United States and Europe, he has graduated from five universities in economics, psychology, and sociology.

Stuart Murray is Associate Professor in International Relations and Diplomacy at Bond University, Australia; Global Fellow at the Academy of Sport, the University of Edinburgh, UK; Honorary Member of the Centre for Sports Law, Policy and Diplomacy at the University of Rijeka, Croatia; and Adjunct Research Fellow at Griffith University Australia. He regularly advises governments, international institutions, and non-state actors on a broad range of matters relating to diplomacy, international affairs, and sport. He is also the co-founder of Sports Diplomacy Alliance, a global advisory and accreditation business that specializes in harnessing the power of sport to generate commercial, diplomatic, and social impact.

Hans Erik Næss is Professor of Sport Management at Kristiania University College, Norway. He is the author of several books on motorsports, politics, and organizational development.

xiv List of Contributors

Michael L. Naraine (PhD, University of Ottawa) is an Associate Professor in the Department of Sport Management at Brock University. His primary research explores digital sport management and marketing, specifically the strategy, engagement, and analytics of new developments in the sport business landscape.

Jeffrey Paller specializes in civic engagement, democratic accountability, and sustainable development in African cities. He curates the newsletter *This Week* in Africa.

Verity Postlethwaite is an early career researcher with extensive industry and higher education research experience. Her main interests and experiences are around how sport and other cultural entities have been used to govern society, with a specialty in international sporting events, inclusion, and international sports governance. Recent outputs include an integrative review of sport diplomacy in *Sport Management Review*.

Josh Rayman is a visual journalist and creative software developer based in London. His work has been published by the *New Statesman, The Times* and the BBC, specialising in election graphics. He competed as a racing driver for karts and cars for many years.

Tobias Ross is Doctoral Researcher in the School of Politics and IR, University of Nottingham, UK, as well as a consultant for international sports marketing projects.

Steven H. Seggie is Associate Professor of Marketing at ESSEC Business School, France, where he is also the Academic Director of the Weekend EMBA. He does research, teaching, and consulting on interorganizational relationships, innovation, and sport, particularly football. He previously hosted a football programme on the nationally syndicated radio station Lig Radyo in Turkey. He is a member of Morton Club Together, the biggest shareholder in Greenock Morton Football Club.

J.P. Singh is Professor of Global Commerce and Policy at the Schar School of Policy and Government, and Richard von Weizsäcker Fellow with the Robert Bosch Academy, Germany. He works at the intersection of technology, culture, and political economy in global contexts. Singh has consulted or advised international organizations such as the British Council, UNESCO, the World Bank, and the World Trade Organization, and conducted field research in 36 countries. In 2022, the International Studies Association named him a distinguished scholar in international communication.

Jonathan Sullivan is Associate Professor in the School of Politics and IR, and Head of China Programmes in the Asia Research Institute, University of Nottingham, UK.

List of Contributors **xv**

Kristian Coates Ulrichsen is Fellow for the Middle East at Rice University's Baker Institute for Public Policy, USA. His research spans the history, political, and international political economy, and international relations of the Gulf States and their changing position within the global order.

Carles Viñas is Associate Serra Hunter Lecturer at the University of Barcelona (UB), Spain. His main research interests are sport, hooliganism, and political movements. He is a member of the International Historical Studies Centre Research Group (GREC-CEHI) at UB.

Donna Wong is Associate Professor in Graduate School of Sport Sciences at Waseda University, Japan. Her research focuses on the managerial aspects of sport. She has researched and published extensively on sports mega-events, digital sports media, and esports. She is holder of both the International Olympic Committee Postgraduate Research Grant and FIFA Research Scholarship. Additionally, her co-authored research on esports with Dr Meng-Lewis has won the Best Paper award at the 2019 Annual European Association for Sport Management Conference. She is currently working on her research on digital sports as well as the legacy of the 2020 Tokyo Olympic Games.

Tony Yang is Assistant Teaching Fellow at Bond University, Australia, and is currently undertaking his PhD research in regard to "China's sports diplomacy". Yang has experience in several football clubs from China, England, Australia, and Portugal, and has completed two postgraduate programmes: Master of Sport Management from De Montfort University, UK, and Master of International Relations from Bond University, Australia. Yang is also a qualified and active football referee registered in the Football Queensland.

Dan Zhang is Lecturer in Marketing and Advertising with Coventry University, UK, and wrote for *Sport Business International* as a freelance Chinese journalist.

1

INTRODUCTION

Towards a Geopolitical Economy of Sport

Simon Chadwick, Paul Widdop, and Michael M. Goldman

In late 2021, reports emerged that a Chinese female professional tennis player – Peng Shuai – had posted a message on social media claiming that she had been coerced into a sexual relationship with one of her country's senior government officials. The post was rapidly deleted, and stories then began to circulate that the athlete had disappeared. Many people, including fellow professional tennis players, began demanding to know what had happened to Peng. Shortly afterwards, the International Olympic Committee president – Thomas Bach – appeared in photographs, apparently in a video call with the missing athlete. This was immediately questioned by observers and critics, though Bach was presumably mindful of the potential for a large-scale boycott of the impending 2022 Winter Olympics in Beijing. Calls for a boycott of the event had been a predominant feature of the run-up to the event, notably in response to China's treatment of its Uyghur community. Whatever the IOC president's motives or intentions, the Women's Tennis Association, an organization founded and based in the United States, subsequently announced that it would be suspending its tournaments in China following the Peng episode. In due course, Peng re-appeared in public, though many remained unconvinced that she was in control of her own liberty and free to speak openly. Nevertheless, the tennis player was eventually seen in the front row at an Olympic freestyle skiing event in Beijing, at which Eileen Gu won the gold medal. Gu herself comes with an interesting story: born and raised in the United States to a Chinese mother and estranged American father; a rising star in possession of naming rights deals with the likes of Red Bull, at the same time competing for China and being seen as an instrument of propaganda for the Chinese state.

Once the Beijing Winter Olympics had ended, though even before the Winter Paralympics had started, Russia invaded Ukraine. Within days, the global sport community had responded, with Russian athletes, teams, and governing bodies

DOI: 10.4324/9781003348238-1

being suspended from participation and membership. The response of European football's governing body – UEFA – was especially notable. Its men's Champions League competition had been sponsored for nearly a decade by Russian state-owned Gazprom, which had been using its sponsorship portfolio for political purposes. At the same time, its chairman had been sitting on the board of UEFA's executive committee as a result of his position as president of the Russian Football Union. He had also been president of the Russian football club Zenit Saint Petersburg, itself owned by Gazprom, playing in a stadium owned by the gas corporation, located in a city in which Gazprom has its headquarters. Furthermore, with little more than four months to go, the men's Champions League Final was scheduled to take place at the Gazprom-owned venue. In response to Russia's military action, UEFA unilaterally terminated its Gazprom sponsorship, switched the upcoming match to Paris, and suspended Russia and its teams from all UEFA competitions.

At the end of 2022, Qatar stages the FIFA men's football World Cup – a tournament that has been hugely controversial in its organization. Less than 5 percent the size of Britain, Qatar has been linked to corruption scandals within FIFA, with critics claiming that it is an undeserving host of football's biggest national team competition. Yet Qatar is a gas- and oil-rich state that is going through a period of economic, political, and social transformation, driven by its long-planned staging of the World Cup. What some have seen as nation building on an epic scale, others have dismissed as ostentation driven by vanity. As the government in Doha has sought to project soft power through football, a popular discourse has arisen that frames Qatar as a sport washer. Though the country has worked hard to position itself as a more progressive Gulf nation (albeit underpinned by traditional Islamic values), critics highlight what they see as an archaic labour market system that has resulted in the exploitation and death of countless migrant workers. Yet Qatar is now a prominent and legitimate member of the global sport community, having staged many of sport's biggest international events and gained decision making influence within sport's governing institutions. At the same time, the likes of its state-owned airline – Qatar Airways – have established an impressive array of sport sponsorship properties. Yet at the same time, other sponsors will have stayed away from any association with the World Cup, fearing adverse consequences of being associated with the country in any way.

Adding to this chronology, there are numerous other examples of where sport, economics, politics, and geography interconnect and influence one another. In early 2022, Houthi drones attacked an industrial facility close to the Jeddah Formula 1 circuit in Saudi Arabia. A retaliatory strike against the country, the Houthis were responding to the kingdom's military actions in Yemen. F1 drivers were so concerned that they considered boycotting the race, which would have had significant economic, political, and legal consequences for a multitude of the sport's stakeholders. In both 2020 and 2021, the British government's attempts to facilitate the Saudi Arabian Public Investment Fund's acquisition of

Premier League club Newcastle United whilst establishing a fan-led review of club ownership were as confused as they were striking. Nonetheless, the British government illustrated the economic and political significance of English football, something that has been accumulated over decades and confers a global competitive advantage in football upon Great Britain. Or one can refer to the case of Colin Kaepernick and his taking the knee, which simultaneously became a socio-political matter as well as a business and commercial one. Upon the death of George Floyd, taking the knee became an important symbol of solidarity and demand for change across the world. All of which has thrust the issue of race into the spotlight of global sport ever since.

In these examples drawn from little more than a period of a few years, several things immediately become clear. Firstly, that the world (and, indeed, the world of sport) is densely interconnected, meaning that it is often impossible to create a demarcation between matters of geography, politics, and economics. At one level sport has become an important focal node of networks underpinned by a quest for power and control over important resources. At another level, sport has become the means to an end for countries, businesses, and others that are seeking to achieve goals that extend way beyond it. Sport is undoubtedly shaped by and is therefore an outcome of geography, both physical and human. One need only think of nations that perform well in alpine sports to understand such a statement. That Qatar and Saudi Arabia are spending lavishly on sport is fuelled by the oil and gas deposits that sit beneath their countries. Though people rail against sport and politics mixing, during the first quarter of the 21st century the two appear to be synonymous or in symbiosis rather than being remote from one another. Different ideologies increasingly underpin the organization and governance of sport, whilst countries compete with each other to successfully formulate strategy and policy in sport. For instance, South Korea was the first country in the world to adopt an esports strategy intended to position it as one of the world's leading industrial hubs. Such policy and strategy typically have an economic dimension, whereby contribution to national income, job creation, the generation of tax revenues, and the promotion of exports in sport becomes as important as sports themselves. One need only consider that the US NBA basketball competition is thought to have generated upwards of $500 billion in China alone is a testament to the economic significance of sport.

For the purposes of this book, we define the geopolitical economy of sport as being:

> The way in which nations, states, and other entities engage in, with or through sport for geographic, political and/or economic reasons in order to build and exert power, and secure strategic advantages through the control of resources within and via networks of which sport is a constituent part.
>
> *(Chadwick, 2022a)*

The editors recommend that readers who may wish to familiarize themselves with the origins and features of geopolitical economy read the above article, though one may also find other articles by Chadwick (2022b) and Chadwick and Widdop (2021) to be helpful. The purpose of this book is, nevertheless, not to address issues in its conceptualization. Rather, it is intended to highlight instances and issues that we believe should be classified as being geopolitically economic in nature. In conjunction with formative commentaries about it, this text is implicitly an assertion that this new way of conceiving sport is of paramount importance at this stage's history. Though we acknowledge the 19th-century utilitarian traditions of sport research and appreciate the contribution of neoclassical economics to understanding sport management in the 20th century, this book is intended as a bold assertion that a new conceptualization of sport – a new discipline in which people can engage in scholarly activity – needs to be adopted. It is anticipated that this book will make an important contribution in this regard. It is important that the reader notes both the multidisciplinary nature of sport's geopolitical economy and the diversity of its constituent members.

It is important for the reader to note that although this book does contain a plethora of chapters focusing on countries and states, they are not the extent of its geographic constituency. Cities, communities, and even individual athletes are amongst the other constituents we assert are part of sport's geopolitical economy. Likewise, governments, sovereign wealth funds, and sport governing bodies are amongst the political constituents. While sponsors, broadcasters, and apparel providers are just a small selection of the economic constituents. It is important to note too that, in spite of the mention above of the likes of China and Qatar, the geopolitical economy of sport is not exclusively an Asian phenomenon – it encapsulates the world. Ideology, diplomacy, and soft power are as much characteristics of Brazilian, Canadian, or Nigerian sport as they are of sport in China, India, or Japan. Equally, sport and the countries of Europe, and those in Oceania and elsewhere, are shaped by and are an influence upon the geopolitical economy.

The reader may wish to note that this book has adopted the following themes, into which chapters have been placed:

- Russia and Ukraine;
- China;
- The Gulf and South Asia
- Africa;
- Football;
- Motorsport;
- Peace, diplomacy, and society;
- Implications.

References

Chadwick, S. (2022a), How 2022 will epitomise sport's burgeoning geopolitical economy. *Institut de Relations Internationales et Strategiques*, 21st January, accessed via https://www.iris-france.org/164078-how-2022-will-epitomise-sports-burgeoning-geopolitical-economy/.

Chadwick, S. (2022b), From utilitarianism and neoclassical sport management to a new geopolitical economy of sport. *European Sport Management Quarterly*, 22 (5), pp. 685–704.

Chadwick, S., and Widdop, P. (2021), The geopolitical economy of sport – A new era in play. *Asia and the Pacific Policy Forum*, 13th January, accessed via https://www.policyforum.net/the-geopolitical-economy-of-sport/.

PART I

Russia and Ukraine

2

ATHLETES' EARLY RESPONSES TO THE WAR AGAINST UKRAINE

Leo Goretti

"No War in Ukraine": so read the sign held up by Ukrainian skeleton racer Vladyslav Heraskevych after he finished one of his runs at the Beijing Winter Olympics on 11 February 2022, amidst warnings that a Russian attack against Kyiv was imminent.[1] Less than a month later, on 5 March, while war was raging across Ukraine, Russian gymnast Ivan Kuliak took the podium at an Artistic Gymnastics World Cup event in Doha wearing the infamous "Z" symbol, associated with support for the Russian military.[2] Through their gestures, Heraskevych and Kuliak used international sports events to deliver opposing political messages – one for peace, the other for war – that were widely reported in the media and reached beyond their respective sports' audiences. Heraskevych's and Kuliak's actions were sensational but far from isolated: within a few weeks of the invasion, a significant number of elite athletes – not only Ukrainian and Russian, but also third-country nationals – took a public stand on the war, in most cases against it.

Athletes' public responses to the war on Ukraine are the latest chapter in the long history of athletes' agency – defined as the "capacity to act" for social and political purposes.[3] They highlight the role and limits of athletes' agency in an era marked by greater attention to humanitarian and human rights considerations on the one hand, and rising international tensions and fragmentation of global governance on the other.[4]

A New Era of Athletes' Agency?

Due to their public relevance and global media attention, major sports events such as the Olympics can offer a uniquely spectacular platform for athletes to make statements about wider sociopolitical issues.[5] This is especially the case for highly emotional events such as medal ceremonies, which have provided the stage for some of the most iconic examples of athletes' agency: first and foremost, Tommie

DOI: 10.4324/9781003348238-3

Smith and John Carlos's black-glove salute at the 1968 Mexico Olympics.[6] These on-field enactments of agency openly defy the self-professed "apolitical" and "neutral" nature of sport that has been part and parcel of the Olympic movement since its inception. Indeed, they bring to light political and social cleavages, undermining the belief that sport is pure recreation; furthermore, at the international level, they may highlight geopolitical tensions, thereby threatening the unity and the status quo of international sport. Not surprisingly, international sports organizations such as the International Olympic Committee (IOC) have long been at pains to prevent and sanction on-field exercise of agency, leading to a number of successive regulations, the most recent being Rule 50.2 of the Olympic Charter, mandating that "No kind of demonstration or political, religious or racial propaganda is permitted in any Olympic sites, venues or other areas".[7]

Historically, elite athletes taking a public stand have constituted a minority, even more so on-field. In recent years, however, an increasing number of sportspeople have publicly supported anti-racism, anti-discrimination, gender equality, and social justice initiatives. Especially after the wave of protests in response to the murder of George Floyd in late spring–summer 2020, the gesture of taking a knee before the start of matches, following the example of NFL quarterback Colin Kaepernick, has become fairly widespread among elite athletes, especially from North America.[8]

Hence, pressing questions about athletes' freedom of expression have emerged, leading the IOC to ask its Athletes' Commission "to explore whether a greater appetite exists among athletes worldwide to express themselves [...] during the Olympic Games".[9] A comprehensive survey administered to over 3,500 elite athletes from 185 different National Olympic Committees highlighted that 42 per cent of respondents deem it appropriate to have an opportunity to "express their individual views on political issues and other topics" in the media during the Games, while only 16 per cent find it appropriate to do so on the medal podium and 14 per cent on the field of play. Nonetheless, having an opportunity for "unified messaging around inclusion and solidarity on the field of play" is welcomed by 46 per cent of respondents.[10] Notably, athletes' responses vary significantly according to nationality: while 40 per cent of US athletes support "Allowing physical gestures in an Olympic venue, as a way to demonstrate or express a view", barely 10 per cent of Russian and 4 per cent of Chinese respondents find it important.[11] Furthermore, the Team USA Council on Racial and Social Justice provided detailed recommendations to the IOC Athletes' Commission, asking, among other things, to "Establish a no-punishment-policy for protests and demonstrations that are aimed at promoting human rights/social justice initiatives and advancing the human rights mission of the Olympic and Paralympic movements".[12]

The IOC consultation did not lead to a change in Rule 50.2; however, on the occasion of both the Tokyo 2020 and the Beijing 2022 Olympic Games, the Athletes' Commission published dedicated "Rule 50 Guidelines". The Guidelines clarified that athletes "have the opportunity to express their views" in a number of instances during the Games, not only when speaking to the media, but also "on the field of play prior to the start of the competition", provided that the gesture is "consistent with the Fundamental Principles of Olympism", not aimed at any specific target and not disruptive to the Games.[13]

Overall, already before the outbreak of the war in Ukraine, the number of elite athletes publicly expressing their views or taking a stand on sociopolitical issues – that is, exercising their agency – seemed to be on the rise.[14] This prompted a response by international sports organizations that, while reasserting the principle of sport's neutrality, partly relaxed their rules regarding athletes' activism. Russia's aggression against Ukraine, which was launched during the "Olympic Truce"[15] only a week before the Beijing Winter Paralympics were due to commence, triggered a new wave of statements and gestures by elite athletes. In contrast to anti-racist and anti-discrimination stances, which usually focused on domestic (especially US) matters, pro-peace (or pro-war) demonstrations directly involved issues of international politics. As such, they injected geopolitical tensions into international sports, piercing the veil of its alleged neutrality and universalism.

Elite Athletes and the War on Ukraine

In the early days following Russia's invasion of Ukraine, a substantial number of elite sportspeople expressed themselves against the war through interviews, public statements, and/or social media. Several of them went beyond generic declarations of solidarity and came out in support of a ban on teams and individuals officially representing Russia in international sports, even threatening to walk out of matches and competitions had international sports organizations failed to do so. This attitude was not limited to Ukrainians – many of whom quickly left the sports grounds to join the fight against the invaders[16] – but was shared by other (overwhelmingly Western) athletes: among the most prominent examples was the Polish men's football team, which on 26 February released a statement via social media in agreement with the Polish Football Association, expressing their intention not to compete against Russia in the upcoming World Cup qualifiers. The Polish were soon joined by the Swedish and Czech teams, leading FIFA to eventually ban Russia from all its competitions, including the World Cup.[17]

In the first week of the war, the primary focus of athletes' initiatives was on the upcoming Paralympic Games. On 27 February, a joint statement by several Ukrainian elite athletes – the first signatory being Vladyslav Heraskevych – and Global Athlete – an "athlete start-up movement aiming to inspire and drive change across the world of sport"[18] – was released, calling for the immediate suspension of the Russian and Belarusian National Olympic and Paralympic Committees, as well as a blanket ban on all Russian and Belarusian athletes from international sport, due to the violation of international law and the Olympic and Paralympic Charters by the two countries. A video message making similar demands and featuring Ukrainian Olympians was also released via social media. In the next days, the joint statement was signed by dozens of other sportspeople, both active and retired, in a personal or collective capacity, reaching a total of over 160 signatories on 2 March: among them, athletes from Ukraine, Russia, Belarus, and another 13 (overwhelmingly Western) countries.[19]

For its part, under joint pressure from Western affiliates, national governments, and public opinions, the IOC took action on 24 February ("strongly condemn[ing] the breach of the Olympic Truce by the Russian government"),[20] on 25 February (urging the relocation of all events due to be held in Russia and Belarus),[21] and on 28 February (recommending to all sports federations the outright exclusion of Russian and Belarusian athletes "[i]n order to protect the integrity of global sports competitions and for the safety of all the participants"). As an alternative to the ban, international sports federations were advised to allow the participation of Russian nationals "only as neutral athletes or neutral teams".[22] This approach was adopted in many events where athletes compete in personal capacity rather than as national representatives (such as the ATP and WTA tennis circuits) and was also the initial decision of the International Paralympic Committee (IPC) towards the Beijing Games.[23] The IPC, however, was soon forced to backtrack and exclude Russian and Belarusian players amidst growing tensions in the Paralympic village and signals that entire teams would walk out of competitions and matches featuring Russian athletes.[24] While parallel pressure from national committees and governments was certainly key, there is little doubt that the firm stance taken by several elite athletes contributed significantly to the introduction of the bans.

Notably, the IOC's recommendation to ban Russian athletes was framed by IOC President Thomas Bach not as a sanctioning measure, but rather as a "protective" one, which was also supposedly aimed at preventing the potential "politicisation of sports competitions by athletes or teams, some of them being encouraged by third parties".[25] According to this narrative, allowing the participation of Russian representatives would imply the risk of turning athletes and teams into geopolitical players, bringing conflict and tensions into the sporting fields; an outright exclusion of Russian sportspeople would therefore be less of a violation of sport's neutrality than allowing them to play against Ukrainian and Western athletes.

One may argue that this approach discounted the agency of Russian sportspeople in using international events to express dissenting views on the war. To be sure, in the early days of the war, several Russian athletes (especially tennis players) made pro-peace declarations and gestures, on-field, during press conferences, or via social media: the best-known example was perhaps Andrey Rublev, writing, "No War Please" on the TV camera during the Dubai Tennis Championships on 25 February 2022, while the 2021 French Open finalist Anastasia Pavlyuchenkova tweeted that she was "not afraid to clearly state [her] position [...] against war and violence. Personal ambitions or political motives cannot justify violence".[26] Unlike Pavlyuchenkova's, however, most of these statements remained fairly generic and came short of criticizing their country's government: this was the case, for example, of ice hockey superstar Alexander Ovechkin, who called for "no more war" during a press conference but, when asked whether he still supported Vladimir Putin, simply replied that "he is my President".[27] As the war progressed, the tightening authoritarian grip of Putin's regime substantially limited the space for dissent in Russian sport,[28] although with notable exceptions.[29] In contrast, a number of Russian athletes toed the official line and publicly supported the war: from the aforementioned episode involving Ivan Kuliak to the attendance of numerous high-profile Russian sportsmen and sportswomen – some of them donning jackets with the Z symbol – at the rally celebrating the eighth anniversary of the annexation of Crimea on 18 March.[30]

The issue of athletes' agency, and its limits, resurfaced with the blanket ban on Russian and Belarusian athletes announced by the organizers of the Wimbledon Championships in April. The ban was not compliant with the ATP's policy of allowing participation of Russian players under neutral flag and was immediately criticized as a potential form of "discrimination based on nationality" by the Association.[31] Wimbledon's organizers justified their decision by pointing to "the importance of not allowing sport to be used to promote the Russian regime and [...] broader concerns for public and player (including family) safety". The latter remark hinted at possible retaliation by the Kremlin against dissenting athletes and their families, which, in the organizers' view, made it impossible to ask for assurances about Russian players' opposition to Vladimir Putin's regime, as had initially been suggested by the UK sports minister.[32] Unlike the earlier bans, Wimbledon's decision was not supported by international sports organizations and seemed to drive a wedge between Ukrainian and other Western players. Ukraine's Marta Kostyuk, for example, repeatedly lamented the silence of Russian players about their country's war of aggression and welcomed the ban.[33] Instead, top Western athletes, such as Rafael Nadal and Andy Murray, opposed the ban initially, although they did not ultimately boycott the event.[34]

One of the reasons for the strong controversy behind the Wimbledon ban is its direct impact on a number of Russian players (like Andrey Rublev and Anastasia Pavlyuchenkova) who had previously taken a stand against the war. As tennis legend Martina Navratilova – who escaped from Communist Czechoslovakia to the United States in 1975 – noted, penalizing players who had "actually spoken out against the war at some potential personal cost" looked "hypocritical", especially considering that countries with a "questionable human rights record" had been systematically "validated" by being granted the organization of mega sports events in the recent past. In her view, the Wimbledon ban highlights once more how deeply "politics and sport are intertwined".[35]

Conclusion: Potential and Limits of Athletes' Agency in a Fragmented World

Much to the chagrin of those who would like them to simply 'shut up and dribble', elite athletes can leverage their fame and media attention to make powerful statements about social and political issues at both the domestic and international levels. When athletes take a stand on issues pertaining to the sphere of international politics, such as an armed conflict or the violation of human rights in another country, however, this implies the risk of heightened confrontation and fragmentation in international sport, undermining its self-professed neutrality and unity. Therefore, international sports organizations have historically tried to minimize the potential disruption of athletes' agency, as evidenced by their firm handling of anti-Israel boycotts at the Olympics and other international events.[36]

In the case of Russia's aggression against Ukraine, however, this was not the case. Not only were athletes' public stances against the war not sanctioned,[37] they effectively played a role in the decision of international sports organizations to introduce sanctioning measures against Russia and Belarus. To be sure, this was only possible due to the concurrent pressure from Western federations, governments, and public opinions denouncing a major violation of international law and of Olympic values (first and foremost, the Olympic truce). In effect, the public stance taken by Western federations and governments on the matter arguably facilitated and enhanced Western athletes' agency, and vice versa.

Significantly, the eventual ban on Russian athletes and teams from most international sports competitions was explicitly motivated by an attempt to prevent further politicization of international sport. Ivan Kuliak's infamous behaviour in Doha somehow hints at the level of tension that the presence of individuals and teams officially representing Russia (and its pro-war propaganda machine) may cause; at the same time, the exclusion of tennis players who had previously opposed the war from Wimbledon 2022 highlights how such bans may also suppress potential opportunities for dissenting Russian athletes to express agency. This is not to overlook, however, that the primary factor constraining the latter has undoubtedly been increased domestic authoritarianism in Russia.

Indeed, to properly understand its potential and limits, athletes' agency must be situated within structural boundaries set at both the domestic (regime type, foreign policy, sports policy) and international levels (international environment, rules, and politics of international sports organizations). These boundaries can facilitate, enhance, constrain, or even suppress athletes' agency altogether. Overall, greater attention to human rights among sportspeople and the general public, as well as rising international tensions and ongoing fragmentation of global governance,[38] suggests that athletes' agency in international sports may be destined to become more and more salient in the coming years.

Notes

1 *CNN* (2022).
2 Pavitt (2022); *BBC* (2022).
3 Braun *et al.* (2019), 788. Relatedly, and with specific reference to athletes' activism, see Totten (2016); Magrath (2022).
4 Chadwick and Widdop (2021).
5 Boykoff (2014), 41–44; Kilcline (2017), 4.
6 Boykoff (2017), 8–9.
7 Boykoff (2014), 51–57; International Olympic Committee (2021b), 94.
8 Ghani (2022); Haislop (2022); *The Guardian* (2020).
9 International Olympic Committee (2021a), 2.
10 Publicis Sport & Entertainment (2021), 10, 18.
11 Ibid., 41, 51, 53.
12 Team USA Council on Racial and Social Justice (2021).
13 International Olympic Committee (2021c), 3; International Olympic Committee (2022e), 3.
14 Lubbers (2021).
15 The Olympic Truce, supported by a resolution of the United Nations General Assembly, is a period running from the seventh day before the start of the Olympic Games until the seventh day following the end of the Paralympic Games, during which states are invited "to promote and strengthen a culture of peace and harmony" and, if involved in armed conflicts, "to boldly agree to true mutual ceasefires" (United Nations 2022).
16 Jack (2022).
17 McLaughlin (2022); Czech Football National Team (@ceskarepre_eng) (2022); FIFA (2022).
18 Global Athlete (2022b).
19 Global Athlete (2022a); Global Athlete (@GlobalAthleteHQ) (2022). The author is grateful to Jasmine Wu for her support in collecting these data.
20 International Olympic Committee (2022d).
21 International Olympic Committee (2022c).
22 International Olympic Committee (2022b).
23 International Tennis Federation (2022); International Paralympic Committee (2022).
24 Pells (2022); Heroux (@Devin_Heroux) (2022).
25 International Olympic Committee (2022a).
26 Holmes (2022); Newman (2022).
27 *CTV News* (2022).
28 *Reuters* (2022b).
29 *The Insider* (2022); Badshah (2022).
30 *AP News* (2022).
31 Association of Tennis Professionals (2022a); Association of Tennis Professionals (2022b).
32 Wimbledon (2022); *Reuters* (2022a).
33 Kostyuk (@Marta_Kostyuk) (2022); Sessions (2022).
34 Boren (2022).
35 Schmitz *et al.* (2022).
36 Close *et al.* (2021); Reiche (2018), 35–39.
37 The sign flashed by Vladyslav Heraskevych during the men's skeleton final, for example, was defined by IOC sources as "a general call for peace" and thus was not sanctioned (Reynolds 2022).
38 Acharya (2016), 453–460.

Bibliography

Acharya, Amitav (2016). 'The future of global governance.' *Global Governance* 22, no. 4: 453–460. DOI: 10.1163/19426720-02204001.

AP News (2022). 'Russian Olympians face backlash after Vladimir Putin rally.' 23 March. https://apnews.com/article/russia-ukraine-putin-winter-olympics-sports-skating-22860075081be288ceb96f328b226ca2.

Association of Tennis Professionals (2022a). 'ATP statement on decision to ban Russian & Belarusian players.' *ATP Tour*, 20 April. https://www.atptour.com/en/news/atp-statement-wimbledon-british-grass-swing-april-2022.

Association of Tennis Professionals (2022b). 'ATP statement on removal of ranking points at 2022 Wimbledon.' *ATP Tour*, 20 May. https://www.atptour.com/en/news/atp-statement-removal-of-ranking-points-wimbledon-2022.

Badshah, Nadeem (2022). 'Ex-Russian football captain Igor Denisov condemns invasion of Ukraine.' *The Guardian*, 15 June. https://www.theguardian.com/uk-news/2022/jun/15/former-footballer-igor-denisov-condemns-russias-war-in-ukraine.

BBC (2022). 'Russian gymnast Ivan Kuliak investigated for wearing pro-war symbol on podium next to Ukrainian.' 6 March. https://www.bbc.com/sport/gymnastics/60641891.

Boren, Cindy (2022). 'Rafael Nadal, Andy Murray oppose Wimbledon ban of Russians, Belarusians.' *The Washington Post*, 2 May. https://www.washingtonpost.com/sports/2022/05/01/rafael-nadal-rips-wimbledons-ban/.

Boykoff, Jules (2014). *Activism and the Olympics*. Rutgers University Press. https://www.rutgersuniversitypress.org/activism-and-the-olympics/9780813562018.

Boykoff, Jules (2017). 'Protest, activism, and the Olympic Games: An overview of key issues and iconic moments.' *The International Journal of the History of Sport* 34, no. 3–4: 162–183. https://doi.org/10.1080/09523367.2017.1356822.

Braun, Benjamin, Schindler, Sebastian, and Wille, Tobias (2019). 'Rethinking agency in international relations: Performativity, performances and actor-networks.' *Journal of International Relations and Development* 22: 787–807. https://doi.org/10.1057/s41268-018-0147-z.

Chadwick, Simon, and Widdop, Paul (2021). 'The geopolitical economy of sport.' *Policy Forum*, 13 January. https://www.policyforum.net/the-geopolitical-economy-of-sport/.

Close, David, Barnes, Taylor, and Najiim, Aqeel (2021). 'Algerian Olympian withdraws from games due to potential matchup with Israeli competitor.' *CNN*, 24 July. https://edition.cnn.com/2021/07/24/sport/algerian-olympian-withdrawal-israel-intl/index.html#:~:text=(CNN)%20Algerian%20judo%20athlete%20Fethi,can%20offer%20the%20Palestinian%20cause.%22.

CNN (2022). 'Ukrainian skeleton star goes from Winter Olympics to war zone in weeks.' 23 March. https://edition.cnn.com/videos/sports/2022/03/23/vladyslav-heraskevych-skeleton-ukraine-spt-intl.cnn.

CTV News (2022). '"Please, no more war": Alex Ovechkin addresses Russian invasion'. *YouTube*, 25 February. https://www.youtube.com/watch?v=vYoQfeed1-Q.

Czech Football National Team (@ceskarepre_eng) (2022). 'The Czech FA executive committee, staff members and players of the national team agreed it's not possible to play against the Russian national team in the current situation, not even on the neutral venue.' *Twitter*, 27 February. https://twitter.com/ceskarepre_eng/status/1497875324947865605.

FIFA (2022). 'FIFA/UEFA suspend Russian clubs and national teams from all competitions.' 28 February. https://www.fifa.com/tournaments/mens/worldcup/

qatar2022/media-releases/fifa-uefa-suspend-russian-clubs-and-national-teams-from -all-competitions.

Ghani, Faras (2022). 'Black lives matter: Should sports and politics mix?'. *Al Jazeera*, 6 July. https://www.aljazeera.com/features/2020/7/6/black-lives-matter-should -sports-and-politics-mix.

Global Athlete (2022a). 'Open letter to IOC and IPC from Ukrainian athletes.' 5 March. https://globalathlete.org/our-word/open-letter-from-ukraine-athletes.

Global Athlete (2022b). 'What is global athlete.' https://globalathlete.org/about.

Global Athlete (@GlobalAthleteHQ) (2022). 'Global Athlete has been asked by the Ukrainian Athletes to post this video addressed to the #IOC and #IPC.' *Twitter*, 28 February. https://twitter.com/GlobalAthleteHQ/status/1498284091892023297.

Haislop, Tadd (2022). 'Colin Kaepernick kneeling timeline: How protests during the national anthem started a movement in the NFL.' *The Sporting News*, 13 September. https://www.sportingnews.com/us/nfl/news/colin-kaepernick-kneeling-protest -timeline/xktu6ka4diva1s5jxaylrcsse.

Heroux, Devin (@Devin_Heroux) (2022). 'Here are the Latvian wheelchair curling coaches. Today they told me about how the team would not to take to the ice to play Russia if they stayed at the Paralympics.' *Twitter*, 3 March. https://twitter.com/Devin _Heroux/status/1499396948109176836.

Holmes, Tracey (2022). 'With Russian athletes speaking out against the Ukraine invasion, what good would banning them Do?' *ABC News*, 28 February. https:// www.abc.net.au/news/2022-02-28/russian-athletes-against-war-in-ukraine-fifa-ioc -measures/100866956.

International Olympic Committee (2021a). *Athlete Expression Consultation: IOC Athletes' Commission Report*. Lausanne. https://olympics.com/athlete365/app/uploads/2021/04 /IOC_AC_Consultation_Report-Athlete_Expression_21.04.2021.pdf.

International Olympic Committee (2021b). *Olympic Charter*. Lausanne. https://stillmed .olympics.com/media/Document%20Library/OlympicOrg/General/EN-Olympic -Charter.pdf?_ga=2.124487945.2023251344.1656669469-1710853960.1647007559.

International Olympic Committee (2021c). *Rule 50.2 Guidelines: Olympic Games Tokyo 2020*. https://olympics.com/athlete365/app/uploads/2021/07/Rule-50.2-Guidelines -Olympic-Games-Tokyo-2020-Final.pdf.

International Olympic Committee (2022a). 'Give peace a chance.' *Olympics.com*, 11 March. https://olympics.com/ioc/news/-give-peace-a-chance.

International Olympic Committee (2022b). 'IOC EB recommends no participation of Russian and Belarusian athletes and officials.' *Olympics.com*, 28 February. https:// olympics.com/ioc/news/ioc-eb-recommends-no-participation-of-russian-and -belarusian-athletes-and-officials.

International Olympic Committee (2022c). 'IOC EB urges all International Federations to relocate or cancel their sports events currently planned in Russia or Belarus.' *Olympics.com*, 25 February. https://olympics.com/ioc/news/ioc-eb-urges-all-ifs-to -relocate-or-cancel-their-sports-events-currently-planned-in-russia-or-belarus.

International Olympic Committee (2022d). 'IOC strongly condemns the breach of the Olympic Truce.' *Olympics.com*, 24 February. https://olympics.com/ioc/news/ioc -strongly-condemns-the-breach-of-the-olympic-truce.

International Olympic Committee (2022e). *Rule 50.2 Guidelines: Olympic Winter Games Beijing 2022*. https://olympics.com/athlete365/app/uploads/2021/11/Rule-50.2 -Guidelines-Olympic-Winter-Games-Beijing-2022-Nov-2021.pdf.

18 Leo Goretti

International Paralympic Committee (2022). 'IPC makes decisions regarding RPC and NPC Belarus.' *Paralympic.org*, 2 March. https://www.paralympic.org/press-release/ipc-makes-decisions-regarding-rpc-and-npc-belarus.

International Tennis Federation (2022). 'ITF suspends Russia, Belarus from ITF membership and team competition.' *ITF Tennis*, 1 March. https://www.itftennis.com/en/news-and-media/articles/itf-statement-itf-suspends-russia-and-belarus-from-itf-membership-and-international-team-competition/.

Jack, Victor (2022). 'From ballerinas to boxers, Ukrainian sports stars sign up to fight Russia.' *Politico*, 9 March. https://www.politico.eu/article/ukraine-sports-stars-ballerina-boxer-fight-russia/.

Kilcline, Cathal (2017). 'Sport and protest: Global perspectives.' *The International Journal of the History of Sport* 34, no. 3–4: 157–161. https://doi.org/10.1080/09523367.2017.1373001.

Kostyuk, Marta (@Marta_Kostyuk) (2022). 'Dear tennis community, Ginetta Sagan once said, 'Silence in the face of injustice is complicity with the oppressor.' This could not be any more true right now.' *Twitter*, 20 April. https://twitter.com/marta_kostyuk/status/1516757492516196354.

Lubbers, Payne (2021). 'Olympic athletes are testing rules and taking a knee for BLM.' *Bloomberg*, 29 July. https://www.bloomberg.com/news/articles/2021-07-29/black-lives-matter-racial-justice-protests-take-stage-at-tokyo-olympics-2021#xj4y7vzkg.

Magrath, Rory (ed.) (2022). *Athlete Activism: Contemporary Perspectives*. London: Routledge.

McLaughlin, Luke (2022). 'Poland and Sweden will refuse to play Russia in World Cup 2022 playoffs.' *The Guardian*, 26 February. https://www.theguardian.com/football/2022/feb/26/poland-will-refuse-to-play-russia-in-world-cup-2022-playoff-robert-lewandowski.

Newman, Richard (2022). '"I am in complete fear': Russian Anastasia Pavlyuchenkova condemns Moscow's assault on Ukraine'. *Eurosport*, 28 February. https://www.eurosport.com/tennis/i-am-in-complete-fear-russian-anastasia-pavlyuchenkova-condemns-moscows-assault-on-ukraine_sto8821882/story.shtml.

Pavitt, Michael (2022). 'Russian gymnast Kuliak faces disciplinary action after displaying symbol linked to Ukrainian war.' *Inside the Games*, 6 March. https://www.insidethegames.biz/articles/1120185/kuliak-disciplinary-action-war-symbol.

Pells, Eddie (2022). 'Athletes force a change in ban of Russians at Paralympics.' *AP News*, 3 March. https://apnews.com/article/russia-ukraine-sports-europe-beijing-vladyslav-heraskevych-409d6e5467b6f024a52b69b0368b0a05.

Publicis Sport & Entertainment (2021). *Athlete Expression Consultation: Quantitative Research Result*. https://olympics.com/athlete365/app/uploads/2021/04/21042021-Athlete-Expression-Consultation-PSE.pdf.

Reiche, Danyel (2018). 'Not allowed to win: Lebanon's sporting boycott of Israel.' *Middle East Journal* 72, no. 1 (Winter): 28–47. https://doi.org/10.3751/72.1.12.

Reuters (2022a). 'Medvedev Wimbledon hopes could hinge on political assurance – UK Minister.' 15 March. https://www.reuters.com/lifestyle/sports/medvedev-wimbledon-hopes-could-hinge-political-assurance-uk-minister-2022-03-15/.

Reuters (2022b). 'Russia fights back in information war with jail warning.' 4 March. https://www.reuters.com/world/europe/russia-introduce-jail-terms-spreading-fake-information-about-army-2022-03-04/.

Reynolds, Tim (2022). 'Ukrainian flashes 'No War in Ukraine' sign after competing.' *AP News*, 11 February. https://apnews.com/article/winter-olympics-skeleton-vladyslav-heraskevych-sign-3866f2f1c193d00f147752fee965ca68?utm_source=Twitter&utm_campaign=SocialFlow&utm_medium=AP.

Schmitz, Robin, Fuller, Jason, and Kenin, Justine (2022). 'Tennis legend Martina Navratilova talks about Wimbledon's ban on Russian players.' *NPR*, 27 April. https://www.npr.org/2022/04/27/1095100365/tennis-legend-martina-navratilova-talks-about-wimbledons-ban-on-russian-players.

Sessions, George (2022). 'Marta Kostyuk: I stand with Wimbledon in its decision to ban Russian players.' *Independent*, 24 June. https://www.independent.co.uk/sport/tennis/marta-kostyuk-harriet-dart-elina-svitolina-england-wta-b2108666.html.

Team USA Council on Racial and Social Justice (2021). *Recommendations for IOC Rule 50/IPC Section 2.2.* https://olympics.com/athlete365/app/uploads/2021/02/Team-USA-Council-on-Racial-and-Social-JusticeIOC-Rule-50-and-IPC-Section-22-Recommendation-FINAL-02012021.pdf.

The Guardian (2020). 'Taking a knee: Athletes protest against racism around the world – In pictures.' 27 August. https://www.theguardian.com/sport/gallery/2020/aug/27/nba-strike-athletes-kneeling-black-lives-matter-protest.

The Insider (2022). 'Ex-Russia football captain calls on Putin to stop war.' 15 June. https://theins.ru/en/news/252225.

Totten, Mick (2016). 'Sport activism and protest.' In Alan Bairner, John Kelly and Jung Woo Lee (eds.), *Routledge Handbook of Sport and Politics.* Taylor and Francis.

United Nations (2022). *Solemn Appeal made by President of the General Assembly in Connection with the Observance of the Olympic Truce.* https://www.un.org/pga/76/2022/01/20/solemn-appeal-made-by-the-president-of-the-general-assembly-in-connection-with-the-observance-of-the-olympic-truce/.

Wimbledon (2022). 'Statement regarding Russian and Belarusian individuals at the Championships 2022.' *Wimbledon.com*, 20 April. https://www.wimbledon.com/en_GB/news/articles/2022-04-20/statement_regarding_russian_and_belarusian_individuals_at_the_championships_2022.html.

3

SPORT SANCTIONS AGAINST INVASIVE RUSSIA

Daryl Adair

Vladimir Putin's invasion of Ukraine in 2022 extended the Russian incursion of Crimea in 2014. However, whereas the annexation of Crimea was "quietly" achieved in a matter of days (Simpson, 2014), Putin's so-called Special Military Operation has become a drawn-out martial conflict (Mackinnon, 2022). NATO countries reacted by providing Ukraine with military equipment, thereby asserting a defensive posture. For ordinary Russians, the most consequential NATO response has been economic sanctions (Valentine, 2022). The intent is to pressure Putin to withdraw troops without direct NATO military involvement (Marlow, 2022). Even the perennially neutral Switzerland, a country outside both the European Union and NATO, has imposed economic sanctions against Russia (Revill, 2022; Wintour, 2022). As we will now see, international sport has also featured sanctions against Russia, though this has overwhelmingly been at the behest of sport organizations rather than governments.

The deployment of sport sanctions during war is not unprecedented, though they have been applied inconsistently. After World War I, the Central Powers were not invited to the 1920 Olympics, while in the wake of World War II, Germany and Japan were not invited to the 1948 Games. However, whereas in 1920 the IOC supported the exclusion of aggressor nations (Mallon and Bijkerk, 1998), it did not do so in 1948 – the Organising Committee for the XIV Olympiad London took that position (New York Times, 1947). Indeed, by contrast to 1920, the IOC tried to insist that Japan – which (unlike Germany) had applied to send a team to London – be accepted (Vrchoticky, 2021). Johannes Edstrom, the IOC president, complained to Games' organizers: "I am surprised that you take this attitude three years after the war has ended. We men of sport ought to show the way for the diplomats" (Rosenwald, 2021). Seven decades later, the IOC is again wrangling with the impact of war on sport and questions

DOI: 10.4324/9781003348238-4

about eligibility for athletic competition. But it is more complex because Russia's invasion of Ukraine is ongoing.

At the closing ceremony of the 2022 Winter Olympics in Beijing, IOC President Thomas Bach spoke of the "unifying power" of the Olympic Games and urged the world to "give peace a chance" (IOC, 2022b). A backdrop to his message was the IOC's expectation that nations abide by the aspirational Olympic Truce; indeed, a UN resolution to that effect had already been signed by 193 member states, including Russia (IOC, 2021). Yet, as Bach was speaking in Beijing on 20 February, Putin was contemplating an invasion of Ukraine (Talmazan et al., 2022), consistent with his dream of restoring territory lost to "historical Russia" after the collapse of the Soviet Union (Osborn and Ostroukh, 2021).

When Putin sent in his troops four days after the Beijing Games, Bach was incensed. The IOC Executive Board met immediately, announcing three verdicts. First, awards of the Olympic Order would be retracted from anyone with "an important function in the government of the Russian Federation or other government-related high-ranking position", which impacted both Putin and his deputy (IOC, 2022a). Second, both Russian and Belarusian athletes should not be invited or allowed to participate in international competitions, while sport federations were advised to not contribute to any sport event in Russia or Belarus. Third, where at short notice it was not possible to exclude athletes or teams from those countries, they must not compete under the auspices of their nation – they should be classified as "neutral" competitors (IOC, 2022a). Rather than the Russian flag, the only permitted symbol was that of the Russian Olympic Committee.

How did the IOC justify sanctions? First, Russia, by invading Ukraine, and Belarus, whose government supported Russia, had violated the Olympic Truce (Associated Press, 2022).

Second, the war would negatively impact competition integrity in sport. While athletes from Russia and Belarus could routinely travel to take part in sport events, competitors from Ukraine may well be prevented from doing so because of impediments wrought by the invasion of their country. There was also the thorny prospect of Russian and Ukrainian athletes pitted against each other in sport competition during a time of war (Gillespie, 2022).

The impact of the IOC's edict was swift. Nearly 100 international sport federations followed the IOC lead, with most of them excluding Russians and Belarusians from competition. Some sports federations still allowed athletes and teams from those countries, though under the IOC proviso they are designated "neutral" competitors. However, Russian and Belarusian sport officials were mostly unaffected by sanctions, with only 7 of 40 international federations suspending them. This was consistent with the IOC's own approach, whereby the national Olympic committees of both Russia and Belarus were permitted to operate as normally (Weinrich, 2022).

Meanwhile, the Beijing Paralympics, which had been slated to accept neutral athletes from Russia in the wake of the 2016 doping scandal, changed its tune after many athletes declared they would withdraw from the program rather than compete against representatives of Russia or Belarus. Hence, no Paralympian from either of those countries was permitted to take part (Pells, 2022). Putin and his deputy Dmitry Chernyshenko were furious with what they took to be the pro-NATO politicization of sport by the IOC and IPC. Chernyshenko argued that countries had "wiped their feet" on the Olympic Charter, using sanctions to unfairly discriminate against Russia by defying the right to free participation in sport. After the rebuff, Russia quickly staged its own Paralympic event, "We are together. Sport", with participation by Belarus, Armenia, Kazakhstan, and Tajikistan (RT, 2022b).

With Russia now excluded from many international sport competitions (for details, see Colucci and Cottrell, 2022; Katsarova, 2022), various substitute events were organized for locals. In a nostalgic twist, the Spartakiad, made famous during the Soviet era when the country refused to take part in the "bourgeois" Olympics (Riordan, 1998), was revived in modern form – crucially, with participation from Russian-annexed Crimea. This all-Russian event is a multi-sport festival, featuring some of the world's best swimmers and gymnasts, along with competitions in volleyball, cycling, taekwondo, and golf (Jack, 2022). Another key initiative has been the Solidarity Games, focusing on swimming, diving, and artistic aquatics, which began in Kazan in July this year (Solidarity Games, 2022b). That event, while intended to provide meaningful competition for Russian athletes prevented from taking part in FINA World Championships, has a further purpose – to involve other nations. Thus far there are sixteen member countries, including regions from the former Soviet Union but also a spattering from other continents, such as Venezuela, Sudan, and Vietnam. No surprise that Russia dominated the medal count at the July meet, though the presence of competitors from a handful of other countries offered the appearance of an invitational contest staged in Russia rather than a closed, parochial event (Solidarity Games, 2022a). There is no doubt that Russia, while ostracized from numerous global and European sport competitions, will continue to stage its own events, thereby seeking to entice countries outside of the NATO alliance to participate (RT, 2022a, 2022c).

No surprise that twelve Russian sport federations and the Russian Olympic Committee appealed bans at the Court of Arbitration of Sport (CAS), arguing that sanctions are, in essence, ideologically driven discrimination (Houston, 2022). Before CAS, the two biggest global sports bodies, the IOC and FIFA, had undoubtedly compared notes and come to a common position. Cleverly, they had positioned sanctions as "protections", which Bach described as "measures to protect the integrity of sport competitions" (Bushnell, 2022), this meaning the inability of Ukrainians to participate without impediment. Furthermore, FIFA pointed out that football federations and players from the three countries slated to play Russia in World Cup qualifying said, "they would refuse to take the same field as Russia" (Bushnell, 2022). CAS agreed: its verdict in the FIFA case focused squarely on the impact of the Russian invasion on sport competitions and what it described as "the secure and orderly conduct of football events for … the world" (Colucci and Cottrell, 2022). From that perspective, the presence of a Russian team would be antagonistic to the collegial purpose of a World Cup or similar sport event.

For Russian athletes, there is the delicate question of their own position on their country's invasion of Ukraine. Ivan Kuliak, a gymnast, made clear his support by adding a Z symbol to his tunic during a medal presentation at the World Cup even in Doha. The letter Z is an explicit symbol of support for the war, appearing on Russian tanks in Ukraine. Brazenly, Kuliak made this gesture while standing beside a Ukrainian competitor (Ingle, 2022a). He later told reporters that he had "no regrets" doing so and would "even do the same again" (Ingle, 2022b). Kuliak is now prevented from doing so, for the International Gymnastics Federation suspended him for 12 months, annulled his bronze medal, and demanded the return of prizemoney (Sankar, 2022).

Meanwhile, though, Russian athletes bold enough to explicitly oppose their country's invasion face the prospect of criticism or even retaliation from Putin (JAM News, 2022). Ice hockey player Alex Ovechkin, the captain of the NHL's Washington Capitals, was able to articulate from the safety of America, where he publicly pleaded, "please, no more war!" (Holmes, 2022). Yet he was not prepared to speak directly about the invasion of Ukraine, and his Instagram profile still features the ice hockey star alongside Putin. Perhaps this is because, as an observer in the *Washington Post* theorized, "Ovechkin's family is in Russia, which could make them vulnerable. All Russian athletes … [are] in a very compromised position if they speak out" (Svrluga, 2022).

For the IOC, a critical element of sport sanctions (which it describes as protections) is that sport organizations must be in control of that process. While Næss reminds us that sport is not neutral, and that politics is very much at the core of how these bodies operate (Næss, 2018), the "autonomy of sport" is jealously guarded by the IOC (Geeraert et al., 2014). This position is underpinned by a determination that governments, though they provide funds to sport, should not "interfere" with the governance of sport organizations (Carpenter, 2013; Morgan, 2020). A speech by Bach in June 2022 illustrates this view while positioning it in the context of sport protections. At a meeting of the Association of Summer Olympic International Federations (ASOIF), Bach insisted that this group take the lead in terms of its own response to the Ukraine invasion, because prevarication risked sport "becoming a political tool" of governments (Barker, 2022). Olympic Movement members, he argued, should be the sole judges of participation eligibility. The autonomy of sport was therefore necessary to protect it from politicization by state actors (Meier and García, 2019). Grand Slam tennis, Bach insisted, was a case in point: "In Paris, Russian players can play as neutral athletes, [though] in London, at Wimbledon, the Government is saying no way". He argued that governments should not be "deciding according to their own political interests, who can take part in a competition and who cannot take part". "Today", he warned gravely, "it is Russia and Belarus, tomorrow it is your country" (Barker, 2022). Bach therefore feared that the Russian crisis might be used as a precursor for nation states to wield power over Olympic bodies.

There is now pressure on the IOC to ban Russia from the 2024 Paris Olympics (Berkeley, 2022). Such a decision would complement that of UEFA, which has banned Russia from Euro 2024 (Braidwood, 2022). However, the IOC now wants to find a way to bring back Russian athletes to international sport, which would have flow-on effects for the Olympics. At the very moment Putin announced the mobilization of 300,000 troops, the IOC was confecting a position in which the world of war and the world of sport ought to again be separated. With fanciful rhetoric, the IOC desired to bring all athletes of the world together and thus to "emphasise the role of sport as a unifying factor in today's much-divided world" (Shefferd, 2022). There was, however, a complicated aspect to this: Bach clarified that "Russian athletes could be allowed back to compete at Olympic Games … only if they don't support their country's war in Ukraine" (Euronews, 2022). The logistics of this process have yet to be explained, but Bach was not shying away from the underlying rationale:

> This war has not been started by the Russian athletes. But we saw that some governments did not want to respect anymore the autonomy of international sports … this is why we've had to take these protective measures to be at least still a little bit in the driving seat and not lose all autonomy.
> *(El-Shaboury, 2022)*

In conclusion, sport sanctions against Russia and Belarus – whether on the part of the IOC, FIFA, or international federations – have negatively impacted athletes and teams. Some observers contend that Russian athletes, who have had no influence on Putin's military policy, should not be made scapegoats (Holmes, 2022). Others point out that economic sanctions hurt ordinary Russians, yet they are also not responsible for Putin's invasion. War, in that sense, is unfair (Adair, 2022). Global sport bodies, meanwhile, are trying to navigate a situation in which one of the world's athletic superpowers is operating extravagantly as a military superpower, and thus in a manner that defies both the rule-based global order (Eilstrup-Sangiovanni and Hofmann, 2019) and the spirit of fair play inherent to sport.

References

Adair D (2022) Is banning Russian tennis players from Wimbledon the right call? Available at: https://theconversation.com/is-banning-russian-tennis-players-from-wimbledon-the-right-call-179551 (accessed 3 October 2022).

Associated Press (2022) Ukraine athletes defend country, demand sanctions against Russia. Available at: https://www.usatoday.com/story/sports/2022/02/27/ukraine-athletes-defend-country-demand-sanctions-for-russia/6965665001/ (accessed 1 October 2022).

Barker P (2022) Bach hits out at Wimbledon ban and political interference in Ukraine response. Available at: https://web7.insidethegames.biz/articles/1124190/bach-asoif (accessed 10 July 2022).

Berkeley G (2022) Russian sports leaders slam suggestion of possible Paris 2024 ban by Reedie. Available at: https://www.insidethegames.biz/articles/1125614/russian-athletes-may-face-paris-2024-ban (accessed 3 October 2022).

Braidwood J (2022) Russia banned from Euro 2024 as international suspension continues | The Independent. Available at: https://www.independent.co.uk/sport/football/russia-euro-2024-qualifying-uefa-fifa-b2171299.html (accessed 3 October 2022).

Bushnell H (2022) Court rules for FIFA over Russia, paving way for continued sports bans amid war. Available at: https://www.msn.com/en-us/sports/olympics/court-rules-for-fifa-over-russia-paving-way-for-continued-sports-bans-amid-war/ar-AAZCaot (accessed 3 October 2022).

Carpenter K (2013) IOC, national governments and the autonomy of sport: An uneasy relationship – LawInSport. Available at: https://www.lawinsport.com/topics/item/ioc-national-governments-and-the-autonomy-of-sport-an-uneasy-relationship (accessed 3 October 2022).

Colucci M and Cottrell S (2022) *Sport and Diplomacy in the Aftermath of the Russia Ukraine War. A Sports Law and Policy Centre and Lawinsport Joint Survey.* Available at: https://tinyurl.com/2p8rhskm.

Eilstrup-Sangiovanni M and Hofmann SC (2019) Of the contemporary global order, crisis, and change. *Journal of European Public Policy* 27(7): 1–13. DOI: 10.1080/13501763.2019.1678665.

El-Shaboury Y (2022) Paris 2024: Russian athletes who do not support invasion of Ukraine could be allowed to compete. Available at: https://www.eurosport.co.uk/olympics/paris-2024-russian-athletes-who-do-not-support-invasion-of-ukraine-could-be-allowed-to-compete-ioc_sto9167117/story.shtml (accessed 3 October 2022).

Euronews (2022) Russian athletes "could be allowed back in Olympics" says IOC chief. Available at: https://www.euronews.com/2022/09/30/russian-athletes-could-be-allowed-back-in-olympcs-says-ioc-chief (accessed 3 October 2022).

Geeraert A, Mrkonjic M and Chappelet J-L (2014) A rationalist perspective on the autonomy of international sport governing bodies: Towards a pragmatic autonomy in the steering of sports. *International Journal of Sport Policy and Politics* 7(4): 473–488. DOI: 10.1080/19406940.2014.925953.

Gillespie T (2022) Ukraine invasion: IOC recommends Russian and Belarusian athletes should be banned from all international competitions. Available at: https://news.sky.com/story/ukraine-invasion-ioc-recommends-russian-and-belarusian-athletes-should-be-banned-from-all-international-competitions-12554151 (accessed 1 October 2022).

Holmes T (2022) With Russian athletes speaking out against the Ukraine invasion, what good would banning them do? Available at: https://www.abc.net.au/news/2022-02-28/russian-athletes-against-war-in-ukraine-fifa-ioc-measures/100866956 (accessed 3 October 2022).

Houston M (2022) Twelve National Federations and Russian NOC appeal to CAS over competition bans. Available at: https://web7.insidethegames.biz/articles/1124864/russian-olympic-committee-cas-sports (accessed 3 October 2022).

Ingle S (2022a) Russian gymnast with 'Z' symbol on podium next to Ukrainian faces long ban. Available at: https://www.theguardian.com/sport/2022/mar/07/shocking

-behaviour-russian-gymnast-shows-z-symbol-on-podium-next-to-ukrainian -winner (accessed 3 October 2022).

Ingle S (2022b) Unrepentant gymnast Ivan Kuliak would show 'Z' insignia for Russia again | Gymnastics | The Guardian. Available at: https://www.theguardian.com/ sport/2022/mar/08/gymnast-ivan-kuliak-says-he-would-show-support-for-russia -again (accessed 3 October 2022).

IOC (2021) UN General Assembly adopts Olympic Truce for Beijing 2022, highlighting the contribution of sport to the promotion of peace and solidarity. Available at: https://olympics.com/ioc/news/un-general-assembly-adopts-olympic-truce-for -beijing-2022 (accessed 10 July 2022).

IOC (2022a) IOC EB recommends no participation of Russian and Belarusian athletes and officials. Available at: https://olympics.com/ioc/news/ioc-eb-recommends -no-participation-of-russian-and-belarusian-athletes-and-officials (accessed 9 July 2022).

IOC (2022b) IOC president's speech – Beijing 2022 closing ceremony. Available at: https://olympics.com/ioc/news/ioc-president-s-speech-beijing-2022-closing -ceremony (accessed 9 July 2022).

Jack (2022) Spartakiad marches across the country: Intrigue, tension, drama. Available at: https://eprimefeed.com/sports/spartakiad-marches-across-the-country-intrigue -tension-drama/157466/ (accessed 2 October 2022).

JAM News (2022) Persecution of war opponents in Russia is in full swing. Available at: https://jam-news.net/putin-told-us-to-kill-you-how-opponents-of-the-war-are -persecuted-in-russia/ (accessed 3 October 2022).

Katsarova I (2022) Russia's war on Ukraine: Impact on athletes and sports competitions – European Parliamentary Research Service. Available at: https://epthinktank.eu /2022/04/21/russias-war-on-ukraine-impact-on-athletes-and-sports-competitions/ (accessed 2 October 2022).

Mackinnon M (2022) How Ukrainian resistance continues to disrupt Vladimir Putin's plans to take over. Available at: https://www.theglobeandmail.com/world/article -russia-ukraine-war-ukrainian-resistance/ (accessed 9 July 2022).

Mallon B and Bijkerk AT (1998) *The 1920 Olympic Games: Results for All Competitors in All Events, with Commentary.* Jefferson, NC: McFarland, Inc. Available at: https://books .google.com.au/books?id=wYIwCgAAQBAJ.

Marlow B (2022) Vladimir Putin will be livid as Russia defaults on its foreign debt. Available at: https://www.smh.com.au/business/the-economy/putin-will-be-livid -as-russia-officially-becomes-an-economic-basket-case-20220628-p5ax3d.html (accessed 10 July 2022).

Meier HE and García B (2019) *Collaborations between National Olympic Committees and Public Authorities.* University of Münster, Germany. Available at: https://tinyurl.com /4x5yzrwn.

Morgan L (2020) Is it time for the IOC to rethink its rule on Government interference in NOCs? Available at: https://www.insidethegames.biz/articles/1090027/ioc -government-interference-nocs (accessed 27 November 2021).

Næss HE (2018) The neutrality myth: Why international sporting associations and politics cannot be separated. *Journal of the Philosophy of Sport* 45(2): 1–17. DOI: 10.1080/00948705.2018.1479190.

New York Times (1947) Germany and Japan are banned as participants in '48 Olympics. Available at: https://timesmachine.nytimes.com/timesmachine/1947/01/24 /88741838.pdf?pdf_redirect=true&ip=0.

Osborn A and Ostroukh A (2021) Putin rues Soviet collapse as demise of "historical Russia." Available at: https://www.reuters.com/world/europe/putin-rues-soviet-collapse-demise-historical-russia-2021-12-12/ (accessed 10 July 2022).

Pells E (2022) Athletes force a change in ban of Russians at Paralympics. Available at: https://abcnews.go.com/Sports/wireStory/athletes-force-change-ban-russians-paralympics-83231629 (accessed 1 October 2022).

Revill J (2022) Analysis: Neutral Switzerland leans closer to NATO in response to Russia. Available at: https://www.reuters.com/markets/europe/neutral-switzerland-leans-closer-nato-response-russia-2022-05-15/ (accessed 2 October 2022).

Riordan J (1998) The sports policy of the Soviet Union, 1917–1941. In: Arnaud P and Riordan J (eds) *Sport and International Politics*. Routledge, pp. 67–78. Available at: https://www.taylorfrancis.com/chapters/edit/10.4324/9780203476581-6/sports-policy-soviet-union-1917–1941-james-riordan.

Rosenwald MS (2021) Japan, Germany were banned from 1948 Olympics after WWII. Available at: https://www.washingtonpost.com/history/2021/07/23/japan-olympics-history/ (accessed 10 July 2022).

RT (2022a) Kremlin reveals 'emphasis' from Putin amid sporting bans. Available at: https://www.rt.com/sport/562271-putin-russia-domestic-sports-events/ (accessed 2 October 2022).

RT (2022b) Putin praises Russian Paralympians after Siberian showpiece ends. Available at: https://www.rt.com/sport/552406-russian-paralympic-games-ban-putin-beijing/ (accessed 2 October 2022).

RT (2022c) Russia working on new BRICS sports formats – Minister. Available at: https://www.rt.com/sport/560078-russia-brics-sporting-cooperation/ (accessed 3 October 2022).

Sankar V (2022) Russian gymnast Kuliak appeals against suspension for sporting "Z" symbol. Available at: https://www.insidethegames.biz/articles/1124227/kuliak-appeals-against-suspension (accessed 3 October 2022).

Shefferd N (2022) Bach says Olympics can set example to the world as Putin escalates Ukraine war. Available at: https://www.insidethegames.biz/articles/1128303/putin-mobilisation-bach-sets-exam (accessed 3 October 2022).

Simpson J (2014) Russia's Crimea plan detailed, secret and successful. Available at: https://www.bbc.com/news/world-europe-26644082 (accessed 9 July 2022).

Solidarity Games (2022a) *Multidisciplinary International Competitions in Swimming, Artistic Swimming, and Diving, Kazan (RUS) 2022*. Available at: https://dspkazan.com/wp-content/uploads/2022/09/Bulletin_ENG_-V_16_09_mini.pdf.

Solidarity Games (2022b) *Solidarity Games: Swimming, Diving, Artistic Swimming*. Available at: https://sportssolidarity.com/en#game-stages (accessed 2 October 2022).

Svrluga B (2022) Alex Ovechkin's situation isn't as simple as 'Putin is my president.' Available at: https://www.washingtonpost.com/sports/2022/05/17/alex-ovechkin-putin-ukraine/ (accessed 3 October 2022).

Talmazan Y, Chistikova T and Williams A (2022) U.S. warns that Russia could attack Ukraine "at very short notice" as troop buildup grows. Available at: https://www.msn.com/en-us/news/world/us-warns-that-russia-could-attack-ukraine-at-very-short-notice-as-troop-buildup-grows/ar-AASVRws (accessed 9 July 2022).

Valentine A (2022) Are sanctions actually hurting Russia's economy? Here's what you need to know. Available at: https://www.npr.org/2022/07/01/1109033582/are-sanctions-actually-hurting-russias-economy-heres-what-you-need-to-know (accessed 9 July 2022).

Vrchoticky N (2021) All the times countries have been banned from the Olympics. Available at: https://www.grunge.com/452177/all-the-times-countries-have-been-banned-from-the-olympics/ (accessed 10 July 2022).

Weinrich J (2022) Olympic federations suspend Russian athletes not officials. Available at: https://www.playthegame.org/news/most-olympic-federations-suspend-russian-athletes-but-officials-go-free/ (accessed 1 October 2022).

Wintour P (2022) Switzerland adopts wholesale EU sanctions against Russia. Available at: https://www.theguardian.com/world/2022/feb/28/switzerland-adopts-wholesale-eu-sanctions-against-russia (accessed 9 July 2022).

4

WHAT FUTURE FOR PUTIN'S SPORT POWER?

Lukas Aubin

And the Sports Movement Came Out of Its Apolitism ...

On the 24th February 2022, the world is in shock. At the initiative of Vladimir Putin, the Russian army has just invaded Ukraine. Kyiv is under siege. Several million Ukrainians have fled the country at the onset of war, whilst others have taken up arms to defend themselves and the homeland. Faced with this geopolitical crisis, the international community is mobilizing. In quick succession, tens or even hundreds of sanctions are taken against Russia to stop "the special military operation", in the words of the Russian president: closure of airspace, increased control of imports and exports, limitation of Russian visas, sanctions against the oligarchs, and so on. The West is mobilizing. Diplomatic, economic, and political, the sanctions are plural and polymorphic. Among them, sport astonishes by its ability to mobilize. Indeed, international sports bodies are at the forefront of sanctions and are rapidly becoming an actor in the conflict. For many, these decisions are surprising. Until then, sport shone by its apoliticism and its neutrality of facade. For example, despite one of the biggest doping cases in sports history, Russian athletes have continued to compete in major competitions since 2014. However, in Russia as in many authoritarian or semi-authoritarian countries, sport is used not in a rational economic logic but in a geopolitical logic of balance of power. Thus, in light of the politico-economic-sports system built by Vladimir Putin – the Sportokratura (Aubin, 2021) – the banishment of Russia from world sport becomes a major political weapon to stop the invasion.

In the days following Russia's invasion of Ukraine, the IOC, UEFA, Formula 1, and even FIFA quickly called for Russia to be excluded from world sport. On the initiative of the United Kingdom, on 5 March 2022, 37 nations sign a joint declaration to prohibit Russia and Belarus from organizing, bidding, or being awarded international sporting events. Among them, France, Germany,

DOI: 10.4324/9781003348238-5

30 Lukas Aubin

Australia, the United States, and Canada are the main Western nations that wish to sanction Russia. The press release is clear: "Russia's unprovoked and unjustifiable war of choice against Ukraine, permitted by the Belarusian government, is odious and a flagrant violation of its international obligations". Unprecedented in their scope and systematism, these decisions constitute a novelty in the history of modern sport. Until then, the global sports movement claimed to be neutral despite an inherently political reality (Defrance, 2000).

Vladimir Putin's Philosophy of Judo

In this context and aware of this paradox, Vladimir Putin does not hesitate to use the elements of language of international sports institutions by recalling that "sport must be apolitical". Like a judo hold, he uses the strength of his opponent to his advantage. Thus, he does not hesitate to explain that the exclusion of Russian and Belarusian athletes following the invasion of Ukraine "not only violated the fundamental principles of sport, but also openly and cynically violated the rights fundamental human rights, the Universal Declaration of Human Rights, adopted by the UN in 1948 – where everything is written. It is not about the status of the athlete: not about the political, legal or international status of the country the athlete represents. It is about the man himself. These rights have been violated". According to him, these decisions are all Russophobic acts stemming from a modern sport controlled by Westerners, led by the United States.

This discourse, which has been remarkably consistent since the end of 2014 and the beginning of the revelations of Russian doping, constitutes the common thread of an alternative narrative thought up by the Kremlin. The objective is to sow doubt as to the legitimacy of international sports bodies. Therefore, this rhetoric uses the apolitical hiatus on which modern sport is based to seize it. Abroad, the effects of this strategy are poor. Overall, most states in the deep south need and use international sports institutions to exist (Qatar, Brazil, China, etc.). However, on a national scale, this has the effect of further isolating the Russian population from the rest of the world through the creation of this parallel information space.

Towards a New Revival of Russian Sport?

However, if Vladimir Putin wants sports to remain politically neutral, he made it a political weapon when he came to power in 2000. For Putin, sport is an instrument of power inherited from the Soviet era. He was born in Leningrad, where he started to play judo very young. Later, when he becomes President, he explains that his success came thanks to the Soviet Sporting System. He wants to resuscitate it. In 2002, he calls the legendary retired soviet ice hockey defenseman who is living in the United States to offer him to become the head of the Ministry of sports. Then, he explains that the glory of Russia is based, among other things, on the sporting victories of the National Team. In 2014, he brings back the Soviet training programme called Ready for Labour and Defence (GTO). Slowly, he builds a new sporting system. Its vertical political-economic-sports system – the Sportokratura – uses oligarchs, politicians, and athletes to make Russian influence efficient throughout the world (Aubin, 2021). Therefore, at the national level, the stake is more important than it seems because a lot of people in Russia are still living in between Soviet and post-Soviet world. This Soviet nostalgia through sports is a strong vector to recreate the West and East antagonism and to call for the emergence of a multipolar world where Russia would play a predominant role. For Putin, sport was a means to make Russia one of the main powers of the planet and a patriotic tool of social control. Since the 24th of February, it is the symbol of a country that has become a pariah.

In this context, the Kremlin is looking for solutions. He found it shortly after the announcement of Russia's exclusion from the Paralympic Games in Beijing, On 5 March 2022, he ordered the organization of a parallel sports competition in the city of Khanty-Mansiysk, in Western Siberia: "We are together: sport". The Deputy Prime Minister of the Russian Federation, Dmitry Chernyshenko, instructed the Ministry of Sports and the Ministry of Finance, as well as the town hall of Khanty-Mansiïsk, to implement these alternative Paralympic Games as soon as possible with the assistance of Armenia, Tajikistan, Kazakhstan, and Belarus, allies of the Russian regime. The aim, according to Sports Minister Oleg Matytsin, is to show that Russia is "a strong and self-sufficient sporting power". Within the Russian population, a joke then circulated: "Beijing prepared its Paralympic Games in seven years, Khanty-Mansiïsk prepared its own in seven days".

The competition took place over four days, from 17 to 20 March. Russian athletes won in the medal standings against the four other participating states. In the process, the Deputy Minister of Sports, Odes Baisultanov, clarified the Russian vision: "We must develop a national project, we must develop our sport, including through the BRICS (Brazil, Russia, India, China, and South-Africa), and the Shanghai Cooperation Organization, so that we can organize international competitions."

Then, on Friday, 18 March, many Olympic medallists took part in the meeting "For a world without Nazism! For Russia! For the President!" in the Luzhniki stadium in Moscow. All but a coincidence, it is the famous sports commentator Dmitri Guberniev who is the Ringmaster of this event held in the presence of 100,000 spectators and broadcast almost live on television. Guberniev did not hesitate to declare about Russian sportsmen: "There is this kind of profession: defending the fatherland". A slogan from a Soviet patriotic film from 1971, widely taken up since by the Soviet and then Russian army, and whose use concerning athletes shows the military dimension that was attributed to the world of sport under Vladimir Putin.

In the aftermath, the second edition of the Pervy Kanal Figure Skating Cup is brought forward to 25–27 March in Saransk to coincide with the 2022 World Championships, from which the Russians and Belarusians have been excluded.

Again, the goal is to unite the Russian population and athletes around the flag to avoid their potential defection. As a sign of the importance of the event, the star Kamila Valieva and the Beijing Olympic champion Anna Chtcherbakova were present to send a strong message both inside and outside the country. This time, the organization is only Russian, but the services are world-class.

The Three Scenarios of the Future Russian Sport

Nevertheless, despite all these attempts, the Kremlin does not seem to have decided on the future of its Sport Power. For the moment, it navigates on sight and oscillates between maintaining contact with international sports federations, returning to a Soviet Sports system, or building a new model. Therefore, these three potential scenarios seem to be taking shape, some of which may potentially overlap.

The "Return to Normal"

The first and most likely is the "back to normal scenario". In other words, international sports bodies would return to Russia once the situation had calmed down. The Russian power would then continue to want to participate in the construction of the current modern sport while knowing that it could be excluded from it. Consequently, he would again construct an alternative narrative to represent his "power of the imagination" and save appearances with his own population when a legal decision, a bad sporting result, or a political affair concerned him. According to this scenario, Russia could therefore both remain in the concert of sporting nations and retain its otherness at the end of the war. This scenario has been seen twice in the past. South Africa (1970–1991) and Yugoslavia (1992–1995) have been banned from the sporting world respectively because of Apartheid and the war. Both have been reintegrated into another political form then. Yugoslavia disappeared in 1995 and has been replaced with Slovenia, Croatia, Bosnia, Serbia, Montenegro, and Macedonia. In South Africa, the system of institutionalized racial segregation – the Apartheid – was officially over in 1991. In both examples, the sporting institutions decided to reintegrate the countries after a major systemic change. We could conclude that it will take a major change in Russia too for sports authorities to re-enter the country. But since a new era of sport has dawned, it's very difficult to predict what could be the future of Russian Sports.

The "Soviet Model"

The second scenario is the "Soviet scenario". As mentioned by Igor Levitin, Assistant to the President of the Russian Federation, during the forum "We are together. Sport" in March 2022, it would consist of withdrawing Russia from all international sports structures and using the experience of Soviet isolationism to rebuild an autarkic and military sports model. The objective would be to use sport to participate in the defence of the country. According to Levitin:

> The events of the past few months show that the law and the spirit no longer exist today. There are clear violations of the Olympic Charter, which sets out the prohibition of discrimination. All of these offenses suggest that we need to return to the origins of Soviet national sport. During the Soviet era, our sports had experienced similar sanctions, but despite everything, we had always maintained a high standard. From now on, international sport is not so much managed by officials as by advertising agencies. We must return to the system that prevailed in the USSR. There is nothing wrong with that. This will bring us self-sufficiency.

Myth or reality? At a time when Russian sport is excluded from the global sports movement, the Kremlin is looking for solutions and digging alternately from the past, the present, and the future.

The "New World Order of Sport"

Indeed, the third scenario is also that of a third voice: it is the "scenario of the new world order of sport". As we have seen, in words and in deeds, the option favoured by the Russian authorities since the start of the invasion remains that of the creation of an alternative sports centre on a world scale to counterbalance the international sports federations such as the IOC or FIFA.

Concretely, the idea would be to dispense with, replace, and/or compete with world sport. In Russia, for example, the idea of splitting the Olympic movement is gaining ground. It would be a question of separating the Olympic Games in two: in the West, the Western Games; and in the East, the "traditional" Russian Games. These Russian Olympics would be held in summer in Crimea and in winter in Sochi. They would draw their legitimacy from the more or less proven historical links of these regions with ancient Greece. In 2007, to obtain the Sochi Olympics, Vladimir Putin had indeed reminded the members of the IOC that "the ancient Greeks lived in the vicinity of Sochi. I saw there the rock near Sochi on which according to legend, Prometheus was chained. Prometheus who gave fire to men, the fire which is ultimately the Olympic flame". Since then, the register of myth is regularly used to evoke this Russian region composed of the Caucasus but also of the Crimean Peninsula. According to Vladimir Putin, these lands have a sacred character, and they could constitute the theatre of a new world order of sport.

Within the framework of this scenario, and to weigh politically and sportingly heavy enough to compete with the Olympic movement, the Russian authorities are already looking for allies. During the Russian Paralympic Games parallel to those in Beijing, the Russian authorities invited Armenia, Tajikistan, Kazakhstan, and Belarus. But Russian ambitions are not limited to these four former Soviet

34 Lukas Aubin

republics. For Matytsine, the objective is to challenge the member countries of the Commonwealth of Independent States (CIS), emerging countries (BRICS), and the Shanghai Cooperation Organization (SCO) so that they are stakeholders in this ambition. These three organizations include several tenors of world sport, of which China is the flagship. If this Russian project were successful, we could see the creation of a new world order of sport intended to compete with the historical institutions of modern sport such as the IOC or FIFA.

This strategy would contribute to the creation of a Eurasian sporting microcosm which would confirm the Russian pivot towards the East (*povorot na vostok*) began in the 2000s and accelerated since 2014 and the annexation of Crimea. Already in February 2007, Vladimir Putin denounced American unilateralism and called for the advent of a "polycentric" world.

The Past as a Model?

To understand the current representations of sport according to Vladimir Putin, we must delve into the Soviet past. Indeed, the leaders of the USSR have already tried, with very relative success, to create sporting microcosms parallel to that ordered by the West.

In 1921, Lenin and Stalin participated in the creation of the Red Sports International (IRS) to compete with the IOC. The goal is to offer a proletarian alternative to the "bourgeois" international sports organizations. It is a question of forming a reserve of revolutionary fighters, and of organizing the Spartakiads to supplant the Olympic Games and promote "healthy emulation between the physical vanguards of the world proletariat" (Le Guellec, 2002). The USSR organized the first Spartakiads in Moscow on 12 August 1928, the closing day of the Amsterdam Olympics. The ambition is clear: to use sport to show the superiority of the Soviet model over the capitalist model whose faults are symbolized by bourgeois sports competitions. The Russian encyclopaedic dictionary *Grenat* explains in its 1932 edition the differences between the traditional Olympic Games and the Spartakiads:

> The Olympic Games are intended to show the success of physical culture and to identify record achievements in the field of purely individualistic sports. Unlike the Olympic Games in bourgeois capitalist countries, the IRS organizes international workers' sports festivals (Spartakiades), which aim to promote physical culture as a means of healing the proletariat and educating the workers to their class. (...) Mass performances are offered here.

A few decades later, during the Cold War, the Friendship Games were organized by the Soviet authorities to compensate for the boycott of the 1984 Olympics in Los Angeles. Officially, the objective of Amitié-84 is also to give athletes whose countries are boycotting the LA Olympics the opportunity to display the fruit of their years of training. However, states around the world can participate. A total of 49 countries, including France, are taking part. Unsurprisingly, it was the USSR that won the competition by winning 126 gold medals. But, more importantly, 50 world records are beaten there against 11 at the Los Angeles Olympics.

More recently, in 2008, the creation of the Kontinental Hockey League (KHL) at the initiative of Moscow had the eminently geopolitical objective of casting the Russian shadow over the post-Soviet space and even beyond. Indeed, the KHL aimed to bring together the best ice hockey teams from the former USSR, former Warsaw Pact countries, Scandinavia, and even Central Asia and China. The winner gets the Gagarin Cup, in reference to the Soviet space conquest. While Croatia, Latvia, Ukraine, the Czech Republic, Finland, and even China have joined the competition over the years, the war in Ukraine which has been going on since 2014 has gradually prompted foreign clubs to leave. Today, only the clubs of Red Star Kunlun (Beijing), Barys (Nursultan), and Dinamo Minsk (Minsk) remain to participate in the championship, with 19 Russian clubs.

It is from this perspective that we must understand the current dilemma facing the Russian authorities. On the one hand, it is a question of continuing to compete with Westerners on their territory. On the other hand, the Russian historical and geopolitical position should allow the authorities to create, disseminate, and organize a new world order of sport.

Nevertheless, this desire for asymmetrical expansion on the part of the Kremlin reflects the imbalance that exists between Russian ambitions and the geopolitical reality of a country that can only count on a few allies. In addition, the power of international sports institutions is such that it seems illusory to be able to compete with them on their field. To enter the new system desired by Moscow, a country like the People's Republic of China (PRC), for example, would have to give up a sports strategy that runs until 2049, with the ultimate objective of hosting and winning a football World Cup to celebrate the centenary of the establishment of the PRC. Would it risk being banned from FIFA to satisfy Vladimir Putin? It's unlikely.

At a crossroads, Russian sport has an uncertain fate. To exist, the authorities seek new geopolitical solutions. The resurrection of the myth of the new world order of sport is for the moment akin to a fantasized ambition, while the consequences of the war in Ukraine on Russian athletes are already very real.

Bibliography

Aubin, L. (2021), *La sportokratura sous Vladimir Poutine: une géopolitique du sport russe*, Bréal, Paris.

Defrance, J. (2000), « La politique de l'apolitisme. Sur l'autonomisation du champ sportif », *Politix*, 2000/2 (n° 50), p. 13–27.

Guellec (Le), G. (2002), « Les guerres olympiques de l'URSS », *Regard sur l'Est*, 2002. URL: https://regard-est.com/les-guerres-olympiques-de-lurss#:~:text=La%20seconde %20guerre%20mondiale%20va,%2C%20%C3%A0%20Londres%2C%20en%201948. Viewed 11 May 2022.

5

GOVERNANCE DYSFUNCTION IN WORLD SPORT

Issues Raised by the Conflict in Ukraine

Sergey Altukhov

Introduction

The start of the paramilitary conflict in Ukraine unexpectedly became another important point for assessing the legal status, the depth of management dysfunctions, and politicization of the activities of the International Sports Federations (ISFs) and the International Olympic Committee (IOC). Within one week, IOC President – Thomas Bach – condemned the Russian authorities' actions in Ukraine and recommended the International Sports Federations to cancel or postpone all international tournaments that were to be in Russia and Belarus and to deprive Russian and Belarusian winners and prizewinners of the right to perform the national anthems and raise the national flags on the pedestal. Mostly the reaction to these recommendations was predictable but still unambiguous.

IOC Recommendations and Timeline of the Consequences

Putting aside the emotional background of the statements, almost all the ISFs supported the point of view and suggestions of Thomas Bach. Still there were some exceptions. For example, the International Aquatic Federation (FINA) and the International Judo Federation (IJF) refused to impede international starts for Russian athletes despite the backdrop of general anxiety. The International Football Federation (FIFA) at the 72nd Congress unexpectedly decided to make the Russian language one of the six official languages of FIFA. After that, the Executive Committee of the World Olympians Association (WOA) issued a condemnation of the ISF sanctions against Russian and Belarusian athletes, stating that "the fundamental principles of Olympism, set out in paragraphs 4 and 6 of the Olympic Charter, must always be respected, and that the right of Olympians

DOI: 10.4324/9781003348238-6

and Athletes, as individuals to participate in sports activities should be supported and encouraged".

Following the officials' statements, news of legal decisions began to arrive. On 11 April, the International Luge Federation (FIL) Arbitration Court stated that the decision to not allow Russian athletes to compete was legally unacceptable. The FIL executive committee declared they would try to circumvent the decision of the court about removing the Russians.

The European Table Tennis Union (ETTU) also did not expect that the ETTU Board of Appeal would rule on the discriminatory exclusion of the Russian clubs Fakel-Gazprom and UGMK from participation in the semi-final and final of the Champions League's last season.

CAS has registered ten appeal cases of Russian organizations and individuals against decisions to suspend Russian athletes from participating in international competitions. Appeals were filed by the Russian Olympic Committee, the Russian Football Union, the Russian Skating Union, the Russian Figure Skating Federation, the Russian Biathlon Union, the Russian Rowing Federation, the Russian Rugby Union, the Russian Artistic Gymnastics Federation, Olympic champion in short track Semyon Elistratov, world champion speed skating champion Angelina Golikova, Olympic medallists in figure skating Evgenia Tarasova and Vladimir Morozov, Olympic champions in artistic gymnastics Angelina Melnikova and Nikita Nagorny, double mini-trampo world champion Mikhail Zalomin, judge in artistic gymnastics Vitaly Ivanchuk, and member of the executive committee of the Jumping Federation on the Russian trampoline Irina Karavaeva. At this rate, we will see the Olympic Games between lawyers very soon.

Outline of the Problem

Modern sport is a phenomenon with many meanings and definitions in historical, sociological, philosophical, economic, legal, and other aspects. Desmond Morris (Morris, 1981), 40 years ago, described sports as "a cultural-ritual form of sublimation of baser instincts" and even "a substitute for radical political activity". Modern sport has become much more attractive, but, speaking about its development, all the same "base instincts" and "political activity" are being replicated – the concentration of resources, the transfer trade in slave athletes, manipulations to achieve results, doping, etc. Sport eludes an unambiguous definition and causes three hardly compatible aspects of perception: semantic ambiguity, ambivalence of values, paradox of goals (Bourg, 2016).

As a result of this kind of age-old evolution, the structure of World Sports Governance has lined up, like the Solar System, around the International Olympic Committee (the sun), with the International Sports Federations – the main copyright holders for all sports – rotating in the orbits. Some of the ISFs (planets) form the programme of the Olympic Games. Therefore, they are located closer to the sun and receive a larger supply of energy, while others are content with the formal recognition of the IOC and exist as conditional comets, asteroids, and nebulae, occasionally relying on the favour of a heavenly body. The level of relations between the subjects of international sports, their mutual influence, and legal regulation become the key problem of management in such configuration.

To further discuss dysfunctions in the operation of the ISFs, some clarifications ought to be made regarding the main element of the system – the IOC. Firstly, let us turn our attention to the factor of financial independence. The IOC (the sun) is an independent nonprofit international organization that feeds its batteries not from galactic energy, but, to a greater extent, from American business. The IOC quickly responded to the American victory in the Cold War (Altukhov & Nauright, 2018) at the end of the 20th century and reformatted the business model of the Olympic movement during the reign of Juan Antonio Samaranch to the rails of a capitalist economy. The idea of developing the humanitarian values of Olympism and promoting peace is a thing of the past. Profits, efficiency, revenues, and contracts have become new benchmarks for Samaranch and his followers Jacques Rogge and Thomas Bach, who, in fact, grew into the hostages of American politics. The persuasion and influence of Richard Pound and his American business partners led to the signing of an incredible agreement, USOC-IOC, in 1990 (15). USOC receives 12.75% of the funds obtained by the IOC from the television contracts' sale, plus 20% of the funds transferred to American sponsors in the IOC. Consequently, the IOC voluntarily agreed to be dependent on US sponsors and television.

After 19 years, the Assembly of the Association of Summer Olympic International Federations at the SportAccord Forum, held in Colorado Springs (the USA), in 2009, demanded the termination of this agreement, and in May 2012, a new USOC-IOC agreement was signed, endorsing the new rules for the distribution of funds from American companies to the IOC, estimated for 20 years – from 2020 to 2040. Under this agreement, the USOC's share of TV revenue is reduced to 7%, and 10% of revenue is transferred from the IOC sponsorship programme to the USOC (16). Generally speaking, USOC funding from the IOC has not changed considerably due to the increase in the cost of TV contracts, while the dependence of the IOC management structure and the entire Olympic Movement on American stakeholders has remained the key element of the business model.

The second aspect is political independence. History knows several precedents when athletes from Germany, Austria-Hungary, the Ottoman Empire, the Bulgarian kingdom, Japan, South Africa, Yugoslavia, and Afghanistan were suspended from Olympic starts. But the IOC has never suspended the US athletes for the US military actions in Afghanistan, Yugoslavia, Iraq, or Syria, since the United States created a legal basis for its actions in advance in the form of UN resolutions. An additional reason for questioning the legitimacy of the ISFs' decisions was the fact that the citizens of a country that is a member of the UN Security Council were removed from professional activity.

Case Analysis

Russian and Belarusian sports found themselves in isolation. In the directives and recommendations, the IOC refers to the consensus reached on the resolution of the UN General Assembly of 2 December 2021, "Promoting peace and building a happier life on the planet through sport and the embodiment of the Olympic ideals", which approved the Olympic truce. Later, IOC President Thomas Bach tried to explain his policy as a desire to preserve the integrity of the sport. According to him, athletes from other countries do not want to participate in competitions along with Russian and Belarusian athletes. In addition, he worries about the safety of the Russian and Belarusian athletes.

In fact, this call by Bach has returned us all to political and ethnic segregation, when people are artificially divided into first and second grades depending on their citizenship, violating the provisions of the International Convention on the Elimination of All Forms of Racial Discrimination (1965). Athletes from Russia and Belarus no longer have equal rights with other athletes. The prohibitions prescribe neutral status for them, neutral equipment and neutral flags and anthems. These athletes are deprived of their self-identity and isolated from the global sports community as inferior humans or dangerous animals. Formally speaking, the IOC did not violate anything at all – they only recommended the implementation of sanctions on Russia and Belarus, and the decision was made by the International Federations.

All the ISFs were created to regulate the calendar, enforce the rules and organize international sport competitions. Over time, their powers have expanded by spreading their activities and acquiring political influence (to varying degrees for each federation) at the global level. In this context, the International Sports Federations can legitimately be seen as subjects of international sports policy regimes (Houlihan, 2009).

International Sports Federations are essentially established by self-governing private norms (Casini, 2015), and position themselves as families. Leo Tolstoy noted that "all happy families are alike, each unhappy family is unhappy in its own way" (Tolstoy, 2020). The redoing of the business model of the Olympic movement according to the canons of the American market has led to changes in the business processes of the ISF, when, along with positive processes and growth in income, all the vices of humanity poured into sports – drug use, doping, match-fixing, fraud, violence, and corruption. Endless scandals, investigations, arrests, and trials began. Most sports federations were not ready for such misfortunes. The principles of management's autonomy and activity's self-regulation turned out to be insufficient for global decision-making.

In international regime theory, Stephen Krasner's classic definition conceptualizes regimes as "the implicit or explicit principles, norms, rules, and decision-making procedures around which the expectations of actors in a given area of international relations converge" (Krasner, 1982). The activities of the ISF are not only classified as international or continental, but also, they are directly

40 Sergey Altukhov

related to the interpenetration of international law, national legislation, and the soft law of sports regulations. Sports management scholars argue that ISF governance structures that have gained a monopoly on the regulation of sports and competition at the international level are not able to deal effectively with these challenges (Henry & Lee, 2004; Pieth, 2014).

The conflict of form and content emerged against the background of the scaling of the ISFs' activities and the inability to regulate these activities in any way. Presumably the concern of the IOC regarding the effectiveness of the ISFs' management and the subsequent implementation of the principles of good governance in the ISFs was related to this. In 2009, the "Basic Universal Principles for the Good Governance of the Olympic and Sports Movement" (PGG) proposed by the IOC and in 2016 the "Key Governance Principles and Key Indicators" (KGP) proposed by the General Assembly of ASOIF, including 28 Summer Olympic ISFs (ASOIF, 2016a), were adopted. Later KGP was supported by seven Winter Olympic ISFs.

The taken measures did not achieve the desired effect. The main reason was the lack of legal status in the relationship between the IOC and the ISFs and direct subordination. There was no regulator or supervisory body for the ISF before – there is none now. The IOC's powers to recognize the status of ISFs from among the organizations applying for this (Rule 25 of the charter) are sufficient for the dominance of the IOC among the subjects of world sports and the legal protection of the interests of the Olympic movement at the global level.

The ISFs, in turn, oversee their autonomy and include self-regulation when there is a risk of governmental interference or reputational costs from the actors of civil society (Isailovic & Pattberg, 2016; Vogel, 2006). Additionally, there are no cases in history where any ISF has benefitted from the compliance of other ISFs. Consequently, the ISFs have no incentive to delegate enforcement powers to the IOC or anyone else to ensure good governance (Abbott & Snidal, 2000). Thus, a situation emerges where there are clearly not enough mechanisms and tools within the system for strategic development in the context of a crisis in the growth of individual entities. External regulators may well include public oversight or governmental sanctions to secure control (Geeraert, 2018).

Conclusion

The rise of the Olympic movement around the world, the growing economic performance of the IOC, the high popularity, and recognition of the symbols of Olympism among the globe's population gradually led to a crisis in the entire system. This looks intriguing. We observe a lack of hierarchy in the structure of international regimes. The changing world order right in front of us highlights the helplessness and vulnerability of the outdated business model of the Olympic movement and the monopolies of ISFs trying their best to survive.

The introduction of compliance for the ISFs has a barely noticeable effect, as there is no completely independent external mechanism for monitoring compliance with the requirements, imposing sanctions, and their implementation. Various types of sports federations have individual compliance mechanisms. Compliance can be achieved through co-regulation, where the governance and persuasion mechanisms of the ISFs are complemented by sanctions from the public or civil society.

The main lesson of the globalization of sports is that the social models of the United States and Europe, recognized as "reference" ones, are not applicable globally. The conflict went beyond economic contradictions. Under these conditions, the priority is not investment or the creation of new markets (sources of value) – it is the new images and meanings of life.

References

Abbott, K., & Snidal, D. (2000). Hard and soft law in international governance. *International Organization*, 54(3), 421–456.

Altukhov, S., & Nauright, J. (2018). The new sporting Cold War: Implications of the Russian doping allegations for international relations and sport. *Sport in Society*, 21, 1120–1136.

ASOIF. (2016). *ASOIF Governance Task Force (GTF) Report Approved by ASOIF General Assembly 2016*. Lausanne: Author. Retrieved from http://www.asoif.com/sites/default/files/basic_page/asoif_governance_task_force_report.pdf

Bourg, J.-F. (2016). Dopage et mondialisation financière du sport: ce que nous apprend l'analyse économique. *Drogues, santé et société*, 15(1), 66–84.

Casini, L. (2015). The emergence of global administrative systems: The case of sport. *Glocalism: Journal of Culture, Politics and Innovation*, 1. https://doi.org/10.12893/gjcpi.2015.1.4

Geeraert, A. (2018). The limits and opportunities of self-regulation: Achieving international sport federations' compliance with good governance standards. *European Sport Management Quarterly*. https://doi.org/10.1080/16184742.2018.1549577

Henry, I., & Lee, P. C. (2004). Governance and ethics in sport. In S. Chadwick & J. Beech (Eds), *The Business of Sport Management* (pp. 25–41). Harlow: Pearson Education.

Houlihan, B. (2009). Mechanisms of international influence on domestic elite sport policy. *International Journal of Sport Policy and Politics*, 1(1), 51–69. https://doi.org/10.1080/19406940902739090

https://m.sport-express.ru/newspaper/2009-04-01/7_1/

https://www.championat.com/business/article-3172515-ssha-poshli-na-ustupki-mok-radi-domashnej olimpiady.html

Isailovic, M., & Pattberg, P. (2016). Private governance. In C. Ansell & J. Torfing (Eds.), *Handbook on Theories of Governance* (pp. 468–476). Cheltenham: Edward Elgar.

Krasner, S.D. (1982). Structural causes and regime consequences: Regimes asintervening variables. *International Organization*, 36(2), 185–205.

Morris, D. (1981). *The Soccer Tribe*. London: Jonathan Cape, p. 276.

Pieth, M. (2014). The responsibility of the host country. In M. Pieth (Ed.), *Reforming FIFA* (pp. 23–30). Zürich: Dike Verlag.

Tolstoy, L.N. (2020). *Anna Karenina*. Publisher ACT. –M., p.6.

Vogel, D. (2006). *The Market for Virtue: The Potential and Limits of Corporate Social Responsibility*. Washington, DC: Brookings Institute.

6

PUBLIC REMEMBERING OF SOCHI 2014 AT A TIME OF WAR

The Kremlin's Soft Disempowerment through Sport

Vitaly Kazakov

Introduction

Academics tend to assign past sporting mega-events (SMEs) into the firm categories of positive, negative, or mixed with respect to their broad impacts (Thomson et al., 2018). This is evident when exploring the domain of sporting events' reputational legacy. Considering the case of the Olympics, the 1936 Berlin Games are an example of an event remembered commonly with disdain. The 1964 Tokyo Olympics and 1992 Games in Barcelona are among those frequently evoked when discussing cases of roaring reputational "victories" for their hosts, while most others have complex symbolic histories. The aim of this chapter is to explore how a case of a contemporary SME with a negative reputation – the Sochi Olympic Games – is informed and further shaped by the geopolitical economy of sport through ongoing public negotiation of the event in the years after its conclusion.

SMEs and Soft (Dis-)Empowerment

The recently proposed conceptual scale between soft power and "soft disempowerment" through sport (Brannagan and Giulianotti, 2018) is a helpful tool to approach the public interpretation of the legacies of past sporting competitions. The concept of soft power, used so ubiquitously, refers to the perceived ability of such events to aid sponsoring states in promoting their interests through attraction rather than coercion. International broadcasting is one tool used by states to showcase their SMEs in favourable ways, mimicking or even surpassing the effect of in-person attendance to global audiences, which can, in turn, contribute to a state's soft power (Crilley et al., 2022). Typically, within the broad parameters of the geopolitical economy of sport, such an envisioned effect is used to

DOI: 10.4324/9781003348238-7

justify the investment into hosting major sporting events like the Olympics or the World Cup. However, the opposite outcome – soft disempowerment – has been more prominently discussed in recent years, whereby hosting SMEs can also "upset, offend or alienate others, leading to a loss of attractiveness or influence" (Brannagan and Giulianotti, 2015: 706). Qatar has proven to be a case in point, as this country's hosting of the 2022 Men's Football World Cup has drawn negative international attention to the state's human rights record, "leading audiences to question the state's integrity and adding further to its perceived lack of credibility" (Brannagan and Giulianotti, 2018: 1156; Crilley et al., 2022).

While discussions on soft power, disempowerment, and the less well-developed concept of sportswashing are becoming more nuanced and plentiful within the broader study of the geopolitical economy of sport (see Chadwick et al., Chapter 1, this volume), one significant angle of enquiry is still surprisingly underdeveloped: namely, the comparative analysis of short-, medium-, and long-term reputational consequences and the effects of soft power (or otherwise) linked to the SMEs after they concluded. Much of the literature makes assessments of such events' effects before they take place and very shortly after they conclude. Few scholars ask what becomes of the soft power effect once the spotlight of international attention moves onto new SMEs and political issues interlinked with them. This chapter bridges this gap by analysing the case of the Sochi 2014 Winter Olympics nearly a decade after their conclusion and in connection to subsequent extreme political turbulence surrounding the Games' host nation.

The State of Russian Nation Projection through Sport in 2022

In early 2022, following the bans on the participation of Russian teams and athletes in most international competitions due to the Russian invasion of Ukraine, the Russian national sports broadcasting network MatchTV aired a promo clip for the channel with a caption in Russian reading, "sanctions are temporary, victories are forever". The clip included footage of high-profile victories of Russian teams and athletes from the recent past, interspersed with overtly political visuals such as the American flag falling from the rafters of a stadium. The visuals, together with the caption, were a tongue-in-cheek effort to "protect" Russian athletes and play up past sporting glories, including from the Sochi Olympics. This clip targeted the domestic audience of the network with an ostentatiously double-voiced reference to victories not only in stadia but also on the battlefield by only showcasing the former and alluding to the latter via overt references to political conflicts. One of the most baffling attempts to project the nation via sports to international audiences at this time was the Russian sports authorities' declaration of their interest to bid to host the UEFA 2028 European Football Championship. Given this statement came in the midst of the Russian invasion of its neighbour, UEFA promptly shut down this audacious proposal (Braidwood,

2022). The international sporting community and public took this, at best, as a delusional attempt at sports diplomacy at a time of war, and at worst as a cynical and calculated provocation by a hostile state.

Perceptions of such nation projection efforts through sport in the conditions of an active war in Europe are very much in contrast to those concerning the Russian SME hosting just under a decade ago. Both the Sochi Games and the 2018 FIFA World Cup, held in Russia, aimed to project an image of a "new", cosmopolitan host country to audiences both at home and abroad (Kazakov, 2019). At the end of the Sochi Olympics, for example, a senior Kremlin official declared that the "Games have turned [Russia's] culture and the people into something that is a lot closer and more appealing and understandable for the rest of the world" (Grohmann, 2014). Despite such optimism, hard power developments like the annexation of Crimea and the doping scandal – both of which shortly followed Sochi 2014 – tarnished the immediate legacy and lasting soft power effects of Russia's first post-Soviet SME (Orttung and Zhemukhov, 2017).

In his recent analysis relying on the benefit of hindsight, Richard Arnold suggested that

> the speed and willingness with which Russia sacrificed any soft power returns from the Sochi 2014 Olympics [suggest] that "soft power" was not the main reason Russia wanted to host such events, and the prestige of the event itself was instead the trophy sought.
>
> *(Arnold, 2022)*

Moreover, further studies explained that unlike other cases, domestic – rather than foreign – audiences and regime legitimacy were the primary targets of Russia's "unique" soft power strategy in hosting SMEs (Grix and Kramareva, 2017; Wolfe, 2021). The apparent short-termism, opportunism, and a sharper focus on domestic, rather than foreign, audiences in the Kremlin's pursuit of SMEs, however, do not negate the need to understand the lasting and ongoing effects of Sochi and similar events. They remain a site where soft power and disempowerment effects simultaneously accrue and dissipate over time as new related developments come to light and the public is reminded of the spectacle of the past SMEs.

I argued previously that mega-events resist straightforward utilization as tools of soft power, nation branding, or regime legitimation and do not inevitably produce desirable effects (Kazakov, 2019); rather, to some degree they live a life of their own upon their official conclusion. One way to understand the ongoing relevance and political significance of past SMEs is to study the way they are remembered and discussed by members of the public at various points in time in the SME's aftermath. Such an enquiry helps to complete the picture of the geopolitical economy of a particular sporting competition and complements analyses within other domains that explore SMEs' impacts in the economic, social, and political spheres.

The Evolution of Public Memory of Sochi: From 2014 to 2022

The remainder of the analysis in this chapter provides a brief overview of the volatile dynamics in public interpretation of the Sochi Games at three points after their conclusion: the outbreak of the doping scandal in the immediate aftermath of the Games, the Tokyo 2020 hacking affair, and the 2022 Russian invasion of Ukraine. The discussion is based primarily on social media analysis, and as such is not representative of the public opinion at large, but rather reflective of just one dimension and several platforms, sites, and temporal points of renegotiation for the symbolic legacy of the SME by various publics. Such an explorative discussion offers insights into the ongoing negotiations of the significance of a past SME with a negative reputation.

Any reactions traced need to be judged against the initial vision and message shared by the sponsors and organizers of the event. To have any positive and lasting effect, communications around an event like the Olympics need to craft a resonant effect upon the audiences, meaning they are not just noticeable and visible, but also coherent and persuasive (Liang, 2019). The image of "new Russia" projected by state-aligned actors in the lead-up to and during the 2014 Games was that of a respected member of the international community and a great power capable of efficiently organizing a world-class event; one that relies on strong popular support, a stable political and social order, and a flourishing economy to succeed (Kazakov, 2019). When the Games ended in February 2014, some social media analyses showed initial responses to the Olympics were indicative of a "soft power victory" for Russia. The authors of one such study observed that some of the initial negative commentary on Twitter in relation to the corruption, #SochiProblems, and Russian "anti-gay legislature" narratives that were prevalent prior to the Games' kick-off reduced in public conversations over time and gave way to a more general discussion about sports (Kirilenko and Stepchenkova, 2017). However, this is consistent with the general patterns of reporting on and discussing other similar sporting events (Liang, 2019). Furthermore, the breakout of the Crimea affair, the war in Donbas, and the eventual doping scandal all prompted academics to suggest that the Sochi Games were "quickly forgotten" (Orttung and Zhemukhov, 2017: 1), and that any prospects of soft power dissolved (Grix and Kramareva, 2017) immediately following the Games' conclusion.

My analysis of a popular site of reflection on the Sochi 2014 legacy in its aftermath showed that such assessments oversimplified the picture. At the time, I studied public comments users left under the official video recording of the Sochi 2014 Opening Ceremony, as shared by the official IOC Olympic Channel YouTube account. By mid-2016 – more than two years after the Games' conclusion and amid doping scandals and international conflict – the YouTube recording had over 1,600 public comments. My qualitative assessment of these comments showed that, contrary to one's expectation of finding a community of democratic polemic about the controversies surrounding the Games, the thread was rather a community of cosmopolitan affection towards the Games and Russia, and it reflected some of the messaging put out by the Olympics' organizers. It may have been the case that the comment thread was moderated by the IOC's social media managers and that Russian bots and trolls inflated the number of positive reflections on the 2014 Games. However, taken at face value, the commentary amounted to an imprint of a "soft power effect" generated by the Games which existed in a public domain. For example, "doping" only appeared once in the English language comments between 2014 and 2016, and none in Russian. Some users favourably compared the Sochi Ceremony to Rio's in 2016. Others expressed affection from around the world, such as "It was a great opening ceremony! Love Russia! from China" [*sic*] (Kazakov, 2019). This online community, however, did not survive the test of time. Shortly after the initial analysis of the comments shared, the IOC took down the recording of the full Sochi opening ceremony broadcast, thus erasing this archive of Sochi's "soft power affection".

Many other sites of public negotiation and remembering of Sochi 2014 have emerged since. The public commentary on the recording of the PyeongChang 2018 Opening Ceremony, for example, drew comparisons and reflections on the Sochi Games. Comments like "Great job South Korea! You guys made good use of the money for the opening ceremony [...] I enjoyed this more than Sochi!" [*sic*] were commonplace and indicate the effects of soft disempowerment rather than any reputational gains for the hosts of the 2014 Games. Another poignant moment in the public renegotiation of the Sochi memory came in 2020, when Moscow was accused of sponsoring cyberattacks against the subsequent Olympics (Wintour et al., 2020). A small-scale analysis of public engagement with this story and its reflection on the Sochi legacy, as expressed through Twitter engagement, helped me to further test the soft (dis-)empowerment dynamics surrounding a past mega-event in the conditions of a newly breaking political story. One assessment (Kazakov, 2021) found that a significant proportion of public commentary on Twitter evoking the Sochi 2014 Games reflected on the nefarious nature of actions linked to the Russian government. Specifically, about a quarter of all tweets in this sample that mentioned Sochi 2014 blamed the authorities in Moscow for its interference in the Tokyo Games and other recent cases of disreputable actions on the international stage, including the doping scandal. This was direct evidence of soft disempowerment through sport and the sponsoring of SMEs. Another significant proportion of messages simply commented on the sporting competitions at Sochi, or otherwise reflected either neutrally or even positively on the 2014 Olympics and their hosts. This meant that even in the conditions of a major international scandal implicitly and explicitly linked to a past mega-event, the effects of soft power and soft disempowerment continued to co-exist.

Finally, the 2022 Russian invasion of Ukraine provided the most recent and poignant opportunity to explore how the public remembers the 2014 SME in the conditions of active hostility by the former host state, sharply juxtaposed against their "soft power offensive" just eight years prior (Rutland and Kazantsev, 2016). I collected Twitter messages between February and June 2022 that included references to Sochi 2014 and its memory or remembering in English and Russian. Here, a section of the posts still only discussed the sporting results of the Sochi competitions, highlighting that the sporting element of the SME remains a significant mnemonic reference even at a time of war. However, the rest of the engagement clearly indicated the dynamics of soft disempowerment through the SME, rather than any positive reputational legacy. One simple metric helped to showcase this. While the tweets sympathetic towards Russia or its government's narratives generated under 50 likes combined from other members of the Twittersphere, those messages with a negative sentiment towards the Sochi Games, or the Russian government's power narratives generated over 5,000 external likes in total.

Soft disempowerment through sport was evident here not only through simple quantitative metrics, but qualitative ones as well. Some of the same members who had previously shown affection towards Russia in 2014 now explicitly rejected the narratives of "new Russia" that were initially proposed through the Sochi Games. One such Twitter user wrote,

> it is very sad for Russia to think what could have been. 2014 Sochi Olympics, the magnificent presentation showing all of Russia's many people, the vastness, beauty, the greatness of her art & science […] Your narrative was excellent. You charmed the world. Sad.

Clearly, the soft power effect existing immediately following the Games turned into regret in the new geopolitical reality surrounding the host state.

Conclusion

Overall, this chapter highlighted that the effects of soft power and disempowerment co-exist at various points in the aftermath of an SME. Both dynamics shape the geopolitical economy of a particular event and have ripple effects on the perceptions of other events, sports more broadly, and related political narratives. The analysis of public memory of past SMEs can therefore help us to trace these dynamics. While the example of Russia is one of the extremes, in which active war has all but erased the soft power effect of their SME hosting, it is noteworthy that Russian authorities are nevertheless still attempting to use sport as a venue for nation projection activity (as examples of the MatchTV promo and a failed bid for the 2028 Euros illustrate). In such severe circumstances, however, the international sporting audience no longer seems to find sympathy for this cause. Ultimately, all SMEs have complex and fluid reputational legacies, and these need to be studied better as part of our exploration of the geopolitical economy of sport.

Bibliography

Arnold R (2022) The most consequential world cup in history? *PONARS: Eurasia PolicyMemo* (799).

Braidwood J (2022) Russia banned from making Euro 2028 bid as part of Uefa measures. *The Independent*, 2 May. Available at: https://www.independent.co.uk/sport/football/russia-uefa-euros-2028-bid-b2069982.html (accessed 17/10/2022).

Brannagan PM and Giulianotti R (2015) Soft power and soft disempowerment: Qatar, global sport and football's 2022 World Cup finals. *Leisure Studies* 34(6): 703–719. DOI: 10.1080/02614367.2014.964291.

Brannagan PM and Giulianotti R (2018) The soft power–soft disempowerment nexus: The case of Qatar. *International Affairs* 94(5): 1139–1157. DOI: 10.1093/ia/iiy125.

Crilley R, Gillespie M, Kazakov V and Willis A (2022) 'Russia isn't a country of Putins!': How RT bridged the credibility gap in Russian public diplomacy during the 2018 FIFA World Cup. *The British Journal of Politics and International Relations* 24(1): 136–152. DOI: 10.1177/13691481211013713.

Grix J and Kramareva N (2017) The Sochi Winter Olympics and Russia's unique soft power strategy. *Sport in Society* 20(4): 461–475. DOI: 10.1080/17430437.2015.1100890.

Grohmann K (2014) Sochi broke ice of scepticism over Russia. Available at: https://uk.reuters.com/article/olympics-sochi-kozak/sochi-broke-ice-of-scepticism-over-russia-deputy-pm-idINDEEA1L02O20140222 (accessed 1/02/2018).

Kazakov V (2019) *Representations of 'New Russia' through a 21st Century Mega-Event: The Political Aims, Informational Means, and Popular Reception of the Sochi 2014 Winter Olympic Games.* PhD Dissertation. University of Manchester, UK.

Kazakov V (2021) What does the hacking of the Tokyo Olympics mean for Russia's reputation? *Commentary, The Royal United Services Institute.* Available at: https://rusi.org/explore-our-research/publications/commentary/what-does-hacking-tokyo-olympics-mean-russia%E2%80%99s-reputation (accessed 10/04/2021).

Kirilenko A and Stepchenkova S (2017) Sochi 2014 Olympics on Twitter: Perspectives of hosts and guests. *Tourism Management* 63: 54–65.

Liang L (2019) Crafting resonance in a sports media event: The Olympic games as a transnational social drama. *Journalism Studies* 20(3): 401–422.

Orttung R and Zhemukhov S (2017) *Putin's Olympics: The Sochi Games and the Evolution of Twenty-First Century Russia.* London: Routledge.

Rutland P and Kazantsev A (2016) The limits of Russia's 'soft power'. *Journal of Political Power* 9(3): 395–413. DOI: 10.1080/2158379X.2016.1232287.

Thomson A, Cuskelly G, Toohey K, Kennelly M, Burton P and Fredline L (2018) Sport event legacy: A systematic quantitative review of literature. *Sport Management Review* 22(3): 295–321.

Wintour P, Borger J and McCurry J (2020) Russia planned cyber-attack on Tokyo Olympics, says UK. *The Guardian*, 20 October. Available at: https://www.theguardian.com/world/2020/oct/19/russia-planned-cyber-attack-on-tokyo-olympics-says-uk (accessed 14/07/2022).

Wolfe SD (2021) *More Than Sport: Soft Power and Potemkinism in the 2018 Men's Football World Cup in Russia.* Lausanne: Verlag Münster.

7

TRANSNATIONAL LEAGUES AND THEIR ROLE IN PROJECTING SOFT POWER

Olivier Jarosz, Konstantin Kornakov, and Adam Metelski

Introduction

On Thursday, 13th of December, 2012, in RIA Novosti's Moscow Office, a press conference is hosted by Sergei Pryadkin, head of the Russian Football Premier League, together with chiefs of three leading Russian clubs: Alexander Dyukov of Zenit, Evgeni Giner of CSKA, and Konstantin Remchukov of Anzhi (RIA Novosti, 2012). What they announce is not quite revolutionary and has been speculated on for many years by fans of post-Soviet football, but it is nevertheless a bombshell of regional and potentially global significance – the launch of preparation for a new unified football championship of the Commonwealth of Independent States (CIS), the political heir to the former USSR, which was dismantled just over 20 years before that press conference.

What was outlined over the more than two hours of this media event by the men captured some of the key narratives of the moment, and was the result of a convergence in a single space and time of several different threads of development in the modern European football industry, including the increasing commercialization and polarization of European football, financial fair play mechanisms, regional football competitions, and optimal calendars for leagues, as well as Russia's own transformation over the post-Soviet period. It was expected that as a direct result of this media event the Russian and Ukrainian top divisions would merge to create a mega (or super) league with significantly enhanced sporting and commercial potential compared to the standalone leagues of Russian and Ukraine.

Today, less than a decade later and armed with the power of hindsight, we know that this project was doomed to failure from the very beginning for multiple reasons, not least that within a year and a half from that press conference at RIA Novosti, Russia was engaging in open hostile actions against Ukraine,

DOI: 10.4324/9781003348238-8

including the annexation of Crimea and covert military action in the Donbas region, which since February 2022 has become overt and increasingly destructive. Knowing all of this makes it even more fascinating to consider the motivations of all the sides involved in such a mega project, and compare it to other transnational competitions to find out if political aims can realistically be a good starting point, or whether business rationale should always set the tone.

All this described above fits in the context of the geopolitical economy of sport, i.e. "the way in which nations, states and other entities engage in, with, or through sport for geographic and politico-economic reasons" (Chadwick, 2022a). At this point, it is also worth explaining that soft power is the ability to get what one wants through attraction (Nye, 2004). In summary, it can be said that "in so exerting soft power, the goals of nations are myriad, including the building of political and commercial influence" (Chadwick, Widdop, and Burton, 2020). Sport and sport-related mega-events have typically been seen as one of the tools through which soft power can be projected, but leagues have not generally been considered in academic research, with preference normally going to the likes of World Cups and Olympics (Grix and Lee, 2013). But the case of the United League is clearly worth examining in this dimension, as it came during a turbulent period in Russo-Ukrainian political relations that preceded overt military conflict, and sport was being used for political purposes by the Russian state at the time (Golubchikov, 2017).

Genesis of the United League

Back in 2012, Russian football, and sport in general, was riding high: since 2007, when the Winter Olympics of 2014 were officially granted to the Black Sea resort of Sochi, the Russian football club Zenit won the UEFA cup in a final against Rangers in 2008, the Summer Universiade of 2013 was awarded to Kazan just two weeks later. In June that same year the Russian National Team finished joint third in its best showing in international football for two decades, and then on 2 December 2010, Sepp Blatter announced the awarding of the FIFA World Cup finals in 2018 to Russia at the home of football in Zurich.

Actually, in what was a very big year for Russian sport, 2008 also saw the creation of two of the forerunners of the United League project – the KHL, or Kontinental Hockey League, modelled on the NHL, and the VTB United League, which was Russian basketball's NBA equivalent. The ice hockey project was long in development, as it was originally proposed by legendary Soviet player Vyacheslav Fetisov in 2005 when he was heading the Russian Federal agency on physical culture and sport. The opening KHL season had 21 Russian teams and a representative each from Belarus, Kazakhstan, and Latvia. Over the years, this international dimension of KHL expanded, in a similar way to US leagues opening up new franchises, and in the various seasons had competing teams from the likes of China, Croatia, Czech Republic, Finland, Slovakia, and Ukraine.

The VTB United League was an even more international affair, including a larger proportion of non-Russian teams on its roster. Similarly, to the KHL, from an initial focus on top clubs from former Soviet republics (Belarus, Estonia, Georgia, Kazakhstan, Latvia, Lithuania, and Ukraine), a move was also made to include teams from other European countries such as the Czech Republic, Finland, and Poland, although they were also within the USSR's orbit of influence during the Soviet period, and came from what was known during that time as Russia's "near abroad". It is worth adding that there are several transnational sports leagues in the world, and some of them are presented in Table 7.1.

The big Russian strategy of leveraging massive sports events as a serious development and marketing tool was clearly making big strides, so much so that it was even mentioned as one of his top-10 priorities by the then President of the Russian Federation, Dmitry Medvedev, at his Davos speech in 2011:

> Tenth, we have launched the implementation of large-scale infrastructure projects including having obtained the right to host major sporting events. This is not just a victory for sports lovers, this is a realistic chance for us to realize the development of major infrastructure projects that will enhance the lives of Russian citizens and develop individual regions of Russia, giving people the opportunity to visit Russia and understand its willingness to open itself to the world.
>
> *(Upbin, 2011)*

As Medvedev clearly stated, this strategy was not only about national showmanship or positioning Russia back at the top global table of influencers – it was also a mechanism of physically developing the country (or parts thereof) in what Oleg Golubchikov terms as "spatial governance" (2017). Organizing top club competitions in various sports, able to compete with the best leagues in the world, with their infrastructure, transport, human resource, finance, branding, and other needs, on a transnational level, was "spatial governance" not only domestically but exported to other countries. All of this was a result of many years of work and seemed to fall neatly into a consistent thread of using sport, and in particular, football, to extend Russia's soft power globally, and in the process confirm the re-branding of the country as a new, modern, dynamic, and competitive global power (Bogdanova, 2014).

Russia's football, in particular, was becoming a boom destination for many international stars: from Anzhi, who captured former Barcelona striker Samuel Eto'o in season 2011/12, to Rubin Kazan and last but not least to huge spenders Zenit with big transfers of the likes of Bruno Alves, Hulk, and Axel Witsel, records were being set and a new gold rush was building up a head of steam for those clubs, players, and agents that seemed keen to take part. With the Russian state very keen to continue making use of sport as an important tool in its political, economic, and social development, it was only a matter of time that the domestic football competition would also get brought in for scrutiny as

TABLE 7.1 Different transnational leagues across the world

Short name	Full name	Sport	Origin	Main sponsor	Number of countries from the beginning	Teams in total	Estimation of the main objective
ABA	Adriatic Basketball Association	Basketball	Croatia	AdmiralBet	10	14	Commercial
A-League	A-League	Football	Australia	ISUZU	2	12	Commercial
KHL	Kontinental Hockey League	Hockey	Russia	SOGAZ	10	22	Mixed
MLS	Major League Soccer	Football	USA	–	2	28	Commercial
NBA	National Basketball Association	Basketball	USA	–	2	30	Commercial
SEHA	South East Handball Association League	Handball	Croatia	Gazprom	13	10	Mixed
VTB	VTB United League	Basketball	Russia	VTB	11	10	Mixed

something needing improvement. Despite the obvious development of Zenit's success in Europe in 2008 and the emergence of some ambitious clubs, particularly in the Caucasus and Tatarstan, public attendance was still lagging well behind European competitors. Market-generated commercial revenues were still rather low, broadcasting revenue was nowhere near the leading competitions like the English Premier League, and the spending of Russian clubs on transfers and coaches was not delivering an acceptable ROI (Sports.ru, 2012). The position of the Russian league in the UEFA ranking and the average audience at matches are presented in Table 7.2.

Despite an upturn in transfer spending in the aftermath of the 2008 global economic crisis, which impacted the existing European football ecosystem especially by creating the conditions for major changes in club ownership, Russia's professional club football was still not competitive enough to challenge the biggest European leagues such as the Premier League in England, La Liga in Spain or even the French Ligue 1, or such prestigious tournaments as UEFA's continent-wide Champions League. Unlike ice hockey or basketball, where there already were local equivalents (for better or worse) of the best leagues globally, the NHL and NBA, in football, the domestic Russian product both on and off the field was of inferior quality even compared to its US equivalent (Kozlovsky, 2015), and this would have been painfully obvious to many eyes.

For the Russian football (and national) authorities this was clearly an issue to be addressed if they did not want to be completely sidelined by other more successful sports or sporting events. In the lead-up to 2012, Russian clubs were trying to find some solutions, and the first big one was to switch the traditional league calendar from a spring–autumn schedule to an autumn–spring season with a long winter break in the middle. This allowed the competition to become synchronized with most of its European counterparts and was also proof that big change was possible both strategically and operationally. But it was clearly not enough to satisfy all the big ambitions, and could not deliver the same impact as hosting an Olympics or World Cup.

Russian club football needed something big: something that could solve all those issues, and do it in such a way that would be noticed both at home and abroad. And here, as with many other things in Russian modern history, the solution was to look at the past, but using all the latest visual and marketing methods: revisit the idea of the old Soviet football league, which had all the best clubs from the Soviet republics and had the aura of extremely high-level competition. Veteran Dynamo Moscow player from the 1950s and 1960s Vladimir Kesarev, who also participated in that famous press conference in Moscow in December 2012, was probably brought there to say as much: He said nostalgically:

> I participated in the USSR championship and can state that the games were so interesting and so high energy in the attempts to win [by the competing teams] that today it is rare to see a game like that, which could compete in interest with those times.

TABLE 7.2 Average attendance in the Russian top football league and Russia's UEFA country position

Season	2003	2004	2005	2006	2007	2008	2009	2010	11/12[a]	12/13
Average attendance	11,309	11,560	11,997	12,014	13,127	12,914	12,434	12,375	13,009	13,261
Russia's UEFA country ranking	10	18	21	13	9	9	6	6	7	7

Source: transfermarkt.de and uefa.com.

[a]This was a transition season beginning in March 2011 and lasting until May 2012, comprising two parts, which enabled the Russian league to move from a spring–autumn league calendar to an autumn–spring season.

Clearly, the calculation was that a combined league should once again produce such high-energy and competitive games, which would, in turn, generate a "completely different level of product" and one that "could be sold for, say, a billion US dollars", according to another participant of the press conference, Konstantin Remchukov of Anzhi.

A combined league would bring together the best football clubs in Eastern Europe, including three winners of the UEFA cup: CSKA Moscow, Zenit St Petersburg, and Shakhtar Donetsk. The theory was simple: a cross-border league will be more attractive for football fans and that means more interest from TV and sponsors. There were predictions that more than 30% of the league's income would come from selling television rights and a significant amount would also come from selling tickets (Lidster, 2013). The intention to build a Russian–Ukrainian league in 2013 was very realistic after the league announced its budget, formed an organizing committee, opened an office in the centre of Moscow, and even created official pages on social media. Gazprom, Russia's natural gas monopoly which owns Russian champions Zenit St. Petersburg and used to (until the beginning of war in 2022) sponsor the UEFA Champions League, proposed an impressive €1 billion budget for the Russian–Ukrainian league and could award an attractive €92m prize for the league's winner. Interestingly, Gazprom doesn't sell anything directly to consumers, instead sells gas to countries (Chadwick, 2022b), so it is best characterized as a G2G (government-to-government) deal. Undoubtedly the Champions League matches enabled Gazprom unique diplomatic and networking opportunities (Chadwick, 2021). In the case of a joint league of Russia and Ukraine, representatives of Gazprom would have direct access to representatives of the national and local authorities of Ukraine via the backdoor of sport. Undoubtedly, it could be an opportunity to exert some influence on them and entangle them in a network of dependencies – an example of soft power. This soft power, in turn, may well have been intended to, for instance, play a role in securing Gazprom's control over Ukraine's gas transport network, which was meant to be unbundled as part of the adherence of Ukraine to the EU's Third Energy Package and was actively worked on by the relevant Ukrainian authorities already in 2012 (Ministry of Energy and Coal Industry of Ukraine, 2012).

Ukraine's top clubs FC Shakhtar Donetsk and FC Dynamo Kyiv publicly expressed their interest in the united Russian–Ukrainian football league but underlined that it should follow a joint decision among all the clubs in the Ukrainian Premier League. In the meantime, the president of the Ukrainian Football Federation – Anatoliy Konkov, expressed a firm "no" to this project. His main argument was that by taking part in the United League Ukraine will lose the opportunity to participate in European competitions (Lidster, 2013).

Apart from the more long-term strategic aspects of improving the competitiveness of Russian club football (Russian Football Federation, 2006) and making it more economically sustainable (i.e. without significant inputs from club sponsors, which were by that time supporting most, if not all, Russian clubs), there was also another interesting, albeit rather more personal, back story to this United League concept. It stemmed from a disciplinary action taken against Zenit St Petersburg for an incident that happened in its match against Moscow rivals Dynamo, where Zenit fans threw fireworks onto the field, which ended up injuring Dynamo's goalkeeper. This led to the Control Disciplinary Committee of the Russian Football Union awarding the match to Dynamo and punishing Zenit with a fine and two matches behind closed doors (TASS, 2012). In a rather unexpected twist, this led Zenit fan and Gazprom CEO Alexei Miller to declare that Zenit might choose to leave the Russian league and go play somewhere else, which was openly publicized on Zenit club communication channels. One of the possible destinations mentioned at the time was the Ukrainian Premier League, where it was said that Zenit could represent the Crimean city of Sevastopol (Trushin, 2012).

Bearing in mind the role of sometimes unpredictable individual events on global-level historical events (see the entire history of the First World War), coupled with UEFA-inspired talk of a change in its long-standing negative approach to multinational league competitions, which was widely discussed in football circles at the time and had some potential areas of application such as in the Baltic region, Balkans, Czech + Slovak leagues, and Belgium + Netherlands, who knows if Miller's threat was actually the detonator needed for proceeding with the Russian-led United League in football in the first place.

The Committee Begins Its Work

The next important date in the story of the United League was 26 December 2012, when it became publicly known that the person selected to head the project was Valery Gazzaev, one of the most well-known football figures in Russia and the former USSR at the time. After a successful playing career as a busy striker for several Soviet club teams, including spells at home-town Spartak Ordzhonikidze (later to become Spartak-Alania and Alania Vladikavkaz), Lokomotiv, and Dynamo Moscow as well as caps for the USSR national team, Gazzaev became a famous head coach who broke Spartak's early dominance in Russian football in the 1990s by winning the league title with his boyhood club Spartak-Alania and then led CSKA Moscow to domestic and European glory in the early to mid-2000s. Crucially for the project, his CV also included a fairly recent spell as manager of Dynamo Kyiv, which did not bring much silverware but enabled him to firm up on contacts in the Ukrainian game.

According to Gazzaev, the creation of this project was supposed to bring a solution to three key challenges facing Russian football: "First of all, it is to do with the loss of spectator interest. Secondly, many clubs drop out of the championship due to financial problems. Many clubs are threatened by Financial Fair Play", he claimed in the public interview where he announced his new job. In parallel, it was also confirmed that the organizational committee was to be headed by Sergei Pryadkin, with the participation of Dyukov from Zenit, Giner from CSKA, and Suleiman Kerimov, the owner of Anzhi. Gazzaev also identified the steps he wanted to take to convince the stakeholders of the worthiness of the project. He said in his introduction:

> First of all, we need to set up the work with national federations, discuss the format of the new championship, access list to European competitions, the first division, youth championship. We are building quite a good team to be able to decide on these matters. And then we will go to the national and international federations with the idea.

So what was meant to be a joint Russo-Ukrainian project was to be run exclusively by representatives of Russian football! It can therefore be assumed that in a way it was an attempt to impose Russian imperialism through sport and even to take the independent status away from Ukraine (Figure 7.1).

Curiously, the announcement of Gazzaev came hot on the heels of an intervention by Russia's then Minister of Sport, Vitaly Mutko, who had a long trajectory in sports administration, first in Saint Petersburg, where he participated in the organization of the Goodwill Games in 1994 and headed FC Zenit around the turn of the new century, and then in Moscow, moving from the presidency of the Russian Football Premier League to the presidency of the Russian Football Union, and then the Ministry of Sport itself. According to Mutko, the creation of the United League was a "fake target" and was an idea that has not been thought through, taking the attention away from the real problems of Russian football, which were "clubs losing sponsors, dropping attendances, fan troubles, transparency of club budgets, development of new talents" (Andreev, 2012).

All of this hinted suspiciously at a conflict, or at least at a lack of shared vision on how to solve the problems, which were being mentioned by everyone: it seemed like there was a group of long-time sports administrators who wanted to operate within the existing pyramid of football and believed that a united competition would be too difficult to organize (and would probably also threaten the existing order), and a group led by Miller, Gazzaev, and the biggest Russian clubs, who saw the recipe of success in the creation of a new combined league

FIGURE 7.1   Rationale behind the United League.

structure, which would kick-start public interest and guarantee football quality together with commercial success.

Less than a month later, the former group landed a major punch when Sepp Blatter, the then FIFA President, visited Saint Petersburg for the opening of the annual CIS Cup, which was a friendly international tournament between post-Soviet clubs from across the geography of the collapsed USSR. Blatter, sitting together with Nikita Tolstykh, the president of the Russian Football Union, was extremely clear in his assessment of the potential of a new United League: "It's impossible. It goes against the principles of FIFA, therefore FIFA would never support such an idea", he stated to the media (Kyiv Post, 2013).

On 18 February 2013, the United League group hit back: at an event hosted by Alexei Miller, the potential competition began to take some shape. Thirty-two clubs, sixteen each from Russia and Ukraine, were invited. Now it was becoming clear that this was no CIS league to bring back the USSR competition – the focus of this project was exclusively Ukraine, but it was going much deeper than a Superleague between the best clubs of both nations. It was really a complete merger of professional football of Russia and Ukraine. However, there was a clear issue emerging with the project: even though all 32 top division clubs from both Russia and Ukraine were invited to this presentation and meeting of the United League organizational committee, it was graced by 14 out of 16 Russian clubs (Mordovia Saransk and Terek Grozny were the absentees), but only one Ukrainian club chose to appear: Tavriya Simferopol. The Ukrainian side was also represented by the executive director of the UPL, Petr Ivanov, but the major clubs were not there (Ria Novosti, 2013).

Alexei Miller, in the aftermath of the meeting, stated that they were hoping to be able to begin the new championship as early as in season 2014–15, but certainly in 2015–16 at the latest (Rsport, 2013), with nine Russian and nine Ukrainian clubs joining up a lucrative division that would compete with the Champions League itself. To achieve this kind of speed, the organizers would need to put everything in place in the space of a few months, since the season beginning in 2013–14 would have been the last under old domestic rules. So, Gazzaev set out to convince the parties, especially the missing Ukrainians. And here it would be appropriate to look at the project through the eyes of both Russian and Ukrainian clubs, as they remember these events today, and some quotes are presented in Table 7.3.

Ahead of the meeting in Moscow on 18 February 2013, Gazzaev travelled to Kyiv on a mission to talk the Ukrainian clubs into supporting the new project (Aleshin, 2013), but as was evident from the attendance list in the Russian capital, the Ukrainian side was extremely weary of jumping off the fence, at least publicly. According to direct participants in those events, the main (and only) argument from Gazzaev was the expected €1bn financial windfall, which was meant to entice Ukrainian clubs to join by solving all their financial problems, which at the time meant that several clubs had to withdraw from the competition due to lack of funds. This was echoed by FFU Vice-president Sergei

TABLE 7.3 Perspective on the United League from the Ukrainian and Russian sides

Ukrainian club view from inside	*Russian club view from inside*
"The idea to play with Russian clubs made sense to have a boost and be more competitive in the UCC". "Not many details were shared to us, as we understood that there is a political principle at the genesis". "When reforms are made by bureaucrats you do not have much concern on football, when reforms are made by football bureaucrats, they do not have much concern on the commercial".	"We played regularly with Ukrainian teams and due to their high level it made sense to play more often". "The whole idea has not been developed at the origin amongst the football circles, we were discovering slice by slice".

Storozhenko later on in the year, in an interview with the Russian sports newspaper *Soviet Sport* (Lokalov, 2013). However, those siren calls were enough to organize a friendly pre-season tournament that included two top clubs from both Russia and Ukraine during June and July 2013 (LB.ua, 2013a), where the Ukrainian clubs each received 1/1000th of the promised cumulative revenue of the future United League for their participation, presumably to demonstrate the serious nature of the project (LB.ua, 2013b). Not surprisingly, this followed the template set by the VTB United League in basketball, which also started as a friendly tournament that evolved into a full-blown official competition.

As the year was progressing, it was becoming clear that the Ukrainian football authorities would not support the proposed merger, as Storozhenko and also FFU President Anatoli Kon'kov clearly stated in their interviews with Russian media (Interfax, 2013), which seemed more interested in this project than the Ukrainian side. Even the leaders of Dynamo Kyiv, which would have been one of the flag bearers of the new competition from the Ukrainian side, were not convinced (LB.ua, 2013c). The fans of Dynamo were certainly clear in their rejection of this project: in a statement, they underlined the political nature of this, termed it a "betrayal of the national interests of the citizens of both countries [Russia and Ukraine]", and declared a boycott to the friendly competition (Fanstyle.ru, 2013). At the same time, the organizational committee led by Gazzaev progressed with their operational development and first opened its headquarters in Moscow in April, located in the rather infamous Lubyanka street (Airapetov, 2013), which during Soviet times was also home to the KGB organization, later to be followed by a foothold in Kyiv in October 2013 (TASS, 2013), just weeks before the outbreak of the Revolution of Dignity. By then, however, it was becoming clear that the project was not succeeding. In a major press conference with Russian media in Moscow at the end of September 2013 Gazzaev once again tried to paint a positive picture, making a public plea – "let's try it, we are not risking anything!" he said to the increasingly sceptical journalists, who were

60 Olivier Jarosz, Konstantin Kornakov, and Adam Metelski

also incredulous at the assertion by Gazzaev that this was not a political project in any shape or form (Sports.ru, 2013).

At the end of November 2013, political events in Kyiv forced football to take backstage, but Gazzaev was still working on the project and promoting it to the Russian public (Agapov, 2013). By February 2014, though, as the Revolution of Dignity triumphed on the streets of Kyiv and Ukrainian President Viktor Yanukovich was fleeing the country, the project was clearly dead in the water. By summer 2014, when Crimea was already annexed and the Donbas region was on fire, even the ever-optimistic Gazzaev accepted the project's defeat (LB .ua, 2014). In 2022, when the entire country of Ukraine has gone in flames after open Russian aggression, football in Russia is now at its most isolated since the early days of the Soviet regime in the 1920s and 1930s, and football in Ukraine is clinging to life-support, with Shakhtar suffering its second displacement in eight years, and all competitions being stopped since the invasion. The mirage of the failed "United League" is now merely a curious footnote of football history, but also a piece of the jigsaw of this bloody conflict.

Conclusion

Sport plays an important political role because through sports countries can build their soft power, which centres on the ability to get what one wants through attraction rather than coercion, and which is an exercise directly practised by nations and their governments to engage in global affairs. What played out ten years ago as a proposal to merge the Russian and Ukrainian top divisions can be interpreted as a sports development project of two countries that were being left behind on the football business front. In this sense, creating a mega league was the strategy that would enable them to compete with the best in the world on a sporting and economic level. On a more sinister level, it could also be interpreted as one of the series of attempts by Russia to "infiltrate" Ukrainian society, in this case through the means of football, which is the most popular global sport. If you subscribe to the view that it plays an important identity-building role in modern society, such an attempt can dilute one of the visible features of an independent state – the domestic football competition. In this narrative, the "United League" project has a firm place in the line of precursor events that were meant to bring Ukraine close to Russia's orbit and eventually lead to it being swallowed up, beginning from the cultural/sport sports space.

Today from the perspective of the ongoing war between Russia and Ukraine we can surmise that this was no simple football project: from the line-up of individuals who were instigating and driving it on the Russian side, to a lack of consultation within Russian football itself and a lukewarm reaction at best from the Ukrainians, where public support from the Ukrainian side was never forthcoming, it never felt right. The lack of any significant Ukrainian representatives in the steering group or Gazzaev's team made it obvious they were not involved in the decision-making, which is rather curious for a merger project where two supposedly independent parties are meant to come together for mutual benefit. And a €1bn revenue projections were not at all in line with the deficiencies of both the Ukrainian and Russian sport business markets. Having said that, there are several transnational leagues in the world that have been able to achieve success, particularly in the case of North America or Australia, and even in Russia, there are transnational competitions in ice hockey and basketball that have a continued existence for more than a decade and are recognized as among the best in Europe.

So why did the joint league ultimately fail? Arguably, the answer lies in the fact that it was a project that did not start with a clear business rationale behind it but was rather an attempt, on one hand, to recreate something from the past (i.e. the USSR championship) based on nostalgia, and on the other hand, the political aims were too obvious but were trying to hide behind a €1bn revenue smokescreen, which created a sense of growing unease from the Ukrainian side. Ultimately, it did not have a transparent logic to generate universal support. And when the guns started to talk, it was obvious the project would not go forward any time soon. Today, just a decade later and looking beyond the unspeakable human suffering and misery caused by the war, the consequences of Russian aggression have also produced a major impact on football in both countries. Crimean football clubs, who had the only direct representative from amongst all the Ukrainian clubs to show their face in the Russian pantomime, have been functioning outside of the global pyramid since 2014 (Homewood, 2014). Russian clubs have been banned from European competition, and the Russian national football team has not been able to play in official matches under the auspices of FIFA or UEFA (Reuters, 2022a). It is currently unable to take part in qualification for Euro-2024 (Reuters, 2022b), meaning that Russian football will be beyond the pale at least until then. Ukrainian clubs, especially those from the Donetsk and Luhansk regions, have also been displaced since 2014, including major ones like Shakhtar Donetsk and Zorya Luhansk, whilst several teams have lost coaches and players as casualties of war (Yangoly, 2022), as well as had their infrastructure destroyed (Hunder, 2022). And when thinking about leagues, we may actually be much closer to a completely different United League now, that of Ukraine and Poland, and on the basis of a Poland and Ukraine combined league, adding the Visegrad league and the Baltic League you could end up with an Intermarium league, where you could have other competitions of a roughly similar size, which could also fit into that pyramid: one group being Belarus/Czech/Hungary and the other Slovakia/ combined Baltic countries – but this is a topic for another story.

Bibliography

Agapov, A. (2013) *Valery Gazzaev: 'Holding the United Cup is Inappropriate'*. Available at: https://m.sport-express.ru/football/osk/news/642664/ (Accessed: 17 June 2022).

Airapetov, V. (2013) *The Office of the Organizing Committee of the United Championship Will be Located in Lubyanka*. Available at: https://www.sport-express.ru/football/news /572332/ (Accessed: 17 June 2022).

Aleshin, P. (2013) *Gazzev Held Negotiations in Kyiv*. Available at: https://m.sport-express.ru/newspaper/2013-02-16/2_2/ (Accessed: 17 June 2022).

Andreev, I. (2012) *'There is No Motive in the CIS Championship'*. Available at: https://www.gazeta.ru/sport/2012/12/25/a_4905381.shtml (Accessed: 15 June 2022).

Bogdanova, S. (2014) *Sochi Winter Olympics 2014: Soft Games Lost*. Available at: https://www.academia.edu/28692171/Sochi_Winter_Olympics_2014_Soft_Games_Lost (Accessed: 22 May 2022).

Chadwick, S. (2021) *Gazprom and its Sponsorship of Football. From Sex Without a Condom to Major Strategic Threat*. Available at: https://www.iris-france.org/154279-gazprom-and-its-sponsorship-of-football-from-sex-without-a-condom-to-major-strategic-threat/ (Accessed: 27 March 2022).

Chadwick, S. (2022a) 'From utilitarianism and neoclassical sport management to a new geopolitical economy of sport', *European Sport Management Quarterly*, pp. 1–20. doi: 10.1080/16184742.2022.2032251/FORMAT/EPUB.

Chadwick, S. (2022b) *How 2022 Will Epitomise Sport's Burgeoning Geopolitical Economy*. Available at: https://www.iris-france.org/164078-how-2022-will-epitomise-sports-burgeoning-geopolitical-economy/ (Accessed: 27 March 2022).

Chadwick, S., Widdop, P. and Burton, N. (2020) 'Soft power sports sponsorship – A social network analysis of a new sponsorship form', *Journal of Political Marketing*, 21(2), pp. 196–217. doi: 10.1080/15377857.2020.1723781.

Fanstyle.ru (2013) *Fans of Kyiv Dynamo Call to Boycott the United Tournament*. Available at: https://fanstyle.ru/news/23168-fanaty-kievskogo-dinamo-prizyvayut-bojkotirovat-obedinennyj-turnir/ (Accessed: 17 June 2022).

Golubchikov, O. (2017) 'From a sports mega-event to a regional mega-project: The Sochi winter Olympics and the return of geography in state development priorities', *International Journal of Sport Policy and Politics*, 9(2), pp. 237–255. doi: 10.1080/19406940.2016.1272620.

Grix, J. and Lee, D. (2013) 'Soft power, sports mega-events and emerging states: The Lure of the politics of attraction', *Global Society*, 27(4), pp. 521–536. doi: 10.1080/13600826.2013.827632.

Homewood, B. (2014) *UEFA Bans Crimean Clubs from Russian League*. Available at: https://www.reuters.com/article/soccer-uefa-crimea-idINKCN0JI23U20141204 (Accessed: 21 September 2022).

Hunder, M. (2022) *Ukraine Set to Restart Soccer League as War Rages on*. Available at: https://www.reuters.com/lifestyle/sports/ukraine-set-restart-soccer-league-war-rages-2022-08-22/ (Accessed: 21 September 2022).

Interfax (2013) *FFU is Still against Holding the Joint Championship of Ukraine and Russia – Konkov*. Available at: https://interfax.com.ua/news/sport/159679.html (Accessed: 17 June 2022).

Kozlovsky, P. (2015) *Why Russia is not America, or Why MLS is Better than RFPL*. Available at: https://www.sport-express.ru/se-money/football/reviews/858743/ (Accessed: 17 June 2022).

Kyiv Post (2013) *FIFA Head Dismisses Plans to Resurrect Old Soviet League*. Available at: https://www.kyivpost.com/article/content/sport/fifa-head-dismisses-plans-to-resurrect-old-soviet-league-319100.html (Accessed: 15 June 2022).

LB.ua (2013a) *Dynamo Beat Spartak to Win the United Tournament*. Available at: https://lb.ua/sport/2013/07/08/211182_dinamo_obigrav_spartak.html (Accessed: 17 June 2022).

LB.ua (2013b) *Shakhtar and Dynamo Will Receive $1 million Each for Participating in the Unified Tournament*. Available at: https://lb.ua/sport/2013/07/05/210794_shahter_dinamo_poluchat_1_mln.html (Accessed: 17 June 2022).

LB.ua (2013c) *Surkis: United Championship? This is Not My Parish*. Available at: https://lb.ua/sport/2013/07/08/211296_surkis_obedinenniy_chempionat.html (Accessed: 17 June 2022).

LB.ua (2014) *Gazzaev: The Combined Championship has Lost its Relevance*. Available at: https://rus.lb.ua/sport/2014/08/27/277352_gazzaev_obedinenniy_chempionat.html (Accessed: 17 June 2022).

Lidster, A. (2013) *Russia's Grand Football Designs*. Available at: https://www.aljazeera.com/sports/2013/5/18/russias-grand-football-designs (Accessed: 27 March 2022).

Lokalov, A. (2013) *FFU First Vice-President: Blatter Told Me: "A Unified Championship is Impossible"*. Available at: https://www.sovsport.ru/amp/2:479866 (Accessed: 17 June 2022).

Ministry of Energy and Coal Industry of Ukraine (2012) *Order N291*. Available at: http://consultant.parus.ua/?doc=086UBF3FAE&abz=DDPSB (Accessed: 21 September 2022).

Nye, J. (2004) *Soft Power: The Means to Success in World Politics*. New York: Public Affairs.

Reuters (2022a) *CAS Dismisses Appeals by Russian FA and Clubs against FIFA, UEFA Bans*. Available at: https://www.reuters.com/lifestyle/sports/cas-dismisses-appeals-by-russian-fa-clubs-against-fifa-uefa-bans-2022-07-15/ (Accessed: 21 September 2022).

Reuters (2022b) *Russia Excluded from Euro 2024 Qualification Draw*. Available at: https://www.reuters.com/lifestyle/sports/russia-excluded-euro-2024-qualification-draw-2022-09-20/ (Accessed: 21 September 2022).

RIA Novosti (2013) *Fedun and Miller Attend a Meeting on the Unified Championship*. Available at: https://rsport.ria.ru/20130218/646063548.html (Accessed: 15 June 2022).

RIA Novosti (2012) *A Press Conference Dedicated to the Creation of the CIS Football Championship was Held at RIA Novosti on December 13*. Available at: https://ria.ru/sng_champ_press_12122012/ (Accessed: 22 May 2022).

Rsport (2013) *Miller Announced the Timing of the Unified Football Championship*. Available at: https://rsport.ria.ru/20130218/646116890.html (Accessed: 15 June 2022).

Russian Football Federation (2006) *Football Development Strategy in the Russian Federation for 2006–2016*. Available at: https://www.prlib.ru/item/682629 (Accessed: 22 May 2022).

Sports.ru (2012) *Sergei Fursenko: 'It is Necessary that Clubs Spend as Much as They Earn'*. Available at: https://www.sports.ru/football/135947279.html (Accessed: 17 June 2022).

Sports.ru (2013) *'Let's Try! We Don't Risk Anything.' How the Unified Championship Keeps Coming*. Available at: https://www.sports.ru/football/153211693.html (Accessed: 17 June 2022).

TASS (2012) *Gazprom Says Zenit Football Club Can Play in Different Championship*. Available at: https://tass.com/archive/685905 (Accessed: 22 May 2022).

TASS (2013) *Valery Gazzaev: Before Negotiations with UEFA Representatives, it is Necessary to Meet with the Leadership of the RFU and FFU*. Available at: https://tass.ru/arhiv/739659? (Accessed: 17 June 2022).

Trushin, E. (2012) *Miller Launched the Gazprom League*. Available at: https://www.gazeta.ru/sport/2012/11/24/a_4866925.shtml?updated (Accessed: 22 May 2022).

Upbin, B. (2011) *Dmitry Medvedev's Davos Keynote: Complete Transcript*. Available at: https://www.forbes.com/sites/bruceupbin/2011/01/26/dmitri-medvedevs-davos-keynote-complete-transcript/ (Accessed: 22 May 2022).

Yangoly (2022) *Sport Angels – Requiem for the Ukrainian Athletes Died*. Available at: https://yangoly-sportu.teamukraine.com.ua/en/ (Accessed: 21 September 2022).

PART II
China

8

THE INTERNATIONAL PARALYMPIC COMMITTEE, BEIJING 2022 WINTER PARALYMPIC GAMES, AND THE INVASION OF UKRAINE

Verity Postlethwaite

Introduction

The 2nd and 3rd of March 2022 became pivotal 48 hours for the International Paralympic Committee and elite disability sport, in what is now, given the Russian invasion of Ukraine, a new era of global sport governance. The timing, and focus of this chapter, is to consider the immediate run-up to the Beijing 2022 Winter Paralympic Games and how the International Paralympic Committee (IPC) handled the situation of Russia invading Ukraine. Notably, the indecision, decisions, and backtracking by the IPC in relation to the inclusion/ability of the Russian and Belarusian Paralympic teams to compete. Following the description of the decision-making timeline, this chapter will outline three views. The viewpoints will show different ways to interpret the IPC's handling of this situation. The first view will be from international media's coverage, the second response from the athletes and National Paralympic Committees, and, finally, the Beijing Organizing Committee's (lack of) response. Through description and interpretation this chapter will highlight how the initial invasion period of the war in Ukraine shaped the governance of elite disability sport and the role that different voices played in the diplomatic aspects of this situation. To ground this piece, the first subsection will identify key debates surrounding the area and conceptualization of para-sport, global sport governance, and diplomacy.

Building on Para-Sport and Global Sport Governance

The modern era of hosting international sports events is often described and analysed in academic and media debate through the dominant prism of the International Olympic Committee (IOC) and the Summer Olympic Games (Postlethwaite et al., 2022). With the growth in status, credibility, and power

DOI: 10.4324/9781003348238-10

the Olympic Movement has buoyed other events along with it. Most notably for this piece is the growth in visibility and status of the Paralympic Games. First hosted in Stoke Mandeville, England, in the late 1940s the Games originated in interventions by medical doctors after World War II when a significant number of injured soldiers returned from war and approaches to rehabilitating injuries, especially spinal cord injuries, improved (Brittain, 2016). The first official Paralympic Games was hosted by Rome in 1960, and since then there have been over six decades of event growth, increase in visibility, and tension around hosting and governing the event (Brittain, 2016; Gold and Gold, 2017; Brittain and Beacom, 2018; Kerr, 2018). The academic and public debate around the Paralympic Games is (thankfully) growing in depth and nuance, as its universal quest to promote equality through sport continues to gain traction in pockets of the global community. Interestingly, for example, the Sochi 2014 Winter Paralympic Games were heralded as a great success, with the beginning of the IPC Excellent Program where the organizing committee exchanges knowledge with previous and prospective hosts (Park and Ok, 2018).

The focus of this chapter is the governance of the Paralympic Games; unlike its counterpart, the IOC, the IPC does not have an equivalent *Olympism* or Olympic Charter philosophy enshrined at the heart of its organization (Chatziefstathiou and Henry, 2012; Postlethwaite and Grix, 2016), nor does it have a multibillion-dollar income stream to leverage its influence on states (Roche, 2017). Instead, it functions as a more traditional non-governmental international organization (see Allison and Tomlinson, 2017; Gerard et al., 2019). In the most recent decades, the IPC has made a conscious effort to formalize its own governance and strengthen ties with the IOC; for example, as Gold and Gold (2017) trace, there were formal agreements in the early 2000s to better integrate (but keep distinct) the Olympic and Paralympic Game bidding and organizing processes. In 2018 the IPC celebrated the long-term agreement with the IOC going through to 2032 (IPC, 2018); then in 2021 the IPC General Assembly approved the new IPC Constitution (IPC, 2021) and continues to maintain that "at the IPC we are very firm believers that sport and politics should not mix" (Houston, 2022). Consequently, 2022 and the Beijing Paralympic Games were very important for the leaders of the IPC as they were the first iteration of Games in the new cycle of the Constitution and after the significantly impacted Tokyo Summer Paralympic Games due to the COVID-19 global pandemic. Moreover, contrary to their fundamental principles, sport and politics definitely did mix!

The Decision-Making Timeline Regarding the Russian Paralympic Committee and the National Paralympic Committee Belarus

The Beijing 2022 Paralympic Games, therefore, should have been an opportunity for the IPC to strengthen its strategic and operational objectives in this new cycle of its Constitution and growing interconnection with the IOC. Alas, the geopolitical incident involving actions from Russia and President Vladimir Putin and the invasion of Ukraine in February 2022, days after the end of the Beijing 2022 Winter Olympic Games and days before the opening ceremony of the Paralympic Games, caused the IPC to consider and take immediate action to uphold the safety and integrity of their event. The handling of this situation will be described briefly in Table 8.1 and then expanded on in the next subsections.

Interpreting the "Handling" of the Situation by the International Paralympic Committee

The description presented in Table 8.1 outlines the truly extraordinary circumstances the IPC found themselves in; in particular they were unable to wait for the IOC's response or follow other trends in International Sports Federations' decision-making. This solo effort put a significant amount of pressure on the governance, leadership, and global community connected to the IPC and the Paralympic Games. By considering the different viewpoints below, this section will highlight how the initial invasion period of the war in Ukraine shaped the governance of elite disability sport and the role that different voices played in the diplomatic aspects of this situation. Based on the discussion, it should be clear that, moving forward, the international media, Paralympic athletes, National Paralympic Committees, and the event's organizing committee need to be consulted by the IPC when making significant decisions around extraordinary political decisions and the hosting of the Games. This broader consultation is necessary as the IPC's attempt to follow protocol and act through the IPC's Board and formal governance processes did not lead to a successful or agreed outcome.

International Media Response

The pace at which the Russian invasion of Ukraine escalated was incredibly quick; the international media therefore looked for interconnected events to report on and create content for the omnipresent "breaking news". The

TABLE 8.1 Significant moments around the Paralympics and Russian invasion of Ukraine

Date	Significance
Thursday, 24th February 2022	Russian invasion of Ukraine
Wednesday, 2nd March 2022	A/RES/ES-11/1 UN General Assembly Resolution, aggression against Ukraine
Wednesday, 2nd March 2022	Press release from IPC to allow for Russia and Belarus to compete
Thursday, 3rd March 2022	IPC news conference to "U-turn" and not allow Russia or Belarus to be present
Friday, 4th March 2022	Start of the Beijing Winter Paralympic Games

high-profile and global nature of the Paralympic Games made it a useful conduit for the media to mirror the relations and reactions in the geopolitical settings through sport. The prospect of Russian and Belarusian teams "mixing" with other nations was a compelling narrative to report on. As a result, the IPC was under incredible scrutiny over its real-time reactions and decisions. It can be observed in the media coverage on the 2nd and 3rd March 2022 that a number of prominent politicians, ex-elite athletes, sponsors, etc. gave named quotes to the international media outlets on what the IPC was doing. For example, Sky News in the United Kingdom had an immediate quote on Thursday, 3rd March, from the Secretary of State for Digital, Culture, Media, and Sport, Nadine Dorries, and British Paralympic Association, who directly stated the IPC's decision was "wrong ... urgently reconsider ... disappointed" (Sale, 2022).

This commentary from non-sport and sporting political voices on the IPC matter is not the norm, as seen in 2015/16 when the Russian doping scandal was reported on around the Rio de Janeiro Summer Olympic and Paralympic Games it was the IOC voice and the Olympic Games in focus in the media. Moreover, the quotes and reporting in 2015/16 were more tempered and delayed as the situation did not directly connect to a geopolitical fallout. For example, Reuters and the *Japan Times* focus on the IOC and the role of the World Anti-Doping Agency and IOC President Thomas Bach (Grohmann, 2016; Odeven, 2016). The content of this controversy was covered by the media in a more considered manner as the sport governing body is seen in the traditional narrative of being "toothless" and not taking a stand. Whereas, in 2022, the IPC was limited in its options as it became embroiled in the broader geopolitical debate and people expected the IPC to take a harsh stance, similar to that of the United Nations and other international bodies.

It can be argued that the IPC underestimated the amount and intensity of media attention and content they would receive around their decisions. Further to this, they did not appear to consult or manage the public relations aspects of their announcements, which can be illustrated by the dissenting quotes from a number of, ordinarily, supportive voices for the IPC and Paralympic Games. The media narrative and headlines of "IPC U-turn" and the quotes from other voices did not strengthen the standing and credibility of the IPC; instead, they arguably became a political chess piece for the media and others to use to illustrate and sensationalize the impact of Russia's actions in Ukraine (Sale, 2022; Houston, 2022).

Paralympic Athletes and Committee's Response

The "U-turn" made by the IPC was influenced most significantly by their membership, i.e., the athletes and the National Paralympic Committees. As described so far, the IPC's decision-making initially was informed by their top-down governance, allowing the Board to negotiate the first decision to allow the Russian and Belarusian athletes to compete. The Board is made up of 14 individuals, 12 of whom are elected by the IPC membership every four years at the IPC General Assembly. The two other members are the Chairperson of the IPC Athletes' Council and the IPC Chief Executive Officer. This Board make-up represents the IPC's sponsors/benefactors and its 206 member organizations. In sports governance theory, this Board should have found a consensus and way forward that was representative of the IPC community and more importantly supported by the wider membership (Allison and Tomlinson, 2017; Gérard et al., 2019).

Unfortunately, this was not the case, and the initial handling by the IPC was not welcomed or received well by its members. This case is reminiscent of the international sports events during the Cold War and the South African Apartheid era when international sport grappled with threats and enactment of boycotts as a way to use the event to protest on political topics symbolically and actually (Dichter and Johns, 2014). A key issue for the IPC, and they explicitly note this in their press release on 2 March 2022, is that they did not have the precedent or mandate to "suspend or termination of a National Paralympic Committee" on the grounds of breaching the Olympic Truce (IPC, 2022). This issue returns to the relative infancy of the Paralympic movement in comparison to the IOC and Olympic Games. The IOC has an enshrined and heralded Olympic Truce mandate where war does not interfere with the ability for communities to come together and participate in sporting competition; further to this the IOC has vast experiences and learnings from weathering two world wars, the Cold War, and other heinous political issues since their modern inception in 1896.

The point here, therefore, is less about the error in judgement of the IPC's first decision, but more so it underlines that although the IPC has grown in governance stature and influence in the past decade or so, this is still in relative infancy in comparison to other more established sports organizations and competitions, such as the IOC, Commonwealth Games Federation, or the Fédération Internationale de Football Association. The IPC does have a strong *Handbook*, governance system, and newly accepted Constitution, but this does not necessarily compensate for a relative lack of experience in dealing with incredibly complex geopolitical issues, such as Russia's invasion of Ukraine. The IPC will recover from this and act around enshrining the principles and punishments connected to the Olympic Truce. The next IPC General Assembly will be a fascinating event, in particular, to see what members take the lead and responsibility for reflecting on this incident and improving the organization further.

Organizing Committee's (Lack of) Response

The final component to raise in this piece is around the un/fortunate role of the Beijing Olympic and Paralympic Games Organizing Committee (BOCOG). A growing raft of literature demonstrates the significance and potential autonomy of the organizing committee (see Parent, 2008; Gauthier, 2011) in the hosting of international sport events, where they can balance the power of the state and the International Sports Federation to create a successful event. In this case, the role of BOCOG is extraordinary as the Chinese Government did not give them autonomy or the ability to act in any other interest than unilaterally and politically for China. Keys (2018) has written extensively about the political relationship between event hosting and China. Although beyond the scope of this piece to account for this in its entirety, it does raise an important point in relation to the IPC's decision-making and its lack of support in decision-making from the organizing committee.

It could be expected that if the Winter Paralympic Games in 2022 had been hosted by a different country, such as Canada, South Korea, and Italy (all recent previous or next hosts), then the organizing committee could have acted as an ally for the IPC. Although it is not the organizing committee that can take decisive action, it has the ability to negotiate and communicate with national governments, the athlete's village, the accredited press core, etc. to manage the situation. Given China's geopolitical positioning in the world and its – neutrality to arguably enabling – position for Russia, the IPC could not rely or use the BOCOG position to ease the pressure on them to decide and communicate the decision. There is much debate around the role of the hosting nation and their local/national governments in influencing the political nature of the sporting event (see Postlethwaite et al. 2022 for a review on sports diplomacy and other pieces in this edited collection for more on sports diplomacy). Ironically, in this case it is arguably the lack of role and willingness to be involved in decision-making that hindered the IPC's options and access to allies in the quest to take the most accepted course of action around allowing Russia and Belarus teams to compete.

In the coming bid cycles for the Olympic and Paralympic Games, it will be incredibly interesting to see how this incident and the dynamic between BOCOG and the IPC may influence the IPC's guidance (formally/informally) around how an organizing committee should behave during a geopolitical crisis. In particular stretching or revising the governing principles around their "commitment to political neutrality and impartiality" (IPC, 2022). If the IPC is to learn from what happened in March 2022 it is the need for allies and a split decision-making platform, notably here the backing of the host nation's government and/or the organizing committee.

Conclusion – Whose Responsibility Is It Anyway?

The origins of the IPC and the Paralympic Games lie in the teeth of war, as World War II influenced the creation and growth of the sporting movement. Alas, it is another war and geopolitical incident in 2022 that has set the momentum of the organization and movement back. The perceived and framed "U-turn" decision on 3rd March 2022, the dissenting voices on the handling of the incident, the lack of allies, and the international press scrutiny all serve to demonstrate the (mis)shaping of governance of elite disability sport and the role that different voices played in the diplomatic aspects of this situation.

Moving forward, the IPC must answer and reflect on the question – whose responsibility is it anyway? This question will challenge the IPC's *Handbook*, Constitution, i.e., formalized governance and diplomatic processes they cultivated, against the voices and political opinions of its members and wider commentators, i.e., the informal aspects of governing and diplomatic affairs. The first decision by the IPC took the formal governance and the "by the book" diplomatic approach, yet it had to retreat to a more informal and uncodified reaction when there was pressure on it to act in a political, rather than a logical, way. Reflections on the handling of this situation will be needed in the coming years as the IPC (and other sporting bodies and events) will face questions around reintroducing Russia and Belarus athletes and/or teams. Plus, as other sport organizations have done in the past (mostly the IOC), a developed understanding of who their allies are in international sport and international politics.

References

Allison, L. and Tomlinson, A. (2017) *Understanding International Sport Organisations: Principles, Power and Possibilities.* Abingdon: Routledge.

Brittain, I. (2016) *The Paralympic Games Explained.* 2nd edn. Abingdon: Routledge.

Brittain, I. and Beacom, A. (eds.) (2018) *The Palgrave Handbook of Paralympic Studies.* Basingstoke: Palgrave Macmillan.

Chatziefstathiou, D. and Henry, I. (2012) *Discourses of Olympism: From the Sorbonne 1894 to London 2012.* Basingstoke: Palgrave Macmillan.

Dichter, H.L. and Johns, A.L. (eds.) (2014) *Diplomatic Games: Sport, Statecraft, and International Relations since 1945.* Lexington, Kentucky: University Press of Kentucky.

Gauthier, R. (2011) International sporting event bid processes, and how they can be improved. *The International Sports Law Journal*, 3(1–2), pp. 3–15.

Gérard, S., Legg, D. and Zintz, T. (2019) The governance of the paralympic movement: An institutional perspective. In *Research Handbook on Sport Governance.* Cheltenham, UK: Edward Elgar Publishing.

Gold, J.R. and Gold, M.M. (2017) The paralympic games. In Gold, J.R. and Gold, M.M. (eds.), *Olympic Cities: City Agendas, Planning and the World's Games, 1896–2020.* 3rd edn. Abingdon: Routledge, pp. 114–137.

Grohmann, K. (2016) Russia escapes IOC blanket ban for Rio Olympics. *Reuters*, 24th July 2016. Available at: https://www.reuters.com/article/us-sport-doping-russia -idUSKCN1040N7 (Accessed 30th June 2016).

Houston, M. (2022) Paralympic athletes from Russia and Belarus banned from competing at Beijing 2022 after IPC U-turn. *Inside the Games*, 3rd March 2022. Available at: https://www.insidethegames.biz/articles/1119989/russia-belarus (Accessed 24th April 2022).

International Paralympic Committee (2018) IOC and IPC to partner until 2032. Available at: https://www.paralympic.org/news/ioc-and-ipc-partner-until-2032 (Accessed 30 August 2018).

International Paralympic Committee (2021) IPC members approve new constitution at General Assembly. Available at: https://www.paralympic.org/news/ipc-members -approve-new-constitution-general-assembly (Accessed 30 January 2022).

International Paralympic Committee (2022) IPC makes decision regarding RPC and NPC Belarus. Available at: https://www.paralympic.org/press-release/ipc-makes-decisions-regarding-rpc-and-npc-belarus (Accessed 5th March 2022).

Kerr, S. (2018) The London 2012 paralympic games. In Brittain, I. and Beacom, A. (eds.), *The Palgrave Handbook of Paralympic Studies*. London: Palgrave Macmillan, pp. 481–505.

Keys, B. (2018) Harnessing human rights to the Olympic games: Human rights watch and the 1993 'stop Beijing' campaign. *Journal of Contemporary History*, 53(2), pp. 415–438.

Odeven, E. (2016) IOC's decision on Russia a disgrace. *Japan Times*, 30th July 2016. Available at: https://www.japantimes.co.jp/sports/2016/07/30/general/iocs-decision-russia-disgrace/ (Accessed 30th August 2016).

Parent, M.M. (2008) Evolution and issue patterns for major-sport-event organizing committees and their stakeholders. *Journal of Sport Management*, 22(2), pp. 135–164.

Park, K. and Ok, G. (2018) 2018 PyeongChang paralympic games and the South Korean political intention. In Brittain, I. and Beacom, A. (eds.), The Palgrave Handbook of Paralympic Studies. London: Palgrave Macmillan, pp. 555–77, at 574.

Postlethwaite, V. and Grix, J. (2016) Beyond the acronyms: Sport diplomacy and the classification of the International Olympic Committee. *Diplomacy & Statecraft*, 27(2), pp. 295–313.

Postlethwaite, V., Jenkin, C., and Sherry, E. (2022) A gendered focused review of sports diplomacy. In Molnár, G. and Bullingham, R. (eds.), *The Routledge Handbook of Gender Politics in Sport and Physical Activity*. Abingdon: Routledge, pp. 137–148.

Postlethwaite, V., Jenkin, C. and Sherry, E. (2022) Sport diplomacy: An integrative review. *Sport Management Review*, online first, pp. 1–22.

Roche, M. (2017) *Mega-Events and Social Change: Spectacle, Legacy and Public Culture*. Oxford: Oxford University Press.

Sale, Ian (2022) Ukraine invasion: Russian and Belarusian athletes to compete as neutrals at Winter Paralympics. *Sky News*, 2nd March 2022. Available at: https://news.sky.com/story/ukraine-invasion-russian-and-belarusian-athletes-to-compete-as-neutrals-at-paralympics-12555512 (Accessed 7 March 2022).

9
ISRAEL'S WINTER SPORTS DIPLOMACY AND BEIJING 2022

Yoav Dubinsky

Introduction

The Israeli–Arab dispute often overshadowed Israel's participation in international sports, resulting in boycotts, exclusions, protests, competitions cancelled, postponed, or moved abroad, and even terrorism (Dubinsky, 2021). The centrality of the conflict manifested as well through the Olympic Movement with boycotts or athletes withdrawing when drawn to compete against Israelis, protests against Israel and calls for exclusion, and of course the Munich Massacre – the terror attack by Palestinians kidnapping and murdering 11 Israel athletes, coaches, and referees during the 1972 Munich Olympic Games (Dubinsky, 2021; Dubinsky and Dzikus, 2021). The massacre and its commemorations are part of the socialization process of Israeli Olympic athletes (Dubinsky and Dzikus, 2019). Yet, when it comes to winter sports, the narrative about Israel's participation is a different one. As seen in Table 9.1, Israeli athletes have been participating in the Winter Olympic Games since Lillehammer 1994 (National Olympic Committee of Israel, n.d.(, including six in the Beijing 2022 Winter Olympic Games (National Olympic Committee of Israel, 2022). Additionally, in Beijing 2022, an Israeli athlete competed in the Winter Paralympic Games for the first time (Burke, 2022). This chapter discusses Israel's use of winter sports for nation branding and public diplomacy purposes through Beijing 2022. The chapter uses Fan's (2010) nation branding framework, including political branding through public diplomacy lenses, cultural branding through national identity lenses, export branding through country-of-origin and product-country-image lenses, and place branding through tourism-destination-image lenses. Despite not being a winter sports country and not winning any medals in the Winter Olympic Games as of Beijing 2022, Israel sees value in participation. Participating in the Winter Olympics portrays Israel outside a polarizing armed dispute, telling a story about Jewish immigration and the possibilities of building bridges between East and West.

DOI: 10.4324/9781003348238-11

76 Yoav Dubinsky

TABLE 9.1 Israel at the Winter Olympic and Paralympic Games[a]

Winter Olympic and Paralympic Games	Number of Athletes	Sports	Notable Landmarks
Lillehammer 1994	1	Figure skating	First participation (Michael Shmerkin, figure skating)
Nagano 1998	3	Figure skating	First pair competition (Galit Chait and Sergei Sakhnovski, ice dancing)
Salt Lake City 2002	5	Figure skating, Speed skating	Best achievement on ice (6th place Chait and Sakhnovski)
Turin 2006	5	Figure skating, Alpine ski	First snow-event participation (Mikahil Renzhin, men's slalom and men's giant slalom)
Vancouver 2010	3	Figure skating, Alpine ski	Israeli siblings Roman and Alexandra Zaretsky stake to the music of *Schindler's List* as a tribute to family members killed in the Holocaust
Sochi 2014	5	Figure skating, Alpine ski, Speed skating	Held memorial service commemorating the Munich Victims with the Jewish Community
PyeongChang 2018	10	Figure skating, Alpine ski, Speed skating, Skeleton	Largest Israeli delegation, first team competition (figure skating)
Beijing 2022	7 (6 Olympic, 1 Paralympic)	Figure skating, Alpine ski, Speed skating	First participation in the Winter Paralympic Games (Sheina Vaspie, Para-alpine ski)

[a] Data in Table 9.1 and Table 9.2 was taken from officially published information by the National Olympic Committee of Israel, the International Olympic Committee, or media coverage referenced in this chapter. See the references list for the sources.

Political Branding

Political branding (Fan, 2010) pertains to public diplomacy – communication with foreign publics to try and achieve a more favourable image that will serve foreign policy goals (Cull, 2010). Because of the long history of boycotts, exclusions, and protests against Israel, for Israel, participating in international sports events and marching in the opening ceremony with the Israeli flag has a normalizing significance of being acknowledged as a legitimate country among others (Dubinsky, 2021). With that said, the ongoing criticism and calls for boycotting the Olympics in China due to human rights violations and sports-washing (Chadwick, 2022; Dubinsky, 2022b) challenge Israel's positionality in Beijing 2022. Amid the silent boycotts Israeli athletes face and a history of exclusions and political interferences, Israeli sports has a policy of competing against anyone regardless of political differences, trying to both create a practical path to compete in international sports and normatively position itself as inclusive and non-discriminative (Dubinsky, 2021). Joining the US-led Moscow 1980 boycott was an exception (Dubinsky, 2021). When questioned about the diplomatic boycotts against China, the National Olympic Committee of Israel reaffirmed its policy of focusing on the athletic competitions and leaving international politics to other actors (Somfavli & Ayad, 2022). This policy might not be aligned with the growing waves of athletes' activism and their demand for more freedom of speech, especially as athletes use their platform to support Palestinian causes (Dart, 2022) and the International Olympic Committee allowing some forms of protests during the Olympic Games (International Olympic Committee, 2021).

Yet, focusing on the Israeli–Arab dispute will not do justice with the Israeli winter delegations to Beijing. The majority of athletes who represented Israel since 1994 in the Winter Games were not born in Israel and lived and trained in different countries. So, the impacts of boycotts, or even the collective trauma of the Munich Massacre, are less central in their socialization process. Israel's winter sports traditions have mostly been shaped by Jewish athletes, coaches, and administrators who immigrated from Eastern Europe and by the support of the North American Jewish community. Due to the lack of elite-level facilities in Israel, the country's top figure skaters train and develop in New Jersey, under national coach and Israeli-born three-times Olympian Galit Chait and the guidance of the head of the Israeli Ice Skating Federation (Peled, 2017) – her father Boris Chait. Boris was born in Moldova, immigrated to Israel in the 1970s, and resides in the United States, where he develops Israeli figure skating along with his wife and daughter (Peled, 2017; Rakovsky, 2022). There are few ice-skating rinks in Israel that meet international regulations, including Canada Centre in the northern city of Metula – which was built thanks to contributions and donations from the Canadian Jewish community (Canada Centre, n.d.). These internal challenges and melting pots create a unique fusion of East and West coming together through Israeli winter sports culture. For example, figure skater Evgeni Krasnopolski was born in Kyiv in 1988 when Ukraine was still under the Soviet Union, immigrated to Israel at the age of three, moved to train under Chait in New Jersey when he was 20, and competed with 3 different American Jewish female partners in Sochi 2014, PyeongChang 2018, and Beijing 2022 (National Olympic Committee of Israel, n.d.; Talshir, 2014). So, in the case of Beijing 2022, with Western countries applying diplomatic boycotts against China, and Russia invading Ukraine during the Paralympic Games and violating the Olympic Truce (Dubinsky, 2022b; IOC News, 2022), such a fusion between Eastern Europe and North America with Middle Eastern flavour is the unique diplomatic value proposition Israel offers to the Winter Olympic Games.

Cultural Branding

From the sociological lens of nation branding, Fan (2010) uses cultural branding to refer to national identity. The social identity theory argues that individuals see themselves as part of a collective, adopting social characteristics of their collective social groups (David and Bar-Tal, 2009). Nation identity is a specific case of a collective identity, in which the identity is also constructed by nationality, shared history, culture, symbols, religions, etc. Israel's participation in the Winter Olympic Games is unique, as it portrays a different narrative about Israeli identity and Judaism. As seen in Table 9.2, out of the seven athletes who represented Israeli in Beijing 2022, only Winter Paralympian Sheina Vaspi was born in Israel, while all the Winter Olympians were born elsewhere.

Jewish athletes who immigrated to Israel at a young age or were naturalized as teenagers or adults received Israeli citizenship through the Law of Return – an Israeli law enabling every Jewish person to receive Israeli citizenship and to make Aliyah (immigrate to Israel) and return to their Jewish Homeland (Dubinsky and Dzikus, 2019). While it is not uncommon that countries naturalize athletes to represent them in the Olympics (Brownell, 2022), in the case of Israel the naturalization process is tied to the country's identity and to diplomatic goals to connect between the State of Israel and the Jewish Diaspora. Although the winter delegations do not go through the same socialization process as the summer ones around the commemoration of the Munich Victims (Dubinsky and Dzikus, 2019), in Sochi 2014 the delegation held a memorial service with members of the local Jewish community and IOC representatives (Aharoni, 2014). This also shows the significance of connecting the delegation and the Jewish Diaspora, with the Israeli diplomatic narratives. Yet, overplaying the significance of Israel in the Winter Olympics and over-naturalizing also leads to domestic backlash. Before PyeongChang 2018, when Israel sent a full figure skating team, sports administrators took pride in being among the best in the world, which was received with criticism and even cynicism by Israeli media as most athletes were not born in Israel and train abroad (Peleg, 2017).

There is no one template for who represents Israel and why. Krasnopolski and speed skater Vladyslav Bykanov made Aliyah as children in the early 1990s from Ukraine after the collapse of the Soviet Union, grew up in Israel, speak Hebrew,

TABLE 9.2 Israeli Athletes in the Beijing 2022 Winter Olympic and Paralympic Games

Athlete	Year/Place of Birth	Sport	Comments
Barnabas Szollos	1998/ Budapest, Hungary	Alpine ski	6th place in combined downhill in Beijing 2022 – tied best achievement for Israeli athlete in Winter Olympics. Trains in Austria.
Noa Szollos	2003/ Budapest, Hungary	Alpine ski	Won silver and bronze medals in the Lausanne Winter Youth Olympic Games – the first Israeli medals in any Olympic winter competition. Trains in Austria.
Alexei Bychenko	1988/Kyiv, Ukrainian SSR	Figure skating	Represented the Ukraine until 2009. Represented Israel in three Winter Olympics. Trains in New Jersey.
Hailey Kops	2002/New York City, NY, USA	Figure skating	First Orthodox Jew to represent Israel in the Winter Olympics. Studied in a Jewish seminary in Jerusalem. Trains in New Jersey.
Evgeni Krasnopolski	1988/Kyiv, Ukrainian SSR	Figure Skating	Made Aliyah at the age of 3. Served in the Israeli military. Represented Israel in three Winter Olympics. Trains in New Jersey.
Vladislav Bykanov	1989/Lviv, Ukrainian SSR	Speed skating	Made Aliyah in 1994, grew up in Israel, and served in the army. Represented Israel in three Winter Olympics. Trains in the Netherlands.
Sheina Vaspi	2002/Yesud HaMa'ala, Israel	Para-alpine ski	First Israeli to compete in the Winter Paralympic Games. Born to a Hasidic family. Withdrew from one competition in Beijing 2022 because of Shabbat. Trains in Colorado.

and served in the Israeli army (Deuel, 2015; Talshir, 2014). Alexei Bychenko represented Ukraine until 2009 before receiving Israeli citizenship in 2010 (Burack, 2022). All three represented Israel in Sochi 2014, PyeongChang 2018, and Beijing 20222. Alpine skiers Barnabas Szollos and his younger sister Noa Szollos moved to represent Israel after the family had disputes with the Hungarian Ski Federation (Aharoni, 2020). Both siblings made an impact on Israeli winter sports: Noa winning silver and bronze medals in the Lausanne 2020 Winter Youth Paralympic Games before making her senior's Winter Olympic debut in China, and Barnabas finishing in the sixth place in the combined downhill ski competition in Beijing 2022 – equalling the best place of an Israeli athlete in the Winter Olympic Games (National Olympic Committee of Israel, n.d.).

Beijing 2022 also showed some of the different complexities in different streams of Judaism. Hailey Kops became the first Orthodox Jew to compete in the Winter Olympics (Burack, 2022). Kops classifies herself as a "modern Orthodox Jew" (Rakovsky, 2022) when explaining how she balances religious traditions and the demands of her sport that requires physical contact with her male partner Krasnopolski, wearing what in Orthodox eyes might be considered a revealing outfit, and at times competing on Shabbat. Israeli-born Para-alpine skier Sheina Vaspi became the country's first athlete to compete in the Winter Paralympic Games, finishing 15th in the giant slalom (Burke, 2022). Vaspi, coming from a Hasidic family, competes wearing a skirt out of modesty and does not ski on Shabbat. In Beijing 2022 she had to withdraw from the women's slalom event for religious reasons after it was rescheduled to Saturday due to the weather conditions (Burke, 2022). Israel has a rich history in the Paralympic Games, going back to the strong connection with the Jewish founder of the Movement, Dr Ludwig Guttman, hosting the Games in Tel-Aviv in 1968, and developing innovative rehabilitation centres for soldiers (Dubinsky, 2021). Thus, Israel's participation in Beijing 2022 also manifests nuances and complexities in Jewish and Israeli identities with diplomatic implications.

Export Branding and Place Branding

From business management and marketing lenses, nation branding is often analyzed through two facets: (a) export branding as a product-based approach also referred to as country-of-origin or product-country-image and (b) place branding as a tourism-based approach which is also referred to as tourism-destination-image (Fan, 2010). In the product-based approach, Israel has been trying to rebrand itself as a start-up nation, creating a bypassing message to the Israeli–Arab dispute by emphasizing its developed technology and history, and culture of adaptation and innovation. Dubinsky (2022a) uses the term "sport-tech diplomacy" to refer to the growing sport-tech ecosystem in Israel, to align such branding attempts with diplomatic goals. In winter sports, Intelligym patented technologies that were used in Israeli Air Force simulators and applied them to neuroscience technologies to improve athletes' cognitive skills, especially in soccer and ice hockey, working with some of the most prestigious leagues and federations, including USA Hockey and Hockey Canada (Intelligym, n.d.). One example regarding the Olympics was with Replay Technologies which developed multidimensional video recording and was purchased by Worldwide Olympic Partner Intel who enjoys category exclusivity in 3D, virtual reality, and other forms of innovative broadcasting (Gilead, 2021; International Olympic

Committee, 2021). Yet, in August 2021, a few days after the closing ceremony of Tokyo 2020, Intel announced they were removing its video sports technologies from its portfolio (Gilead, 2021). Regarding the 2022 Winter Olympics, Israeli-founded live streaming company LiveU took pride in supporting the broadcasting of the Games from Beijing 2008 to Beijing 2022 (Wasserman, n.d.).

From a place branding and a tourism-based approach (Fan, 2010), the branding of Israel is limited as athletes train and compete abroad, the country lacks the infrastructure to host significant internationally attractive competitions that will draw tourists and media, and have very few snow-days to become a tourism venue for winter sports enthusiasts. There was some use of winter sports through ice hockey in the Maccabiah Games – the quadrennial international multi-sport event for Jewish people that is nation branding and public diplomacy oriented (Dubinsky, 2021). Israel also does not have Olympic Houses (Dubinsky, 2021) – rented venues in the host city where countries hold events for different stakeholders and also expose their music, food, culture, and products (Dubinsky, 2021). Yet, due to the strict COVID-19 measures in Beijing, this was not a realistic possibility anyway. About Israeli music, Israeli rhythmic gymnasts often use Israeli and Hebrew songs in their routines in the Olympics, which can also be done in figure skating, yet that was not the case in Beijing 2022. In past Winter Olympics, some Israeli skaters competed to music with historical and cultural heritage, such as the soundtrack of *Schindler's List* as a tribute to family members murdered in the Holocaust and to the significance of Yom HaShoah – the annual Holocaust Memorial Day in Israel, or to the much happier and upbeat Jewish folk song "Hava Nagila" (Krieger, 2010; Olympics, 2019). So, from business lens, despite not being a winter sports country, Israeli technology continued to add some authenticity to the country's sport-tech diplomacy and the country's start-up nation branding around Beijing 2022, but from a tourism-destination approach, cultural diplomacy attempts were missing.

Conclusion

Israel's participation in the Winter Olympic Games, including in Beijing 2022, tells a different story about the country, not embodied in the Israeli–Arab dispute, terrorism, occupation, or accusation of Apartheid policies. Implications of the Israeli–Palestinian conflict or even the branding attempts of Israel as a start-up nation through sport-tech diplomacy are marginal. Israel's participation in Beijing 2022 pertains mostly to the identity and complexities of Israel as a self-defined Jewish state and homeland for Jewish people. Through this melting pot, there are diplomatic implications such as manifesting a fusion of East and West into politically charged Games and navigating different streams, branches, and traditions of Jewish identities. Yet, Beijing 2022 also confronted Israel with the question of diplomatic boycotts against a sports-washing country amid the growing support for athletes' activism (Chadwick, 2022; Dart, 2022; Dubinsky, 2022b). Despite continuing the tradition of participating in each

Winter Olympics since 1994 and making its Winter Paralympic Games debut, with zero medals won, Israel is not one of the most recognized winter sports countries. In fact, from broader international relations lenses, Israel's participation in Beijing 2022 might not be much different than dozens of other countries who marched in the ceremonies, competed peacefully, and returned safely without major achievements or incidents. In the politically charged climate and under the restrictive conditions of Beijing 2022, normalization is a favourable outcome for Israel's nation branding and public diplomacy.

References

Aharoni, O. (February 2, 2014). Sochi: A memorial service was held for the Munich Victims. *Ynet*. Retrieved from https://www.ynet.co.il/articles/0,7340,L-4486319,00.html [Hebrew].

Aharoni, O. (January 12, 2020). Blue white: On Israel's most surprising achievement ever. *Ynet*. Retrieved from https://www.ynet.co.il/articles/0,7340,L-5658010,00.html [Hebrew].

Brownell, S. (March 25, 2022). Citizenship swapping at the Beijing 2022 Winter Olympics. *Georgetown Journal of International Affaris*. Retrieved from https://gjia.georgetown.edu/2022/03/25/citizenship-swapping-at-the-beijing-2022-winter-olympics%EF%BF%BC/.

Burack, E., JTA. (February 3, 2022). Skating to the sounds of "Schindler's List": The Jewish athletes in the Winter Olympics. *Ynet*. Retrieved from https://www.ynet.co.il/judaism/article/s17i00gfrk [Hebrew].

Burke, P. (March 12, 2022). Vaspi forced to miss slalom at Beijing 2022 after schedule change cause clash with Shabbat. *Inside the Games*. Retrieved from https://www.insidethegames.biz/articles/1120436/vaspi-beijing-2022-slalom.

Canada Center. (n.d.). *English*. Retrieved from https://www.canada-centre.co.il/html5/sbs.py?_id=9709&did=1165&G=.

Chadwick, S. (2022). From utilitarianism and neoclassical sport management to a new geopolitical economy of sport. *European Sport Management Quarterly*, 1–20. https://doi.org/10.1080/16184742.2022.2032251.

Cull, N. J. (2010). Public diplomacy: Severn lessons for its future from its past. *Place Branding and Public Diplomacy*, *6*, 11–17. https://doi.org/10.1057/pb.2010.4.

Dart, J. (2022). From Ferguson to Gaza. Sport, political sensibility, and the Israel/Palestine conflict in the age of Black lives matter. *European Journal for Sport and Society*, *19*(2), 151–169. https://doi.org/10.1080/16138171.2021.1917183.

David, O., & Bar-Tal, D. (2009). A sociopsychological conception of collective identity: The case of national identity as an example. *Personality and Social Psychology Review*, *13*, 354–379. https://doi.org/10.1177/1088868309344412.

Deuel, E. (March 14, 2015). Ice man: Vladislav Bykanov conquers Europe. *Ynet*. Retrieved from https://www.ynet.co.il/articles/0,7340,L-4636737,00.html [Hebrew].

Dubinsky, Y. (2021). From start-up nation to sports-tech nation? A SWOT analysis of Israel's use of sports for nation branding. *International Journal of Sport Management and Marketing*, *49*(1/2), 49–75. https://doi.org/10.1504/IJSMM.2021.114168.

Dubinsky, Y. (2022). Sport-tech diplomacy: Exploring the intersections between the sport-tech ecosystem, innovation, and diplomacy in Israel. *Place Branding & Public Diplomacy*, *18*(2), 169–180. https://doi.org/10.1057/s41254-020-00191-2.

Dubinsky, Y., & Dzikus, L. (2021). The 1972 Munich Massacre and Israel's country image. *Journal of Olympic Studies, 2*(1), 90–109. https://doi.org/10.5406/jofolympstud.2.1.0090.

Dubinsky, Y., & Dzikus, L. (2019). Israel's country image in the 2016 Olympic Games. *Place Branding and Public Diplomacy, 15*, 173–184. https://doi.org/10.1057/s41254-018-0105-y.

Fan, Y. (2010). Branding the nation: Towards a better understanding. *Journal of Place Branding and Public Diplomacy, 6*(2), 97–103.

Gilead, A. (August 19, 2021). Intel shuts down Israeli co Replay Technologies. *Globes.* Retrieved from https://en.globes.co.il/en/article-intel-shuts-down-israeli-co-replay-technologies-1001382306

Intelligym. (n.d.). *Intelligym.* Retrieved from https://www.intelligym.com/.

International Olympic Committee. (July 2, 2021a). IOC extends opportunities for athlete expression during the Olympic Games Tokyo 2020. *Olympics.* Retrieved from https://olympics.com/ioc/news/ioc-extends-opportunities-for-athlete-expression-during-the-olympic-games-tokyo-2020.

International Olympic Committee. (2021b). *Olympic Marketing Fact File – 2021 Edition. International Olympic Committee.* Retrieved from https://stillmed.olympics.com/media/Documents/International-Olympic-Committee/IOC-Marketing-And-Broadcasting/IOC-Marketing-Fact-File-2021.pdf.

IOC News. (February 28, 2022). IOC EB recommends no participation of Russian and Belarusian athletes and officials. *International Olympic Committee.* Retrieved from https://olympics.com/ioc/news/ioc-eb-recommends-no-participation-of-russian-and-belarusian-athletes-and-officials.

Krieger, H.L. (February 19, 2010). Zaretsky's Olympic dance a tribute to their Holocaust losses. *The Jerusalem Post.* Retrieved from https://www.jpost.com/sports/zaretskys-olympic-dance-a-tribute-to-their-holocaust-losses.

National Olympic Committee of Israel. (n.d.). *Journey over Time.* Retrieved from https://olympic.localtimeline.com/index.php?lang=he# [Hebrew].

National Olympic Committee of Israel. (2022). *Israeli Olympic Delegation Beijing 2022.* Retrieved from https://www.olympicsil.co.il/wp-content/uploads/2022/01/%D7%97%D7%95%D7%91%D7%A8%D7%AA-%D7%91%D7%99%D7%99%D7%92%D7%99%D7%A0%D7%92-2022.pdf.

Olympics. (October 24, 2019). Full men's figure skating short program | PyeongChang 2018 | throwback thursday. *YouTube.* Retrieved from https://www.youtube.com/watch?v=WtfxFNBPKUY.

Peled, S. (December 22, 2017). Eskimo kiss: The Israelis who try to bring a medal in ice skating. *News13.* Retrieved from https://13news.co.il/item/news/domestic/ntr-1278947/ [Hebrew].

Peleg, A. (December 21, 2017). Joke of the year/ Peleg on thursday. *Ynet.* Retrieved from https://www.ynet.co.il/articles/0,7340,L-5059888,00.html [Hebrew].

Rakovsky, I. (February 17, 2022). The religious skater came to Israel for a year in the Midrasha. Now she represents it in the Olympics. *Haaretz.* Retrieved from https://www.haaretz.co.il/sport/other/2022-02-17/ty-article-magazine/.highlight/0000017f-e2e9-df7c-a5ff-e2fbde8d0000 [Hebrew].

Somfavli, A., & Ayad, M. (February 2, 2022). Yael Arad: "Olympics under the coronavirus? It's no longer fun". *Ynet.* Retrieved from https://www.ynet.co.il/sport/article/hy9jh1acf [Hebrew].

Talshir, U. (February 7, 2014). Who dares to tell Krasnopolski he is not Israeli? *Haaretz*. Retrieved from https://www.haaretz.co.il/sport/other/2014-02-07/ty-article/0000017f-db86-db5a-a57f-dbee70320000.

Wasserman, S. (n.d.). From Beijing 2008 to Beijing 2022: Driving the paradigm shift in live broadcasting. *LiveU*. Retrieved from https://www.liveu.tv/resources/blog/from-beijing-2008-to-beijing-2022-driving-the-paradigm-shift-in-live-broadcasting.

10

THE GLOBAL SPORTING POWER ELITE

Eileen Gu

Donna Wong and Yue Meng-Lewis

> When I'm in the U.S., I'm American, but when I'm in China, I'm Chinese.
>
> Eileen Gu

Introduction

The famous quote by Eileen Gu (Gu Ailing in Chinese) sums up the epitome of a modern-day successful elite athlete when asked about her nationality by the media. Gu, an 18-year-old who became the youngest Olympian champion in freestyle skiing, enjoyed a meteoric rise to fame with her haul of two golds and a silver medal in the 2022 Beijing Winter Olympic Games (hereafter Beijing 2022). In addition to her athleticism, what drew international attention was the San Francisco native's decision to compete for China instead of the United States at a time of intense geopolitical tensions. Born to a Chinese mother and an American father, she claims US citizenship. However, China's state media had previously reported that Gu renounced her US citizenship when she became a Chinese national at 15 (Pretot, 2022). With no government record of her renunciation of US citizenship and yet Chinese law prohibits dual citizenship (The Economist, 2022), it sparked a raging debate on her nationality and patriotic allegiance to China and the United States. Gu evaded the question with the now-famous reply, which settled as the Games closed. This dyadic debate is reignited when the Salt Lake City Winter Olympic Games Bid Committee recently announced Gu's ambassadorial role for their bid for the 2030 or 2034 Games (The Guardian, 2022). This series of events brings into focus the current geopolitical environment elite athletes are experiencing, which needs their careful management to ensure a sustained successful career. Gu is exemplary of a modern, successful young athlete caught in the conflict between two superpowers as she navigates her dual identity in the eyes of the public. This chapter examines

DOI: 10.4324/9781003348238-12

the complexities of the geopolitical maelstrom in sport and extrapolates the hall-marks of a contemporary global citizen of sport through Gu.

Background

Sports labour migration, or switching citizenship for sport, is not unusual at international sports events (see, for instance, Maguire, 1994, 2009, 2011). Gu's case is just a drop in the ocean, which caused a significant ripple on three bases. Firstly, Beijing 2022 took place at the height of political tensions between China and the United States. The relationship between these two countries has reached a new low in recent years as Chinese global power grows economically and militarily. President Trump's punitive trade measures against China heightened the tension. The United States also called for and led a diplomatic boycott of the Winter Games over China's alleged human rights abuses (Yeung, 2022). Straddling two countries with her dual identity, Gu's decision came at a particularly fraught time. Secondly, the migratory direction of sports labour has conventionally flown from the East to the West (e.g., Bale and Maguire, 1994; Cornelissen and Solberg, 2007; Lee and Tan, 2019). However, Beijing 2022 saw the representation of 30 naturalized athletes in a 176-strong Chinese delegation (Qin, 2022). Most of these foreign-raised athletes, many of whom are from North America, have no Chinese ancestry or ties with China. Although sports labour migration is common in the international sports arena, China is a latecomer to the party. Fielding its largest-ever contingent of foreign-born Olympic athletes, with Gu among them, this (reverse) sports migratory flow has taken the world by surprise. Thirdly, relating to the above, naturalized athletes are not common in China. Given China's homogeneity and one of the world's tightest immigration laws, the policy move is unusual. China is no stranger in its attempt to acquire international recognition and participate in global development through sports diplomacy (Murray, 2018; Wong and Yue, 2022). China is keen to demonstrate to the world that it has the capability to attract foreign talents, and Beijing 2022 offered a world stage to present a new generation of Chinese athletes. Gu became the poster girl as China looked to broaden its geopolitics limits and spread its power globally by wielding soft power beyond its borders through sports diplomacy. Gu's role comes with challenges as she undertakes a balancing act in handling the complications of a dual identity. The following section reflects how both parties have received her rise to fame as she treads the fine line.

Ailing in China

Accolades and praises for Gu poured in when she won her first gold, followed by her second and third medals. Chinese celebrated her as the nation's pride. Her victory "overwhelmed the Chinese internet"; hashtags related to Gu's triumph received more than 300 million views within an hour, which briefly crashed the Chinese social media as Sina Weibo's servers[1] became overloaded (Wu, 2022).

The Global Sporting Power Elite **87**

In the wake of her success, Gu dominated searches on Weibo, where seven out of ten most popular topics were on her and her triumph. She has since amassed over 6.8 million Weibo followers (Gu, n.d.). Her stature in China is reflected in her celebrity status. She is now a household name in China, with her face gracing billboards and the front cover of magazines. In terms of her business value, before 2021, Ailing had only less than ten sponsors mostly related to skiing (e.g., Anta sports, Faction Skis, Oakley). Between 2021 and June 2022, she managed to amass a rapid succession of endorsement brands, which spanned multiple fields from sports to cosmetics, food, fashion, and automobile. As a new "top stream" (顶流)celebrity, she holds sponsorships and endorsement with both Chinese and global brands. As a top sports idol, Gu represents a new phase of brand endorsement using female athletes in China where the market has previously been dominated by male entertainment celebrities (Xiao, 2022).

Gu's newfound fame in China also led to the rise of the "Gu Ailing phenomenon", where public discussion surrounding her triggered a novel way of thinking about global citizens (Cheng and Cheng, 2022). The "Gu Ailing phenomenon" relates to widespread discussion on her personal life, study, training, competitions, etc., which dominated Chinese social media discussion topics. China's social media users and media comments have responded most positively to her and her sporting performances. There was also an outpour of public adulation over her Chinese heritage – her strong Beijing accent and fluent Chinese, being academically gifted, and success as a model (Qin, 2022). Gu is perceived as a role model for female athletes in China, and also for raising the profile of skiing in China, which is still a nascent sport and inspiring Chinese youths to pursue the activity (Wong, 2022). In particular, Gu's success in both sports and academic areas was the centre of all discussions. There are people who attributed Gu's success to her American educational background. Gu's success enabled Chinese to notice and appreciate the American educational philosophy where an integration of sports training and academic education is encouraged, compared to the Chinese system (Xu and Chai, 2022). In addition, this also leads to a general reflection and instigated debates on China's existing sport talents education and sport elite selection (Fan et al., 2022).

In short, Gu represents the perfect Chinese American, one Chinese people can all be proud of and root for. Narratives from the Chinese officials focused on Gu's Chinese heritage and her patriotism while carefully avoiding the issue of her nationality. She is recognized as an overseas Chinese who belongs to the nation, like other Chinese in China. She has become a symbol of the Chinese dream, with the Chinese government claiming her as one of their own. This is echoed by Gu herself when she proclaimed that "I have very, very deep roots in China" during an interview with the state media CCTV (Chi, 2022). Chinese media portray her as a patriotic athlete, praised for winning glory for her motherland. Amidst Gu's success, there remained criticisms, particularly over her portrayal as a patriotic symbol. Hu Xijin, the influential former editor-in-chief and currently a columnist for the state-run *Global Times* newspaper, is sceptical and commented that her success should not be seen as the "glory of China"; instead, it should be viewed as the "glory of China's Olympic team". He cautioned Chinese media against glorifying Gu on patriotic grounds over her future allegiance as legal complications are ultimately challenging to bypass. Hu warned that any political components associated with her achievements should be minimized as "China's national honour and credibility should not be put at stake in the case of Gu Ailing" (Bloomberg, 2022).

Eileen in America

Walking a tightrope between two cultural identities brings its own challenges. Gu came under fire in the United States for her decision to represent China. Fox News labelled Gu "ungrateful, for her to betray, turn her back on the country that not just raised her, but turned her into a world-class skier with the training and facilities that only the United States of America can provide" (Colton, 2022). Similar sentiments were also found under social media posts for other naturalized Chinese athletes like ice hockey player Jake Chelios (Yeung, 2022). Conservative media in the United States have generally portrayed her as a traitor for turning down the honour of being a Team USA member. They viewed Gu's representation as immoral, suggesting that her identity had to be binary – either an American or a Chinese, but not both. Some were also sceptical and believed her decision was mercenary to cash in on the lucrative business opportunities it offered (Wolken, 2022). However, her move also won the support of Chinese Americans, who felt that Gu's experience resonated with them, articulating the duality of their lived experiences. Some were inspired by the ease with which she could negotiate her dual identity and navigate the intense political friction between the two countries. Supporters also viewed the doubt over her allegiance as an uncomfortable reminder of the stereotypes of Asian Americans as perpetual foreigners during a fraught time when anti-Asian hate crimes were at an all-time high across the United States (Wong, 2022).

Despite the right-wing criticism, Gu's sporting achievements and multicultural background made her a marketer's dream. Her duality represents a particularly ideal proposition for international brands seeking a share of the Chinese market and the Chinese counterparts eyeing international exposure. As someone who straddles two cultures, her unique appeal cuts through both China and the West. In addition to Chinese brands, Gu has contracts with over 30 international brands as brand ambassadors. Many are based in the United States, including Tiffany & Co., Victoria's Secret, Oakley, and Estée Lauder. Experts have put Gu among the ranks of the world's highest-earning female athletes among the likes of Naomi Osaka and Serena Williams (Yang et al., 2022).

Eileen Gu Ailing: The Face of Global Sporting Power Elite

Just as the political proxy fight came to a close with the conclusion of Beijing 2022, Salt Lake City's bid committee for the 2030 or 2034 Winter Olympics revealed in June that Gu has signed on to work for the bid as an ambassador. The announcement divided opinions among social media users in both China and America. The inspiration from or controversy over her divided loyalties elicited reactions ranging from support (e.g., role model) to criticism (e.g., flexible citizenship) of her latest role (Wade, 2022).

In announcing her role with Salt Lake, Gu explained that her appointment with the bid committee was a "beautiful example of globalism" (Wade, 2022). This nicely sums up the changing face of sports labour migration in an increasingly globalized society, which is a clear departure from Bale and Maguire's (1994) seminal work three decades ago. Gu's meteoric rise, particularly in a time of heightened geopolitical tensions between two countries, brought out what athletic talent migration means in the contemporary era. Firstly, the migration patterns are nothing new, but the migratory flow of athletic talent between origin and destination is changing – from Anglo-Saxon countries to the East. It appears to be closely interwoven with the broader global development process as a rising China transforms the global political order. Secondly, international sporting events have become a platform for nationalistic projection, more so than ever, with the rise of nationalism. Athletes are now (re)presented and assessed through the lens of geopolitics. The increased melding of politics and sports ushered in a shift whereby athletes were previously expected to eschew overt political debates. Now, there is seemingly an expectation that they should take a stand and speak out on political issues. Thirdly, national identity continues to be a fluid construct, which can be readily transformed and drawn on. National identities appear to be in flux and do not appear as cohesive as they are sometimes represented. Switching citizenship or taking up the role of an ambassador for an Olympics to be organized in a nation other than their own country is not uncommon. For example, Taiwanese American tennis player Michael Chang was an ambassador for China's bid for the 2008 Olympic Games. Yet Gu's decision came under intense scrutiny, aptly described in news coverage as "navigating two cultures, judged by both of them" (Har and Dilorenzo, 2022).

Gu has steadfastly maintained an apolitical stance and neutral duality in negotiating the delicate bilateral tensions. Instead, she showcased her intercultural competence, focused on inoffensive topics, and presented herself as a bridge-builder, a global ambassador, and a role model for winter sports. With her athletic and international commercial success, the carefully curated public persona has generated a perfect storm of elements that made her an impressive prototype of a global sporting power elite.

Conclusion

The media narratives and reception of Gu in both China and the United States have shed important light on the debate regarding globalization, national identities, and the geopolitics of sport. Globalization induced a set of complexities in society, which, in turn, left a significant impact on the sporting world (Lee,

2010). Gu's global success demonstrates that the complexity of the globalized world does not always match up neatly with geopolitics. While the Olympic Games could be celebrating the sporting achievements and contributions of Chinese American athletes (e.g., Nathan Chen and Zhu Yi, both US-born Chinese ice skaters) for their bridging role to both countries, it has turned out to be otherwise. Gu's representation in particularly tense political circumstances reflects biases and misgivings on the identity diaspora, particularly over Chinese American identity. What Gu also represents is a new phenomenon – where the world is used to the Americans benefitting from the influx of sporting talents from around the world, China has joined the game. With time, the world will be accustomed to it, and Gu is not that unusual. Gu's arrival to the international sports arena also reveals the dilemma for international movement of elite athletes. For the ingress party, the international flow of elite athletes plays a positive role in promoting the economic development of a specific sport, and (hopefully) leaves a positive impact on the existing cultural and political ecology through media and public debates and discussion. For the egress party, the international outflow of elite athletes helps the nation gain more international attention and recognition, and improve their political status and influences (Huang, 2013). Nevertheless, at the same time, the outflow of local elite athletes may lead to the loss of international competitiveness in the exporting nation. For these "global athletes" or "borderless athletes" (Chiba et al., 2001), there may be a danger of receiving a backlash from two countries owing to their multiple identities and how well they fit in and play these roles.

Note

1 Sina Weibo is a Chinese microblogging website, one of the largest social media platforms with monthly active users of 582 million in March 2022.

References

Associated Press (2022, June 8). Chinese freeski star Eileen Gu to join Salt Lake City's Winter Olympic bid. *The Guardian*. Retrieved from https://www.theguardian.com/sport/2022/jun/08/eileen-gu-usa-salt-lake-city-winter-olympics-bid (Accessed 8 June 2022).

Bale, J., & Maguire, J. (Eds.) (1994). *The Global Sports Arena: Athletic Talent Migration In An Interdependent World*. London: Routledge.

Bloomberg (2022, February 14). China warned against treating Eileen Gu like a patriot. *Time*. Retrieved from https://time.com/6147844/eileen-gu-nationality/ (Accessed 10 May 2022).

Cheng, Z., & Cheng, B. (2022). Spiritual call of the future of the Olympic Games – A multiple interpretation of the spirit of the Beijing Winter Olympics. *Journal of Xi'an Institute of Physical Education, 39*(3), 257–262.

Chi, J. (2022, February 3). Freestyle ski star Gu Ailing a super idol among Chinese young people for representing true spirit of sport. *The Global Times*. Retrieved from https://www.globaltimes.cn/page/202202/1251377.shtml (Accessed 3 May 2022).

Chiba, N., Ebihara, O., & Morino, S. (2001). Globalization, naturalization and identity: The case of borderless elite athletes in Japan. *International Review for the Sociology of Sport, 36*(2), 203–221.

Colton, G. (2022, February 2). Eileen Gu's sponsors show 'the corrupt and weak corporations of America': Cain. *Fox News*. Retrieved from https://www.foxnews.com/media/eileen-gu-ski-us-china-corruption-citizenship (Accessed 10 May 2022).

Cornelissen, S., & Solberg, E. (2007). Sport mobility and circuits of power: The dynamics of football migration in Africa and the 2010 World Cup. *Politikon, 34*(3), 295–314.

Fan, K., Wu, S., Lu, Y., Yang, H., Lin, Z., & Wang, Z. (2022). Causerie of the phenomenon of Gu Ailing. *Journal of Sports and Science, 43*(2), 33–42.

Gu Ailing [@青蛙公主爱凌]. (n.d.). Followers [青蛙公主爱凌]. *Sina Weibo*. Retrieved from https://weibo.com/u/3639470012 (Accessed 1 June 2022).

Har, J., & Dilorenzo, S. (2022, February 13). Eileen Gu: Navigating two cultures, judged by both of them. *NBC Los Angeles*. Retrieved from https://www.nbclosangeles.com/news/sports/beijing-winter-olympics/eileen-gu-navigating-two-cultures-judged-by-both-of-them/2826793/ (Accessed 3 May 2022).

Huang, L. (2013). Analysis on the international movement of soccer players on the focus of debate and dilemma. *Zhejiang Sport Science, 35*(5), 1–6.

Lee, S. (2010). Global outsourcing: A different approach to an understanding of sport labour migration. *Global Business Review, 11*(2), 153–165.

Lee, J. W., & Tan, T. C. (2019). The rise of sport in the Asia-Pacific region and a social scientific journey through Asian-Pacific sport. *Sport in Society, 22*(8), 1319–1325.

Maguire, J. (1994). Sport, identity politics, and globalization: Diminishing contrasts and increasing varieties. *Sociology of Sport Journal, 11*(4), 398–427.

Maguire, J. (2009). 'Real politic' or 'ethically based': Sport, globalization, migration and nation-state policies. In Steven J. Jackson and Steven Haigh (Eds.), *Sport and Foreign Policy in a Globalizing World* (pp. 109–124). London: Routledge.

Maguire, J. A. (2011). Power and global sport: Zones of prestige, emulation and resistance. *Sport in Society, 14*(7–8), 1010–1026.

Murray, S. (2018). *Sports Diplomacy: Origins, Theory and Practice*. London: Routledge.

Pretrot, J. (2022, February 8). Freestyle skiing-China's golden Gu dodges U.S. passport question. *Reuters*. Retrieved from https://www.reuters.com/lifestyle/sports/freestyle-skiing-golden-girl-gu-sidesteps-citizenship-question-2022-02-08/ (Accessed 1 May 2022).

Qin, A. (2022, February 16). The Olympians caught up in the U.S.-China rivalry. *The New York Times*. Retrieved from https://www.nytimes.com/2022/02/16/world/asia/olympics-china-american-athletes.html (Accessed 16 May 2022).

The Economist (2022, February 17). Olympic skier Eileen Gu sparks a debate about dual nationality. *The Economist*. Retrieved from https://www.economist.com/china/2022/02/17/olympic-skier-eileen-gu-sparks-a-debate-about-dual-nationality (Accessed 1 May 2022).

Wade, S. (2022, June 8). Chinese Olympian Eileen Gu working for Salt Lake Games bid. *Associated Press*. Retrieved from https://apnews.com/article/eileen-gu-winter-olympics-sports-china-beijing-b1549a2c689f7086af97993dfcadadc3 (Accessed 3 May 2022).

Wolken, D. (2022, February 8). Opinion: Eileen Gu's life gets more complicated after winning gold at Olympics for China. *USA Today*. Retrieved from https://www.usatoday.com/story/sports/columnist/dan-wolken/2022/02/08/chinese-american-eileen-gu-enters-culture-war-consciousness-gold/6701680001/ (Accessed 1 May 2022).

Wong, A. (2022, February 18). Why Chinese Americans are talking about Eileen Gu. *The New York Times*. Retrieved from https://www.nytimes.com/2022/02/18/nyregion/eileen-gu-chinese-american.html (Accessed 3 May 2022).

Wong, D., & Meng-Lewis, Y. (2022). Esports diplomacy–China's soft power building in the digital era. *Managing Sport and Leisure*. DOI: 10.1080/23750472.2022.2054853.

Wu, H. (2022, February 8). Praise for Eileen Gu after gold medal win breaks Chinese social media. *NBC Sports*. Retrieved from https://www.nbcsports.com/washington/beijing-2022-winter-olympics/praise-eileen-gu-after-gold-medal-win-breaks-chinese-social (Accessed 3 May 2022).

Xiao, M. (2022). Gu Ailing: From winter Olympics "gold medallist" to "marketing icon"? *Sales and Marketing, 3,* 20–22.

Xu, Y., & Chai, Y. (2022). The enlightenment of the growth pattern of ethnic Chinese athletes in XXIV Olympic Winter Games to the development concept of sports education integration in China – Take Eileen Gu for example. *Journal of Sports and Science, 43*(3), 50–55.

Yang, J., Yu, E., & Bachman, R. (2022, February 13). Eileen Gu is dominating the Beijing Olympics—In skiing and sponsorships. *Wall Street Journal*. Retrieved from https://www.wsj.com/articles/eileen-gu-beijing-olympics-sponsorships-11644757027 (Accessed 13 May 2022).

Yeung, J. (2022, February 8). Eileen Gu is the poster child for a new type of Chinese athlete. But one wrong move could send her tumbling. *CNN*. Retrieved from https://edition.cnn.com/2022/02/07/china/eileen-gu-olympics-foreign-athletes-mic-intl-hnk/index.html (Accessed 3 May 2022).

11

CHINA'S MOVES TO INFLUENCE THE GEOPOLITICAL ECONOMY OF SPORTS

The Three Axe Strokes

Lingling Liu and Dan Zhang

Introduction

In the past three decades, China has risen from a self-effacing "developing country" profile to the world's No.2 economy. The status of its sports has grown proportionally to wedge firmly into the top three medal rankings of the Olympic summer and winter games. The combined economic and athletic competencies are not about size and scale only but also carry qualitative dimensions. Since its founding in 1949, Communist China has attached sports to politics (Hong and Xiaozheng, 2002; Zhouxiang, 2016). Academics have evidenced the links between Chinese sports and the nationalism ideology (e.g., Jinxia, 2005; Shen, 2020; Zhang, Hong, and Huang, 2018). The global significance of Chinese sports has reached a new level after the successful staging of the 2008 Beijing Olympics. While continuing to hone and display its sporting prowess, China has advanced its economic interests and political agenda in this field.

This chapter contends that China has deliberately and successfully used sports and their peripheral dealings reinforced by the state's economic might to promote and defend national interests for beneficial geopolitical results. Chadwick (2022) calls for scholarly activities in sports to pay attention to the geopolitical economy of sport. Among many implications of the geopolitical economy of sports, this chapter discusses how China means to use sports as the basis for achieving national competitive advantage.

The Three Axe Strokes is a Chinese idiom describing an ancient war hero's attack strategy. Legends say that he charged at the enemy, roaring and swearing intimidatingly, then struck his axe three times. He might have defeated the enemy at the count of three. Or else he would evaluate the result and quickly decide whether to continue or run away. The Three Axe Strokes of General

DOI: 10.4324/9781003348238-13

Cheng Yaojin (AD 589–665) suggest seemingly simple tactics with careful effectiveness calculations.

China's offensives to advance its geopolitical advantages in the sports world fit the analogy of General Cheng's Three Axe Strokes. This chapter finds out that the three deliberated moves are sponsorships, acquisitions, and mega-events used as the cutting edges. We will firstly posit a brief analysis of the geopolitical contentions that China deals with regionally, continentally, and globally. Then we will describe and analyze China's sports expansion using the three moves persistently over the past 15 years and evaluate the effectiveness. Finally, we suggest that China aimed at Europe to have developed the power and influence in what Chadwick (2022) defined as the geopolitical economy in sports. However, it faces challenges in sustaining what it has achieved.

Geopolitical Pinch Points

China has consistently intertwined the state ideology and politics together with sports. It has used sports to rule the people (Brownell, 1995; Hong and Zhouxiang, 2012). Externally, it is not surprising that sports also reflect China's geopolitical positions.

In East Asia, China maintains irksome relationships with its neighbours. Such political relationships are contentious because Japan, South Korea (Republic of Korea), Taiwan, North Korea (Democratic People's Republic of Korea), and China have different and conflicting political and social systems. And there is a complex matrix of economic competition between these nations.

However, the primary geopolitical sports contention is between China and Taiwan, over which the Chinese Communist Party has claimed to have governing sovereignty. So far, China and Taiwan have managed to coexist in sports arenas, with the latter using the name and flag of the Chinese Taipei Olympic Committee. In addition, China has rallied the international sports governing bodies to ensure that Taiwan does not appear as an independent nation. The ultimate plan is for the Chinese NOC to be the sole representative of China and Taiwan, although this is unlikely to happen soon.

In East Asia, China, Japan, and South Korea also engage in sports-related rivalry due to the historical trauma of brutal wars (Mangan et al., 2013). Continentally across Asia, China's position in the geopolitical economy of sports demonstrates a pattern that it contends against the sports nations that are friendly with the United States. This contention is even more evident if the countries happen to be good or better at the sports that directly compete against China. In the case of football in the Asia-Pacific region, Japan, South Korea, and Australia fit this rival profile perfectly. As a counter-example, India and China are direct geopolitical competitors. However, India is not close to the United States, and its sporting routes do not cross with China's. Therefore, the two countries have had few conflicts or tensions in the sporting arenas.

Globally, Chinese sports aim to challenge the US dominance in sports. The aim is consistent with the Chinese government's agenda of catching up with America around 2025 (Nye Jr, 2010). However, China has not directly entered the sports markets in the Americas. Instead, the strategy is to export Chinese influence to Africa and Europe. In Africa, China implements the method of building sports stadiums in exchange for resources, the so-called Sports Stadium Diplomacy (Dubinsky, 2021; Will, 2012). Chinese sports investors have been active in the European market during the first decades of the 21st century. The Chinese sports officials have been the second force after the athletes to be involved in sports governance bodies headquartered in Europe and Asia. In South America, it is relatively quiet, as China does not seem to have much to export in terms of football.

Three Axe Strokes

The Chinese government has the ambition of becoming the world's largest sports economy by 2025 (Chadwick, 2015). The aspiration has driven policies and strategies to build and expand its global geopolitical and economic influences. China knows that to conquer the world of sports, it must aim to win over Europe, where most of the world's sports governance, investors, and influencers are based. There have been three moves aiming at this purpose. The common denominator under these three moves is China's economic power and financial resources.

Big Sponsors

The first move is to offer sponsorships to sports brands, organizations, and individuals. Affluent Chinese brands and companies, including the e-commerce giant Alibaba, in the elite The Olympic Partner (TOP) program, and Wanda Group, a real-estate developer and a FIFA Partner, seem to lead and drive the initiatives. They, however, comply with the central government's directives of encouraging domestic businesses to "go overseas". Such sponsorships reached an apex in 2018, exemplified by the seven Chinese brands sponsoring the FIFA World Cup (Manoli, Anagnostou, and Liu, 2022). Industry data indicate that between 2015 and 2019, the sponsorship spending by Chinese brands grew by 8.9% yearly and will contribute to a third of the future global growth from 2021 to 2030 (Beyond Next, 2021).

The motivations for the Chinese brands to be global sports sponsors could not all be commercial. Companies like Alibaba have international business agenda, so it made sense. However, before it acquired Infront Sports & Media in 2015 and the Ironman triathlon series in 2020, Wanda Group only operated domestically inside China. An argument for the sponsorships is that the intended returns on investment were to enhance the brand equity for China and its influences on sports. Evidence indicates that sponsorships in sports such as football help states build soft power (Krzyzaniak, 2018). Chadwick, Widdop, and Burton (2022) identified the connection between sponsorship soft power and national branding across a few states. There is no reason for China to plan and behave differently.

Shopping Spree

Academics have noticed China's moves to invest in sports assets internationally and have interpreted the moves as a part of the country's financial-backed sports diplomacy (e.g., Dubinsky, 2019; Hong and Xiaozheng, 2002; Miller, 2010) to advance the country's global influence. The activeness of such moves spiked around the mid-2010s, a couple of years after Xi Jinping took the leadership of China and rolled out the Belt and Road Initiatives (BRI), which means to export Chinese influences to Europe and Africa via direct investments (Li et al., 2021). Between 2014 and 2017, Chinese foreign direct investment projects frequently took to the front lines of sports business news. Buyers put AC Milan, Liverpool, Infront Media, Ironman, etc. into their shopping trolley. With the idea that Chairman Xi Jinping was a football fan, Chinese billionaires aimed at football clubs as the most-wanted merchandise. In particular, the Wanda Group was the most active. It purchased a 20% stake in Spain's Atletico Madrid for US$52 million in 2015. According to Bloomberg data, Chinese businesses spent at least US$1.7 billion on sports assets in 2015, mostly in soccer. The following year, the Chinese state-backed financial conglomerate Everbright Group offered Liverpool FC US$1.24 billion, the most notable instance of Chinese overseas direct investment in sports (Turzi, 2020).

The shopping spree carried political and economic ramifications. Taking over the valuable and influential sports assets would, in turn, influence the related stakeholders such as fans, media, and governance bodies. Schweizer, Walker, and Zhang (2019) pointed out the political connections of the cross-border acquisitions by Chinese enterprises. In the sports arena, the buyers appeared to have used their financial assets to buy influence in the politics, culture, and society as a form of soft power push (Lee and No, 2022; Shambaugh, 2015). One of the unspoken goals is to build up the representation of the Chinese influence in global and continental sports governance organizations.

The building of financial diplomacy in sports took a break after 2017 when the Chinese financial regulators tightened the supply of foreign currencies. The tightening measure was due to the more enormous geopolitical tensions between China and the United States after President Donald Trump took office. The Trump administration's trade sanctions squeezed China's US dollar reserve from its 2014 peak to a bottom in 2017. The Chinese government, in turn, scrutinized the billionaires moving cash assets offshore in the name of shopping for the sports soft power.

Mega-events

Despite the controversies surrounding human rights, pandemic control, and press freedom (Dooley, 2022; Ross et al., 2021), hosting the Beijing 2022 Olympic

Winter Games demonstrated China's lure to the global sporting community to have mega games hosted here. Shortly before Beijing 2022, Yu Zaiqing, vice president of the International Olympic Committee (IOC) from China, said that China has at least ten cities capable of hosting the Olympic Games. He hoped that China would continue to bid for the Olympics to improve the country's international status and increase its global influence (Xinhua, 2022).

China has hosted a starry collection of international, continental, and regional games on its soil (Fitzgerald and Maharaj, 2022) with consistent extravaganza displays. However, it would not be a complete collection without the FIFA World Cup. There is a mutual courtship between China and FIFA, as evidenced by Xi Jinping telling FIFA President Infantino in 2017 about his dream of hosting the football World Cup. FIFA tested the water by awarding the 2021 Club World Cup to China but had to cancel it amid the pandemic crisis. Neither side is very keen. The speculated reason for China not being in a rush to get a World Cup is the potential embarrassment by the country's impotent national team, which is unlikely to pass the first round (RFI, 2022). The real reason may be that China does not see hosting the World Cup would make it more influential in football politics than its Asia-Pacific competitors. These competitors are Japan, South Korea, Australia, and a few Middle East countries, including Qatar, which recently hosted the 2022 World Cup.

The Human Factor

China has successfully projected an image of a big spender over the past two decades. Whether the three axes have helped it achieve the intended purposes and whether the momentum would sustain and develop further await further research. But China's weight and influence on the global sports fields are increasing. The Beijing 2022 evidenced this with the behaviours of the IOC President during the Games. The president of the world's leading sports governance organization prioritized two task items during the Games: firstly, to praise Beijing and to endorse the claims that the successes and legacies of the Winter Olympics have made China a winter sports country; and secondly, to soothe the public anger surrounding a tennis player's accusations of sexual assaults by a former Chinese state leader. His ceremonial and complimentary role-playing reflected the host country's influences.

The economics underwrite the geopolitical power and influences in sports that China now possesses in Europe and Africa. Therefore, China must sustain its economic might and cash flow to finance the advancements in the days to come. However, there are worrying signs that the country's draconic pandemic control measures since January 2020 have put its economy, productivity, supply chains, and purchasing power in a doldrums, contributing negative values to what is a global "pandemic depression" (Reinhart and Reinhart, 2020). If the downturns continued, China would have to tighten the cash supplies to finance its soft power push and financial diplomacy in sports. It would be interesting to see the countermeasures and how China would finance its global advancement of sports interests.

It is more intriguing when geography factors in with the intrinsic human and physical geography elements (Goudie, 2017; Massay, 1999). The geopolitical economy of sports refers to activities associated with human geography (Chadwick, 2022) as countries, places, and people commonly are (Marston, Jones, and Woodward, 2005). Notably, we have noticed that when human factors are considered, China has a shortcoming in providing the needed human resources to sustain its ambition to influence and even take over the global sports power. It is in dire need of candidates to represent the country in international sports organizations. Nothing can be more accurate than what the IOC Vice President Yu Zaiqing from China explained how the government intended to change the rules of global sports. He said that to gain the right to speak, Chinese representatives must first enter the international organizations before it is possible to participate in the process of "making the constitutions and amending the constitutions" (Xinhua, 2018). In the past three decades, China managed to have a dozen officials appointed to leadership positions in IOC, federations, and regulatory bodies such as the World Anti-Doping Agency. However, before they could assume and perform influential roles, many had to prioritize developing language skills over diplomacy and people skills. There is little research on Chinese officials' roles and functions in world sports governance and decision-making organizations. It would be a worthy research question to find out how Chinese participation in international sports governance bodies functions as agents of geopolitical economy influences in sports. For China, this is a critical human factor for furthering and sustaining the effectiveness of its used-and-tested Three Axe Strokes tactics.

References

Brownell, S. (1995) *Training the Body for China: Sports in the Moral Order of the People's Republic.* University of Chicago Press. Chicago.

Chadwick, S. (2015) China's Strategy for Sport Yields Intriguing Research Opportunities. *Sport, Business and Management: An International Journal*, 5(3). https://doi.org/10.1108/SBM-05-2015-0017 (Accessed: 26 June 2022).

Chadwick, S. (2022) From Utilitarianism and Neoclassical Sport Management to a New Geopolitical Economy of Sport. *European Sport Management Quarterly*, 22(5), pp. 685–704. Available at: https://doi.org/10.1080/16184742.2022.2032251 (Accessed: 30 June 2022).

Chadwick, S., Widdop, P. and Burton, N. (2022) Soft Power Sports Sponsorship - A Social Network Analysis of a New Sponsorship Form. *Journal of Political Marketing*, 21(2), pp. 196–217. Available at: https://doi.org/10.1080/15377857.2020.1723781 (Accessed: 10 July 2022).

Dooley, B.D. (2022) Sportswashing: The 2022 Beijing Olympics. In *SAGE Business Cases*. SAGE Publications: SAGE Business Cases Originals. Available at: https://dx.doi.org/10.4135/9781529607987 (Accessed: 20 June 2022).

Dubinsky, Y. (2019) From Soft Power to Sports Diplomacy: A Theoretical and Conceptual Discussion. *Place Branding and Public Diplomacy*, 15(3), pp. 156–164. Available at: https://doi.org/10.1057/s41254-019-00116-8 (Accessed: 22 June 2022).

Dubinsky, I. (2021) China's Stadium Diplomacy in Africa. *Journal of Global Sport Management*, ahead-of-print, pp. 1–19. Available at: https://doi.org/10.1080/24704067.2021.1885101 (Accessed: 29 June 2022).

Fitzgerald, T. and Maharaj, B. (2022) Mega-Event Trends and Impacts. In N. Wise and K. Maguire (eds.), *A Research Agenda for Event Impacts*. Edward Elgar Publishing (pp. 181–192). Available at: https://doi.org/10.4337/9781839109256.00022 (Accessed: 20 June 2022).

Goudie, A.S. (2017) The Integration of Human and Physical Geography Revisited. *The Canadian Geographer*, 61(1), pp. 19–27. Available at: https://doi.org/10.2307/621938 (Accessed: 20 June 2022).

Hong, F. and Xiaozheng, X. (2002) Communist China: Sport, Politics and Diplomacy. *International Journal of the History of Sport*, 19(2–3), pp. 319–342. Available at: https://doi.org/10.1080/714001751 (Accessed: 15 June 2022).

Hong, F. and Zhouxiang, L. (2012) Representing the New China and the Sovietisation of Chinese Sport (1949–1962). *International Journal of the History of Sport*, 29(1), pp. 1–29. Available at: https://doi.org/10.1080/09523367.2012.634982 (Accessed: 16 June 2022).

Jinxia, D. (2005) Women, Nationalism and the Beijing Olympics: Preparing for Glory. *International Journal of the History of Sport*, 22(4), pp. 530–544. Available at: https://doi.org/10.1080/09523360500122830 (Accessed: 20 June 2022).

Krzyzaniak, J.S. (2018) The Soft Power Strategy of Soccer Sponsorships. *Soccer and Society*, 19(4), pp. 498–515. Available at: https://doi.org/10.1080/14660970.2016.1199426 (Accessed: 12 June 2022).

Lee, S. and No, S. (2022) China's Overseas Financial Direct Investment (ODI) in European Football Clubs: Revisiting ODI in the Context of Sport Industry. *Journal of Global Sport Management*, 7(3), pp. 391–405. Available at: https://doi.org/10.1080/24704067.2020.1805163 (Accessed: 20 June 2022).

Li, J. et al. (2021) Foreign Direct Investment along the Belt and Road: A Political Economy Perspective. *Journal of International Business Studies*, 53(5), pp. 902–919. Available at: https://link.springer.com/content/pdf/10.1057/s41267-021-00435-0.pdf (Accessed: 11 June 2022).

Mangan, J.A. et al. (2013) Rivalries: China, Japan and South Korea – Memory, Modernity, Politics, Geopolitics – And Sport. *International Journal of the History of Sport*, 30(10), pp. 1130–1152. Available at: https://doi.org/10.1080/09523367.2013.800046 (Accessed: 14 June 2022).

Manoli, A.E., Anagnostou, M. and Liu, L. (2022) Marketing, Sponsorship and Merchandising at FIFA World Cups. In S. Chadwick, P. Widdop, C. Anagnostopoulos and D. Parnell (eds.), *The Business of the FIFA World Cup*. Routledge (pp. 190–202). Abingdon.

Marston, S.A., Jones III, J.P. and Woodward, K. (2005) Human Geography without Scale. *Transactions – Institute of British Geographers (1965)*, 30(4), pp. 416–432.

Massey, D. (1999) Space-Time, Science and the Relationship Between Physical Geography and Human Geography. *Transactions – Institute of British Geographers (1965)*, 24(3), pp. 261–276.

Miller, K. (2010) Coping with China's Financial Power: Beijing's Financial Foreign Policy. *Foreign Affairs*, 89(4), pp. 96–109.

Nye, J.S. (2010) American and Chinese Power after the Financial Crisis. *The Washington Quarterly*, 33(4), pp. 143–153.

Reinhart, C. and Reinhart, V. (2020) The Pandemic Depression: The Global Economy Will Never Be the Same. *Foreign Affairs*, 99(5), p. 84.

RFI. (2022) After Holding Two Olympic Games, China Aims at the World Cup but the National Football Level Is Too Poor. Available at: https://www.rfi.fr/cn/中国/20220221-举办了两届奥运会之后-中国瞄准世界杯但欠国足水平太差 (Accessed: 20 June 2022).

Ross, M., Arkin, Z., Hui, F., Lhamo, C., Biao, T., Heine, M., Peel, A., Lenskyj, H.J., Field, R., Nzindukiyimana, O. and Misener, L. (2021) Critical Commentary: A Call to Boycott the 2022 Beijing Olympic Games and Establish Minimum Human Rights Standards for Olympic Hosts. *Journal of Emerging Sport Studies*, 6. Available at: https://journals.library.brocku.ca/index.php/jess/article/download/3589/2727 (Accessed: 26 June 2022).

Schweizer, D., Walker, T. and Zhang, A. (2019) Cross-Border Acquisitions by Chinese Enterprises: The Benefits and Disadvantages of Political Connections. *Journal of Corporate Finance*, 57, pp. 63–85. Available at: https://doi.org/10.1016/j.jcorpfin.2017.12.023 (Accessed: 20 June 2022).

Shambaugh, D. (2015) China's Soft-Power Push: The Search for Respect. *Foreign Affairs*, 94(4), pp. 99–107.

Shen, L. (2020) Olympic Strategy, Nationalism and Legitimacy: The Role of Ideology in the Development of Chinese Elite Sports Policy in the First Reform Decade, 1978–1988. *International Journal of the History of Sport*, 37(sup1), pp. 26–40. Available at: https://doi.org/10.1080/09523367.2020.1737021 (Accessed: 28 June 2022).

Turzi, M. (2020) The China-Argentina Strategic Soccer Play. *Peace Review*, 32(4), pp. 496–503. Available at: https://doi.org/10.1080/10402659.2020.1921410 (Accessed: 28 June 2022).

Will, R. (2012) China's Stadium Diplomacy. *World Policy Journal*, 29(2), pp. 36–43.

Xinhua. (2018) Xinhua News Agency's Exclusive Interview With IOC Vice Chairman Yu Zaiqing: To Strive for the Right to Speak Internationally, We Must Promote the Reform of Sports Associations. Available at: http://sports.xinhuanet.com/c/2018-02/24/c_1122448678.htm (Accessed: 28 June 2022).

Xinhua. (2022) Interview with Yu Zaiqing, Vice Chairman of The International Olympic Committee and Vice Chairman of The Beijing Winter Olympics Organizing Committee. Available at: http://www.news.cn/sports/2022-01/18/c_1128272260.htm (Accessed: 26 June 2022).

Zhang, H., Hong, F. and Huang, F. (2018) Cultural Imperialism, Nationalism, and the Modernization of Physical Education and Sport in China, 1840–1949. *International Journal of the History of Sport*, 35(1), pp. 43–60. Available at: https://doi.org/10.1080/09523367.2018.1500460 (Accessed: 29 June 2022).

Zhouxiang, L. (2016) Sport and Politics: The Cultural Revolution in The Chinese Sports Ministry, 1966–1976. *International Journal of the History of Sport*, 33(5), pp. 569–585. Available at: https://doi.org/10.1080/09523367.2016.1188082 (Accessed: 20 June 2022).

12

MAKING OF (NOT ONLY) A SPORTS SUPERPOWER

The Chinese Dream

Abhishek Khajuria

Introduction

Over the years, China has proved its might in the world of sports. It has consistently been finishing near the top spots at the Olympics and the Asian games while it continues to train athletes in world-class training facilities to continue that spree. But winning medals and finishing near top spots is not the only objective. There are other aims as well which China wishes to achieve through strategies like stadium diplomacy, football mission, and hosting of mega events which will be covered in this chapter from the lens of the geopolitical economy of sport.

Stadium Diplomacy

For over six decades, China has been practising the "art" of what is called "stadium diplomacy" in journalistic and academic circles. It started in 1958 when the Chinese decided to fund the construction of the National Sports Stadium in Ulaanbaatar, Mongolia (Amaresh, 2020). One of the most recent examples of this policy is the joint venture for building the Lusail Stadium in Qatar for hosting the FIFA World Cup 2022 (Chadwick, 2016a). This policy of the Chinese government hasn't remained confined to one single region, but has covered the globe. Chinese-built stadiums are now found throughout the South Pacific, Latin America, and the Caribbean, Africa, and Asia (countries like Indonesia and Cambodia) (Kellison and Cintron, 2017, p. 121). The capacities range from a couple of thousand to 50,000 (in some cases, even 60,000-seater stadiums). The purposes are varied, from recreational facilities to holding big international events like the Africa Cup of Nations (AFCON), among others (Kellison and Cintron, 2017, pp. 121–122). These have been portrayed as symbols of friendship between China and the recipient countries. Thus, it comes to the mind that if a

DOI: 10.4324/9781003348238-14

country needs a stadium, the process might be a pretty straightforward one. Ask China and enter into an agreement for the type of stadium you need and get it done. However, it isn't that straightforward.

What seems simple on the face of it has, in fact, a lot of layers accompanying it. Building and donating and, in some cases, part-funding stadiums form an important part of the Chinese aid programme, though it might not form a big portion of the aid when it comes to numbers. Stadiums form only 5 per cent of the total projects of the Chinese aid while, when it comes to construction aid, the number is 12.69 per cent (Kellison and Cintron, 2017, p. 122; Xue et al., 2019, 2). But where these stadiums outshine other projects like bridges and highways for example is that stadiums are those grandiose monuments which stand out and their importance in terms of visibility should never be underestimated. They play the role of landmarks and mark an era for a particular country or community. They are intimately connected to the social, political, and cultural lives of the communities they are situated in (Xue et al., 2019, 1). They also have a multiplier effect in terms of the economic activity they are able to generate around them in varied ways. Thus, it can be said that stadiums "convey a sense of citizen health, political equality and emancipation" (Xue et al., 2019, 1).

The reason that countries (especially in Africa) opt for what can be called "stadium aid" from China is that unlike Western countries and financial institutions led by them, Chinese aid doesn't stress on and ask for changes in internal political and economic conditions of the country concerned, however terrible those may be (Xue et al., 2019, 2). This way authoritarian leaders and other states in precarious economic conditions can get the job done without having to answer anyone. This helps to placate the public (in terms of increased employment and economic activity) and for the autocrats to get their images whitewashed. However, nothing comes for free, and the Chinese also seek to derive some benefit from their "generous" donations of stadiums. One thing which immediately comes to mind is the immense soft power which they gain and which goes beyond the heads of states and percolates to the masses in addition to looking the other way when it comes to China's human rights issues. Soft power, then, gives rise to "smart power" (the former when combined with hard power) which China employs to extract concessions from the recipient countries (Dubinsky, 2021, p. 4). One such instance of this has been that China has used this tool in the pursuance of its "One China" policy. So, it has demanded from the beneficiary to cut diplomatic relations from Taiwan in exchange for China getting the stadiums built (Amaresh, 2020; Dubinsky, 2021, p. 4). When Costa Rica ended diplomatic relations with Taiwan and recognized China in 2007, there was a free trade agreement signed between the two (Dubinsky, 2021, p. 4). The newly built Costa Rica National Stadium by the Chinese costing around 100 million dollars was inaugurated in 2011 (Amaresh, 2020). However, Kiribati's case was a bit different. There the Chinese were working on constructing the Betio Sports Complex. But a scandal emerged regarding the Chinese ambassador donating money to an organization linked to the then President Teburoro Tito (Kellison and Cintron, 2017, p. 128).

Though Tito won the election in 2003, within a year, he had to leave office due to a vote of no-confidence against him. His replacement, Anote Tong, initiated diplomatic ties with Taiwan, with the consequence being the Chinese stopping the work on the sports complex (Kellison and Cintron, 2017, p. 128). The Taiwanese then completed the complex instead.

Voting in multilateral institutions in favour of China is another important factor which should be remembered when looking at stadium building by China in other countries. Associated with that only is the inclusion of Wushu in the Dakar Youth Olympics 2026 which the International Olympic Committee (IOC) had repeatedly rejected over the years. This came as a result of the larger sports diplomacy by the Chinese in addition to the stadium diplomacy as a result of which Wushu has become very popular throughout Africa (Dubinsky, 2021, p. 10).

Chinese stadium diplomacy has a resource or, we should say, an economic dimension as well. This type of diplomacy always takes place as part of the wider process of agreements with the beneficiary nations where Chinese stranglehold on their resources is ensured apart from the access to markets by the help of the stadiums which have been referred to as "trojan horses" (Dubinsky, 2021, p. 5; Amaresh, 2020). In many African countries, stadium construction has coincided with increase in trade volumes both ways which then again has led to increase in the number of stadiums being constructed (Dubinsky, 2021, p. 5). The Chinese appetite for raw materials and energy has been increasing every year due to a rapidly growing economy and a burgeoning middle class. Thus, it is no coincidence that some of the countries in Africa where the constructions in the last two decades have taken place have quite a lot of offshore oil reserves: Angola, Equatorial Guinea, and Gabon (Ross, 2014). A case in point is Guinea-Bissau, where construction has been returned with the right to explore the sea and forest of the country (Amaresh, 2020). Same goes for countries like Ecuador and Angola, important oil exporters to China (Kellison and Cintron, 2017, p. 130). Such projects also help to absorb the excess Chinese labour which might lie idle back home. A combination of all this is intended to aid China in its bid to challenge the United States and rise as a superpower where the soft power which China would accumulate through such projects combines with the resources gathered needed to build the economy required to challenge the United States and the wider West.

However, there are certain negative implications associated with stadium diplomacy by the Chinese. Poor treatment of African workers where less wages are paid with no provision of insurance is one such (Dubinsky, 2021, p. 12). Apart from that, the quality of infrastructure constructed hasn't been up to the mark in many cases. The locations of the stadiums have also come under scrutiny, rendering them unusable ultimately, thus gaining the title "white elephants" (Dubinsky, 2021, pp. 12–15). The criticism on the grounds of resource exploitation has remained a constant throughout.

Hence, from the perspective of the geopolitical economy of sport, stadium diplomacy has worked well for China so far. It has boosted its One China policy, got access to resources, built a reserve of soft power all around the world, and has

China: The Football Mission

China is steadfastly pursuing its football mission under the leadership of President Xi Jinping. His dream is to see his country becoming a football superpower (an important component of becoming the actual superpower). The "football development plan in the medium and long term (2016-2050)" points out "football is a sport of global influence" and that "the realization of the dream of becoming a football power" would be a clear demonstration of the "great rejuvenation of the Chinese nation" and a source of "national pride" (Junior and Rodrigues, 2017, p. 121). Its three main goals are: for China to qualify, host, and win the FIFA World Cup, all by 2050 (the male team).

There has been lot of activity on the football front from the Chinese firms all around the globe during the past decade (even before the declaration of the plan), which has contributed to the goals of the plan only. Stakes in European clubs have been bought like the acquisition of Inter Milan by Suning, a 20 per cent stake in Atletico Madrid in 2015 (17 per cent was sold in 2018), and a 13 per cent stake in Manchester City by China Media Capital (CMC) for 265 million pounds (Chadwick, 2016b). The Wanda group also sponsors the Wanda Metropolitano Stadium of Atletico Madrid. An explanation which has been provided for this buying spree, especially by Suning and Wanda, is that the push is to create a vertically integrated global business (Chadwick, 2016b). There, the former's e-commerce business and the latter's entertainment business could very well complement their football acquisitions. Alibaba has been the sponsor of the FIFA Club World Cup for the best part of the last decade. All these would immensely contribute to China's soft power push and sportswashing. On the other hand, in the case of CMC, the acquisition should be seen in the context of the overall ownership of City by the Abu Dhabi United Group. The latter's oil reserves could be a significant help for the Chinese while the Chinese might offer some reciprocity by awarding air routes to Etihad Airways in the medium to long term (Chadwick, 2016b). The rising ambition of China in football also signals an attempt at shift in the balance of power in the football world where Qatar and China seem to be the stalwarts (Chadwick, 2016a).

Back home, huge amounts of money have been pumped into the Chinese Super League (CSL). Stars of European football have been brought to the country like Carlos Tevez and Didier Drogba for huge wages in the twilight of their careers although those like Hulk and Oscar also arrived during their peak. All this has made China an attractive market for European football and China has become a fixed destination for pre-season tours of European clubs (Connell, 2018, p. 8). China has also been announced as the host nation of the new 24-team Club World Club, again aiding the sportswashing efforts of the country in addition to the attempts at the realization of economic potential of the game in the country.

However, achieving the three main goals is not going to be easy. Despite having prowess in infrastructure, hosting the World Cup might get difficult due to increased linkage of awarding the hosting rights of such events with the human rights practices of the country concerned. On the other hand, when it comes to qualifying and winning the World Cup, the quality of football played in China still leaves a lot to be desired. Though clubs are improving, the national team still has a long way to go. So far, it has qualified for the World Cup only once, which was in 2002. There, it was eliminated in the group stage after losing all the three matches.

Hosting of Mega Events

In the last 15 years, China has hosted three mega sporting events: Beijing Olympics (2008), Asian Games Guangzhou (2010), and Winter Olympics Beijing (2022). The year 2008 was a watershed moment which announced China's arrival on the world stage. The Olympics were an exercise in public diplomacy and a search for soft power. The motive was to brandish its image as a rising power and "aid its integration and agency in the international system" (Grix and Lee, 2013, p. 531). While placing the impact of hosting on one side, the fact that China was able to win the hosting rights was a momentous achievement in itself. It was seen as a matter of national pride in the country. The successful hosting of the event added to nation building in the country, a raised level of nationalism (Grix and Lee, 2013, p. 532). The attempt was less at presenting a changed nation to the world. Rather, it was a quest to present an alternative model, a different system, to rest of the world and show its success (Grix and Lee, 2013, p. 532). No wonder, it was not only about becoming a sport superpower. It was definitely more than that. But it is also true that the effect on the image of Chinese government was not very great (Beyrer and Peirce, 2022).

Cut to 2022, for the Winter Olympics, the aims were more or less the same but "stakes were higher" (Beyrer and Peirce, 2022). The rise in confrontation with the United States and the wider West, the controversy over the human rights situation in the country and the elephant in the room, the COVID-19 pandemic, and the focus of the government to show the superiority of the China model all contributed to the "high stakes". Then, the diplomatic boycotts by some Western nations, especially the United States and the United Kingdom, brought in geopolitics into the games, while any significant economic benefit could not be drawn due to the situation engendered by the pandemic. And anyway, they did not prove to be a watershed moment as was the case in 2008.

Conclusion

Thus, in conclusion, it can be said that stadium diplomacy and hosting of mega events have worked (as per the wishes of the Chinese) so far. Stadium diplomacy has ensured soft power and access to resources have aided China's quest for becoming a superpower. In addition to that, stadiums have been used as enduring symbols of China's friendship with the countries that have got these. However, there have been downsides to stadium diplomacy as well. Questionable quality of infrastructure, poor working conditions, and the stadiums becoming "white elephants" have been some of the major criticisms levelled at it. These have been glossed over though. With regard to hosting of mega events, China has been able to display the success of an alternative political system and give a renewed push to its efforts at sportswashing. There has been a marked difference, though, in the way the Beijing Olympics 2008 and the Beijing Winter Olympics 2022 are looked at. While the former was a watershed moment and immensely increased the soft power, the latter came at a time when China is at loggerheads with the United States and the wider West (in addition to the effects of the pandemic) and didn't have the effects like 2008 did. Still, China has proved itself as a capable host with hosting three mega events in the space of 15 years in addition to several other sports events. But when it comes to the football mission, the targets are very ambitious to say the least. Hosting the FIFA World Cup can be relatively easy but might become difficult in the years to come due to increased scrutiny over human rights in the country and their linkage to awarding of the hosting rights. Qualifying and winning the World Cup are even more difficult due to the quality of football in the country. Added to that, tilting the balance of power of football in favour of the East is not going to be easy too, whatever the amount of money is pumped in the game in the country by the Chinese government. Conquering the most popular game of the world is an important part of the Chinese power calculus led by a determined leader in Xi Jinping and a confident population behind him. So, it has set up nicely for us to watch and judge for ourselves in a few decades from now about how did the Chinese fare in their quest.

References

Amaresh, P. (2020) *China's Stadium Diplomacy: All that Glitters is not Gold* [Online] Available at: https://diplomatist.com/2020/11/03/chinas-stadium-diplomacy-all-that-glitters-is-not-gold/ (Accessed 10 June 2022).

Beyrer, P. and Peirce, M. (2022) *What Does China Stand to Gain by Hosting the 2022 Winter Olympics?* [Online] Available at: https://www.csis.org/blogs/new-perspectives-asia/what-does-china-stand-gain-hosting-2022-winter-olympics (Accessed 11 June 2022).

Chadwick, S. (2016a) *An East-West One-two for Oil and Power in China and Qatar's Stadium Diplomacy* [Online] Available at: https://www.scmp.com/sport/china/article/2055715/east-west-one-two-oil-and-power-china-and-qatars-stadium-diplomacy (Accessed 15 June 2022).

Chadwick, S. (2016b) Xi Jinping's Vision for Chinese Football [Online] Available at: https://theasiadialogue.com/2016/11/07/xi-jinpings-vision-for-chinese-football/ (Accessed 10 June 2022).

Connell, J. (2018) 'Globalisation, Soft Power, and the Rise of Football in China', *Geographical Research*, 56(1), pp. 5–15.

Dubinsky, I. (2021) 'China's Stadium Diplomacy in Africa', *Journal of Global Sport Management*, [Online] Available at: https://doi.org/10.1080/24704067.2021.1885101 (Accessed 10 June 2022).

Grix, J. and Lee, D. (2013) 'Soft Power, Sports Mega-Events and Emerging States: The Lure of the Politics of Attraction', *Global Society*, 27(4), pp. 521–536.

Junior, E.F.L. and Rodrigues, C. (2017) 'The Chinese Football Development Plan: Soft Power And National Identity', *HOLOS*, 33(5), pp. 114–124.

Kellison, T. and Cintron, A. (2017) 'Building Stadiums, Building Bridges: Geopolitical Strategy in China', in Esherick, C., Baker, R.E., Jackson, S. and Sam, M. (eds.), *Case Studies in Sport Diplomacy*. Morgantown: FiT Publishing, pp. 121–135.

Ross, E. (2014) *China's Stadium Diplomacy in Africa* [Online] Available at: https://roadsandkingdoms.com/2014/chinas-stadium-diplomacy-in-africa/ (Accessed 16 June 2022).

Xue, C.Q.L. et al. (2019) 'Architecture of 'Stadium Diplomacy'- China-aid Sport Buildings in Africa', Habitat International [Online] Available at: https://doi.org/10.1016/j.habitatint.2019.05.004 (Accessed 10 June 2022).

13

CHINESE SUPER LEAGUE

Soft Power, Investment, and Sustainability

Ricardo Gúdel and Emilio Hernández

Overseas direct investment (ODI) in the football industry is a variable that arises from different possible actions with which clubs and owners try to create value and obtain an inevitable return on investment. In the last decade, Chinese companies started to invest in sponsorships in European football clubs and competitions (Chadwick et al., 2020) in the partial or total purchase of clubs (Lee & No, 2020) and also in agreements with European leagues for the training of players, coaches, and referees for the development of national skills (Connell, 2017). In addition, academics have mainly studied in recent years the transfer market and the purchase of players by Chinese Super League (CSL) clubs due to their fluctuations and the attraction of players with high media impact and increased investment (Cockayne et al., 2021; Liang, 2014; Sullivan, 2021). In this regard, the Chinese football industry has implemented various strategies for growth with reforms and national development plans to make such spending more sustainable (Gündoğan & Sonntag, 2018).

The areas in which Chinese investment is concentrated are included in the Chinese five-year plans. Five-year plans are a set of economic and social development initiatives that serve to map out China's strategies for growth over five-year periods. China's five-year plan offers a glimpse of the priorities that central and local governments will adhere to in the next five years. Plans typically include numerical growth targets and provide policy guidelines for reforms. Since the issuance of the 1st Five-Year Plan in 1953, China has published 14 such documents.

Looking at China's outward investment in general, it is noteworthy that the last two five-year plans, while differing in some respects, share standard features in this regard. In the 13th Five-Year Plan (2016–2020), a reference to the Belt and Road Initiative (BRI) appears for the first time. More significant outward investment, infrastructure activities along the BRI route, and demonstrating actual

DOI: 10.4324/9781003348238-15

results through foreign aid are crucial points (United Nations Development Programme, 2016). The 14th Five-Year Plan (2021–2025) includes a long-term development goal for 2035 to comply with openness policies in the future, attract ODI flows, and promote ODI through the BRI, albeit with greater sustainability. Arguably, the main narrative of the 14th Plan is one of continuity, with some innovations and expanded ambitions (United Nations Development Programme, 2021).

The most ambitious strategy pursued by the Chinese government, the BRI, has among its primary objectives sport. China intends to be one of the largest sports economies in the world. To this end, it has been implementing public policies to develop its sports industry (Leite Junior & Rodrigues, 2020). This strategy is equally applicable to the football industry. It is essential to mention the already well-known Stadium Diplomacy regarding the construction of infrastructures abroad. Since 1958, China has built more than 140 sports facilities worldwide, and the amount of investment destined for the African continent stands out (Vondracek, 2019). In this way, China secures access to certain raw materials and combats overcapacity in its construction sector (Jin et al., 2021). Furthermore, African countries are involved in large-scale projects which, while providing a sense of development, build structures that do not necessarily improve the quality of life of the local inhabitants (Dubinsky, 2021).

This flow of investment for the development of the football industry and sport, in general, has been considered a soft power strategy. However, it can also be considered, like the BRI, an intelligent power strategy with Chinese characteristics: a combination of cultural and economic power. This approach has become a country branding strategy and the *leitmotif* of China's foreign policy, encompassing many investments and projects. Infrastructure, finance, culture, education, interpersonal relations, political relations between states, and the football industry are no strangers to such investments. Hard power elements, such as economic investments, are combined with a soft power strategy, such as promoting Chinese culture or improving China's image. It is the perfect vehicle to propagate its soft power strategy (Brînză, 2018).

If we look at the evolution of the football industry, the lack of sustainability has been one of the determining factors in the government's change of strategy in recent years regarding investments. The expenditure, especially in 2015 and 2016 in terms of the number of player transfers from Europe and partial or total acquisition of clubs, led to a dangerous financial situation due to the maintenance of high player salaries (Gao & Chappelet, 2021). For this reason, the Chinese Football Association (CFA) established the penalties for transfer fees and regulations concerning national U-23 players (Yang & Bairner, 2021).

In their article, Xue et al. (2020) position China's football industry as an instrument that aligns capital flows with political and financial ends aiming to forge debt relationships. However, this planning led to consequences: the difficulty of club payments and the partial insolvency of the competition. It is important to note that, since its professionalization in 1994, the real estate sector has played a significant role in the Chinese football industry (Yu et al., 2017). Companies such as China Fortune Land Development or R&F Properties have used their investments in their CSL clubs, Hebei and Guangzhou, respectively, to secure subsidies from local governments to make profits in the development of urban land (Hesketh & Sullivan, 2020).

In recent years, numerous authors have extensively studied the real estate sector in China in the face of the threat of a real estate bubble (Glaeser et al., 2017; Zhang & Li, 2020; Zhao et al., 2017). Currently, the Chinese real estate sector represents a third of the Asian giant's economy. It includes housing, rental, and brokerage services, industries that produce household appliances, and construction materials. Nevertheless, this phenomenon is not new. In the country's major cities, prices in the sector grew by 13.1% annually from 2003 to 2013 (Fang et al., 2016). Moreover, the ratio of housing prices to household income is among the highest globally. According to Rogoff & Yang (2020), the average family in China needs 27 years' income to buy a standard home.

The main risk today is that there will be a contagion effect and that the banks will stop lending money to construction companies if they believe the sector is sinking. In this sense, the bankruptcy of the financial problems of the sector giant Evergrande (the majority shareholder of Guangzhou FC) has led to a trend change in the Chinese economy. According to this, the Beijing government is committed to boosting domestic consumption by being less dependent on debt, with greater control by the Communist Party (Artigas, 2021).

In 2021, 12 of the 16 CSL teams had a real estate or construction company as one of the majority shareholders (EFI Database, 2022a). Due to this, it is of great importance to analyze how the real estate bubble could affect the football industry in China. To get a first indication of the impact of the real estate bubble on the Chinese football industry, the correlation between the construction and real estate sectors with the football industry was analyzed using the variables described below:

- Total investment of CSL clubs in transfers with owners related to real estate companies (1).
- Total transfer investment by CSL clubs (2).
- Revenues by main activity of Chinese real estate companies (3).
- Operating profit of Chinese real estate companies (4).
- Chinese Net ODI in real estate (5).
- Chinese Net ODI in sport, culture, and entertainment (6).
- Net ODI total for China (7).

For this purpose, data from the "EFI Database" of the Department of Business Organisation and Marketing and Market Research of the University of Valladolid (Faculty of Commerce) has been used in the present study. This research analyzes 472 transfers during ten years in the Chinese first division between the 2011–2012 and 2020–2021 seasons, both inclusive. Data from the official websites of the Chinese Super League football clubs, the specialized website transfermarkt.com, and official data from the Chinese government have also been included in the above-mentioned database.

The real estate and construction sectors have historically, and for obvious reasons, been related, as evidenced by numerous studies that research them in conjunction (Ball, 2006; Kaklauskas et al., 2011; Kamenetskii & Yas'kova, 2018). However, it can be seen in the evolution of Chinese ODI by sector in Figure 13.1 that the pattern of net ODI flow is not similar between the two. The culture, sports, and entertainment and real estate sectors are the ones that are closely related in terms of their behaviour during that period.

To complement the information provided by the ODI data and the strength of the correlation between the variables described above, multivariate analysis has been carried out by extracting a Pearson Product-Moment correlation coefficient.[1] Table 13.1 does not include association values with the variables as ODI in the construction sector or profit of Chinese construction companies. Results seemed to show that their correlation would not be relevant.

However, it is essential to consider the results for the real estate sector. The total investment of clubs with real estate–related owners is highly correlated with total ODI, real estate ODI, culture, sports, and entertainment ODI, and the total investment of all clubs over the period 2011–2019. The latter is also highly correlated with all three ODI variables, as Table 13.1 shows.

Although correlation does not imply causation, Chinese Stadium Diplomacy could reflect that the construction sector does not seem to be related to the Chinese football industry. According to Vondracek (2019), the acceleration of the use of this diplomacy is evident in line with the economy's growth over the last decades. A significant increase from 2010 to 2016 (8.8 cases analyzed per year) compared to 1990–2009 (3.3 cases) reveals that China is building more and more of such infrastructure worldwide if analyzed from a historical perspective.

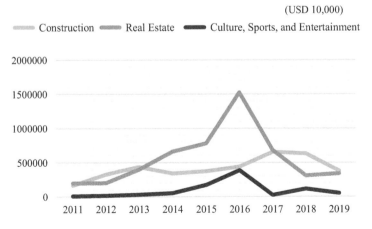

FIGURE 13.1 China's Net ODI by sectors 2011–2020 (EFI Database, 2022b).

112 Ricardo Gúdel and Emilio Hernández

TABLE 13.1 Pearson Product-Moment correlations

	1	2	3	4	5	6	7
1		0.97	0.51	0.22	0.76	0.84	0.87
2	0.97		0.42	0,1	0.85	0.94	0.87
3	0.51	0.42		0.9	0.22	0.29	0.7
4	0.22	0.1	0.9		−0.17	0	0.36
5	0.76	0.85	0.22	−0.17		0.88	0.84
6	0.84	0.94	0.29	0	0.88		0.78
7	0.87	0.87	0.7	0.36	0.84	0.78	

Source: EFI Database (2022c).

TABLE 13.2 CSL bankrupted clubs and owners

CSL Club	Last Main Owners	Owner's Headquarters	Sector	Years Active
Beijing Renhe	Renhe Commercial Holdings Company Limited	Hong Kong	Agricultural	1995–2021
Jiangsu Suning	Suning.com Co., Ltd.	Jiangsu	Household appliances	1994–2021
Shanghai Shenxin	Hengyuan Corporation	Shanghai	Real estate	2003–2020
Yanbian Funde	Yanbian Sports Bureau & Life insurance company Funde Holdings Group	Jilin & Guangdong	Government & Insurance	1994–2019
Tianjin Tianhai	Local Football Association	Tianjin	Governmental	2006–2020
Liaoning Whowin	Whowin & Liaoning Sport College	Liaoning	Real Estate & Local	1994–2020

Source: EFI Database (2022a).

The government has recently sought to increase the sustainability of China's investments abroad. However, the succession of infrastructure constructions in recent years[2] suggests that such a policy behaves independently of the investment in football by CSL clubs and owners over the last decade. The author also associates this with China's possible more excellent utility for its interests in the form of soft power in this type of diplomacy.

The financial problems of CSL clubs stemming from the high salaries incurred and investments made over the last decade have been palpable in the disappearance of several major and even founding clubs from the competition in the first season after its professionalization. As shown in Table 13.2, only two of the six clubs, once participants in the CSL, that have officially ceased their activities since 2019 have a majority shareholder belonging to the real estate sector. Still, it is essential to note that in the case of Shanghai Shenxin, the main reason for the cessation of activities was disqualification by the Chinese Football Association after they failed to submit the salary and bonus confirmation form before the 2020 season. Regarding Liaoning Whowin, the cause was their failure to provide evidence to the authorities that they had settled their debts and paid the employees' salaries (Reuters, 2022). Nevertheless, it is vital to highlight the cases of Guangzhou FC and Hebei FC, two clubs with financial problems due to their owners. Both are real estate companies with a significant accumulation of debt, which has almost cost both teams the possibility of not being able to compete during the CSL 2022 (White, 2021).

Even though the investment of CSL clubs has had a similar trend to the real estate sector in terms of the amount of investment over the last decade, we cannot claim that the causes of the financial difficulties of the teams in the competition are due to the real estate bubble. China is a country deeply indebted (especially in the private sector). This leverage makes the economy vulnerable, and we are still at the beginning of the process regarding defaults. It is necessary to analyze each case on a case-by-case basis as clubs whose owners are not real estate companies have disappeared or had difficulties due to financial problems. The construction sector seems not to be closely related to Chinese football either. Although it is essential to note that, even if there appears to be no similar behaviour between sectors, any event that leads to financial problems in the sector of the club owners can also provoke fatal consequences for the clubs. The business lines that the clubs represent for these companies are dispensable to the extent that they do not involve added profitability or revenue from their core business.

Furthermore, the consequences of the policies pursued in the Chinese football industry are still palpable, observable in the evolution of the Chinese ODI in sport, culture, and entertainment, and the lack of sustainability generated, especially by the players' high salaries. The current transfer system has been in place since 2010. Despite its similarities to European transfer systems, restrictions on the participation of foreign players,[3] and policies to encourage the development of domestic talent, it has failed to prevent the economic drift of the participating teams.

The investment flows in the football industry present a mixture of hard power and soft power strategies through economic acquisition and the transmission of the values and image of China as geostrategic tools for positioning on the world stage. In this regard, as a geopolitical tool, the football industry has most likely prevented the forging of a sustainable development strategy capable of competing with the top Asian leagues. A high return does not usually accompany such policies on investment. Moreover, there does not seem to be a strategy of internationalization and networking of Chinese companies at the level of sponsorship, acquisitions, or player transfers that have generated or currently generate high added value to the competition in the short term.

Notes

1 The closer the correlation between variables is to 1 or −1, the greater the association, positive or negative, between the variables. A significant coefficient was considered to be ±0.68 or higher.
2 E.g., the construction of Stade Olympique Alassane Ouattara in Côte d'Ivoire by the Chinese company Beijing Construction Engineering Group inaugurated in 2020, or the Bingu National Stadium in Malawi by the contractor Anhui Foreign Economic Construction Group inaugurated in 2017 (StadiumDB, 2022)
3 According to statistics reflected in the EFI Database (2022d), the number of foreign players has decreased over the last decade despite the significant increase in investment during the years in question.

References

Artigas, I. A., 2021. The Evergrande crisis marks a change of model in China. *Economic Alternatives SCCL*, Issue 96, pp. 24–25. https://dialnet.unirioja.es/servlet/articulo?codigo=8152525

Ball, M., 2006. *Markets and Institutions in Real Estate and Construction*. s.l.: Blackwell Publishing.

Brînză, A., 2018. *The Diplomat*. [Online] Available at: https: //thediplomat.com/2018/03/redefining-the-belt-and-road-initiative/ [Accessed 21 May 2022].

Chadwick, S., Widdop, P. & Burton, N., 2020. Soft power sports sponsorship – A social network analysis of a new sponsorship form. *Journal of Political Marketing*, 21(2), pp. 196–217.

Cockayne, D., Chadwick, S. & Sullivan, J., 2021. Chinese football – From a state-led past to a digital future. *Journal of Global Sport Management*, 7(3), pp. 345–354.

Connell, J., 2017. Globalisation, soft power, and the rise of football in China. *Geographical Research*, 56(1), pp. 5–15.

Dubinsky, I., 2021. China's stadium diplomacy in Africa. *Journal of Global Sport Management*, pp. 1–19.

EFI Database, 2022a. *CSL Owners*. University of Valladolid: s.n.

EFI Database, 2022b. *China's Net ODI by Sectors and Regions (2011–2020)*. Universidad de Valladolid: s.n.

EFI Database, 2022c. *Chinese Investment Variables Correlations*. Universidad de Valladolid: s.n.

EFI Database, 2022d. *CSL Transfer Market Evolution*. University of Valladolid: s.n.

Fang, H., Gu, Q., Xiong, W. & Zhou, L.-A., 2016. Demystifying the Chinese housing boom. *National Bureau of Economic Research*, 30, pp. 105–166.

Gao, Z. & Chappelet, J.-L., 2021. Evolution of professional football management in the People's Republic of China from 1992 to 2016. *Asian Journal of Sport History & Culture*, 37(17), pp. 1863–1883.

Glaeser, E., Huang, W., Ma, Y. & Shleifer, A., 2017. A real estate boom with Chinese characteristics. *Journal of Economic Perspectives*, 31(1), pp. 93–116.

Gündoğan, I. & Sonntag, A., 2018. Chinese football in the era of Xi Jinping: What do supporters think?. *Journal of Current Chinese Affairs*, 47(1), pp. 103–141.

Hesketh, C. & Sullivan, J., 2020. The production of leisure: Understanding the social function of football development in China. *Globalizations*, 17(6), pp. 1061–1079.

Jin, C. et al., 2021. Measurement for overcapacity and its influencing factors on the construction industry-evidence from China's provincial data. *Environmental Science and Pollution Research*, Issue 28, pp. 7883–7892.

Kaklauskas, A. et al., 2011. Crisis management in construction and real estate: Conceptual modeling at the micro-, meso- and macro-levels. *Land Use Policy*, 28(1), pp. 280–293.

Kamenetskii, M. I. & Yas'kova, N. Y., 2018. Construction and real estate markets: From crisis to growth. *Studies on Russian Economic Development*, 29(1), pp. 35–40.

Lee, S. & No, S., 2020. China's Overseas Financial Direct Investment (ODI) in European football clubs: Revisiting ODI in the context of sport industry. *Journal of Global Sport Management*, 7(3), pp. 391–405.

Leite Junior, E. & Rodrigues, C., 2020. Belt, road and ball: Football as a Chinese soft power and public diplomacy tool. In: F. Leandro & P. Duarte, eds. *The Belt and Road Initiative. An Old Archetype of a New Development Model.* Singapore: Palgrave Macmillan, p. 62.

Liang, Y., 2014. The development pattern and a clubs' perspective on football governance in China. *Soccer & Society*, 15(3), pp. 430–448.

Reuters, 2022. *Chinese Clubs Risk Relegation, Explusion over Unpaid Wages.* [Online] Available at: https://www.reuters.com/lifestyle/sports/chinese-clubs-risk-relegation-explusion-over-unpaid-wages-2022-04-04/ [Accessed 3 May 2022].

Rogoff, K. S. & Yang, Y., 2020. Peak China housing. *National Bureau of Economic Research.* (No. 27697).

StadiumDB, 2022. *StadiumDB.com.* [Online] Available at: http://stadiumdb.com/stadiums/ [Accessed 21 April 2022].

Sullivan, J., 2021. Xi's Soccer dream: Defining characteristics, unintended consequences. In: J. Sullivan, ed. *China's Football Dream.* s.l.: University of Nottingham, pp. 12–17.

United Nations Developemt Programme, 2021. *China's 14th Five-year Plan.* Beijing: United Nations Developemt Programme China.

United Nations Development Programme, 2016. *13th Five-Year Plan: What to Expect from China.* Beijing: United Nations Development Programme China.

Vondracek, H., 2019. China's stadium diplomacy and its determinants: A typological investigation of soft power. *Journal of China and International Relations*, 7(1), pp. 62–86.

White, J., 2021. *South China Morning Post.* [Online] Available at: https://www.scmp.com/sport/china/article/3155413/struggling-chinese-side-hebei-fc-thank-fans-amid-uncertain-csl-future [Accessed 6 May 2022].

Xue, H., Watanabe, N., Chen, R., & Yan, G. (2020). Football (as) Guanxi: a relational analysis of actor reciprocity, state capitalism, and the Chinese football industry. *Sport in Society, 23*(12), pp. 2005–2030. doi:10.1080/17430437.2020.1755959

Yang, S. & Bairner, A., 2021. Can the foreign player restriction and U-23 rule improve Chinese football? In: J. Sullivan, ed. *China's Football Dream.* s.l.: University of Nottingham, pp. 29–38.

Yu, L., Newman, J., Xue, H. & Pu, H., 2017. The transition game: Toward a cultural economy of football in post-socialist China. *International Review for the Sociology of Sport*, pp. 1–27.

Zhang, X. & Li, H., 2020. The evolving process of the land urbanization bubble: Evidence from Hangzhou, China. *Cities*, 102.

Zhao, S. X. B., Zhan, H., Jiang, Y. & Pan, W., 2017. How big is China's real estate bubble and why hasn't it burst yet? *Land Use Policy*, 64, pp. 153–162.

14

DOING SPORTS BUSINESS IN CHINA

Still a Slam Dunk?

Jonathan Sullivan and Tobias Ross

International sport, like most other sectors, has been attracted by the size, growth potential, and increasing wealth of the Chinese market since the reform era began in 1979. For much of the reform period, China's economy grew at break-neck speed, numerous economic sectors liberalized, and, post-Tiananmen, Jiang Zemin (1993–2003) and Hu Jintao (2003–2013) oversaw a comparatively liberal approach to the management of Chinese society. However, until the 1990s, most of China's sport industry was controlled and funded by the state, almost completely excluding foreign brands. As China became richer, more concerned by growing health problems (Wu et al., 2017) and interested in the "soft power" (Giulianotti, 2015) and economic (Liu et al., 2017) potential of sport, international sports organizations, leagues, clubs, and adjacent brands were increasingly welcomed and consequently rushed in, hoping to leverage the purchasing power of a large and expanding middle class. Further driven by globalization and international market competition, these entities increasingly looked into global markets to outplay their competitors (Horne & Manzenreiter, 2004). With Chinese modernization waxing in international consciousness, symbolized by futuristic cityscapes and the immaculate Beijing Olympics in 2008, the cost-benefit calculation for international sport was straightforward.

Chinese sporting preferences do not map exactly onto the mainstream Euro-American offering – table tennis, badminton, and gymnastics are among China's most popular sports. But the markets for TV, streaming, commercial tie-ups, merchandising, online shopping, experience packages, sports betting (though technically illegal), sponsorship, and dense and active digital spaces are lucrative and relatively untapped. Compared to many western economies, the Chinese sport industry's contribution to its national economy is very low and still in its infancy stage (Liu et al., 2017). For some sports, the Chinese market has been transformative, often representing a substantial share of their global value, like

DOI: 10.4324/9781003348238-16

illustrated in Table 14.1. Snooker, for instance, a sport with minimal traction in China before the 2000s, now has a multi-tournament swing, multiple Chinese sponsors, and an exciting generation of young Chinese players with millions of fans. Other sports have failed to establish themselves, but for every ICC frustrated by cricket's lack of appeal, there is an FIA giddy about a Chinese driver competing at the Shanghai Grand Prix.

Approaching the end of the first decade of Xi Jinping's rule, China is an economic and diplomatic superpower and a central component in the globalized economy, its wealth and middle classes larger than ever. Yet, the promise of continuing liberalization and progress towards a market economy has stalled, and sudden and heavy-handed state interventions have become the norm. Systematically repressive policies have been enacted in Xinjiang, alongside the

TABLE 14.1 Selected international sport activity in China

Entity	Entry	Activity	China Value	Global Value
Premier League	1992	Youth training; Asia Trophy Cup; exhibition games, shops, experiences	€30–35m (2021/22) (broadcasting)	€5.13b (2019/20)
LaLiga	2002	Academy; youth tournaments; marketing joint venture; exhibition games	€30–50m (2021/22) (broadcasting)	€3.11b (2019/20)
NBA	1986	NBA China company; exhibition games; Junior NBA league; academies; entertainment parks; shops	>$500m (2019)	$8.76b (2018/19)
WTA	2004	9 major events (2019), incl. record prize money (Shenzhen); office; major Chinese sponsors	>$20m (2018)	$102.6m (2018)
ATP	1996	4 major events (planned for 2022); major Chinese sponsors	$20m (2015) (broadcasting)	$107.1m (2014)
UFC	2012	Academy, 6 fights to date; 12 fighters	$20m (2021) (broadcasting)	$930m (2021)
World Snooker	2005	Academy; 6 major events; 20+ top-100 players; major Chinese sponsors	£1.13m (2017) (streaming)	£18.4m (2017)

Sources: Deloitte (2021); Escobar (2021); Insider Media Limited (2018); Jiemian News (2017); Sohu (2017); Sports Business Journal (2015); Statista (2022); Tifosy (2022); Wall Street Journal (2021); Xue (2018); Yahoo Sports (2021; 2021a).

118 Jonathan Sullivan and Tobias Ross

circumscription of freedoms in Hong Kong and crackdowns across many sectors of society. "Assertive" policy and posture in foreign affairs has been accompanied by rapid deterioration of China's foreign relations and image in the west. International sports entities are adept at sidestepping political tensions, but the trajectory in China's relations with the west is increasingly salient.

During Xi's tenure it has become more difficult to operate in China. The leeway that foreign operations enjoyed in the past has decreased as a powerful and confident China no longer sees the need to give special treatment. The state and consumers alike are aware of the power yielded by the Chinese market. The state can restrict or effectively "cancel" foreign sport brands, behoving them to avoid Chinese "internal affairs" like human rights or repression in Xinjiang, and to adopt government-approved "politically correct" positions on issues like Hong Kong or Taiwan. Hyper-vigilant cybernationalists capitalize on any faux pas that "hurts the feelings of the Chinese people" or "insults China". Resulting furores can result in "informal sanctions" (Reilly, 2012) and do irrevocable harm to brand image (Nyiri, 2009).

Assuaging the Chinese state and Chinese publics is one thing. Doing so without provoking outrage and associated reputational damage "at home" is another. When the US president declares that China is committing genocide in Xinjiang, does a sports league want to be seen toeing the Party line? Is a club tainted when it disowns one of its athletes and makes abject apologies to Chinese netizens? Is it possible to square being "woke at home" and supportive of authoritarianism abroad? Adept public relations and the inherent capacity of high-level sporting competition to mesmerize are powerful assets. But a further complication is the rise of socially conscious athletes with huge individual platforms. Athletes like Serena Williams, Lewis Hamilton, Megan Rapinoe, Steph Curry, and Marcus Rashford possess cultural power and social influence that transcends sport. Others, like Enes Kanter, Mesut Özil, and Sonny Bill Williams, have explicitly contravened Chinese "red lines" to criticize repression in Xinjiang and Tibet. Two recent case studies illustrate these complexities.

Daryl Morey and the NBA

In October 2019, shortly before the NBA's pre-season China Games, Houston Rockets executive Daryl Morey posted from his device in Japan an image in support of a protest movement in Hong Kong to the American social media platform Twitter. Thousands of Hong Kong citizens were at that moment on the streets protesting a proposed extradition bill they believed represented a devastating encroachment by Beijing on the city's remaining political freedoms. The protests were framed by the pro-Beijing establishment in Hong Kong, and throughout China's controlled information environment, as violent mob riots facilitated by malicious "foreign forces".

Morey's tweet could not be seen directly in China, because the platform is unavailable behind the Great Firewall that keeps out unsanctioned information.

But many Chinese access the "free internet" using VPNs and salient information easily finds its way into Chinese cyberspaces via domestic platforms. The Rockets had a substantial following in China, being intrinsically linked to the Hall of Fame career of Yao Ming, one of China's biggest sports stars and "soft power" assets. Yao had helped the Rockets, and the NBA, to become major players in the Chinese market, so it was unsurprising that Morey's faux pas was noticed, shared, and quickly went viral. As usual in such cases, the backlash in Chinese cyberspace was picked up by state media and opinion leaders, and subsequently government officials. Ultimately, it led to the suspension of broadcasts and streaming, cancelled sponsorship deals and events, and the decimation of merchandise sales, resulting in revenue losses in excess of $200 million (Escobar, 2021).

China was the NBA's biggest market outside the United States, and the league scrambled to implement the corporate crisis-management playbook, issuing apologies and doubling its efforts to connect with Chinese publics. The NBA had experienced similar difficulties in 1999, following the accidental bombing of the Chinese embassy in Belgrade by US/NATO forces, which many people in China believed was deliberate. The team and the league quickly distanced themselves from Morey's "personal views", as did Yao Ming, even as American publics, media, and politicians voiced their support and criticized the NBA's lack of spine (O'Connell, 2021). LeBron James put out a mollifying statement to the effect that Morey should further educate himself on the issue, a mealy-mouthed stance at odds with James' tireless social activism and celebrated championing of racial justice in the United States.

Joe Tsai, an executive at the Chinese e-commerce giant Alibaba and part-owner of the Brooklyn Nets, similarly opined that Morey "was not as well informed as he should have been". From one perspective this was correct: Morey should have known that supporting the Hong Kong protests would provoke trouble in China. Properly informed, he would have recognized that doing business in China requires acquiescence or acceptance of certain "facts" and narratives. On the other hand, "informed" by Tsai's definition was disingenuous: Had Morey made the objectively uninformed, but "politically correct", statement that (paraphrasing Chinese state media) 'Hong Kong rioters under the guidance of foreign black hands are seeking to undermine Chinese sovereignty by fomenting a colour revolution,' he would likely have been lauded in China.

Morey deleted the tweet and apologized, and temporarily remained in his role. He was subsequently removed, but the Rockets brand was irredeemably damaged in China. Now president of basketball operations at the Philadelphia 76-ers, Morey remains "cancelled" in China. Streaming partner Tencent has edited or halted coverage to avoid transmitting political messages on signs or T-shirts worn by fans at the stadium. Guilty by their association with Morey, Sixers' games are unavailable to stream. The Boston Celtics have been blacklisted due to the outspoken human rights activism of Center Enes Kanter, who wears game shoes supporting Xinxiang, Tibet, and Taiwan. NBA Commissioner

Peng Shuai and the WTA

In November 2021, Grand Slam doubles champion Peng Shuai posted an earnest and detailed claim of sexual assault to her personal Weibo account. The allegation was levelled against a recently retired member of the Politburo, i.e. one of China's most powerful politicians, 75-year-old Zhang Gaoli, with whom Peng had once had a consensual relationship. The post quickly disappeared into the black hole of Chinese internet censorship, and Peng herself disappeared from public view for several weeks. During that time foreign journalists raised concerns about her whereabouts and wellbeing. Naomi Osaka was one of several athletes to amplify calls for her safe return. Clumsy attempts by Chinese state media, and an ignoble intervention by the IOC concerned to avoid bad publicity before the Beijing Winter Olympics, failed to assuage growing international concern. Peng subsequently reappeared, giving scripted media interviews and choreographed public appearances. Her repeated protestations that she had never alleged sexual assault, and other incongruous statements, prolonged fears that her performances were coerced and her freedom contingent.

The WTA response was immediate and unequivocal. Chairman and CEO Steve Simon was consistent and adamant that WTA operations in China would be put on pause until both the proximate issue of Peng's safety was resolved and the sexual assault allegations were investigated. Lauded by athletes and much of the international sports community, the WTA's stance brought it into direct conflict with the Chinese authorities' narrative that Peng was fine and that the allegation had not happened or was a misunderstanding. A public accusation against a high-ranking official, by one of the country's most famous athletes no less, was unprecedented. Outside of Party-led purges, the private lives of elite politicians are strictly taboo. The Party and state information control and propaganda apparatus went into overdrive. China's sensitivity and rejection of outside interference, in combination with the Party's intense proclivity for self-preservation (Tsang, 2009), clashed with the WTA's principled stand and left no room for compromise. The WTA cancelled its China-based tournaments.

The WTA invested substantially in expanding its China operations since the first tournaments were held there in the early 2000s. Shortly before the decision to pull its tournaments from China, the WTA had signed several long-term deals with Chinese broadcasters, sponsors, and almost a dozen host cities. It had made Shenzhen the home of the WTA Finals, with a record-breaking $14 million in prize money. Supporting women in sport has been a core pillar of the WTA's mission since its foundation in 1973 (Szto, 2015). Taking a stand on the apparent disappearance of a woman athlete, her potential mistreatment by an authoritarian government and the cover-up of a sexual assault would thus appear to be the requisite response. But given that China accounts for roughly 20–30% of the

WTA's total income (Yahoo Sport, 2021a) and the propensity of other sports entities, firms, and governments to compromise or capitulate rather than risking access to the Chinese market, the WTA's case was unusual. The ATP, for example, has signalled its intent to continue "business as usual" in China. Once Peng reappeared and said in effect, "I'm fine, there's nothing to see here", a more cynical and less principled organization might have backed off and surreptitiously returned to business as usual.

The Peng case was the first test of a foreign sports league since the COVID-19 pandemic and the emergence of aggressive "wolf warrior diplomacy" (Sullivan and Wang, 2022), a rather confrontational style of foreign diplomacy which is increasingly used under Xi Jinping. It occurred at a moment when there is widespread global awareness of the repression in Xinjiang, crackdowns in Hong Kong, intimidation of Taiwan, and the general authoritarian grip being exerted domestically. In this period, China's foreign relations environment has significantly deteriorated, and in western democracies China's international image has been tarnished and public opinion turned sharply negative. In this broader context, the WTA was widely lauded for standing up for its athlete and standing by its principles. American health technology firm Hologic subsequently signed on as the WTA tour's new title sponsor, stating that strong support for Peng was a factor (New York Times, 2022).

Conclusion

The Chinese government welcomed foreign sports because it amplified the idea that China was global and modern, while simultaneously helping develop the domestic sports industry. It was another way to demonstrate to the Chinese people that the country had become rich, strong, and respected under the Party's guidance. The need for external affirmation of Chinese progress has receded, and as China has become more self-confident it is less willing to make concessions or accept interference in its affairs. Foreign governments, firms, individuals, and sport either heed that message, or they will pay a price. As the saying goes, "you can't eat our rice and smash our pots". Chinese people love sports, but few love sports more than they love China; hence, public demand to punish transgressors who "insult China" will always supersede fans upset at missing broadcasts or exhibition games.

Market access as a tool of foreign policy is not new (Baldwin, 2020), but we have not seen a situation where a country has the power to influence freedom of speech to the extent that China possesses within and outside its borders. It isn't just companies doing business in China that will have to modify their and their employees' behaviour. Every sector that deals with Chinese consumers will be motivated to self-censor to avoid offending with "uniformed" opinions that hurt the bottom line. Not even university lecturers feel exempt from the pressure to conform (Greitens and Truex, 2020). To date, most foreign companies that have triggered reactions in China for their faux pas have apologized and tried to make amends. Failure to do so can be devastating and even precipitate market exit. Companies like Nike, H&M, and Adidas that were subject to Chinese bans for their statements on Xinjiang Cotton and forced labour practices in March 2021 experienced substantial revenue losses, lasting reputational damage, and ceded ground to domestic Chinese competitors. While the Chinese market retains substantial potential, the cost-benefit calculus for foreign sports entities operating there has become more complicated than the slam dunk it once was.

References

Baldwin, David A. (2020). *Economic Statecraft*. Princeton: Princeton University Press.

Deloitte (2021). Annual review of football finance 2021. Available at: https://www2 .deloitte.com/uk/en/pages/sports-business-group/articles/annual-review-of-football -finance.html (accessed 19.04.22).

Escobar, Christopher J. (2021). The billion dollar tweet: Assessing the impact of the fallout between the NBA and China. *Sports Lawyers Journal*, 28, 1–18.

Giulianotti, Richard. (2015). The Beijing 2008 Olympics: Examining the interrelations of China, globalization, and soft power. *European Review*, 23(2), 286–296.

Greitens, Sheena Chestnut, and Truex, Rory. (2020). Repressive experiences among China scholars: New evidence from survey data. *The China Quarterly*, 242, 349–375.

Horne, John and Manzenreiter, Wolfram. (2004). Football, culture, globalisation: Why professional football has been going East. In Horne, J. & Manzenreiter, W. (eds.) *Football Goes East* (pp. 17–34). Abingdon: Routledge.

Insider Media Limited (2018). World Snooker ups prize fund after "unprecedented" revenue growth. 24 April. Available at: https://www.insidermedia.com/news/ south-west/world-snooker-ups-prize-fund-after-unprecedented-revenue-growth (accessed 19.04.22).

Jiemian News (2017). 十年世界斯诺克新媒体版权仅卖出千万元，这项运动在中国还能好吗 [Ten years of World Snooker new media rights have been sold for only 10 million yuan, is this sport still good in China?]. 15 August. Available at: https://www .jiemian.com/article/1548837.html (accessed 19.04.22).

Liu, Dongfeng, Zhang, James J., and Desbordes, Michel. (2017). Sport business in China: Current state and prospect. *International Journal of Sports Marketing and Sponsorship*, 18(1), 2–10.

New York Times (2022). Strong stance on China and Peng Shuai helps land WTA a new title sponsor. 3 March. Available at: https://www.nytimes.com/2022/03/03/sports/ tennis/wta-hologic-china.html (accessed 15.04.22).

Nyiri, Pal. (2009). From Starbucks to carrefour: Consumer boycotts, nationalism and taste in contemporary China. *Portal*, 6(2), 1–25.

O'Connell, William D. (2021). Silencing the crowd: China, the NBA, and leveraging market size to export censorship. *Review of International Political Economy*, 29(4), 1112–1134.

Reilly, James. (2012). China's unilateral sanctions. *The Washington Quarterly*, 35(4), 121–133.

Sohu (2017). 因欠款超过1亿元，乐视体育ATP转播合同被终止 [LeTV sports' ATP broadcast contract was terminated due to arrears exceeding 100 million yuan]. 25 April. Available at: https://www.sohu.com/a/136359894_116132 (accessed 19.04.22).

Sports Business Journal (2015). ATP outstrips WTA in revenue growth. Available at: https://www.sportsbusinessjournal.com/Journal/Issues/2015/11/23/Leagues-and -Governing-Bodies/ATP-revenue.aspx (accessed 19.04.22).

Statista (2022). National Basketball Association total league revenue from 2001/2 to 2020/1. 3 March. Available at: https://www.statista.com/statistics/193467/total -league-revenue-of-the-nba-since-2005/ (accessed 19.04.22).

Sullivan, Jonathan, and Wang, Weixiang. (2022). China's "wolf warrior diplomacy:" The interaction of formal diplomacy and cyber-nationalism. *Journal of Current Chinese Affairs*. DOI: 10.1177/18681026221079841.

Szto, Courtney. (2015). Serving up change? Gender mainstreaming and the UNESCO– WTA partnership for global gender equality. *Sport in Society*, 18(8), 895–908.

Tifosy (2022). How the UFC is becoming the ultimate fighting championship. 11 February. Available at: https://www.tifosy.com/en/insights/how-the-ufc-is -becoming-the-ultimate-fighting-championship-3558 (accessed 19.04.22).

Wall Street Journal (2021). Chinese sponsor distanced itself from women's tennis before WTA pulled events from China. 3 December. Available at: https://www.wsj.com/ articles/wta-china-peng-shuai-iqiyi-11638553096 (accessed 19.04.22).

Wu, Sa, Luo, Yufeng, Qiu, Xue, and Bao, Mingxiao. (2017). Building a healthy China by enhancing physical activity: Priorities, challenges, and strategies. *Journal of Sport and Health Science*, 6(1), 125–126.

Xue, Wenting. (2018). 体媒人物: 体媒人物: 新中国体育新闻转播口述史 *[Media Figures: New China's Oral History of Sports News Broadcasting]*. Beijing: Tsinghua University Press.

Yahoo! Sport (2021). UFC's five-year Chinese media deal valued at 'high eight figures' as promotion expands. 24 February. Available at: https://sports.yahoo.com/ufc-five -chinese-media-deal-161337967.html (accessed 19.04.22).

Yahoo! Sport (2021a). The WTA's hundred-million-dollar statement to China. 2 December. Available at: https://uk.sports.yahoo.com/news/the-wt-as-hundred -million-dollar-statement-to-china-043514815.html (accessed 15.04.22).

PART III

The Gulf and South Asia

15

QATAR AND THE 2022 FIFA WORLD CUP

Soft Power, State Branding, or Nation Building?

Kristian Coates Ulrichsen

This chapter examines the various factors that lay behind Qatar's decision to bid for the 2022 FIFA World Cup and assesses whether the 12-year-long cycle of preparation and planning met or defied the expectations of Qatari officials since 2010. Three opening sections explore the degree to which the hosting of the FIFA World Cup has been guided by (and intended to contribute to) a desire to extend Qatari soft power, state branding, or nation building. A common thread in each of the sections is whether the long 2022 World Cup cycle has supported or undermined the broader geopolitical objectives of a country and a leadership that has consistently sought for itself an outsize role in regional and international affairs.

While Qatar became a fully sovereign state only in 1971, since the 1990s its leadership (under the hereditary rule of the Al Thani family) has developed the country's enormous reserves of natural gas to become a global gas giant that in 2006 surpassed Indonesia as the world's largest exporter of liquefied natural gas (LNG) (Roberts 2017: 50). The largest non-associated gas field in the world straddles the Qatar–Iran boundary, and shipments of LNG from the Qatari share of the North Field began in 1996 – one year after the then–Heir Apparent, Sheikh Hamad bin Khalifa Al Thani, had ousted his father as Emir and assumed power in Doha (Gray 2013: 94). Qatar's small landmass and population meant that, as recently as 2006, the country was labelled a "micro-state" (in one of the earliest academic studies of its branding and soft power initiatives, which defined a "micro-state" as one with a population of less than half a million people, as was the case in Qatar until the late 1990s) (Peterson 2006: 735). One indicator of the rapidity of growth in this period was the doubling of the population in the decade to 2007, when it exceeded one million, and subsequent doubling again to two million by 2013 (Doha News 2013).

DOI: 10.4324/9781003348238-18

The decision by FIFA to award the hosting rights to the 2022 World Cup in 2010, at the same time as the rights to the 2018 tournament, has created a significant backlash for Qatar by providing ample scrutiny of allegations of corruption in securing the rights and extending the timeframe of the hosting cycle. Not since the FIFA Congress in England in 1966, when the hosting rights for three tournaments – 1974, 1978, and 1982 – were decided simultaneously has a host country had such a long run in the glare of the spotlight. A succession of investigative reports and even book-length studies have explored in detail the bidding process for the 2022 World Cup and cast Qatar – and Qatari officials – in an unflattering light, while other journalists and human rights groups have focused unrelentingly on the conditions faced by migrant workers (cf. Blake and Calvert 2015, Conn 2017, Human Rights Watch 2022).

Qatar's Pursuit of Soft Power

Beginning in the 1990s, Qatari policymakers have taken advantage of a broader evolution in the nature and structure of "power" and "influence" that has enabled small states to overcome the "traditional" constraints faced by the small states in the international system (Cooper and Momani 2011: 117). Concepts of power became more multidimensional and relative and derived from the assets that a state can leverage to shape developments to their advantage as well as the political decisions of what to do with those assets (Juneau 2014: 40). Joseph Nye also pioneered and popularized the notions of "soft" and "smart" power, with soft power denoting the ability to appeal to and persuade others using the attractiveness of a country's culture, political ideals, and policies, and smart power encompassing the use of both soft power of co-optation and the hard power of coercion (Nye 2011: xiii).

Nye listed Switzerland and Norway as examples of states adept at "smart" power. Norway deployed military force in addition to diplomatic and humanitarian instruments of power as part of the NATO-led intervention in Libya that ousted the Gaddafi regime in 2011. Like Norway, Qatar participated in *Operation Odyssey Dawn* and *Operation Unified Protector,* the two phases of the air campaigns, and Qatar co-chaired (with the UK) the inaugural meeting of the International Contact Group on Libya in April 2011 (Henriksen 2016: 135). Writing in 2016, a team of Qatari and Qatar-based researchers listed Al Jazeera and Qatar Airways as examples of Qatari "soft" power alongside Qatari mediation in regionwide conflict zones and government-linked initiatives such as Reach Out to Asia and Education Above All (Al Horr et al. 2016: 355).

The Libya intervention was part of Qatar's expansive response to the Arab Spring which included non-stop coverage on Al Jazeera as the uprisings in Egypt, Libya, and Syria unfolded in early 2011 and sometimes partisan news coverage that led Qatar's detractors to accuse it of bias toward Islamist movements (Coates Ulrichsen 2014: 151). While there is no evidence of any link between the award of the World Cup hosting rights on 2 December 2010 and Qatar's policy responses to the Arab uprisings which began with the self-immolation of a Tunisian street vendor 15 days later, Qatari decisions in 2011 were taken at a time when Qatar's self-confidence was at its zenith after the success of the World Cup bid. Moreover, the subsequent backlash against Qatar's Arab Spring-era "activism", led by Saudi Arabia and the United Arab Emirates (UAE), dominated the regional dimension of much of the ensuing decade, with a coordinated withdrawal of ambassadors from Doha for nine months in 2014 and a far more serious economic and political boycott of Qatar between June 2017 and January 2021 (Coates Ulrichsen 2020: 10).

It is difficult to conclude that the long cycle of the Qatar World Cup between 2010 and 2022 has contributed positively to the state's pursuit and projection of soft power. Media coverage of the run-up to the tournament was overwhelmingly negative as the initial focus on the allegations of corruption during the bidding process that dominated reporting between 2010 and 2014 gave way gradually to a spotlight on the conditions faced by the migrant workforce constructing the stadia and related infrastructure. The tournament itself became a target during the 2017–2021 blockade as one prominent Emirati appeared to suggest that the rupture in relations would go away if the tournament was moved from Qatar, while suggestions abounded in 2018 about allegedly Saudi-backed plans for FIFA to bring forward the planned expansion of the tournament from 32 to 48 teams (scheduled for the 2026 World Cup), which would have made it more logistically difficult for Qatar to host the tournament without involving neighbouring states (Coates Ulrichsen 2020: 243–244). If the Qatari leadership perceived in 2010 that hosting the World Cup would raise the bar in a region already replete with "mega-projects", it also placed them firmly in the glare of an unforgiving regional and international spotlight.

State Branding and the 2022 World Cup

Winning the bid to host the 2022 World Cup placed Qatar firmly "on the map" of global consciousness in ways that went far beyond the state's early attempts at branding itself as a mediator in regional conflict zones (Kamrava 2011: 540). An element of state branding has run through Qatari policymaking since the early 2000s when a permanent constitution unveiled in 2003 placed the "peaceful resolution" of disputes at the heart of Qatari foreign policy. This was evident as well in the closure of the Ministry of Information and the creation of Al Jazeera in 1996 which sought to position Qatar as a nation distinct from its regional neighbours, especially Saudi Arabia (Rathmell and Schulze 2006: 52–53). Another aspect of branding was the multibillion-dollar commitment to developing the Qatar Foundation and its Education City initiative which attracted world-leading universities to open branch campuses in Doha (Vora 2017: 4–5).

Sport emerged alongside diplomacy, mediation, Al Jazeera, and educational initiatives as a key pillar of Qatari efforts to present and narrate itself to the world. Qatar's use of sport as a potent tool of branding, able to reach audiences worldwide due to its mass appeal, began well before the bid for the 2010 World Cup. As early as 1979, the then–Heir Apparent, Sheikh Hamad bin Khalifa, predicted that Qatar would develop into a specialized hub for athletics, 16 years before he became Emir (Scharfenort 2012: 217). Qatar also began to bid for and host sporting events, beginning at the regional level with the Gulf Cup of Nations (1976, 1992, and 2004), the Asian Football Championships in 1988, before moving onto the global stage with the FIFA U-20 World Cup (1995), the Handball World Junior Championships in 1999, the World Weightlifting Championships in 2005, and the Asian Games – the world's second-largest multi-sport event after the Olympic Games – in 2006 (Brannagan and Reiche 2022: 56).

The pace of hosting major sports events – across a wide spectrum of sporting disciplines and age ranges – picked up considerably in the 2010s when Qatar also garnered international headlines over the acquisition of Paris Saint-Germain by Qatar Sports Investment (QSI) and the Qatar Foundation became shirt sponsor of FC Barcelona. The Qatar Foundation's tie-up with Barcelona in 2010 was notable for the fact that it paved the way for Qatar Airways to become Barcelona's first commercial shirt sponsor partner in 2013 (Reiche 2014: 7). Qatar Airways is one of the most internationally visible Qatari entities that has contributed to the branding of Qatar on the global stage, and in 2017 it succeeded a regional rival, Emirates, as FIFA's official partner airline for the 2018 and 2022 World Cups (The National 2017).

Qatar's hosting of the 2019 World Athletics Championships provided a portent of some of the challenges to state branding that have become apparent in the run-up to the FIFA World Cup, and which may overshadow much of the (western) reporting of the tournament itself. Media coverage of the World Athletics Championship was dominated by discussion of the poor attendance and seeming lack of local interest, which called into question Qatar's suitability as a tournament host, with one article, representative of the broadly critical coverage, bluntly entitled "Doha Disaster" (Daily Mail 2019). The general tone of the reporting of the event served as a reminder that states' investment in branding can only go so far in shaping public narratives and media discourse. This became manifest during the World Cup as well as allegations of "sports-washing" – a poorly defined term which has gained wide currency in recent years – dominated much of the European reportage (NPR 2022).

Aspects of Nation Building

Qatar became a fully sovereign state in 1971, so the 2022 World Cup cycle spanned its fifth decade of national development. In 2008, around the same time that the 2022 bid was being prepared, the Qatari authorities unveiled Vision 2030, a long-range, multi-decade development plan that was in vogue in neighbouring Gulf countries as well (with Bahrain unveiling its own Vision 2030 in the same year and Saudi Arabia following suit with its 2030 vision in 2016) (Coates Ulrichsen 2016: 3). Responsibility for drawing up and delivering Vision

2030 was entrusted to the then-Heir Apparent, Sheikh Tamim bin Hamad Al Thani, as part of the process of bringing him into significant aspects of decision-making prominence in the period before he succeeded his father as Emir in 2013. Although the launch of Vision 2030 preceded by two years the award of the hosting rights to the World Cup, much of the urban development and related infrastructure and investment in human and social capital contained within Vision 2030 were consistent with the subsequent preparations for the tournament (Brannagan and Reiche 2022: 37).

To be sure, the success of the World Cup bid in 2010 upended part of the Vision 2030 timeline just as the economic and trading dislocation of the 2017 blockade necessitated the acceleration of an agricultural and industrial strategy designed to increase Qatari self-sufficiency in certain areas (Al Ansari 2018: 35–36). In addition, the sharp fall in oil and gas prices after 2014 led to a paring back of budgets in several key areas, including the Qatar Foundation/Education City ecosystem, as well as in the energy sector. It is also the case that major infrastructure projects such as the construction of Hamad International Airport and the Doha Metro would have happened regardless of whether Qatar hosted the World Cup or not. Entities such as Qatar Airways similarly evolved into global brands and established Qatar as a regional hub and a critical nexus in the international political economy of the twenty-first century irrespective of 2022 (Kamrava 2016: 61).

And yet, the preparations for and hosting of the 2022 World Cup is consistent with the broader focus that Qatari policymakers have, for at least two decades, placed on establishing Doha as a player in the lucrative global "MICE" (Meetings, Incentives, Conferences, Exhibitions) circuit (Roberts 2017: 103). A primary objective for decision-makers in Doha has been to develop niche markets rather than the uncontrolled, mass-market approach pioneered by Dubai in the tourism and entertainment sector (Roberts 2017: 139). This is evident in the growth of a museums and heritage sector in specialist areas such as Islamic Art and Arab contemporary art and the region's first museum focused on the history and legacy of slavery in the Gulf (Exell 2016: 262).

Although the World Cup is a departure from that norm, in the sense that it is a mass-market event, the modular design of several of the stadia, enabling their disassembly and/or downsizing after the tournament is over, reduces the risk that Qatar will be left with a series of "white elephants" thereafter. Significant investment by the Supreme Committee for Delivery and Legacy in the Josoor Institute, as its training and educational arm, and Generation Amazing, as a World Cup legacy entity, further indicates a policy intent to absorb lessons from the hosting experience to develop and share best-practice information in the sports and events sectors and channel legacy initiatives in directions that align with Vision 2030 and Qatar's regional goals, including sports diplomacy and sustainable development. Their success (or not) will be tested ahead of the preparations for the 2030 Asian Games in Doha and any potential bids for the (summer) Olympic Games later in the 2030s.

132 Kristian Coates Ulrichsen

Bibliography

Al Ansari, T. (2018), 'Food Security: The Case of Qatar,' in R. Miller (ed.), *The Gulf Crisis: The View from Qatar*. Doha: Hamad bin Khalifa University Press, pp. 28–38.

Al Horr, A., Al Thani, G., Evren Tok, M., and Besada, H. (2016), 'Qatar's Global-Local Nexus: From Soft to Nested Power?' in M. Evren Tok, L. Al Khater, and L. Pal (eds.), *Policy-Making in a Transformative State: The Case of Qatar*. London: Palgrave Macmillan, pp. 1–36.

Blake, H. and Calvert, J. (2015), *The Ugly Game: The Corruption of FIFA and the Qatari Plot to Buy the World Cup*. New York: Scribner.

Brannagan, P.M. and Reiche, D. (2022), *Qatar and the 2022 FIFA World Cup: Politics, Controversy, Change*. Cham: Palgrave Pivot.

Coates Ulrichsen, K. (2014), *Qatar and the Arab Spring*. London: Hurst & Co.

Coates Ulrichsen, K. (2016), 'Economic Diversification Plans: Challenges and Prospects for Gulf Policymakers,' *Arab Gulf States Institute in Washington*, policy paper series.

Coates Ulrichsen, K. (2020), *Qatar and the Gulf Crisis*. London: Hurst & Co.

Conn, D. (2017), *The Fall of the House of FIFA: The Multimillion-Dollar Corruption at the Heart of Global Soccer*. New York: Nation Books.

Cooper, A. and Momani, B. (2011), 'Qatar and Expanded Contours of Small State Diplomacy,' *The International Spectator: Italian Journal of International Affairs*, 46(3), pp. 113–128.

Daily Mail (2019), 'Doha Disaster: How the World's Finest Athletes Are Battling for Golds In Front of a Pitiful Number of Fans at Qatar's Soulless World Championships in an Eerily Empty Stadium,' 2 October.

Doha News (2013), 'QSA: Qatar's Population Has Nearly Doubled Since 2007,' April 7.

Exell, K. (2016), 'Desiring the Past and Reimagining the Present: Contemporary Collecting in Qatar,' *Museums & Society*, 14(2), pp. 259–274.

Gray, M. (2013), *Qatar: Politics and the Challenges of Development*. Boulder: Lynne Rienner.

Henriksen, D. (2016), 'The Political Rationale and Implications of Norway's Military Involvement in Libya,' in D. Henriksen and A.K. Larssen (eds.), *Political Rationale and International Consequences of the War in Libya*. Oxford: Oxford University Press.

Human Rights Watch (2022), 'FIFA: Pay for Harm to Qatar's Migrant Workers,' May 18.

Juneau, T. (2014), 'U.S. Power in the Middle East: Not Declining,' *Middle East Policy*, 21(2), pp. 40–52.

Kamrava, M. (2011), 'Mediation and Qatari Foreign Policy,' *Middle East Journal*, 65(4), pp. 539–556.

Kamrava, M. (2016), 'Contemporary Port Cities in the Persian Gulf: Local Gateways and Global Networks,' in M. Kamrava (ed.), *Gateways to the World: Port Cities in the Persian Gulf*. London: Hurst & Co., pp. 43–78.

NPR (2022), 'How Countries Use Sports to Improve Their Image,' March 15.

Nye, J. (2011), *The Future of Power*. New York: Public Affairs.

Peterson, J.E. (2006), 'Qatar and the World: Branding for a Micro-State,' *Middle East Journal*, 60(4), pp. 732–748.

Rathmell, A. and Schulze, K. (2006), 'Political Reform in the Gulf: The Case of Qatar,' *Middle Eastern Studies*, 36(4), pp. 47–62.

Reiche, D. (2014), 'Investing in Sporting Success as a Diplomatic and Foreign Policy Tool: The Case of Qatar,' *International Journal of Sport Policy and Politics*, published online.

Roberts, D. (2017), *Qatar: Securing the Global Ambitions of a City-State*. London: Hurst & Co.

Scharfenort, N. (2012), 'Urban Development and Social Change in Qatar. The Qatar National Vision 2030 and the 2022 FIFA World Cup,' *Journal of Arabian Studies*, 2(2), pp. 209–230.

The National (2017), 'Qatar Airways to Sponsor FIFA World Cup After Vacancy Left by Emirates,' July 21.

Vora, N. (2017). *Teach for Arabia: American Universities, Liberalism, and Transnational Qatar.* Stanford: Stanford University Press.

16

GEOPOLITICS OF SPORT IN THE MENA REGION

Mahfoud Amara and Sara Mehanna Al-Naimi

The Middle East and North Africa (MENA) region offers a number of venues to reflect upon the question of geopolitics and sport. First, its geography located between the Atlantic Ocean in the west, the Mediterranean Sea, to the Arabian (or Persian) Gulf. The region is located in two continents: Africa and Asia. North Africa's closeness to Europe in the north and sub-Saharan Africa in the south has its significance when studying the North–South power dynamics in sport. The same is true for the Middle East (The Mashreq), the Levant, and the Gulf region, with the presence of Israel and Iran. Egypt – and North Sudan to some extent – being the bridge, somehow, between North Africa and the Middle East. It is not always a comfortable position to be in, considering the rivalry between Egypt and other North African countries, namely Algeria, Tunisia, and Morocco. The countries of the MENA are majority Arab and Muslim, with most countries having religious and ethnic minorities. The societal make-up of the MENA region impacts on the norms and value system around sport. We cannot ignore, in addition to geography and ethnicity, the dimension of demography. It is a crucial aspect when it comes to sport participation and development of elite sport in particular. Moreover, the variable of economy and different source of revenues of countries in the region are to be taken into account in shaping countries' national and international strategy in sport. The aim of this chapter is to explore some of these different aspects to make sense of the geopolitics of sport in the region, including the specificity of sport in North African versus the Middle East contexts and the concept of soft power in the Gulf Cooperation Council (GCC) countries.

DOI: 10.4324/9781003348238-19

North Africa

History, Modernization, and Internationalization of Sport

The geographical closeness of North African countries to Europe explains the diffusion and modernization of sport which was a product of colonial history starting from the 19th century, and which ended (at least military) in the 1960s. Egypt, being the first to gain independence in 1922, explains its earlier engagement with the emerging modern sport structures, including its first participation as an Arab nation in the 1934 FIFA World Cup. French colonialism of Morocco (including Spanish occupation of its northern part), Tunisia, and Algeria (which was for 132 years three departments of France) contributed to the diffusion of modern sport by military and European settlers. First through the introduction of physical education in schools and the formation of sport clubs and leagues. The beginning of the 20th century, with the globalization and professionalization of sport, witnessed the integration of indigenous population into the growing professional sport. Local population, having sensed the significance of sport and its internationalization, started to form sport clubs as a space to express their nationalist sentiment for independence. A case in point is the FLN national team established in 1958 in exile by the FLN party, the leader of the Algerian struggle for independence, to represent the Algerian cause for independence internationally. The other example of sport and internationalization agenda as well as the use of sport as a platform to express the growing Arab nationalist sentiment is the boycott by Arab nations of the 1956 Melbourne Olympics, the purpose of which was to protest against Israel, Great Britain, and France's attack of Egypt over the Suez Canal crisis, and President Gamel Abdel Nasser's support of the Algerian revolution (Fates, 1994; Amara, 2012; Nauright and Amara, 2018).

The independence of countries in North Africa in the 1960s was consolidated by their adhesion to international sport federations and the International Olympic Committee. Moreover participation in regional/continental and international sport competitions became a means to strengthen their nation-state building, and position in the bipolar world, divided between eastern and western blocs. This was followed by an active strategy to host regional and international sport events (Pan-African, the Mediterranean, and Francophonie Games, to name but a few). An example of this strategy is the successive (unsuccessful) bids of Egypt and Morocco to host the FIFA World Cup. The 2022 FIFA World Cup in Qatar is the first mega sport event to be hosted by a Middle Eastern and a majority Arab and Muslim country.

Sport Migration and Women Sport

The geographical closeness to Europe, the southern Mediterranean, and sub-Saharan Africa has contributed in shaping the narrative around sport and migration in North Africa, the region being a transit for players, including from sub-Saharan Africa, to European professional leagues (and football leagues in particular). The region is in the midst of international geography of sport migration characterized by the influx of players to Europe, and the import of European coaches to North African domestic leagues and national teams. Many selected players for national teams in North Africa are playing in Europe or holding dual nationality. This provokes a debate in domestic leagues in North Africa about the rationale for football development as only few players from domestic leagues are selected for the national team. Selection of players and athletes in football and in other sports from the North African diaspora in Europe to play for national teams of their country of origin poses the question of belonging. Players with mixed cultural background are under pressure to be accepted in both societies. For these players accepting to play for the country of origin is a way to honour their parents. It is also an opportunity for these players to have an international career and raise their value as professional players in the international sport market.

The other important dimension is that of gender question and women sport in particular. The ranking of nations from North Africa in the Olympics would not be the same without women athletes' performance in international sports competitions. Their participation in sport is a reflection of geopolitical debates about their body which go back to the colonial era. This includes colonial orientalist narrative about North African (Arab and Berber) women's body as revealed in orientalists' painting and photography. Participation of Arab and Muslim women in (western-dominated) sport is usually explained as a form of their emancipation and liberation from traditions and patriarchy. The same narrative has been reproduced post-independence by secular governments in North Africa. Women sport continues to be at the centre of debate about secularalization and Islamization (in opposition to westernization) of North African societies. It is also positioned in relation to international movement of feminism and post-feminism, as well as commodification, mediatization, and embodiments of women athletes (Walseth and Fasting, 2003; Amara, 2012; Sehlikoglu, 2014).

Elite Sport

Countries in North Africa, Tunisia, Morocco, and Algeria, in particular, have been active in participating in international sport competitions and the integration of decision-making positions within continental and international sport organizations. The striking example is that of Egyptian Hassan Mostafa, the president of the International Handball Federation since 2000. The other key figure of women sport in the region is Ms Nawal El Moutawakel, the first Arab Muslim to win a gold medal in the Olympics (the 1984 Los Angeles Olympics Games). She is member of the Executive Board (2008–2012 and 2020–) and IOC Vice President (2012–2016). She chaired and participated in a number of IOC Commissions. Considering aspects of demography and national GDP Tunisia with about 11 million inhabitants has outperformed other North African countries' sport performance at regional and international levels. The best performance for Morocco and Algeria internationally has been in football which receives more funding from the state due to its political significance, and in track and field. The six medals (three by female athletes) in the 2021 Tokyo Olympics is considered to be the best performance of Egypt since 1936. Egypt is also known for its international performance in squash and handball. There has been a tradition in Morocco in the past in producing good professional tennis players, the example of Younes El Aynaoui highest ranking in ATP of 14 in 2003 and Hicham Arazi's highest ranking of 22 in 2021. The fourth position in Women Tennis's Association by Ons Jabeur from Tunisia is the best performance in international tennis so far. The other sports where North African athletes are showing good performance for both male and female are boxing and martial arts (e.g. judo, taekwondo, and karate).

Elite sport offers another venue to address geopolitics of sport and power relation between the so-called centre and periphery. Elite sport system is dominated in terms of access to financial resources, corporate money, as well as sport science provision for athletes, equipment, and sport venues, by industrial countries. Countries in North Africa, as do other developing countries, have limited opportunities to compete at the highest level in collective and individual sports. Qualifications criteria to international championships are not always in favour of countries in the so-called Global South. For instance, the qualification tournament to the FIFA World Cup for Africa, with a total of 45 countries, allows only 5 African countries to qualify. The competition can turn into a real battle on and off the pitch (including in mainstream and social media), thus escalating the rivalry between North African countries particularly in football which is defined around historical and political legitimacies. As well illustrated by Rommel (2021) in his ethnographic work on Egypt in mid-2000 and up to the 2011 revolution, which is also applicable to other North African countries, football is a primary concern of political circles, represented by the dominant ruling party and its close military and business elites.

The Gulf Cooperation Council (GCC)

This part aims to investigate the intersection of sport and geopolitics in GCC countries. It explores how this connection impacted the conduct of these countries and the intra-competition among them. It examines this process as witnessed in several aspects, namely identity, media, economy, and society. A concise overview of the newcomers in the sport arena in the GCC context can help visualize the unique features and shifts in the interaction between sport and the GCC's geopolitics. Kuwait has been on the frontier of the GCC sports. One could attribute that to the fact that Kuwait was the first GCC country to gain its independence from Britain in 1961 (Crystal, 1989). The Kuwaiti Olympic committee was a pioneer in the GCC region, as it was created in 1957 (Bromber et al., 2013). Kuwait invested in sport and, in particular, football. The Kuwaiti football team, The Blue Team, was considered one of the top GCC football teams in the 1980s. It holds the highest record of winning the Gulf Cup, the premier football men's championship organized every two years among the GCC state members, as it won it ten times. Unfortunately, however, the golden age of Kuwaiti excellence in sports drew to a close with the Iraqi invasion in the 1990s. After the invasion, the GCC countries shifted their tools to reposition themselves in the international arena. As a unique strategy, this projected image functioned as an alternative identity marker, distinguishing these countries from unstable states in the broader region. Hosting Sport Mega-events (SMEs) represents the first instrument to achieving this purpose. The starting point for achieving this aim was launched by Bahrain, followed by the UAE. In 2004 Bahrain started hosting Formula 1 races in Manama in 2004. In 2009, UAE's Abu Dhabi began competing with Manama in hosting Formula 1 races, followed in 2021 by KSA and Qatar which signed partnership with Formula 1 to hosting, respectively, Jeddah and Doha Grand Prix.

Competition and Rivalry Inside and Outside Sporting Arena

In 2010, the rivalry among small GCC countries increased with FIFA's announcement of Qatar as the upcoming host of the 2022 World Cup. It reached its peak with the blockade imposed by UAE, Saudi Arabia, Egypt, and Bahrain on Qatar (2017–2021), based on indictments of Qatar for "supporting terrorism". However, the blockade did not stop Qatar from continuing its preparations for hosting the 2022 World Cup (Ulrichsen, 2021). The second strategy is illustrated by the emergence of sport cities and zones in GCC states, such as the UAE's Zaid Sport City and Qatar's Aspire Zone, to name just two. Both of them are equipped with modern sports infrastructure and high-tech equipment. This urbanization process demonstrates the GCC states' desire to fashion themselves as new destinations for sports enthusiasts. Furthermore, specializing in this type of tourism helps diversify their hydrocarbon-based economies, which is essential since hydrocarbon resources still fuel 80% of GCC governments' revenues (Mishrif, 2018).

Furthermore, GCC states promoting themselves as recuperative zones for sport medicine and injuries helps attract foreign investments and well-known sports stars. Investing in sport abroad demonstrates the third strategy pursued by GCC countries. The GCC's involvement in sport investments abroad includes a harmonious mixture of visible state and non-state actors. The GCC's non-state actors involve prominent GCC royals, elite businessmen, and airline companies. However, this confluence of actors involves other non-revealed actors that interfere with backing up those apparent ones. This might lead to the hypothesis that an unwritten code of cooperation organizes the relationship between the myriad of sponsoring GCC actors. Koch (2020) renders the example of when Sheikh Mansoor Bin Zayed Al Nahyan, a UAE royal family member, managed to take over Manchester City football Club with Abu Dhabi's Investment Authority SWF in 2008. Indeed, GCC airlines, such as Qatar Airways and UAE's Etihad and Emirates airlines, have been sponsoring several elite European football teams (Chadwick, 2019; Barzani, 2022).

Between Modernization and Tradition

The rapid transformations that the GCC region has gone through, such as "modernization, educational reforms, and the influx of wealth from oil revenues" (Harkness and Islam, 2011, p. 64), have influenced the different segments in the GCC communities, including females. Through its values, such as fairness and promotion of social inclusion, sport can be regarded as an agent of social change. Furthermore, the GCC countries aimed to enhance female inclusion in their modernization narrative through sport. By advocating the quota of GCC women's participation in sport, GCC countries' reputations for supporting GCC females' rights will be enhanced. AlKhalifa and Farello (2021) emphasize that the GCC's soft power project has many facets. One of these aspects is increasing the participation of the GCC females in sport – an originally male-dominated domain in the GCC Muslim countries. The involvement of GCC females in sport would shift the image of the GCC states as less oppressive countries towards females. In a new chapter of a modern and liberal Saudi Arabia in 2018, Crown Prince Mohammed bin Salman allowed Saudi women to drive and participate in sports competitions (Lysa, 2020; Ishac, 2020).

On the other hand, sport can also play the opposite role of becoming a space to express the GCC conservatives' fear that the participation of GCC females in sports would demonstrate a form of resistance that can endanger social values of the GCC societies. After all, the hijab is considered the conventional head cover for GCC females. As a result, the empowerment of GCC women in sport is still in its early stages (AlKhalifa and Farello, 2021). In order to create a balance between the modernity efforts in the GCC states and the traditional societal values, the ruling elites are utilizing several strategies to legitimize and normalize the participation of females in sports events and athletic competitions in the eyes of the GCC societies. The encouragement of the least controversial sports and initiating health-related campaigns manifest some of these government-led projects.

Conclusion

As highlighted in this chapter, the region of the Middle East and North Africa offers a rich context and space to the study and analysis of sport and geopolitics. The legacy of colonial history and geographical position between east and west (Mashreq and Maghreb) and location between the south Mediterranean, the horn of Africa, and the gulf Arabian (Persian) have shaped the engagement of North African countries with international sport system for nation-state building, identity formation, sport migration, and elite sport development, in the region and beyond (within diaspora in Europe). In the GCC region, the impact of geopolitics and geographical borders on the GCC states can be examined through understanding of sport's soft power. Tracing the shifts and the transformations that the GCC region has witnessed since the 1990s can help in understanding the complex reality that led to the rise of certain GCC countries as influential players in regional and international sport. Their motives are diverse, but within the spectrum of improving their image as modern states and diversifying their economies.

References

AlKhalifa, Hussa and Farello, Anna. (2021). The soft power of Arab women's football: Changing perceptions and building legitimacy through social-media. *International Journal of Sport Policy and Politics*, 13(2), pp. 241–257.

Amara, Mahfoud. (2012a). *Sport, Politics and Society in the Arab World*. London: Routledge.

Amara, Mahfoud. (2012b). Veiled women athletes in the 2008 Beijing Olympics: Media accounts. *International Journal of the History of Sport*, 29(4), pp. 638–651.

Barzani, Hezha. (2022). Many European Soccer teams are owned by Gulf states. But why? [online] Available at < https://www.atlanticcouncil.org/blogs/menasource/many-european-soccer-teams-are-owned-by-gulf-states-but-why/> [accessed 20 June 2022].

Bromber, Katrin, Krawietz, Birgit, and Maguire, Joseph (Eds.). (2013). *Sport Across Asia: Politics, Cultures, and Identities*. London: Routledge.

Carl, Rommel. (2021). *Egypt's Football Revolution: Emotion, Masculinity, and Uneasy Politics*. Austin, TX: University of Texas Press.

Chadwick, Simon. (2019). The business of sports in the Gulf cooperation council member states. In Danyel Reiche and Tamir Sorek (Eds.), *Sport, Politics and Society in the Middle East*. Oxford: Oxford Scholarship Online.

Crystal, Jill. (1989). Coalitions in oil monarchies: Kuwait and Qatar. *Comparative Politics*, 21(4), pp. 427–443.

Fates, Youcef. (1994). *Sport et Tiers Monde*. Paris: Presses Universitaires de France.

Harkness, G., and Islam, S. (2011). Muslim female athletes and the hijab. *Contexts*, 10(4), 64–65.

Ishac, Wadih. (2020). Arab countries' strategies to bid and to host major sport events. In Fan Hong and Lu Zhouxiang (Eds.), *The Routledge Handbook of Sport in Asia*. London: Routledge, pp. 437–446.

Koch, Natalie. (2020). The geopolitics of Gulf sport sponsorship. *Sport, Ethics and Philosophy*, 14(3), pp. 355–376.

lrichsen, Kristian. (2021). The impact of the lifting of the blockade on the Qatar World Cup. [online] Available at < https://cirs.qatar.georgetown.edu/the-impact-of-the-lifting-of-the-blockade-on-the-qatar-world-cup/> [accessed 19 June 2022].

Lysa, Charlotte. (2020). Fighting for the right to play: Women's football and regime-loyal resistance in Saudi Arabia. *Third World Quarterly*, 41(5), pp. 842–859.

Mishrif, Ashraf. (2018). Challenges of economic diversification in the GCC countries. In Ashraf Mishrif and Yusuf Al Balushi (Eds.), *Economic Diversification in the Gulf Region*. Volume II: The Political Economy of the Middle East. Singapore: Palgrave Macmillan.

Nauright, John and Amara, Mahfoud (Ed.). (2018). *Sport in the African World*. London: Routledge.

Sehlikoglu, Sertaç and Samie, Sumaya. (2014). Strange, incompetent and out-of-place: Media representations of Muslim sportswomen during London 2012. *Feminist Media Studies*, (15), 3. Published Online.

Walseth, Kirstin and Fasting, Kari. (2003). Islam's view on physical activity and sport: Egyptian women interpreting Islam. *International Review of Sociology of Sport*, 38(1), pp. 45–60.

17

SPORT AND SAUDI ARABIA

Mimetic Isomorphism, Soft Power, and Disempowerment

Nicholas Burton and Michael L. Naraine

Introduction

The 21st century has signalled a new era of sport business and management. The turn of the millennium witnessed a shift away from the corporatization of sport and towards the geopoliticization of global sport, including state ownership of global sporting institutions, strategic investments in mega-sporting event ownership by developing economies (e.g., BRICSAM) and rentier states, and extensive state-funded sponsorship and broadcast investment throughout the sporting ecosystem. Central to this geopolitical era has been sport's ability to cultivate and convey *soft power* for nations. First proposed by Nye (1990, 2004) as a counterbalance to nations' typical reliance on *hard power*, soft power is defined as a nation or individual's ability to "attract and co-opt [others] to want what you want" (Nye 2004). Soft power in this capacity represents a form of reputational politics and diplomacy and reflects a nation's power of attraction (Grix and Lee 2013) – influencing both internal and external perspectives of the state to foster goodwill and build political, economic, and cultural influence.

This chapter explores soft power and the geopolitical era of sport within the context of the Kingdom of Saudi Arabia's (KSA) broadening efforts to cultivate and exploit soft power. In so doing, the nature of soft power and soft disempowerment are discussed, and the mimetic isomorphism behind Saudi Arabia's investments and interests in global sport is explored.

Soft Power

Sport as a source of soft power is well established. Nations have sought to secure the hosting rights of mega-sporting events such as the Olympic Games and the FIFA World Cup for geopolitical means, seeking to alter both internal

DOI: 10.4324/9781003348238-20

and external audiences' impressions and perspectives of the nation by aligning with global sporting bodies and thus growing the nation's reputation internationally (Manzenreiter 2010). Examples of such soft power–driven sport hosting include China's hosting of the 2008 Beijing Summer Olympic Games (Grix and Lee 2013); Brazil's dual hosting of the 2014 FIFA World Cup and 2016 Rio de Janeiro Summer Olympic Games (Grix, Brannagan, and Houlihan 2015); Russia's political aspirations behind the 2014 Sochi Winter Olympic Games (Grix and Kramareva 2017); and Qatar's extensive soft power strategy as hosts of the 2022 FIFA World Cup (Brannagan and Giulianotti 2015).

Similarly, the growth of state-owned sponsorship and property ownership has been guided by geopolitical and economic motives, emphasizing the potential for states to leverage multiple sport stakeholders for strategic gain. Soft power sponsorship, as described by Chadwick, Widdop, and Burton (2022), entails the sponsorship of a sports property by a state or state-owned corporation with the intent to promote the nation-state's attractiveness, culture, or policies. Such agreements have become commonplace in global sport, affording nations an opportunity to engage with established and respected sporting bodies, and to enter into diplomatic and economic relations with diverse markets. Examples include Dubai-owned airline Emirates' vast sponsorship portfolio across European football, rugby, and tennis; Russian state oil corporation Gazprom's extensive investments in German and European football, including partnerships with UEFA and FC Schalke 04; and Azerbaijan's former sponsorship of Atlético Madrid.

Such sporting strategies illustrate soft power's particular focus on reputation management, attractiveness, legitimacy, and relationship development. Unlike nation branding or similar constructs of state-identity creation and marketing, soft power is commonly derived of economic, political, and diplomatic partnerships enabling a nation to engage with other nations, major economic or commercial stakeholders, as well as both internal and external audiences. How nations have approached the strategic exertion and exploitation of soft power, however, remains an area in need of greater examination. Which nations are best suited to leverage sporting partnerships for geopolitical gain? What strategic partnerships and investments afford the greatest reputational benefits? What external pressures inform countries' soft power efforts? In these respects, the example of Saudi Arabia may provide some important insight.

Saudi Arabia and Sport

Amongst the most prominent recent examples of soft power exertion through sport, Saudi Arabia's approach has been multifaceted, comprising a diverse array of property partnerships and event hosting, strategic investment in foreign sport, and new property creation. Saudi Arabia's investments have included a 15-year partnership agreed with Formula 1 which saw the kingdom host its first Grand Prix (GP) in 2021 in Jeddah, as well as an extensive motorsports sponsorship portfolio. The kingdom's relationship with F1 has been reported as being worth up to $65 million per year to Formula 1, in addition to state-owned Aramco's sponsorship agreement with F1 worth more than $40 million per year to grant the Saudi oil corporation title sponsor status for the Spanish, Hungarian, and American GPs (Edmondson 2022). Aramco's sponsorship portfolio also includes Aston Martin's F1 team and the title sponsorship of the Indian Premier League's Orange and Purple Caps awards, further diversifying Saudi Arabia's economic network beyond the Gulf region.

As well as their investments in motorsports, Saudi Arabia has also partnered with World Wrestling Entertainment to host and promote events in the kingdom since 2014, including a marquee pay-per-view event known as "Crown Jewel"; professional golf circuits on the men's Asian Tour and Ladies European Tour (first hosting annual events in 2019 and 2020, respectively); and a $146 million agreement with the Spanish Football Association to host the Spanish Super Cup (Dixon 2021).

Perhaps most significant, however, have been the kingdom's two most recent developments in their sports strategy: a growing network of Saudi-owned football clubs globally, including the purchase of England's Newcastle United Football Club in October 2021; and the founding of the LIV Golf tour in 2022, a Saudi-funded men's professional circuit intended to compete with the PGA Tour and European Tour. Negotiations with Newcastle's previous ownership, the Premier League, and the UK government lasted 18 months, following concerns regarding Saudi sportswashing (the use of sport event hosting, ownership, sponsorship, and more to improve an actor's questionable or tarnished reputation), potential impropriety in the new ownership's Owners' and Directors' Test which all English club owners must pass, and disputes within the Premier League and its broadcast partners over Saudi Arabia's BeOutQ, a pirate channel which rebroadcast Qatar's beIN illegally in response to diplomatic tensions between Qatar and Saudi Arabia.

The creation of LIV Golf has proven similarly fractious, challenging the PGA Tour's hegemony in professional golf and attempting to upset the status quo on the men's side. Originally proposed as the Saudi Golf League, LIV Golf was created with the explicit aim of attracting men's golf's top players through substantial guaranteed event purses and appearance fees, spearheaded by former great Greg Norman and co-designed by Phil Mickelson. The circuit succeeded in partnering with the Asian Tour to grant the league legitimacy, and secured partnerships with championship-level clubs as hosts across the United States and Europe. Central to its creation and allure to professional golfers has been Saudi Arabia's considerable wealth and spending power, including former major champions Phil Mickelson and Dustin Johnson who received a reported $200 million and $120 million, respectively, for agreeing to join the new circuit (Ferguson 2022).

Alongside these more prominent investments, high-ranking members of the royal court have further extended Saudi state-funded involvement in sport through various club ownership agreements, including Spanish football club UD

Alméria (owned by royal advisor Turki Al-Sheikh), and English club Sheffield United, French club FB Chateauroux, Belgian team KFCO Beerschot Wilrijk, Kerala United of India, and Al-Hilal United in the UAE (all owned by Prince Abdullah bin Mosaad bin Abdul Aziz al-Saud).

These purchases have followed the Saudi state's 2030 strategic vision, which specifically outlines sport and the use of sporting properties (both internal and external to Saudi Arabia) as political, economic, and diplomatic assets to be employed by the nation and the Saudi royal family. This followed Qatar's 2020 strategic vision, which described the Qatari royal family and political leaders' intended use of sport in the nation's redevelopment and reputation-building on a global stage. Accordingly, the case of KSA should not solely be viewed as ambition derived unilaterally, but rather as a strategy strongly influenced by their Gulf rivals, the UAE and Qatar, and their use of sport to exert greater geopolitical influence in the region; such an approach is reflective of a form of mimetic isomorphism and provides a useful lens through which to examine sport's geopolitical evolution.

Mimetic Isomorphism and Soft Disempowerment Through Sport

Isomorphism is the process by which entities operating in a similar environment achieve homogeneity in their practice (Greenwood et al. 2008). Typically, isomorphism occurs through two stages: (1) an entity surveys its environment and implements a new practice or behaviour to ascertain competitive advantage and (2) additional entities in a similar environment implementing the identical course of action to resemble one another. In sport, isomorphism is well established. For example, risk-averse sport organizations are known to follow each other's lead, as has been the case with digital advancements like the adoption of social media (Naraine and Parent 2016). There are three pressures known to instigate isomorphism, none more applicable in this context than the mimetic isomorphic pressure. In this regard, entities implement the actions of others in their environment because they perceive those practices to be successful and seek to mimic the competitor to stay relevant: the UAE and Qatar initiate new practices, and the KSA follows suit. With the former states, there has been a tradition of soft power exertion through sponsorship and club ownership, accelerated by Qatar's aggressive pursuit of sport event hosting opportunities. With Qatar's relative success in this capacity, it is unsurprising that the latter would embark on a similar trajectory. Consequently, KSA's sporting ambitions are as much keeping up with the Qatari royal family and that nation's increasing soft power activities as wanting to chart their own course of sport development, physical literacy, and entertainment for its citizens.

As well as illustrating the mimetic isomorphism of Gulf States' geopolitical strategies in exploiting global sport investments and event hosting, the Saudi Arabian example equally provides evidence of the tangible risk posed to nations in seeking to cultivate soft power – namely, soft disempowerment. First proposed by Brannagan and Giulianiotti (2015), soft disempowerment refers to those instances where a nation's attempts at cultivating or manifesting soft power may instead result in audiences taking offence, grow alienation from that nation, or cause upset, in turn negatively affecting the nation's perceived attractiveness. Such risks have long been component to event hosting: a poorly organized event brings with it the potential for negative publicity or loss of attractiveness on the part of a host city or country. However, for nations seeking to employ sporting events or investments as a geopolitical tool through which to grow international reputation, these risks are magnified.

Whilst Saudi Arabia's sporting investments have been strategic as a mechanism for exploiting soft power and achieving geopolitical objectives, in line with prior efforts by Qatar and the UAE, both the purchase of Newcastle United and the Saudi investment firm's creation of new men's professional golf circuit (amongst others) have been met with active resistance and forceful opposition within sport and media. Media, Amnesty International, and athlete participants have been vocal in condemning the Saudi royal family's perceived sportswashing, the murder of journalist Jamal Khashoggi, and its efforts to conceal and cleanse the nation's human rights record. These concerns have proven valid in light of Newcastle supporters' active promotion and celebration of the Saudi takeover and rejection of criticism regarding human rights and civil liberties in the country, alongside public statements by pro golfers Phil Mickelson and Lee Westwood justifying their participation in the Saudi league prioritizing the financial rewards offered over and above known human rights abuses in the state. Such rationalizations and justifications exemplify sportswashing and have cast negative light on Saudi Arabia's actions within the global press. The widespread condemnation received is indicative of the risks of attempting to use sport as a soft power vehicle for nations, and the potential soft disempowerment faced by states actively seeking to use sport to cleanse their image and redefine their reputation on a global scale.

Soft disempowerment most commonly manifests as a result of three primary sources: (i) a nation's contravention of international laws and rules; (ii) that nation failing to uphold international conventions or standards on global development; and (iii) the state acting in ways that have direct and negative impacts on other individual nations or communities of nations (Brannagan and Giulianotti 2018). In the Saudi context, the state's active role in the Yemeni conflict, BeOutQ's piracy of Qatar's beIN broadcasts, and long-standing concerns regarding the country's treatment of women and marginalized groups each serve to illustrate Saudi Arabia's contentious global reputation.

These concerns of soft disempowerment are not unique to Saudi Arabia, however. Other Gulf nations (e.g., Qatar, the UAE) have faced similar criticism decrying sportswashing and serious issues with the kafala labour system and women's rights. Qatari's winning bid to host the 2022 FIFA World Cup, for example, resulted in aggressive media coverage and criticism from the international community regarding the country's labour rights and treatment of migrant workers, corruption and collusion within FIFA, and concerns regarding the state's ability to expend tremendous wealth as a means to paper over its perceived cracks rather than effectuating actual societal, economic, or political change (Brannagan and Rookwood 2016). The successes of the state in securing the World Cup, however, alongside Paris Saint-Germain's considerable accomplishments and the UAE's ability to leverage Manchester City and City Football Group for global expansion, suggest that soft disempowerment can be overcome through investment and reputation management.

Brannagan and Giulianotti (2015) argued that the success of a nation in adopting a soft power strategy through sport will ultimately depend on their ability to overcome and address those issues posed by disempowerment, to confront the challenges highlighted by both internal and external audiences, and to effectuate change that is conveyed and communicated in a positive light on an international stage. For Saudi Arabia, then, in order to mitigate the considerable negative publicity and allegations of sportswashing attracted by the kingdom's recent investments in sport, the nation and its leadership must use sport as a vehicle through which to effectuate political, economic, and social change within the country. This could include significant sociocultural and sociopolitical advances in the nation's treatment of women and the LGBTQ community, economic and trade diversification beyond fossil fuels, or a modernization of the nation's image through cultural influences such as music or the arts.

Conclusion

The potential loss of attractiveness and diminished reputation is a sizeable risk for nations seeking to adopt a sporting soft power strategy. Despite Saudi Arabia's immense wealth and important standing within the Gulf region as a major economic, diplomatic, and cultural driver for both the Arab and Muslim worlds, engaging with sport on an international stage has invited considerable media and public scrutiny of Saudi domestic and diplomatic policy. Allegations of sportswashing and concerns regarding the country's motives in engaging with sport event hosting and ownership, and criticism from non-governmental agencies such as Amnesty International over the nation's human rights record and its treatment of women, the LGBTQ+ community, and migrant workers, are indicative of the challenges faced by Saudi leaders and the royal family. However, as the Qatar and UAE examples have illustrated, soft disempowerment can beget soft power where progress is achieved – and more importantly – communicated, or where investment in beloved sporting institutions and events outweighs the criticisms faced.

References

Brannagan, P. M. and Giulianotti, R. (2015) Soft power and soft disempowerment: Qatar, global sport and football's 2022 World Cup Finals. *Leisure Studies* 34(6): 703–719.

Brannagan, P. M. and Giulianotti, R. (2018) The soft power-soft disempowerment nexus: The case of Qatar. *International Affairs* 94(5): 1139–1157.

Brannagan, P. M. and Rookwood, J. (2016) Sports mega-events, soft power and soft disempowerment: International supporters' perspectives on Qatar's acquisition of the 2022 FIFA World Cup finals. *International Journal of Sport Policy and Politics* 8(2): 173–188.

Chadwick, S., Widdop, P. and Burton, N. (2022) Soft power sports sponsorship – A social network analysis of a new sponsorship form. *Journal of Political Marketing* 21(2): 196–217.

Dixon, E. (2021, June 7) Report: Spanish Super Cup staying in Saudi Arabia until 2029. *SportsProMedia*, https://www.sportspromedia.com/news/spanish-super-cup -saudi-arabia-hosting-2029-rfef/.

Edmondson, L. (2022, March 31) It's F1's 'duty' to continue racing in Saudi Arabia, says CEO Stefano Domenicali. *ESPN*, https://www.espn.com/f1/story/_/id/33637311/ stefano-domenicali-f1-duty-continue-racing-saudi-arabia.

Ferguson, D. (2022, June 6) Phil Mickelson joins field for 1st evet of breakaway Saudi-funded golf tour. *CBC News*, https://www.cbc.ca/sports/golf/golf-phil-mickelson -joins-liv-field-1.6479227.

Grix, J., Brannagan, P. M. and Houlihan, B. (2015) Interrogating states' soft power strategies: A case study of sports mega-events in Brazil and the UK. *Global Society* 29(3): 463–479.

Grix, J. and Kramareva, N. (2017) The Sochi Winter Olympics and Russia's unique soft power strategy. *Sport in Society* 20(4): 461–475.

Grix, J. and Lee, D. (2013) Soft power, sports mega-events and emerging states: The lure of the politics of attraction. *Global Society* 27(4): 521–536.

Greenwood, R., Oliver, C., Suddaby, R. and Sahlin-Andersson, K. (2008) *Handbook of Organization Institutionalism*. London: Sage.

Manzenreiter, W. (2010) The Beijing Games in the Western imagination of China: The weak power of soft power. *Journal of Sport and Social Issues* 34: 29–48.

Naraine, M. L. and Parent, M. M. (2016) "Birds of a feather": An institutional approach to Canadian national sport organizations' social-media use. *International Journal of Sport Communication* 9: 140–162.

Nye, J. S. (1990) Soft power. *Foreign Policy* 80: 153–171.

Nye, J. S. (2004) *Soft Power: The Means to Success in World Politics*. New York, NY: Public Affairs.

18

SPORT WASHING AND THE GULF REGION

Myth or Reality?

Simon Chadwick and Paul Widdop

Introduction

Over the last two decades, countries in the Gulf region have spent considerable sums of money investing in sport – domestically, regionally, and globally. Indeed, the Qatari government has spent US$240 billion on preparing to stage the 2022 FIFA men's World Cup; Saudi Arabia's Public Investment Fund has instigated the highly controversial LIV golf series, which pays total prize money of US$25 million per event; Abu Dhabi owns the football club Manchester City, of the English Premier League, which has spent US$1.7 billion on acquiring talent; and Bahrain's sovereign wealth fund owns a 60% stake in the McLaren Formula 1 team (the other shares being held by Saudi Arabia's PIF).

Some activist groups, members of the media, and commentators often label such activities as being sport washing; that is, the deployment of sport by a state entity for the purposes of laundering a country's image and reputation. Instead of seeing human rights abuses, the suppression of minority groups, or aggressive military campaigns, it is said that by investing in sport countries like Qatar and Saudi Arabia make attempts to distract people's attentions away from their crimes, political ideology, and misdemeanours by staging a global sport mega-event, buying a high-profile sport team, or engaging in a high-profile sponsorship deal.

However, the concept of sport washing is elusive, in that, it hasn't really been empirically identified or validated, and even less is known about the micro mechanisms that underpin it. Furthermore, beyond accusations that countries sport wash, there is little work of any systematic note that scientifically or satisfactorily examines the supposed phenomenon. As such, it is unclear what forms sport washing can take, how sport washing works, what motivates countries to

DOI: 10.4324/9781003348238-21

engage in sport washing, and what outcomes can be achieved by countries that seek to capitalize upon sport washing.

As such, this chapter examines how the term "sport washing" emerged, what it means, what it involves, and the issues associated with its use.

The Nature of Sport Washing

During British colonial rule in South Africa, it is estimated that as many as 150,000 people were held in concentration camps, of which 28,000 may have died in the 40 camps the British had constructed. At the same time, the British government was encouraging its sports teams to visit South Africa, one media outlet at the time noting that

> The Bakers Cup, Suzman Cup, and Godfrey South African Challenge Cup were national [soccer] competitions that electrified crowds in Johannesburg and Durban. Tours by professional clubs from Britain added to the enormous excitement, an atmosphere sustained by popular discourse and improving sports coverage in the press.

Whether sport was deployed by the British as a means of cultural imperialism, or either to suppress South Africans or as a means through which to shift attention away from its infractions and abuses, the current global discourse employed in this context would surely have seen the British being labelled as sport washers. Throughout the history of the eighteenth and nineteenth centuries, Britain's use of sport in the Indian subcontinent and other commonwealth nations would perhaps see them as the architects of sport washing, long before oil was found in the Gulf. In other words, the country may have been using sport (specifically soccer, cricket, and rugby) to cleanse its image and reputation by washing away what the British government didn't want South Africans and the other citizens under colonial rule to see or think.

Indeed, there have been other, similar such episodes; for instance, Germany's hosting of the 1936 Olympic Games appears to fit the template of what is now commonly referred to as sport washing. Adolf Hitler seemingly deployed the event as a means of projecting his political ideology and worldview, burnishing his reputation, and legitimizing his malicious intentions. However, it was not until the twenty-first century's second decade that the term appears to have first been used. Indeed, there are specific contexts within which the label is commonly applied, notably among autocracies with questionable human rights records or with significant domestic problems that are either ignored or otherwise not satisfactorily addressed, at least to outside observers. Typically, this has meant that Gulf nations are often described as being sport washers, though countries such as Great Britain have historically avoided being associated with what is now often seen as being an insidious, deceitful practice.

In 2018, the murder of journalist Jamal Ahmad Khashoggi in Saudi Arabia's embassy in Istanbul caused a global outcry, which appeared to take even government officials in Riyadh by surprise. At the time of writing this chapter (in 2022), the matter is still widely discussed, framing Saudi Arabia in the eyes of many as a threatening, villainous nation. Later, in early 2020, reports began to emerge that the country's sovereign wealth fund PIF was trying to acquire English Premier League football club Newcastle United. Immediately, the popular discourse and prevailing narrative began to assert that Saudi Arabia was seeking to use sport to divert attention from Khashoggi's killing (amongst other things). Amnesty International even weighed into the debate, asserting that the deal was a distraction from human rights abuses. For a variety of reasons, the purchase of Newcastle United wasn't completed until October 2021, during which time debate raged about whether the purchase was an example of sport washing. Some observed that United fans were weaponized by Saudi Arabia to represent its interests; indeed, some of the club's fans attacked critics on social media, at times aggressively so.

It remains a moot point whether Saudi Arabia deliberately and strategically intended to use its purchase of Newcastle United as an instrument of sport washing; there is no scientifically derived evidence to prove the case either way. Indeed, more than a cursory analysis of Saudi Arabia's investments in sport reveals a country amidst profound socio-economic changes. It is spending upwards of US$1 trillion on sport and sport-related projects, which would appear to be an inordinately large amount of money simply for the purposes of changing people's perceptions of the country. Sport in Saudi Arabia is seen as a way of diversifying the country's economy, of rebranding what many see as an antiquated nation, and of effecting positive change in spheres such as gender equality. Within the kingdom there is also a growing health and obesity problem, and in fact the nation has one of the lowest physical activity levels recorded globally. There are other domestic reasons for the commitment to engaging in sport; indeed, through the exposure to and diffusion of sport, its population will become central to the more active lifestyles and healthier living. Therefore, to reduce a policy commitment by a significant regional and international power to only being sport washing has been somewhat naive and misguided. The issue of whether sport washing is real or perceived is therefore an important one that needs to be addressed. Nevertheless, it also warrants observers and analysts contemplating whether sport washing is a deliberate or a strategic act, or if it can be unintentional and, therefore, accidental.

The Process of Cleansing

The prevailing popular discourse about sport washing thus far appears to be rooted in the Global North, particularly Europe. In countries characterized by liberal democratic values – such as Denmark, Germany, and Great Britain – the labelling as sport washing of what Gulf nations engage in is perhaps most

Sport Washing and the Gulf Region **151**

vehement. Indeed, it has become a tagline for both media and social commentary. Usage of the term is rather less well established in the United States, where awareness of it has only recently begun to grow following the Saudi Arabian Public Investment Fund's creation of the LIV golf series. Perhaps, this in and of itself is significant. Golf in the United States has a certain cultural capital and embedded within certain sections of its population – popular with elites and the transnational classes. Donald Trump, George Bush, and Jeff Bezos, amongst others, all have significant levels of interest in the sport. As the Saudi government begins to invest in and restructure the game, the country's intentions have started to register with US audiences. An awareness of sport washing is becoming established in the United States.

In the Gulf itself, indeed across the Global South more generally, there seems to be little, if any, debate about sport washing. Indeed, Yasir Al-Rumayyan – Governor of Saudi Arabia's Public Investment Fund and Chairman of Newcastle United – has even said that he does not recognize or understand the term. Rhetoric aside, this does raise two important questions: Firstly, how does one's politico-cultural lens shape the deployment of sport washing as a label for another country's investments in sport? Secondly, to what extent is use of the term "sport washing" co-created by activist groups, the media, football fans, and others? Perhaps the Global North set in motion a self-fulfilling prophecy whereby it has co-created political narratives around sport washing, that wasn't the intention of the countries' use of sport, which then ultimately leads to that country being accused of using sport to blindside the world.

Both questions are highly pertinent as in the cases thus far mentioned above, rather than becoming a supposed distraction from malicious acts, investment in sport by Gulf nations has become prominent in discussions about and analyses of them. This would appear to contradict what we are told is the purpose of sport washing, though it does raise further important issues. Though the initial scrutiny associated with an investment in sport may shine a spotlight on the country making that investment, through processes of legitimization and normalization, there may be a point at which mass attentiveness to suspicions of sport washing eventually ceases. Indeed, following once vehement criticism of Bahrain's and Abu Dhabi's initial staging of Formula 1 races, both events are far less questioned and more firmly embedded in the sport's annual calendar. This implies that a process of legitimization has taken place, suggesting that rather than seeking to wash their images or reputations, such countries are instead seeking to attain legitimacy in the eyes of others. Some observers might alternatively frame sport washing as soft power projection – a way of engaging key target audiences via the power of attraction – by demonstrating that you share the same values and ambitions as they do. For those with an interest in sport washing, it is important that clarity and understanding exist in any comparisons or distinctions made between the two phenomena.

Assuming sport washing exists and is a deliberate, strategic act (whilst retaining a notion that it could also be accidental and unintended), the implication is that there is a conceptual basis underpinning to its deployment by policymakers. Put another way, in arguing that sport washing exists also assumes that government decision-makers are clear about their motives for undertaking it, who their target audiences are, how the process of sport washing takes place, and what outcomes it delivers. Currently, no evidence exists to either prove or disprove any of these things. The academic literature in this field is poorly developed, whilst observers postulating about sport washing have done so without offering any detailed, coherent, or systematically collected data. At one level, this casts doubt upon sport washing's existence; at another it emphasizes the need for a rudimentary understanding of how it might work. In simple terms an understanding of human behaviour is required, linking the motives of people with their attitude formation and, ultimately, their behaviours. Put another way: researchers need to create and test the validity of models that seek to explain sport washing and how it works.

Returning to the case of Newcastle United and the club's acquisition by the Public Investment Fund, this would mean that in the first instance Saudi Arabian government officials had an insight into the motives of the club's fans. That is, why people from the North-East of England would jump to the defence of and become advocates on behalf of the Gulf state. In studies of human psychology, motives shape attitudes – the mindset, outlook, and feelings that people have towards something. If this is, perhaps, the essence of sport washing, then the Riyadh government's purchase of the English club worked from the outset. In fact, throughout the protracted acquisition process, United fans became something akin to online warriors fighting on behalf of the Saudi cause, many of them taking to social media as they sought to advocate on behalf of both the takeover and the Gulf state.

The Twitter weaponization of Newcastle's fans, be it deliberate or accidental, represents a clear opportunity for researchers to establish the role in sport washing played by social media platforms, and by fans. The journey from attitude formation to the public display of pro-Saudi Arabian behaviours was a relatively short one. Indeed, as the takeover neared completion in late 2021, some United fans took to wearing a Saudi Arabian thobe (white robe) and a ghuthrain (head covering) on match days. Yet behaviours need not always be so crass and may extend to the ways in which people talk about a country and the purchase of products from that country. We speculate that there may even be a country-of-origin effect associated with the behavioural outcomes of sport washing. This effect has been widely studied as, when making associations between a country and the products it produces, there is clear evidence that people's consumption behaviours in relation to that country are influenced by their attitudes towards it. Considerable doubts must, however, remain about the power of Newcastle United fans alone and the club itself to effect positive changes in general attitudes and behaviours towards Saudi Arabia. At best, this surely can be effective only if it is part of a wider programme of activities aimed at repositioning a country's image and reputation.

The "Whataboutery" of Sport Washing

Sport's current debate about sport washing, one could refer to it as an obsession, is immature and marked by the inflammatory language of binary ideologists intent on asserting their own position rather than understanding a complex phenomenon. In the Global North, attempts to compare-and-contrast the likes of colonial-era Britain with twenty-first-century Qatar are sometimes met with derision and claims of "whataboutery". Yet examining the ways in which countries have deployed sport for political purposes is not an attempt to sidestep serious issues nor to excuse one country or another for the misdemeanours in which they have engaged. Instead, it is about establishing a breadth of knowledge and depth of understanding, which the present diatribe fails to do. Those who make the most noise about sport washing or else plead ignorance to its existence are typically both disingenuous: unverified, unvalidated suppositions do not establish a phenomenon's existence, nor its absence. In failing to establish a shared understanding about sport washing, the next time that a Gulf nation hosts a sport mega-event, observers in the Global North will rally to the dog whistle call of popular condemnation. Yet, so long as the likes of Qatar and Saudi Arabia fail to make satisfactory progress in changing labour market laws or improving the rights of women, then they expose themselves, perhaps rightly so, to claims of sport washing.

As researchers and analysts, we must be careful to include other evidence in our analyses of sport washing. Great Britain has long used sport to engage important audiences around the world, which its government often labels as soft power projection. However, with more than one hundred thousand modern slaves currently living in the country and the government committed to deporting immigrants to Rwanda, it would be remiss of commentators not to examine the proposition that Britain has always been a sport washing nation. In the same way, we should not forget Rwanda itself, a country that has been widely accused of indulging in the practice, most notably through a series of state-led sponsorships with the likes of Arsenal of the English League. Yet little attention has been paid to the National Basketball Association's activities in Rwanda or, for that matter, in Abu Dhabi. Commentators in the Global North may not like it, but there are grounds also for labelling the United States as a sport washing nation.

However, this chapter is not intended as a litany of speculation or grievance; instead, it is intended as the basis for asking difficult questions about an important matter, something we still know very little about. For the sake of sport, we must establish a more sophisticated understanding. We never hear about "movie washing" or "tourism washing", it is always a problem within sport; hence, it is important to move on from perpetuating the myths of sport washing to understanding the realities. We must strive to remove the term as a catch-all phrase, with zero grounding in empirical evidence, or understanding of its mechanisms – that is, if it even actually exists. If not, those commentators in the Global North who deploy the term face being accused of cultural imperialism or orientalism.

Bibliography

Chadwick, S. (2018). Sport-washing, soft power and scrubbing the stains. *Asia and the Pacific Policy Forum*. 24th August. Retrieved from https://www.policyforum.net/sport-washing-soft-power-and-scrubbing-the-stains/

Chadwick, S. (2021). Are nations playing the game of 'sport washing?'. *The Hill*. 15th December. Retrieved from https://thehill.com/opinion/international/585890-are-nations-playing-the-game-of-sport-washing/

Lauletta, T. (2022). LIV Golf has brought 'sportswashing' into everyday conversation. But what is the Saudi government really doing and why should people care? *Insider*. 2nd August. Retrieved from https://www.insider.com/what-is-sportswashing-liv-golf-saudi-government-2022-7

19

GEOPOLITICS OF CRICKET IN INDIA

Mohit Anand

In India, cricket often blurs the lines between passion and obsession. India has emerged as the key economic player in world cricket which is now leveraged more than ever towards its political objectives. As the geopolitical tensions with its nemesis China occurred in 2020, it has its commercial implications for Chinese mobile company "Vivo" which was replaced as the title sponsor of the Indian Premier League (IPL) for cricket by the "TATA" – India's leading conglomerate. This is reflective of the use of economy of sport as a geopolitical ploy to signal its adversaries that countries can go above and beyond diplomatic, military, and informational means to achieve its objectives. Cricket as a sport is an example of the use of emotive passion, leveraging its massive commercialization and consumption as a geopolitical economy of sport towards its ongoing tensions with its adversaries.

Celebrated Australian cricketer Steve Waugh commented,

Few nations have a relationship with sport such as India's connection to the sport of cricket. The sport has become so ingrained in the culture that to many it could be considered a religion, with superstars like Sachin Tendulkar and Virat Kohli reaching almost legendary status amongst their fellow countrymen.

(Waugh, 2020)

If at all it has to be compared, cricket as a sport can be somewhat attributed to as to what soccer (or football) is for Brazil. India may not do well in multidisciplinary sports like athletics, soccer, and swimming. For example it just won one gold medal in Tokyo Olympics, but it is a powerhouse in cricket. India has won

DOI: 10.4324/9781003348238-22

the cricket World Cup twice, in 1983 and in 2011; it also won the inaugural Twenty20 World Cup in 2007 and the Champions Trophy in 2002 and 2013. India is consistently ranked among the top competing teams across all three formats of one day, T20, and five day Test series (ICC, 2022).

The British brought cricket to India in the early 1700s, with the first documented instance of cricket match played in 1721 (Clement, 1924). Although cricket's origins have been linked to the colonial times, it gained tremendous popularity and was accepted as a mainstream sport in the country. It has become much more popular than hockey (the national sport of the country). Ashis Nandy – a well-known political psychologist and social theorist – rightly pointed out that "Cricket is an Indian game accidentally discovered by the British". In his book, he analyses the origins of cricket and puts forward the theory that cricket was actually invented by the Indians and then adopted by the British (Nandy, 1989).

Irrespective of its origins, it is without doubt that India has helped popularized and commercialized cricket to a large extent. With almost 1.4 billion people (1/6th of the world population), cricket commands immense popularity in India as a sport for the masses. Every park, club, maidan (open spaces), and gully (roadside alleys) of the country is dotted with children playing cricket. In a country which is so diverse and multifaceted, where nothing is or can be generalized about its society, culture, and people, cricket is one rare and common idea that galvanizes and binds its people like nothing else. Cricket, therefore, draws a lot of passion and emotion among the people here. In this cricket-obsessed nation, cricketers like Sachin Tendulkar, M.S. Dhoni, and Kapil Dev are cult figures, so much so that many Bollywood movies have been made on their life (e.g. *M.S. Dhoni, 83, Azhar*).

Over the past two decades, cricket has ushered in a lot of commercial interests, raking in billions of dollars from sponsorships, TV and broadcasters, online streaming rights, royalty fee, etc. It lies at the centre stage of this commercialization of this often called "gentleman's game". Historian Ramachandra Guha (2002) opined that the live coverage of cricket, as well as India's success, broadened the sport's "catchment area" and "got more housewives involved in watching cricket, as well as more people outside the big cities". At a time when other Indian sports were languishing, television made cricket central to the Indian sport fan's imagination. BCCI (Board of Control for Cricket in India) is the governing body for cricket in India. It is the richest and most influential cricket board in the world; it is in fact richer than the International Cricket Council (ICC) – the global governing body for cricket. Estimates suggest that 70% of global cricket revenues come from the Indian market (Wilson, 2017); this, along with over a billion-plus viewership of cricket, gives the country and its governing board an unprecedented power and clout in international cricket. Every cricket playing nation wants to play with India as it brings in much needed revenues for them as well.

In 2008, BCCI launched the "Indian Premier League" (IPL) – the world's most lucrative Twenty20 cricket tournament. It runs annually for two months, usually from March to May, bringing in Indian and foreign cricketers to play among different franchises. IPL brings in more prize money for the winning team than the official World Cup organized by the ICC. The winner of the IPL 2021 received $2.60 million while the ICC T20 World Cup 2021 winner, Australia, got $1.6 million (Ali, 2022). On 15 June 2022, the media rights for IPL 2023–2027 seasons went for a cumulative figure of over $6.2 billion after a three-day online auction saw the league's broadcast value triple from the last one in 2017. IPL is now the second most valued sporting league in the world in terms of per-match value (Jamkhandikar and Ganguly, 2022). With a combined per-game value of $15.1 million, the IPL vaults past the English Premier League ($11.23 million per game between 2022 and 2025), Major League Baseball, and the NBA ($9.57 million and $2.12 million per game, respectively, according to a 2020 estimate). It trails only the NFL, which is believed to average a staggering $36 million per game with its 11-year deal from 2022 to 2033 (Lavalette, 2022). In coming years, IPL aims to become the biggest sporting league in the world in terms of revenue, participation, and performance – said BCCI Honorary Secretary, Mr Jay Shah (BCCI, 2022). IPL as a "sportainment" is construed to its potential to provide exciting and titillating space; whether through cheerleaders or through its "30 seconds dugout interviews" in between the play sessions; blurring the line between leisure, sport, and entertainment. While the IPL is reflective of contemporary Western sports frameworks, it incorporates the highly stylized visual aesthetic and potent celebrity cachet of Indian cinema culture, with its match entertainment and team branding (Thakur, 2012, pp. 25–27).

Cricket accounts for almost 85% of the Indian sports economy (Raman, 2020). As evident, this massive economic and commercial weight of cricket is also reflected towards exuding political overtones by leveraging it to address geopolitical objectives. Here two examples are interesting. The first example is about how the Indian cricket board wielded its financial muscle on ICC and other national cricket boards to coerce them to fall in line with their political agenda. We saw that during the Kashmir Premier League (KPL), when in August 2021 the Indian cricket board (BCCI) asked the ICC not to recognize the Pakistan Cricket Board–promoted KPL, the first edition of which was played in Pakistan-administered Kashmir. In its letter, the BCCI expressed concerns about the status of Kashmir as a disputed territory. The Indian cricket board also cited the political and diplomatic ties between India and Pakistan which have been fluctuating post-Independence in 1947. BCCI had issued informal warnings to all cricket boards around the world that those participating in KPL would be barred from playing in leagues in India or from having any commercial connection with the BCCI (Chakrabarty, 2021). Former England spinner Monty Panesar pulled out of the KPL in 2021, citing "political pressure" and "advice" from the BCCI, terming his participation in the KPL "too risky a decision" for him. South African batsman Herschelle Gibbs accused the BCCI of attempting to prevent him from participating in the inaugural KPL. He added that the BCCI had also threatened with denying him entry in India if he participated in the league (Dawn, 2021). BCCI commented that it was well within their rights to take decisions with respect to the cricketing ecosystem in India and to defend its posturing on the disputed Kashmir territory – by accusing Pakistan of using cricket (sport) as a ploy to achieve political gains.

In October 2021, PCB Chairman Rameez Raja told his country's Senate Standing Committee that India's clout in the ICC, based on the world body's sponsorship money generated from India-based multinational companies, was impacting Pakistani cricket. He said that 50% of the funding for PCB comes from ICC. The global body gets its 90% of its revenue from India, which necessarily means that Indian business houses run Pakistan Cricket, and that "if tomorrow the Indian Prime Minister decides he will not allow any funding to Pakistan, this cricket board can collapse" (Ali, 2022).

The second example is as to how the 2020 border skirmish with China impacted cricket sponsorship in India. In 2020, the decades-long border dispute spread across the 3,700-kilometre-long Himalayan range between China and India precipitated into an armed clash between both the armies for the first time in over 45 years. The incident happened at the border post in Galwan Valley (Union Territory of Ladakh), resulting in the death of 20 Indian soldiers while China didn't reveal causalities on its side (it is said to be anything between 20 and 35 as per US and Russian Intelligence) (TASS, 2021).

Despite several rounds of negotiations between Special Representatives, the dispute is nowhere near a solution. The two sides are carrying out one of the biggest conventional military build-ups along their borders. In a strong response to this apparent Chinese aggression, India banned 273 Chinese apps, including TikTok, PUBG, SHAREit, etc. (Garg, 2022), put restrictions on Chinese investments, and cracked down on Chinese companies in the country (e.g. Xiaomi) while also not allowing Huawei's 5G technology in India. Civil society in India also called for boycott of Chinese products and companies. The tensions were further aggravated when China's People's Liberation Army's regimental commander, who had suffered severe injuries during the Galwan clash, became the torchbearer at the Beijing 2022 Winter Olympics Torch Relay (Pathak, 2022). India announced a diplomatic boycott of the Games. The Ministry of External Affairs spokesman commented that "It is indeed regrettable that the Chinese side has chosen to politicize an event like the Olympics" (Marlow, 2022).

Interestingly, since 2016 the title sponsor of the IPL (Indian Premier League) was Vivo, a China-based smartphone company. Vivo had a deal of approx. $293 million (Rs 2200 crore) for title sponsorship rights initially from 2018 to 2022. But as a fallout of the Galwan clash in 2020, there was a lot of criticism of the BCCI (India's cricket board) for retaining the sponsorship of Vivo and, amidst public backlash, calls were made to cancel Vivo's sponsorship of the IPL. Vivo was caught on the back foot and eventually walked away from the 2020 IPL season due to rising anti-China sentiments across the nation and sensing the fact that in the current environment, sponsoring IPL will do more harm than good to the their brand (Laghate, 2020).

However, the 2021 season saw their return as the principal sponsor, anticipating that things might have normalized a year after the military stand-off (DNA, 2022). They were far from reality; the sustained heightened tensions between two Asian giants made sure that the anti-China sentiment was not going anywhere. There were heightened tax scrutinies on Chinese mobile phone makers in the country. In December 2021, the Indian tax department searched several handset makers, including Xiaomi and Oppo. Oppo and Vivo are brands owned by the same parent company—China-based BBK Electronics Corp (Khosla, 2022). The ongoing COVID pandemic and global supply chain issues further exasperated the troubles for Vivo in India. Hence sponsoring the IPL in India for Vivo was not a good option, from both a political and a commercial perspective.

On 11 January 2022, the IPL governing council agreed to terminate Vivo's sponsorship for the remaining two years after the company requested to exit the IPL sponsorship deal. The IPL sponsorship in turn was given to TATA (India's leading business conglomerate) in 2022 and 2023. BCCI Secretary Jay Shah said:

> This is indeed a momentous occasion for the BCCI IPL as the Tata Group is the epitome of global Indian enterprise with an over 100 year old legacy and operations in more than 100 countries across six continents. The BCCI like the Tata Group is keen to promote the spirit of cricket across international borders, and the growing popularity of the IPL as a global sporting franchise bears testimony to the BCCI's efforts. We are truly happy that India's largest and most trusted business groups has believed in the IPL growth story and together with the Tata Group, we will look to take Indian cricket and the IPL forward to greater heights.
>
> *(Oinam, 2022)*

The majority of IPL stakeholders were happy to see the back of Vivo as most of them weren't comfortable with a Chinese company on board after the 2020 incident that heightened diplomatic tensions between the two countries. A BCCI source said:

> This was supposed to happen sooner or later as Vivo's presence was bringing bad publicity for both the league as well as the company. With negative sentiment around Chinese products, the company had to pull out of the sponsorship with one season left for the deal to be completed.
>
> *(Business Standard, 2022)*

Anti-Pakistan or anti-China sentiment is not a new thing in India; what is interesting is the greater leverage of sports (cricket in this case) by the nation state through its sport entities or institutions as a tactical weapon to feed its political objectives. Whether it's wielding of the massive financial muscle of the BCCI to coerce other cricket boards and their players not to participate in the KPL or Vivo's exit from the IPL sponsorship, they are consequences of the geopolitical

160 Mohit Anand

friction between nations. Thereby engaging economic and commercial aspects of the sports that helps to further the political rhetoric.

This chapter reflects as to how sports and its economy are not just being used for achieving commercial objectives, but more and more towards serving political intentions behind it. Nations, institutions, businesses, and political leaders are using sports and their emotive and financial clout as a tactical tool to exert power, control, and/or influence beyond the sports arena. The example of Vivo suggests that companies need to be cognizant of their operations and cautiously position and promote their brand and advertising in a sporting event that might turn out to be counterproductive. It should, therefore, not be assumed that sports industry and its ecosystem will be spared from such and similar geopolitical skirmishes. In coming years we will see greater geopolitical economy of sports. Ultimately, *the politics of sports is intertwined with the economics of sports!*

References

Ali, Q.M. (2022) 'Why Indian money rules world cricket'. *South Asia Monitor,* 17 Feb. Available from: https://www.southasiamonitor.org/spotlight/why-indian-money-rules-world-cricket [accessed 19 June 2022].

BCCI (2022) *BCCI Announces the Successful Bidders for Acquiring the Media Rights for the Indian Premier League Seasons 2023–2027.* Available from: https://www.bcci.tv/articles/2022/news/55555891/bcci-announces-the-successful-bidders-for-acquiring-the-media-rights-for-the-indian-premier-league-seasons-2023-2027?type=Latest [accessed 23 June 2022].

Business Standard (2022) *Tata Group to Replace Vivo as IPL Title Sponsor from this Year.* Available from: https://www.business-standard.com/article/pti-stories/tata-group-to-replace-vivo-as-ipl-title-sponsors-from-this-year-122011100691_1.html [accessed 20 June 2022].

Chakrabarty, S. (2021) 'Those part of PoK league can't play or work in India: BCCI'. *Indian Express,* 1 Aug. Available from: https://indianexpress.com/article/sports/cricket/those-part-of-pok-league-cant-play-or-work-in-india-bcci-7432438/ [accessed 17 June 2022].

Clement, D. (1924) *A History of the Indian Wars.* London: Oxford University Press.

DAWN (2021) *Former England Cricketer Monty Panesar Pulls Out from Kashmir Premier League Due to 'Political Pressure'.* Available from: https://www.dawn.com/news/1638389 [accessed 19 June 2022].

DNA (2022) *With VIVO Pulling Out and Handing Rights to TATA, IPL Title Sponsors from 2008 to 2021.* Available from: https://www.dnaindia.com/cricket/photo-gallery-with-vivo-pulling-out-and-handing-rights-to-tata-ipl-title-sponsors-from-2008-to-2020-pepsi-dream11-dlf-2927935/vivo-ipl-2021-2927955 [accessed 20 June 2022].

Garg, A. (2022) 'Garena free fire to TikTok: All the 273 Chinese apps that Indian govt banned so far'. *India Today,* 15 Feb. Available from: ps://www.indiatoday.in/technology/news/story/garena-free-fire-to-tiktok-all-the-273-chinese-apps-that-indian-govt-banned-so-far-1913141-2022-02-15 [accessed 17 June 2022].

Guha, R. (2002) *A Corner of a Foreign Field: The Indian History of a British Sport.* London: Pan Macmillan.

ICC (2022) *Ranking*. Available from: https://www.icc-cricket.com/rankings/mens/overview [accessed 1 August 2022].

Jamkhandikar, S. and S. Ganguly. (2022) 'IPL broadcast deal fetches $6.2 bln; Disney, Viacom18 bag rights'. *Reuters*, 14 June. Available from: https://www.reuters.com/lifestyle/sports/disneys-star-pays-302-bln-ipl-2023-27-tv-rights-2022-06-14/ [accessed 17 June 2022].

Khosla, V. (2022) 'Tata replaces Vivo as IPL title sponsor for final two years'. *MINT*, 12 Jan. Available from: https://www.livemint.com/sports/cricket-news/tata-replaces -vivo-as-ipl-title-sponsor-for-final-two-years-11641926678280.html [accessed 17 June 2022].

Laghate, G. (2020) 'Chinese smartphone manufacturer Vivo pulls out as title sponsor of IPL 2020'. *The Economic Times*, 5 Aug. Available from: https://economictimes .indiatimes.com/news/sports/vivo-pulls-out-as-title-sponsor-of-ipl-2020/ articleshow/77358587.cms?utm_source=contentofinterest&utm_medium=text &utm_campaign=cppst [accessed 17 June 2022].

Lavalette, T. (2022) 'Indian premier league's jaw-dropping $6 billion broadcast deal will have major ramifications in cricket'. *Forbes*, 14 June. Available from: https:// www.forbes.com/sites/tristanlavalette/2022/06/14/the-indian-premier-leagues-jaw -dropping-6-billion-broadcast-deal-will-have-major-ramifications-in-cricket/?sh =684cd37743e6 [accessed 19 June 2022].

Marlow, I. (2022) 'India to boycott Beijing Olympic ceremonies over PLA torchbearer'. *Bloomberg*, 4 Feb. Available from: https://www.bloomberg.com/news/articles /2022-02-04/india-to-boycott-beijing-olympic-ceremonies-over-pla-torchbearer [accessed 23 June 2022].

Nandy, A. (1989) *The Tao of Cricket: On Games of Destiny and the Destiny of Games*. New Delhi; New York: Penguin.

Oinam, J. (2022) 'Indian premier league title rights: Tata group, not Dream11, To replace Vivo from IPL 2022'. *Outlook*, 11 Jan. Available from: https://www.outlookindia.com /website/story/sports-news-ipl-2022-tata-group-to-replace-chinas-vivo-as-indian -premier-league-title-sponsors/409207 [accessed 28 July 2022].

Pathak, S. (2022) 'Beijing Winter Olympics: DD Sports not to live telecast opening, closing ceremonies'. *Zee News*, 3 Feb. Available from: https://zeenews.india.com /india/beijing-winter-olympics-dd-sports-not-to-live-telecast-opening-closing -ceremonies-2433269.html [accessed 23 June 2022].

Raman, S. (2020) 'Impact of covid-19 on revenues of world cricket and Indian sports'. *Mass Communicator: International Journal of Communication Studies*, 14(3), pp. 37–40.

Senate of Pakistan, News Detail (2021) *In the Meeting of the Senate Standing Committee on Inter-provincial Coordination Held under the Chairmanship of Senator Mian Raza Rabbani on 7th October, 2021*. Available from: https://senate.gov.pk/en/news_content.php?id =4061 [accessed 28 July 2022].

TASS (2021) *China, India Commence Withdrawal of Forces from Shared Border – Chinese Defense Ministry*. Available from: https://tass.com/world/1254813 [accessed 23 June 2022].

Thakur, R. (2012) 'Cultural economy of leisure and Indian Premier League (IPL)'. *Dialog* (22) (Spring), pp. 21–29.

Waugh, S. (2020) *The Spirit of Cricket, India*. Macquarie Park, NSW: SAMS Marketing. Available from: https://stevewaugh.com.au/

Wilson, J. (2017) 'India's share of ICC global revenues adjusted after initial vote'. *BBC*, 22 June. Available from: https://www.bbc.com/sport/cricket/40374596 [accessed 17 June 2022].

PART IV
Africa

20

AFRICA IN THE GLOBAL FOOTBALL BUSINESS COMPLEX

Gerard A. Akindes

Introduction

Football is undeniably a colonial legacy in Africa (Alegi, 2010; Darby, 2002). John Sugden and Alan Tomlinson state that "football came to Africa on the wings of empires" (1998)). As discussed, the British, French, and Portuguese introduced football in Africa. From the colonial initiation to the contemporary football business complex, African football evolved with the political, social, and economic transformations of the continent.

This chapter discusses the evolution of African football from its early years until its current position and role in the global football ecosystem where a few stakeholders such as FIFA, selected European leagues and clubs, the UEFA along with a few Arabian Gulf nations, transnational broadcasters, and transnational sponsors constitute the key players. The first part of the chapter is a brief history of African football prior to its post-independence entrance on the world stage. This section of the chapter discusses the post-independence evolution of African football, its institutions, and how African football reached the world stage. The third section presents the transformations and aspects of African football that positioned African football as a stakeholder in the global football business complex. The last section and conclusion describes the power structure and challenges African football faces as an active member of the globalized football business complex.

Accessing the Football Global Stage

As stated by Peter Alegi (2010, p. 3), football started in 1862 in Africa, and the first recorded football game was played in South Africa between whites in the

DOI: 10.4324/9781003348238-24

166 Gerard A. Akindes

Cape and Natal provinces. By the early twentieth century, football was played in Algeria, Egypt, and the Belgian Congo (Leopoldville) (Table 20.1).

Despite some initial reluctance from the colonial institutions, football in Africa diffused and rapidly became an integral activity for groups such as the African-schooled elites, and people in contact with Europeans and the African elite. Alegi posits that starting in the 1990s, football became part of the growing urban Africa. Clubs created at that time remain among the most important clubs in the country. Meanwhile, the game continued to spread among indigenous populations and progressively became the most popular sport across the continent.

Football's Development Along Political Agendas

The early post-independence years were dominated by establishing local leagues, national and continental governing bodies, and joining FIFA. Football's development in Africa evolved rapidly (sprouting clubs and leagues) and quickly became a political instrument. The game primarily offered a unique platform for articulating political matters such as anticolonial protest, nation-building, and anti-apartheid solidarity in South Africa.

In Algeria, the role of football as a political instrument was clearly evident in the formation of a national team that represented the liberation movement from French colonial dominance. The "Revolutionary team" was known as the FLN[1] XI (Darby, 2002) and quickly became highly popular. This team was one of the most symbolic roles of football in nation creation and building in Africa. Ghana (through President Kwame Nkrumah) also used football for nation-building. Alegi notes, "President Kwame Nkrumah fervently believed in the game's capacity to transcend ethnic, linguistic, regional, religious, and generational barriers" (2010, p. 57). The Black Stars symbolized the nation and was its ambassador.

At the continent level, the formation of the Conféderation Africaine de Football (CAF) in Khartoum in February 1957 launched African football to the global stage. Darby calls the confederation a "critical juncture" in the development of football in Africa. In February 1957 four independent nations – Egypt, South Africa, Sudan, and Ethiopia – formed the Conféderation Africaine. In 1961, South Africa was expelled from the confederation by the CAF congress preceding the Third African Cup of Nations in Ethiopia. By these actions, the CAF clearly stated its political stand, and CAF also became the main advocate for African football's global representation.

By the early 1960s, many African countries, then independent, had their local leagues, governing bodies, and national teams, and had become members of CAF and FIFA. While building national and continental structures, African countries' participation in the FIFA World Cup in the 1960s and 1970s was limited to African individuals playing for France and Portugal during the colonial era and after. Those players playing for Europeans clubs and national teams were the main contribution of Africa to the global football labour force.

Contribution to the Global Football Labour Market

As stated above, the first African players to play in Europe were from the former colonies of France and Portugal. Although Arthur Wharton is the first African to play in England in the late 19th century (Vasili, 1998), the more consistent presence of African footballers started only in the early 20th century when footballers such as the Moroccan Larbi, known as Ben Barek (the "Black Bead"), held a European career in France and Spain. Portugal and Belgium also encouraged the integration of their colonies' athletes. For example, in 1954, Mário Esteves Coluna arrived from Mozambique to play in Portugal. Eusebio Ferreira Da Silva followed in 1961. These two players, Mário and Eusebio, are still ranked among the greatest players Portugal has ever had. In Belgium, Paul Bonga Bonga from the Democratic Republic of Congo (DRC) was recruited in the early 1960s to play for the Standard de Liege (Akindes & Alegi, 2014). He was considered one of the best footballers in Belgium and beyond in the 1960s.

During the early years of migration, African footballers played professional football mostly in a few European countries. However, although some leagues and clubs became professional in the early 20th century, the business model and administration of most clubs remained closer to amateur football with paid players. The transfer of African players was on recommendation. Systematic scouting, agents, and transfer fees paid to the club of origin of the players were not current practice. Africa supplied players to European football clubs, but in limited number until the late 1980s. From the 1980s, the competitiveness of African teams on the football world stage was consistent.[2] African teams' performances at FIFA World Cups and FIFA Youth World Championships increased the attention given to African players. As a result, the demand for African talent increased in European football.

Youth Football Achievements

The introduction by the FIFA of new World Cups (the Under 20 in 1977 and the Under 17 in 1987) put young African footballers in the global spotlight. Since the inception of the Under 20 World Cup, African teams have won the Cup once (Ghana, in 2009), played three finals, and completed nine semi-finals. In the Under 17 competitions, African teams have played nine finals and have won five, all by Nigeria. In addition to the already-visible African players in Europe, African youth teams on the continent displayed the young talent and the potential of African football players during these events.

Labour Supply to Global Football

It is significant that less than half a century after becoming independent, a few African nations (Cameroon, Senegal, Egypt, South Africa, Morocco, Algeria, Ghana, Nigeria, and Côte d'Ivoire) have consistently performed well against the best football nations. The successful hosting 2010 FIFA World Cup in South Africa reinforced the status of African football as an integral part of the global narrative of football and simultaneously established the African nations that won some very symbolic victories over European football powerhouses such as France and Germany as forces to reckon with. The world has taken notice of players such as George Weah from Liberia, Didier Drogba from Côte d'Ivoire, and Samuel Eto'o and Roger Milla from Cameroon. African footballers gained in recognition and value, leading to the "scramble for Africa" as described by Darby (Darby, 2000).

After Brazil, Africa is the largest transcontinental exporter of players to European and Asian football (Poli et al., 2022). For African players, it is an attractive incentive for leaving the continent in order to achieve a successful career in Europe. Many African players are also motivated by the quest of better wages and playing conditions often not available in their home countries, especially in the sub-Saharan countries, South Africa excepted. Consequently, African football became a reservoir of talent for clubs in Europe, Asia, and the United States.

The already existing economic gap between European and African football amplified when European television broadcasting rights revenues drastically increased in the late 1980s to early 1990s (Clarke, 2002). Essentially, European professional leagues emerged with an increasingly commercialized football and flourished with an exponential growth in broadcasting rights revenues. In contrast, African football on the continent could not build a similar model of highly professionalized and commercialized football. Given its limited revenue capacity, African football embraced players' development for more lucrative markets. Football academies then emerged as a system for football talent detection and development. Darby, Akindes, and Kirwin (2007) posited that since the early 1990s that the number of academies has increased. One of the first academies, the ASEC (Association Sportive des Employés de Commerce) Mimosas football academy in Côte d'Ivoire was launched in 1994 and achieved remarkable

TABLE 20.1 The oldest clubs in Africa (2010)

Year Created	Club Name	Location
1906	Al Alhy	Egypt
1907	Zamalek	Egypt
1911	Heart of Oak	Ghana
1919	Esperance de Tunis	Tunisia
1921	Jeanne d'Arc de Dakar	Senegal
1921	Mouloudia Algiers	Algeria
1930	Canon de Yaoundé	Cameroun
1930	Diables Noirs and Renaissance de Brazzaville	Congo Brazzaville
1930	TP Englebert of Lubumbashi and AS Vita Club Kinshasa	Democratic Republic of Congo
1937	Orlando Pirates	South Africa

results locally and continentally by 1999 (Darby et al., 2007). As a result of their success, the young talented players were rapidly recruited by S. K. Beveren, a Belgian professional football club. After playing for S. K. Beveren, several first-class players of the ASEC Mimosa football academy, such as Yaya Toure, Kolo Toure, and Emmanuel Eboue, were recruited by prestigious highly competitive and commercialized European football clubs, namely Arsenal FC, Liverpool FC, Manchester City, and FC Barcelona in England and Spain. More recent examples of Sadio Mane and Idrissa Gana Gueye, who were respectively detected and trained by Generation Foot and Diambars academies in Senegal, illustrate the contribution of African football academies to the value chain of the global football labour. A study by Raffaele Poli, Loïc Ravenel, and Roger Besson indicates that Europe as well as Turkey and the United States is a main destination of African footballers from Nigeria, Ghana, Côte d'Ivoire, and Senegal (2022). Although less documented and studied, African players in Asia constitute several hundreds of players in countries like India, Malaysia, Thailand, and Indonesia (Akindes, 2013). North America is now an attractive destination mostly for Ghanaian players (Poli et al., 2022). African football labour contribution to the labour value chain of global football business is undeniably a well-established reality.

Football academies provided a more structured labour supply to the global football labour network. With the increased commodification of the game, including players' management, academies, scouts, and agents, the recruitment of African players integrated the value chain of global football labour. In discussing the labour migration of footballers in Ghana, Darby utilizes the sociology of development perspective, global value chains (GVC), and economic geography global production networks (GPV) (Darby, 2013). Darby explained that the Ghanaian global value chain operates across six phases, including the formal and informal academies, the local league, European leagues, and the post-career. Beyond the Ghanaian case, African footballers who migrated to Europe and other destinations such as Asia and the United States are part of the GVC and GPN. In Poli et al. (Poli, 2007), African football players' trajectories from local football systems, academies, and clubs, to European football clubs are compared to commodities to which value-added occurs mainly in European clubs when transferring from less prominent clubs and leagues to clubs with more financial resources, capacity, and prestige. The recent FIFA Global Transfer Report confirms that the value-added of players' transfer does not occur in Africa (FIFA, 2021, p. 27).[3] The strong presence of African countries in the top 25 supplying countries on the international transfer market (FIFA, 2021, p. 23) is showcased by television broadcasting, and the media business complex facilitates the global viewership of their performances.

African Football, Transnational Television, and Sponsorship

Television broadcasting contributed to African football visibility and recognition. In addition to the presence of African teams and players in global competitions, the most popular football event in Africa (the Africa Cup of Nations) is now shown globally via transnational television broadcasters. According to the African Confederation of Football, the Africa Cup of Nations had a cumulative global audience of 6.6 billion viewers (Confederation Africaine de Football (CAF), 2013). In 2013, all the matches of the same competition were streamed live for the first time (on ESPN3), and the semi-finals and final were shown on tape delay (on ESPN Deportes TV). The most recent AFCON, in Cameroon in 2022, was broadcast in 150 countries (CAF, 2022). Satellite television broadcasting and the transforming economics of football and media gave CAF an opportunity to embrace the broadcasting rights economy and generate media and sponsorship revenues (Alegi, 2010, p. 110).

The AFCON 2022 sponsors and the media rights holders illustrate the global position of CAF and Africa' most commercialized competition. Their long-lasting sponsorship relation with CAF and their operations and business presence across Africa make the French transnational corporations Orange (official sponsor) and Totalenergies (title sponsor) logical sponsors of CAF. For the most recent sponsors Umbro, TikTok, and 1XBET the global reach of the competition through television broadcasting may have provided a valuable platform to reinforce their existing transnational sponsorship portfolio while establishing their brand in Africa. With the exception of "Visit Rwanda", Rwanda's government subsidized sponsorship of Arsenal FC in England and Paris Saint Germain (PSG) in France, African corporations are not represented on the global sponsorship ecosystem dominated by transnational corporations with a global business footprint or a global deployment marketing strategy.

Transnational satellite broadcasting of football competitions is another facet of African football participation in the global football business complex. Pay-TV transnational broadcasters Canal+ Horizons, Supersport, StarTimes, and beIN Sports are the main suppliers of popular football games and competitions to African football fans. As discussed by several authors (Akindes, 2013; Alegi, 2010; Owumelechili & Akindes, 2014), access to satellite pay-TV from Canal Horizons and DStv with Supersport, beIN Sports, and StarTimes has boosted Africans' consumption of European football competitions. African football fans consistently engage with the most prestigious leagues, teams, and competitions, such as the English Premier League and the Spanish LaLiga.

Concluding Thoughts

African football – after several decades of transformation and growth – is well established on the world stage, with its players performing in all the major (and less significant) European leagues and in many Asian championships (Akindes, 2013). African footballers claim a fair representation in world competitions. Despite the undeniable gains and position of African football as part of the global football business complex narrative, the continent remains numerically underrepresented at the World Cup. Moreover, South Africa's successful hosting of the competition did not alleviate the continent's rocky football history and the economic environment of most African countries. The asymmetrical economic competition for talent and resources between Africa and the Global North determined the reality of the position of African football in the global football business complex. African football is mostly present as global labour supplier, then again at the beginning of the value chain with young players who migrate. Those young players, also entering the global GVC and GPN and considered commodities (Darby, 2013; Poli, 2007), generate their highest value-added once on the European football market. Africa's significant and substantial successes and achievements in football show a level of progress and performance. However, despite the success of talented players in the Global North, African football remains at the peripheral football system to the global football business complex as mainly a labour supplier with limited financial return to build and reinforce its local leagues, clubs, and competitions. The achievements and successes of individual players and selected national teams do not seem to close the economic and structural gap. Macro- and micro-economic circumstances continue to challenge African football's capability to be more than a simple talent supplier and media consumer of the global football complex.

Notes

1 Front Nation de Libération (National Front of Liberation)
2 For example, in the 1986 FIFA World Cup in Mexico, after Morocco beat Portugal 3–0, Morocco reached the second round. (They lost to Germany 0–1 in the following round.) Cameroon and Ghana, respectively, reached the quarter-final of the FIFA World Cup in 1990 and 2010. Africans won three consecutive Olympic medals: Ghana in 1992 (silver), Nigeria in 1996 (gold), and Cameroon in 2002 (gold). The subsequent creation of Youth World Cups has provided an additional showcase for African footballers.
3 The report states that "only five of 2021's top 25 associations in terms of total receipts from transfer fees came from outside Europe. There were no member associations from Africa" (FIFA, 2021, p. 27).

References

Alegi, P. (2010). *African soccerscapes: How a continent changed the world's game.* Ohio University Press : Athen, Ohio.

Akindes, G. (2013). South Asia and South-East Asia: New paths of African footballer migration. *Soccer & Society, 14*(5), 684-701..

Akindes, G., & Alegi, P. (2014). From Leopoldville to Liège: A conversation with Paul Bonga Bonga. In *Identity and Nation in African Football: Fans, Community and Clubs* (p. 288). Palgrave Macmillan, London, England.

CAF. (2022, January 9). *Total Energies AFCON 2021 to Be Broadcast in Over 150 Countries as Africa's Biggest Event Kicks Off in Cameroon Today.* CAFOnline.Com. https://www.cafonline.com/total-africa-cup-of-nations/news/totalenergies-afcon-2021-to-be-broadcast-in-over-150-countries-as-africa-s-bigge.

Clarke, R. (2002). *The Future of Sports Broadcasting Rights*. SportBusiness Group, London, England.

Darby, P. (2000). The new scramble for Africa: African football labour migration to Europe. *European Sports History Review, 3*, 217–244.

Darby, P. (2002). *Africa, football, and FIFA : politics, colonialism, and resistance*. F. Cass. London, England

Darby, P. (2013). Moving players, traversing perspectives: Global value chains, production networks and Ghanaian football labour migration. *Geoforum, 50*, 43–53.

Darby, P., Akindes, G., & Kirwin, M. (2007). Football academies and the migration of African football labor to Europe. *Journal of Sport & Social Issues, 31*(2), 143–161.

FIFA. (2021). *FIFA-Global-Transfer-Report-2021-2022-indd.pdf*. FIFA. https://digitalhub .fifa.com/m/2b542d3b011270f/original/FIFA-Global-Transfer-Report-2021-2022 -indd.

Onwumechili, C., & Akindes, G. (Eds.). (2014). *Identity and nation in African football: Fans, community and clubs*. Springer, London, England.

Poli, R. (2007). Migrations de footballeurs et mondialisation: Du système-monde aux réseaux sociaux. *M@ Ppemonde, 88*, 12.

Poli, R., Ravenel, L., & Besson, R. (2022). *Football Players' Export: 2017–2022* (p. 6). CIES Football Observatory. https://www.football-observatory.com/Football-players -export-2017-2022.

Sugden, J. P., & Tomlinson, A. (1998). *FIFA and the contest for world football: Who rules the peoples' game?* Polity Press; Blackwell Publishers. Cambridge, UK

Vasili, P. (1998). *The First Black Footballer, Arthur Wharton, 1865–1930: An Absence of Memory*. F. Cass, Abingdon, England.

21
THE NBA'S PARTNERSHIP WITH RWANDA

Michael M. Goldman and Jeffrey W. Paller

The National Basketball Association (NBA) is aggressively expanding globally and has targeted Africa as an emerging market. In collaboration with the International Basketball Federation (FIBA), the NBA launched the Basketball Africa League (BAL) as a centrepiece of its ambitions in Africa. Economically, the NBA identified seven substantial markets in Africa as the most important – Angola, Egypt, Kenya, Morocco, Nigeria, Senegal, and South Africa – with a combined gross domestic product totalling more than $1.5 trillion (Bhasin & Hoije, 2022). Yet despite these target markets, it launched the inaugural BAL tournament in May 2021 in Kigali, Rwanda, a country with only 12.95 million people that has never had a player in the NBA.[1] This was even more surprising given that the NBA touts civil rights, racial equality, and social justice (NBA, 2022), and Rwanda is considered an authoritarian regime accused of eliminating political opponents, violating human rights, and controlling access to information (Reyntjens, 2015). The most recent Amnesty International report on Rwanda documented continued violations of the rights to a fair trial, freedom of expression, enforced disappearances, allegations of torture, and excessive use of force (Amnesty International, 2022). In response to the BAL announcement, the New York-based Human Rights Foundation appealed to the NBA to deny the Rwandan government the opportunity to use the NBA's global influence to "whitewash its warmongering, war crimes, crimes against humanity, and illegal plunder of natural resources" (Zidan, 2021).

Why did the NBA partner with Rwanda to host the inaugural tournament, and what explains the ongoing partnership between the NBA and Rwanda? The answer to this question contributes to our understanding of the emerging geopolitics of sport, and the organizational choices businesses make in global expansion. We outline three factors that help explain the NBA's partnership with Rwanda: (1) Diplomacy and soft power, (2) Governance over politics, and

DOI: 10.4324/9781003348238-25

(3) Personal relationships. We address how these factors contribute to the NBA's business decisions, as well as how these factors might inform other sports organizations' expansion across the world.

Diplomacy and Soft Power

Firstly, the NBA believes that the BAL will improve the livelihoods of African youth, gender equality, and economic inclusion efforts, which are part of the sport diplomacy and soft power role the NBA sees itself playing in the world (Spears, 2021). BAL president, Amadou Fall, partly explained the hosting of the tournament in Rwanda as an opportunity to "bring people together" (Zirin, 2021). Fall has spoken about the "leadership role wherever we do business in terms of addressing societal issues", with the BAL including social justice initiatives that focus on raising awareness for gender-based violence, supporting women's education, growing female participation in basketball, and social economic inclusion (Ebanks, 2021). Babatunde Folawiyo, Chairman and CEO of the Yinka Folawiyo Group and the leader of the strategic investment consortium in NBA Africa, reinforced this objective: "success will be defined not just by return on investment but by sustainable and long-term impact on the lives of our people" (NBA, 2021). In these ways, the NBA's decision to partner with Rwanda can be seen as the league's role in potentially influencing government and other stakeholders in Rwanda. The US State Department noted how the NBA's presence on the continent can help spread American values:

> The expansion of the NBA into Africa only further serves to connect us socially and economically through the game of basketball. We look forward to supporting increased access, inclusion, capacity, and opportunity for African sports leaders and youth as we continue building bridges through sport.
>
> *(Tyburski, 2021)*

Former US president Barack Obama, who is a strategic partner and minority owner of the BAL, similarly argued that the NBA "has always been a great ambassador for the United States", and that the league would make a substantial contribution in promoting "opportunity and wellness and equality across the continent" (Mizelle, 2021; Bhasin & Hoije, 2022). The goal of social responsibility has been at the forefront of the NBA's foreign efforts since its earliest investments in international basketball (Sharp, 2018). Former NBA stars involved see the Africa initiatives as a chance to give back to their societies. In fact, these efforts are consistent with basketball's missionary roots, a game that was invented at the International YMCA Training School and was spread across the world by YMCA missionaries (Krasnoff, 2017; Gao, 2012).

In launching the BAL, Dikembe Mutombo, a Congolese-American former NBA player and investor in the BAL, argued that African youth "just need the

The NBA's Partnership with Rwanda **175**

opportunity and support to achieve great things … the new NBA Africa is the transformative next step to do just that" (Spears, 2021). Will Mbiakop, Senior Director at NBA Africa, spoke of the "special boost" that sports and diplomacy get in Africa, recalling the role of basketball in unifying Angola after its civil war (Krasnoff, 2020). In this way, Mutombo and Mbiakop's comments demonstrate the NBA's potential contribution to the nation- and peace-building mechanism of soft power (Nygard & Gates, 2013). The NBA's social development and sport diplomacy intentions echo calls by US think tank Freedom House that link long-term corporate success with democracy and call American organizations to use their substantial leverage to discourage authoritarianism and "promote inclusive and sustainable economic development" (Freedom House, 2021). The NBA is therefore providing another example of the enabling diplomacy and soft power of sport, in the same way that the English Premier League has acknowledged the unique reach and influence it provides to the UK government (Rofe, 2016).

Governance over Politics

Secondly, the NBA – and many actors in the international community – values the security, stability, and ease of doing business. Rwanda provides this, as it touts great progress made in good governance, health, education, and gender empowerment. This progress is the result of a long and strategic process of post-Genocide state building led by Rwanda's president Paul Kagame, who has used a combination of sportswashing, guilt, and narratives of self-reliance (Beswick, 2013) to transform Rwanda from a poor, rural society to a strong, modernizing state with the modern capital, Kigali (Straus & Waldorf, 2011).

Kagame's technocratic approach to governance fits the analytically minded business practices of NBA's young and ambitious executives, making him an ideal brand ambassador and entrepôt to an otherwise foreign and difficult-to-navigate environment. The relationship between league executives and Rwanda is similar to that of an international aid agencies and the country. Successful aid delivery mechanisms are those that receive credible commitments from both the donor countries and the recipient countries over the long term (Swedlund, 2017). In this way, donor countries prioritize "cooperation partners" that offer lasting and long-term benefits over the moral and ideological factors that conventional wisdom suggests drive foreign aid. In this way, the international aid agencies prioritize governance over politics (Lancaster, 2007). Recent evidence suggests that aid donors tend to focus on technical governance while ignoring political failures (Winters & Martinez, 2015).

Since 1994, Rwanda has cultivated durable relationships with the international aid industry, becoming "aid darlings" in the eyes of many Western countries. For example, Desrosiers and Swedlund (2019) report on why Canadian donors' preferred working with Rwanda is telling: "Rwandan technocratic leadership continued to feature prominently as a driver. Most Canadian participants insisted that the Rwandan government's capacity to 'get things done' was

176 Michael M. Goldman and Jeffrey W. Paller

key. Rwanda was described as 'a development darling', 'serious' about aid". In this way, Rwanda makes a good "cooperation partner", and the NBA's partnership is consistent with the international aid industry writ large. Global Affairs writer Howard French made a similar point about Kigali being "such a smoothly ordered place" that "reporters feel comfortable there, and by the same token, don't feel comfortable looking very deeply into anything potentially critical" (Zidan, 2021).

It appears that the NBA has prioritized stability and technical capacity over social justice and politics. Victor Williams, NBA Africa's CEO, referred to the BAL as part of the NBA's apolitical effort to further basketball in Africa (Zidan, 2021). Paul Hinks, Co-founder and CEO of New York-based Symbion Power as well as Chairman for Invest Africa, has a history of working with the NBA on the continent. In a 2021 op-ed, he echoes the sentiments of many in the international aid community by writing, "Politics Should Stay Out of the NBA's Basketball Africa League", and continues:

> The selection of Rwanda as the location for the BAL finals is fitting. The no-nonsense leadership of President Paul Kagame's administration has created an enabling environment for investment that makes it among the top destinations in sub-Saharan Africa for the international investor community. There is a serious push against corruption, a burgeoning private sector and foreign investors are welcomed with support from the Rwanda Development Board. In Rwanda there is predictability and stability – key fundamentals that attract Foreign Direct Investment.
>
> *(Hinks 2021)*

Hinks also has a history of conducting business in the country, receiving a 25-year gas concession on Lake Kivu in Rwanda in 2015. Kagame won the 2017 elections in Rwanda with almost 99 percent of the votes, earning a third seven-year term of office, after a constitutional amendment allowed Kagame to run for three more terms of office. Although the US State Department was disturbed by "irregularities observed during voting", some analysis suggests that most Rwandans value the strong leadership Kagame provides: "they uphold their strongman president who has proven capable of balancing ethnic tensions and creating a common Rwandan identity" (Fried, 2017).

The order and strong governance that Rwanda provides was particularly important in the context of the COVID-19 pandemic, when the BAL followed the example of the NBA's bio-bubble in 2020. As Amadou Fall explained, the NBA needed to "move over 500 people of 52 nationalities in the bubble, from our teams from all 12 countries to the different vendors and partners we had to get to Kigali" (Thomas, 2021). Fall continues, "We are holding the inaugural BAL season at a single site in Kigali because Rwanda has the infrastructure and facilities in place to provide the best opportunity for a safe and successful event" (Zirin, 2021). Rwanda's commitment to the NBA is clear; Rwanda built a $104 million, 10,000-person stadium, the Rwandan government is the biggest sponsor of basketball in the country, and the Rwanda Development Board is a foundational sponsor of BAL. These investments signal to the NBA that Rwanda will be a strong partner for the long term.

Interestingly, the strategic trade-off of governance over politics that the NBA is making with respect to Rwanda thus far contrasts the choices the NBA has made to navigate its sensitive relationships in China. In 2019, a social media post in support of pro-democracy protesters in Hong Kong by Daryl Morey, at the time an executive with the Houston Rockets, resulted in a suspension of NBA game broadcasts and other commercial relationships in China. The NBA's policy was confirmed by Commissioner Silver, who acknowledged that "there are consequences from freedom of speech; we will have to live with those consequences. For those who question our motivation, this is about far more than growing our business" (Riley, 2019). Silver also clearly positioned the NBA: "We wanted to make an absolutely clear statement that the values of the NBA, these American values – we are an American business – travel with us wherever we go, and one of those values is free expression" (Deb, 2019). In April 2021, Silver emphasized that "engagement is better than isolation" and that a boycott of China because of "legitimate criticisms of the Chinese system, won't further the agenda of those who seek to bring about global change" (Rigdon, 2021). By June 2022, Silver acknowledged that the NBA had lost hundreds of millions of dollars as a result of the 2019 incident, but that these losses were acceptable as the "cost of free speech" (Smith, 2022).

Personal Relationships

Third, personal relationships are key to how the NBA does business, and the long-term relationship between Paul Kagame and the leagues' most respected powerbrokers paved the way to the inaugural tournament. Commissioner Silver has described the sport industry as an "industry of relationships" (Ourand, 2015). These relationships are built on trust, charisma, and return on investments, and resemble the relationships Rwanda has had with the international aid community, long considered an "aid darling" (Beswick, 2011). In this context, Toronto Raptors' President Masai Ujiri has a decade-long close friendship with Kagame, who helped open the Giants of Africa camp in Kigali in 2018. At a previous NBA Africa Summit in Toronto, Ujiri quoted Kagame: "We do not want to always be victims, we also want to be players" (Ishimwara, 2016). Kagame congratulated his "Brother Masai Ujiri" on his "visionary leadership and determination" when the Raptors won the NBA Finals in 2019 (Kagame, 2019). Kagame is also reported to have granted 2.4 hectares in Kigali to Ujiri by presidential decree in 2021, for the development of a hotel, restaurants, and sporting facilities (Emmanuel, 2021).

Commissioner Silver commented in 2019 that Kagame "and his family are very knowledgeable NBA fans", after the Rwandan president attended an NBA playoffs game in Oakland as a guest of the NBA (Spears, 2019). Kagame also spoke at the NBA Africa Forum in 2019 on the sidelines of the UN General Assembly in New York (The New Times Rwanda, 2019). Kagame's love of basketball runs deep, having attended a number of NBA events, watched broadcasts, and posted on social media about his fandom (Himbara, 2021). This relationship points to the organizational structure and culture of the NBA, demonstrating how personal networks, friendships, and passion for the game shape the league's development.

Conclusion

In spite of the concerning attacks on freedom of expression and human rights in Rwanda, the NBA has partnered with the Rwandan government to host the inaugural BAL tournament, and the finals of the most recent second edition in Kigali. Our analysis outlined three factors that help explain the NBA's partnership with Rwanda: (1) Diplomacy and soft power, (2) Governance over politics, and (3) Personal relationships. While these factors provide an explanation for the NBA's decisions, they also raise further questions that the NBA may need to navigate in the future. For example, what happens when someone in the NBA is critical of Kagame? Considering the example of the NBA's relationship with China, some commentators have questioned the extent to which the NBA is using its platform to really promote freedom of speech, democracy, and human rights, or whether the NBA may be limiting expression as it walks the geopolitical tightrope in its international relationships (Faria, 2022). A strong message of support for democratic voices in Rwanda by an NBA or BAL player or official will test the NBA's commitment to American values of free expression, and the NBA's calculation of an acceptable cost. Will the personal relationships involved be able to smooth over further restrictions of freedoms in Rwanda? How successful will the NBA be in exporting American values to Rwanda through basketball diplomacy?

Note

1 The original pre-COVID inaugural season plan included the semi-final and final games in Rwanda, with regular season games in Egypt, Senegal, Nigeria, Angola, Morocco, and Tunisia. The 2022 season followed a similar structure, with the playoffs hosted in Rwanda.

References

Amnesty International. (2022). *Amnesty International Report 2021/22: The State of the World's Human Rights.* https://www.amnesty.org/en/documents/pol10/4870/2022/en/

Beswick, D. (2011). Aiding state building and sacrificing peace building? The Rwanda-UK relationship 1994–2011. *Third World Quarterly, 32*(10), 1911–1930.

Beswick, D. (2013). From weak state to savvy international player? Rwanda's multi-level strategy for maximising agency. In W. Brown and S. Harman (Eds.), *Africa Agency in International Politics*. Routledge.

Bhasin, K., & Hoije, K. (2022, June 22). The NBA turns to Africa to fuel basketball's next era of growth. *Businessweek*. https://www.bloomberg.com/news/features/2022 -06-22/nba-african-basketball-league-looks-for-next-joel-embiid

Deb, S. (2019, October 17). N.B.A. commissioner: China asked us to fire Daryl Morey. *The New York Times*. https://www.nytimes.com/2019/10/17/sports/basketball/nba -china-adam-silver.html

Desrosiers, M-E., & Swedlund, H. J. (2019). Rwanda's post-genocide foreign aid relations: Revisiting notions of exceptionalism. *African Affairs, 118*(472), 435–462.

Ebanks, J. (2021, December 21). The Basketball Africa League is building its foundation for the present and future. *SLAM*. https://www.slamonline.com/the-magazine/the -basketball-africa-league-is-building-its-foundation-for-the-present-and-future/

Emmanuel, K. (2021, July 23). *Masai Ujiri uyobora Raptors yahawe ubutaka na Leta i Kigali: Menya imishinga ateganya n'umubano we n'u Rwanda*. IGIHE. https://mobile.igihe.com/ amakuru/u-rwanda/article/masai-ujiri-yahawe-inkondabutaka-mu-mujyi-wa-kigali

Faria, Z. (2022, June 6). Adam Silver's latest defense of the NBA's relationship with China falls flat. *Washington Examiner*. https://www.washingtonexaminer.com/opinion/adam -silvers-latest-defense-of-the-nbas-relationship-with-china-falls-flat

Freedom House. (2021). *Reversing the Tide: Towards a New US Strategy to Support Democracy and Counter Authoritarianism*. https://freedomhouse.org/democracy-task-force/special -report/2021/reversing-the-tide

Fried, B. (2017). *President Paul Kagame and Rwandan Democracy*. Berkley Center for Religion, Peace & World Affairs, Georgetown University. https://berkleycenter .georgetown.edu/posts/president-paul-kagame-and-rwandan-democracy

Gao, H. (2012, February 22). From Mao Zedong to Jeremy Lin: Why basketball is China's biggest sport. *The Atlantic*. https://www.theatlantic.com/international/ archive/2012/02/from-mao-zedong-to-jeremy-lin-why-basketball-is-chinas-biggest -sport/253427/

Himbara, D. (2021, July 28). *Kagame Captured the National Basketball Association – Obama is Making a Big Mistake to Join the NBA's Basketball Africa League as a Strategic Partner*. Medium. https://medium.com/@david.himbara_27884/kagame-captured -the-national-basketball-association-obama-is-making-a-big-mistake-to-join-the -6e3fec49d26a

Hinks, P. (2021, May 20). Politics should stay out of the NBA's Basketball Africa League. *U.S. News & World Report*. https://www.usnews.com/news/best-countries/articles /2021-05-20/politics-needs-to-stay-out-of-the-nbas-basketball-africa-league

Ishimwemaria. (2016, February 14). *Masai Ujiri Quotes President #Kagame: We Do Not Want to Always be Victims, We Also Want to be Players* [Tweet by @ishimwemaria]. https://twitter.com/ishimwemaria/status/698807199569702912

Kagame, P. (2019, June 14). *Heartfelt Congratulations to @Raptors for Your Hard Earned and Deserved #NBAFinals Win! My Brother Masai Ujiri, You Have Proven What Visionary Leadership and Determination Can Accomplish. You Made Us Proud!* [Tweet by @]. https:// twitter.com/paulkagame/status/1139595214203576320

Krasnoff, L. S. (2017, December 26). How the NBA went global. *The Washington Post*. https://www.washingtonpost.com/news/made-by-history/wp/2017/12/26/how-the -nba-went-global/

Krasnoff, L. S. (2020). *Basketball Diplomacy in Africa: An Oral History from SEED Project to the Basketball Africa League (BAL)*. Centre for International Studies and Diplomacy,

SOAS University of London. https://eprints.soas.ac.uk/32907/1/BBDipAF2020%20Will%20Mbiakop.pdf

Lancaster, C. (2007). *Foreign Aid: Diplomacy, Development, Domestic Politics.* Chicago: The University of Chicago Press.

Mizelle, S. (2021). Ex-President Obama joins NBA Africa as strategic partner and minority owner. *CNN.* https://edition.cnn.com/2021/07/27/politics/barack-obama-nba-africa/index.html

NBA. (2021). NBA forms new Africa entity, partners with strategic investors. https://www.nba.com/news/nba-forms-new-africa-entity-partners-with-strategic-investors

NBA. (2022). *National Basketball Social Justice Coalition.* https://coalition.nba.com

Nygard, H. M., & Gates, S. (2013). Soft power at home and abroad: Sport diplomacy, politics and peace-building. *International Area Studies Review, 16*(3), 235–243.

Ourand, J. (2015, May 25). Industry of relationships. *Sports Business Journal.* https://www.sportsbusinessjournal.com/Journal/Issues/2015/05/25/Sports-Business-Awards/Sports-Business-Awards.aspx

Reyntjens, F. (2015). Rwanda: Progress or powder keg? *Journal of Democracy, 26*(3), 19–33.

Rigdon, J. (2021). *Adam Silver Talked about Embracing New Technology and the NBA's Broadcast Relationship with China.* AwfulAnnouncing.com. https://awfulannouncing.com/nba/adam-silver-talked-about-embracing-new-technology-and-the-nbas-broadcast-relationship-with-china.html

Riley, C. (2019). NBA chief Adam Silber says profit can't come before the league's principles. *CNN.* https://www.cnn.com/2019/10/08/media/nba-adam-silver/index.html

Rofe, J. S. (2016). Sport and diplomacy: A global diplomacy framework. *Diplomacy & Statecraft, 27*(2). https://doi.org/10.1080/09592296.2016.1169785

Sharp, A. (2018). Coming to America. *Sports Illustrated.* https://www.si.com/longform/2018/nba-international-oral-history/index.html

Smith, K. (2022, June 2). *Adam Silver Said the NBA has Lost "Hundreds of Millions of Dollars" Due to Strained Relations with China. But Silver Added that He Accepts Those Losses as "The Cost of Free Speech"* [Tweet by @KeithSmithNBA]. https://twitter.com/KeithSmithNBA/status/1532519524557373440

Spears, M. J. (2019, May 2). *Rwandan President Paul Kagame Makes Grand Appearance at Oracle Arena.* Andscape. https://andscape.com/features/black-coaches-can-lead-in-college-baseball-if-afforded-the-opportunity/

Spears, M. J. (2021). Adam Silver announces business entity NBA Africa, backed by former star player. *ESPN.* https://www.espn.com/nba/story/_/id/31503611/adam-silver-announces-business-entity-nba-africa-backed-former-star-players

Straus, S., & Waldorf, L. (2011). *Remaking Rwanda: State Building and Human Rights after Mass Violence.* Madison: The University of Wisconsin Press.

Swedlund, H. J. (2017). *The Development Dance: How Donors and Recipients Negotiate the Delivery of Foreign Aid.* Ithaca: Cornell University Press.

The New Times Rwanda. (2019, September 24). *President #Kagame on Tuesday Attended the NBA Africa Forum alongside NBA Commissioner Adam Silver, Toronto Raptors President Masai Ujiri and NBA Africa VP Amadou Fall. The Forum is Held on the Sidelines of the #UNGA19* [Tweet by @NewTimesRwanda]. https://twitter.com/newtimesrwanda/status/1176706540780347392?s=21

Thomas, D. (2021). Slam dunk! Inside the NBA's Basketball Africa League. *African Business.* https://african.business/2021/09/trade-investment/slam-dunk-inside-the-nbas-basketball-africa-league/

Tyburski, L. (2021). The Basketball Africa League has arrived: Here's why it matters. Atlantic Council. https://www.atlanticcouncil.org/blogs/africasource/the-basketball-africa-league-has-arrived-heres-why-it-matters/

Winters, M. S., & Martinez, G. (2015). The role of governance in determining foreign aid flow composition. *World Development, 66*, 516–531.

Zidan, K. (2021, June 1). The NBA's alignment with Rwanda's repressive leader was headscratching. *Guardian.* https://www.theguardian.com/sport/2021/jun/01/the-nbas-alignment-with-rwandas-repressive-leader-was-headscratching

Zirin, D. (2021, April 30). Voices are raised against the NBA launching its new African league in Rwanda. *The Nation.* https://www.thenation.com/article/world/rwanda-basketball-nba/

PART V
Football

22

THE POLITICS OF ALTERNATIVE FOOTBALL

Curious Friends

Steve Menary

The combination of international football with politics and national representation has been a problematic concept since the formation of the Federation Internationale de Football Association (FIFA) in 1904. A number of nations have joined FIFA, played international football, and then disappeared from Czechoslovakia, the Soviet Union, and Yugoslavia to East Germany, the Saar, South Vietnam, and South Yemen.

The entry and withdrawal of these teams at least reflected wider accepted political norms, whereas the development of games played outside of the accepted framework of international football established by FIFA has understandably been more difficult to categorize.

The idea of alternative football first emerged in 2003 with the formation of the Non-FIFA Board. The name was later changed to the New Federation Board so that the organization was not defined in opposition to FIFA, but virtually all of the teams to have taken part on the field have been based on some form of resistance. In 2005, Jens Brinch, the international head of the Greenland Sports Federation, said: "If we all just do what FIFA want, then we are all doing nothing" (Brinch, 2005).

Greenland was, like many of the organizations that initially embraced the alternative football movement, fairly non-contentious. An autonomous country within the Kingdom of Denmark, Greenland is isolated by geography rather than by any political reasons that would at that time have hindered joining one of FIFA's confederations. Participation, rather than representation, drove Greenland, which never fully joined the NF Board but looked to the movement to overcome the lack of opportunities caused by their remoteness.

Other early members of the NF Board included Monaco, where a population of 31,400 made trying to compete with any other European countries almost impossible (CIA, 2022). Monaco is universally recognized as country, but other

DOI: 10.4324/9781003348238-27

186 Steve Menary

early NF Board members had either lost their statehood many years ago or never achieved this aim.

Occitania covers parts of southern France, Monaco, and Italy and is a widely recognized region but never achieved statehood. The only stipulation for membership of the Occitan XI was speaking the Occitan language (Menary, 2007, p 108).

The identity of the indigenous Sámi people of northern Scandinavia was subject to repression at home but a wider notion of Lapland – a term the Sámi dislike – has softer connotations through its association with Christmas. The Sámi wanted to keep alive their languages and culture and were early supporters of the nascent alternative football movement. When Leif Isak Nilut, a Sami theatre director and head of the Football Association of Sápmi, was asked at an NF Board meeting in 2005 what the criteria for membership of this tribe was, he responded with an emotional joik, the traditional Sámi singing style (Menary, 2007, p 26).

In Norway, the Sámi people also had funding for a parliament and newspapers in their language and hosted the 2008 VWC and CONIFA's 2014 World Football Cup but could only host so many tournaments.

The idea of separating football from politics was an early aim of the NF Board and its successor organization, the Confederation of Independent Football Associations (CONIFA), but detaching a need for funding was harder. The NF Board had originally proposed to be a "waiting room" for teams looking to join FIFA (NF Board, 2011), but those federations with a realistic prospect of joining the established football family via membership of one of FIFA's six confederations – and the funds that would bring – such as Gibraltar and Kosovo largely avoided a nascent organization initially based on opposition to the money pot that was FIFA. In 1998, Sepp Blatter took over as FIFA president and introduced regular payments of $250,000 to all national association members that in 2014 were doubled (Reuters, 2014). These funds offered more of an attraction than anything on offer from the NF Board.

The likes of Gibraltar and Kosovo kept their distance from the alternative football movement and what little funding they had to themselves. Both would-be FIFA members knew that engaging in the world of alternative football would place their aspirations in opposition to international footballing norms. The NF Board's need for money to stage tournaments would create tension in the fragile dynamic of this putative world.

This would be an unspoken, but central, criteria for membership of the alternative football movement as more contentious teams were embraced from the Turkish Republic of Northern Ireland (TRNC) – created eight years after Turkey's invasion of the top half of the Mediterranean island in 1974 – to those aspiring for a politically accepted homeland crossing existing boundaries for the Kurdish people. The more controversial teams invariably had more money from backers in the wider geopolitical firmament to stage the tournaments that were a crucial part of the alternative football dream.

The almost universally unrecognized TRNC regime was created through the invasion of northern Cyprus that killed hundreds of people and displaced thousands more from the Turkish and Greek Cypriot communities. Only Turkey recognizes the TRNC, but unlike other NF Board members, the Kıbrıs Türk Futbol Federasyonu (KTFF) had more than 40 member clubs, ran leagues and had significant funding and stadia that would make feasible the NF Board's dream of staging of a first Viva World Cup (VWC) for unrecognized teams in 2006.

By this time, the NF Board's acronym had been changed to the New Federation Board, but a dispute over funding with the KTFF saw the debut VWC moved to Occitania. The Turkish Cypriots had £135,000 to spend on hosting the Equality, Liberty, Fraternity Trophy (Menary, 2007, p.175). Subsidized flights and accommodation brought eight teams to northern Cyprus including the Crimean Tatars, Zanzibar, and a team of exiled Tibetans, whereas only three teams contested the NF Board's VWC.

In 2012, the Turkish Cypriots made their only appearance in an NF Board tournament in what would be a high-point for alternative football, but an end to the original organizers. Iraqi Kurdistan also had sufficient money to stage a tournament and more than 20,000 saw the hosts beat the Turkish Cypriots. The NF Board subsequently descended into disarray due to infighting that ended up in a Belgian court (Play the Game, 2015).

A new body emerged and CONIFA says its aims are to support the "representatives of international football teams from nations, de facto nations, regions, minority peoples and sports isolated territories" (CONIFA, 2022). Those aims all embrace some form of resistance. CONIFA would be more successful in engaging with the media and expounding the notion of alternative football and professed to leave "all politics behind" (CONIFA, 2022), but the fundamental realities remained. Staging football tournaments cost money, and CONIFA too would make some curious friends.

In 2017, the body was planning an ambitious 16-team World Football Cup in London and put the cost at €1.5 million (World Soccer, 2017). While the exact cost to stage that event in London remains unknown, to make this dream happen entailed starting a relationship with betting company Paddy Power and brought betting to a level of football that the Council of Europe's Macolin Convention has expressly suggested are better avoided (COE, 2014). This has continued with crypto betting company Sportsbet.io sponsoring CONIFA events such as the 2020 World Football Cup (Insider Sport, 2019).

These events also needed hosts, and there were only so many putative associations in the world with both facilities and funding to put on the events that CONIFA planned – and would succeed – in staging. More recent invasions and annexations in would-be countries lacking international support would swiftly be forgotten in order to let the people play.

The creation of the independent republics Abkhazia and South Ossetia in 2008 came after a violent dispute with Georgia that saw separatists in both territories – backed with Russian military support – break away to establish independence that remains largely unrecognized. After Gibraltar had applied to join UEFA and FIFA despite the opposition of Spain, membership of both bodies was amended to require recognition from United Nations members (Play the Game, 2013), but Abkhazia and South Ossetia are only recognized by their Russian sponsors plus Nicaragua, Venezuela, and Nauru. Tuvalu and Vanuatu had recognized both breakaway states in 2011 but withdrew this support after establishing relations with Georgia (TASS, 2018).

The world of alternative football sits outside of the constraints of the globally recognized political system and offered both nascent republics an opportunity to promote their independence through a largely unquestioning media. In 2016, Abkhazia hosted CONIFA's second World Football Cup. The tournament attracted significant media attention and was also the subject of a documentary film, *Desert Storm*, about the Kurdistan team, which took part. Abkhazia was sufficiently open to visitors to stage a tournament that generated significant support and also, crucially, was able to provide a budget of around €450,000 (Menary, 2017).

Just as Cypriot objections to the ELF Cup had gone unheard, protests from Georgia over the participation of Abkhazia and South Ossetia were largely ignored by the international community, which at this point was doing little or nothing to confront the expansion of Vladimir Putin's Russia on many fronts, including football. In 2016, Abkhazia even expressed a desire to join FIFA, which, even given the woeful state of the world body, seems unlikely (Interfax, 2016).

Ironically, one of the few obstacles placed in the path of both Abkhazia and South Ossetia in CONIFA events was the denial of visa to its European Football Cup in Hungary in 2015 (CONIFA, 2015). The hosts were the Székely Land, an area of Romania inhabited by a Hungarian-speaking minority. The tournament was staged in the Hungarian city of Debrecen and, given the relatively close relationship between the country's prime minister Viktor Orbán and Putin, this political snub seems ironic. Doubly so, given that Orbán himself has used football to establish a greater sphere of Hungarian influence and spent around €55 million supporting clubs in regions of neighbouring countries where the population speak Hungarian (IJ4EU, 2018).

Alternative representative teams from Hungary have also embraced CONIFA. In addition to Székely Land, Kárpátalja representing Hungarian speakers in western Ukraine's Zakarpattia Oblast and Felvidék in Slovakia have played in CONIFA's main or qualifying competitions (CONIFA, 2018). These three teams along with Délvidék representing Hungarian speakers in Serbia also played in the 2016 Heritage Cup staged at Szarvas in Hungary.

A mediatized involvement with CONIFA boosted Orbán's ideal of a Greater Hungaria, while the participation of Abkhazia and South Ossetia had aided the notion of an expanded Russian sphere of influence as the two de facto states – created with Russia's support – were able to create a form of independence through football. Alternative football would soon be used again.

In 2014, pro-Russian separatist groups in the Ukrainian Donbass region declared their independence through the establishment of "People's Republics" in Donetsk and Luhansk. Football became a post-conflict tool in attempts to establish both statelets long before their "independence" was formally recognized by Russia on the eve of the next stage of Putin's Ukrainian invasion on 24 February 2022 (BBC, 2022).

A team from the so-called People's Republic of Luhansk had played a friendly with Abkhazia in 2015, then a few months later lost 4–1 to a representative side from the Donetsk statelet. Games between Donetsk and Luhansk were included as qualifiers for CONIFA's 2018 Football World Cup in London. South Ossetia has also played Luhansk and both Donbas sides drew 1–1 in Yenakiieve in 2016 in a game categorized by CONIFA as a qualifier for their 2018 Football World Cup, although neither team made it to the finals in London (CONIFA, 2018).

When the Russian army attempted to enlarge their occupation of the Donbass and conquer Ukraine in 2022, football was again a tool in the conflict and the sporting isolation of Russia quickly became a prerequisite. All Russian clubs and national teams were suspended by FIFA four days after the invasion began in February 2022 (FIFA, 2022).

The notion – in the rest of Europe and North America at least – that a universally accepted line had been crossed by Russia did not register in the realms of alternative football. Abkhazia and South Ossetia were both included in CONIFA's proposed Euro 2022 tournament. Asked in February 2022 if Abkhazia and South Ossetia would travel to the proposed host city of Nice in France, CONIFA President Per-Anders Blind said, "Impossible to say at these dark times ... the majority of the players hold Russian passports" (Menary, 2022).

As Russian involvement in all walks of life became restricted, the concept that both teams were widely unrecognized extensions of Putin's empire and should not appear was not considered. Alternative football was outside the accepted universal norms that Putin and any de facto states created through his expansionist plans should be censured for the widely acknowledged atrocities in Ukraine.

While alternative football has supported cultural representation and exchanges in many positive ways, the concept that there should be no borders or limits has both allowed in unlikely "national" teams such as the English counties of Cornwall, Surrey, and Yorkshire and, on another extreme, become a vehicle for contentious teams that are based predominantly on achieving a political aim.

References

BBC. (2022). *Ukraine: Putin announces Donetsk and Luhansk recognition*. Available at: https://www.bbc.co.uk/news/av/world-europe-60470900 Accessed 16 June 2022.

Brinch, J. (2005). Interview with author, Shetland Isles 12 July.

CIA World Factbook. *Monaco*. Available at: https://www.cia.gov/the-world-factbook/countries/monaco/ Accessed 16 June 2022.

CONIFA. (2015). *Looking back and moving forward!* Available at: https://conifaofficial .wordpress.com/2015/07/07/looking-back-and-moving-forward/ Accessed 16 June 2022.

CONIFA. (2018). *WFC 2018 qualification*. Available at: https://www.conifa.org/en/event /conifa-paddy-power-world-football-cup-2018/wfc-2018-qualification/ Accessed 16 June 2022.

CONIFA. (2022a). *Who we are*. Available at: https://www.conifa.org/en/about/ Accessed 16 June 2022.

CONIFA. (2022b). *FAQS*. Available at: https://www.conifa.org/en/faqs/ Accessed 16 June 2022.

Council of Europe. (2014). *Council of Europe convention on the manipulation of sports competitions*. Available at: https://rm.coe.int/16801cdd7e Accessed 16 June 2022.

FIFA. (2022). *FIFA/UEFA suspend Russian clubs and national teams from all competitions*. Available at: https://www.fifa.com/tournaments/mens/worldcup/qatar2022/media -releases/fifa-uefa-suspend-russian-clubs-and-national-teams-from-all-competitions Accessed 16 June 2022.

IJ4EU. (2018). *Hungarian football funds*. Available at: http://www.investigativejourna lismforeu.net/projects/investigating-hungarian-public-money-in-the-football-clubs -of-neighboring-countries/ Accessed 16 June 2022.

Insider Sport. (2019). *CONIFA names Sportsbet.io as World Football Cup 2020 sponsor*. Available at: https://insidersport.com/2019/12/04/conifa-names-sportsbet-io-as -world-football-cup-2020-sponsor/ Accessed 16 June 2022.

Interfax. (2016). *Abkhazia wants to become FIFA member*. Available at: https://interfax.com /newsroom/top-stories/31973/ Accessed 16 June 2022.

Menary, S. (2007). *Outcasts: The lands that FIFA forgot*. Studley: Know The Score.

Menary, S. (2017). Information supplied to author by Abkhazia officials at 2017 at CONIFA Euro 2017 tournament in northern Cyprus, June 4.

Menary, S. (2022). Message to author on LinkedIn, February 28.

NF Board. *History the N.F.-Board genesis*. Available at: https://nfbwebsite.wixsite.com/ nfboard/history Accessed 16 June 2022.

Play the Game. (2013). *Gibraltar no longer an outcast*. Available at: https://www.playthegame .org/news/gibraltar-no-longer-an-outcast/ Accessed 16 June 2022.

Play the Game. (2015). *Non-FIFA football in quarrel*. Available at: https://www.playthegame .org/news/non-fifa-football-in-quarrel/ Accessed 16 June 2022.

Reuters. (2014). *FIFA to give "success" payments to member associations*. Available at: https:// www.reuters.com/article/uk-soccer-world-fifa-finances-idUKKBN0EM1RA20 140611 Accessed 16 June 2022.

TASS. (2018). Countries that recognized South Ossetia's and Abkhazia's independence. Available at: https://tass.com/world/1007058?utm_source=google.com&utm _medium=organic&utm_campaign=google.com&utm_referrer=google.com Accessed 16 June 2022.

World Soccer. (2017). *FIFA-less nations enjoy their moment in the sun*. July, p. 37.

23

THE CONJUNCTURAL POLITICS OF THE 2026 FIFA MEN'S WORLD CUP

United 2026

Adam S. Beissel

Introduction

> I have to inform you that the U.S. is on the verge of becoming the soccer power of the world.
>
> FIFA President Gianni Infantino (quoted in Javers, 2020, para. 1)

On 13 June 2018, the Fédération Internationale de Football Association (FIFA) awarded the 2026 FIFA Men's World Cup (FMWC26) to a joint bid of the United States (US), Mexico, and Canada. FMWC26 will be one of firsts: the first time the tournament features a 48-team format, the first time three countries have shared hosting rights, and the first to completely use already existing stadiums and infrastructure. It will also be the most politically entangled, geographically sprawling, and commercially lucrative FIFA Men's World Cup (FMWC) in history. The North American effort – known as United 2026 throughout the bidding process – proposed an integrated hosting vision and event legacy United as One aimed at strengthening continental partnership between host nations and using FIFA's signature event as a platform to unite the global [football] community. These political aspirations are made particularly salient given the recent presidency of Donald Trump, whose hard-line stances on trade and immigration eroded long-standing political and economic partnerships between the three countries, and diplomatic relations reached their lowest point in decades. FMWC26 will be the first truly regional tournament – a geographic sprawling, trans-continental competition with matches held in 16 cities across three North American countries. FMWC26 will span nearly the entire continent – from Vancouver to Miami, Guadalajara to Boston – and features start-of-the-art stadiums, a substantial experience hosting large-scale sport spectacles and

DOI: 10.4324/9781003348238-28

international sport mega-events (SMEs), and all the pre-existing infrastructure and tourist amenities required to accommodate millions of tourists, event spectators, and tournament participants from around the world. Perhaps most importantly, however, is that FMWC26 will be the largest commercial sport spectacle in modern history. Economic estimates forecast a staggering $11 billion profit for FIFA (Das, 2018a) – more than double that of any previous MWC – based on unprecedented economic certainty from the use of already existing stadiums and unequalled commercial opportunities that could firmly anchor football markets in three of the world's largest 15 economies. Accordingly, FMWC26 promises to leave an unmatched and unrivalled legacy and impact on the people, markets, and communities of the entire North American continent.

I've been researching and writing on the geopolitical economy of FMWC26 for a while now. In this chapter, I bring together my various research findings and observations to concisely discuss the *conjunctural politics of the FMWC26* in order to contextualize the event within the broader historical and cultural conjuncture. The politics of each sport mega-event is, to note, conjunctural in that it will be "affected by different political circumstances at local, national, regional and global scales at different times and places" (Horne, 2017, p. 331). According to Horne (2017), there is a politics *in*, and a politic *of*, international sport mega-events such as the Olympic Games and MWC. The former, he argues, focuses on the *internal politics* of sporting international non-governmental organizations – referred to as SINGOs (Allison and Tomlinson, 2017) – such as the International Olympic Committee and FIFA. This chapter, rather, extends a discussion of the *external politics of* 2026 FMWC as they relate to global political economic forces and relations in combination with, or in confrontation of, local interests and national political agendas. Specifically, my interest lies in examining ways the geographic, political, and economic formations of FMWC26 shape, and are shaped by, the current geopolitical conjuncture. I detail three primary features of FMWC26: a promise of *political unity, a magnitude of economic certainty*, and *an unprecedented commercial opportunity*. The chapter concludes by discussing how FMWC26 relates to sport's burgeoning geopolitical economy.

Political Entanglements – A Promise of Political Unity

In April 2017, the three governing bodies of Canada, Mexico, and the US officially announced their intent to submit a joint bid for FMWC26 in an effort to bring the tournament back to the region for the first time since 1994, when the US last hosted. The formation of the United 2026 bid partnership and the development of the United as One strategic hosting vision were owed to interrelated internal and external contextual forces. As I have discussed elsewhere, the three *internal forces* that guided US Soccer's decision to include Mexico and Canada in the bid were: *practical, strategic*, and *political*. In terms of the *practical reasons* for each nation to join forces, the new 48-team, 80-game format required more state-of-the-art stadiums and modern infrastructure than any previous

MWC. Not only did each federation offer experience and expertise in hosting world-class sporting events, but the increased number of teams and matches for FMWC26 necessitated more infrastructure to support larger fan engagement with in excess of 5.8 million fans expected to attend matches in person and millions more participating in city-hosted FIFA Fan Fests (*United 2026 Bid Book*, 2018, p. 8). There were also *strategic reasons* that guided the joint North American effort. Following the Qatari scandal, USSF was hesitant to commit the time and money – estimated at $10 million of a $60 million annual budget in 2022 – to pursue hosting rights (Murray, 2015). There were also concerns within USSF that FIFA members would seek retribution via MWC hosting rights after the US Department of Justice investigation of FIFA's corruption and a collaborative North American effort could, potentially, shift focus from the US as the main tournament benefactor.

Perhaps most importantly, there were *political reasons* for collaboration. As interrogated shortly, United 2026 bid organizers hoped an integrated hosting strategy of United as One, and the implied symbolic politics (Black, 2007) of unity, would outweigh any concerns about negative perceptions of President Donald Trump, his administration, or American foreign policies. Notwithstanding commercial and diplomatic relations between the three countries reaching their lowest point in decades, the United 2026 bid's vision enabled symbolic reimagining of a truly international partnership amidst growing diplomatic tensions and rising anti-American sentiment (Luce, 2018). In developing the unity narrative, organizers attempted to position the bid as capable of transcending political scruples to provide a common good through football. The United 2026 bid's integrated hosting vision and strategy of United as One was a symbolic reimagining of the US-led bid as a truly international partnership amidst growing tensions in diplomatic relations and a growing anti-American sentiment due to the unpopular policies and spiteful rhetoric of President Trump. From its initial inception, FMWC26 celebrated and promoted *political unity* to provide a signature event legacy, distance the bid from President Trump, and ultimately gain support for the bid from FIFA member associations and the global community.

Of course, this vision of political unity and trans-continental cooperation became increasingly difficult to maintain as Trump became increasingly involved himself with FMWC26. Trump emerged as a vocal public supporter of the United Bid despite his public disagreements with Mexico and Canada, authoring several antagonistic statements and Twitter tirades in order to influence the bid process. Moreover, the *New York Times* reported that Trump began writing letters to FIFA President Gianni Infantino expressing his hosting the event in "the spirit of continental partnership" (quoted in Das, 2018, para. 17) and assuring FIFA officials of visa-free travel, that his Muslim travel ban would not apply, and agreeing to grant FIFA full tax exemptions on all commercial activity during the tournament. As I have written elsewhere with David L. Andrews (2021), Trump's seemingly contradictory embracing of the United Bid was an attempt to advance his particular form of authoritarian populism through the construction of real and imagined threats to the racial and nationalist dominance of America and by destabilizing and restructuring the dominant geopolitical order. In his public sentiments expressing support for the 2026 MWC bid, Trump was able to advance the ideological and affective elements of Trumpism by establishing a compelling definition of the crisis and formulating a proposed conjunctural resolution.

On the other hand, the United 2026 bid and its United as One strategic hosting vision were developed to simultaneously address *external forces* related to FIFA's (corporate) rebranding and consolidation of power as football's global authority. In specific terms, the United as One strategic hosting vision articulates global unity, continental partnership, and inclusivity aligned harmoniously with FIFA 2.0. As I have written elsewhere with Neal Ternes, the release of FIFA's new vision, known as FIFA 2.0, followed one of the highest-profile corruption scandals in modern sports history after the US Department of Justice indicted 27 football officials for wire fraud, racketeering, and money laundering. Released in 2016 by newly elected FIFA President Gianni Infantino, FIFA 2.0 not only promised to implement a stronger governance structure that would resist the corruption scandals that plagued the previous administration, but it promised a new organizational strategy to present a new public purpose for the beleaguered organization as a progenitor and caretaker of global sporting market. Therefore, the United 2026 bid, which promoted cooperation, diplomacy, and transnational (and, by proxy, global) partnership, provided FIFA an acceptable altruistic and public project for rehabilitating its public image. Indeed, the symbolism of FMWC26 would serve as a strategic opportunity for FIFA to consolidate the association's sporting pre-eminence and symbolically (re-)imagine its purpose as a principal agent for growing the game, positive social change, and promoting global diplomacy. Thus, the United 2026 bid not only helped bring FIFA 2.0 to reality, but it also reframed FIFA 2.0's broad allusions to using football for the social good as meaning the productive use of the MWC to bring politically disparate nations together through unity, continental partnership, and public diplomacy.

Amidst these twofold contexts, FMWC26 and the United as One strategic hosting vision has become a metonym for shared cultures, economic trade relations, and transnational government alignment in North America. However, the United as One vision romanticized the potential for football to bring people together and transform lives and communities by invoking clichés about the sport as a global unifier. Notions of continental partnership and global fraternity sit largely as abstract promises and clichés for political unity building. In harmony with the recognized ambiguity of sport mega-event legacy constructions, the hosting vision lacked measurable outcomes for its diplomatic ambitions. More critically, the vision ignored deeply entrenched cultural differences, problematic histories, and the growing contemporary geopolitical divides. Furthermore, the vision normalized football as inherently positive, while ignoring unequal power relations, sports' marginalizing effects, and prevailing sociocultural hegemonies.

Contrary to the organizer's aspiration, from the outset United as One was less euphemistic than a carefully mediated marketing strategy. While diplomatic and political aspirations have featured in other SME bids, the use of unity as a political legacy was a means for bid organizers to confront and break with Trump's discourse and administration and, concomitantly, offer FIFA a political legacy of diplomacy extending beyond competition cessation.

Geographic Expanse – A Magnitude of Economic Certainty

FMWC26 proposes the largest geographic reach of any MWC in recent history. The three host nations combine for a population of 500 million people, 69 Metro areas >1 million inhabitants, and a GDP of $21.5 trillion (*United 2026 Bid Book*, 2018, p. 31). Although the US comprises the majority economic weight (in terms of GDP), both Canada and Mexico rank among the 15 largest global economies (*United 2026 Bid Book*, 2018, p. 103). In terms of trade and commercial relations, the North American Free Trade Agreement (NAFTA) accounts for $1 trillion a year in trade between Canada, Mexico, and the US. The US is the second most popular tourist destination in the world, with more than 75 million annual visitors coming from overseas, contributing over $1.5 trillion in tourism-related spending. Together, the three nations combine for an estimated $20 trillion in total economic output (*United 2026 Bid Book*, 2018, p. 103). Accordingly, the United 2026 bid emphasized specific innovative corporate sectors within the three nations, including: biotechnology, transportation, and smart cities (Canada); agriculture, mathematics, and tech innovation (Mexico); and technology, pharmaceuticals, aerospace, and media production (US).

The United 2026 bid proposal included 23 candidate host cities with all the pre-existing stadiums and necessary infrastructure – notably each candidate city featured stadiums with capacities of 68,000 or greater – thus avoiding need for new constructions (*United 2026 Bid Book,* 2018, p. 21). With more than 125 FIFA-compatible stadiums in existence across the three nations, the bid guaranteed FIFA timely delivery of all stadiums, venues, and facilities. Thus, a tournament of this geographic scale – one which offered more than a hundred FIFA-compatible, already existing stadiums – assured a post-scandal FIFA and its member associations of a level of badly desired *economic certainty*. Bid organizers have long argued that not only do these stadium and infrastructure savings promote economic certainty, but they also enable the event to be an opportunity to invest energy and resources towards improving and scaling existing and to-be-developed spaces and programming, and directly impacting the lives of millions of the countries' constituents (*United 2026 Bid Book*, 2018, p. 35). Such assertions provided an assurance that the tournament would be a commercial success, and the promise to use existing infrastructure presented FIFA a sign of further certainty and sustainability. As one journalist noted, the sheer geographic scope and already existing infrastructure included in the United Bid made it "too big to fail" (Hall, 2018, para. 19).

196 Adam S. Beissel

The FMWC26 host city selection process followed a particularly unique set of circumstances. Prior to 2026, the competitive bid process was typically an *inter-nation competition* between aspirant hosts in which the host cities were pre-determined as part of the official bid. Local organizers would include a complete list of host cities as part of the official bid proposal, and FIFA's evaluation process would consider the economic reach and political support of each constituent city as part of the entire bid's evaluation. However, FIFA's evaluation of individual host cities for 2026 was divided into two separate evaluations, with the host cities selected multiple years after the nation's bid rights were confirmed. Thus, the process for an *inter-nation competition* between prospective North American host cities began nearly as soon as United 2026 won the hosting right. Over the four years between the United 2026 bid's successful awarding in 2018 and the announcement of host cities in June 2022, public and private leaders across North American lined up with tax exemptions, government guarantees, amendments to local laws, and millions of dollars of public and private investments in the prospect at landing at least some FMWC26 matches. An official FIFA delegation, led by FIFA Vice President Victor Montagliani, conducted systematic visits of all candidate host cities in order to evaluate the city's existing stadiums and infrastructure, assess the commercial opportunities, and privately negotiate with local leaders (Goff, 2021). By staging an internal bid competition – in which there were more candidate cities than host sites – FIFA was able to negotiate the most generous terms for staging the event. Not only did this inter-nation competitive bid process allow FIFA to rationally map out the geographic reach and expanse of the tournament, but also carefully consider the bids that offered the most favourable political guarantees, public and private funding, and economic certainty.

The geographic expanse of the first FMWC held across three nations became evident when FIFA announced the FMWC26 host cities in June 2022. At a public ceremony in downtown Manhattan, FIFA President Gianni Infantino revealed the host cities at a televised spectacle, with 11 venues chosen in the US, 3 in Mexico, and 2 in Canada. The host cities are divided into three zones: Western (Vancouver, Seattle, San Francisco, Los Angeles, and Guadalajara); Central (Kansas City, Dallas, Atlanta, Houston, Monterrey, and Mexico City); and Eastern (New York/New Jersey, Boston, Philadelphia, Miami, and Toronto) (Goff, 2022). Six cities were ultimately unsuccessful in the competitive hosting process: Baltimore/D.C., Cincinnati, Denver, Edmonton, Nashville, and Orlando. The US will host 60 of the 80 matches in the tournament, including every game from the quarterfinal onwards. Canada and Mexico will host 10 matches each. As of this writing, FIFA has yet to announce which of the cities and venues will host matches in the knockout stages, including the final, though it is expected the tournament's final match will be in either New York or Los Angeles.

More broadly, the reliance on already existing stadiums and facilities across 16 North American cities serves as a *risk-averse strategy* allowing FIFA to escape the public criticism and backlash associated with strategies of urban placemaking and the spectacular construction of World Cup space(s). As I have written elsewhere with Neal Ternes (2022), a seemingly ready-made FMWC26 could avoid any of the major construction delays, displacement effects, white elephant stadiums, and sporting Trojan horses that have characterized the hosting of recent MWCs in South Africa, Brazil, and Russia, and Qatar. Such a risk-averse approach was particularly attractive to FIFA, whose newly adopted *FIFA 2.0-Vision for the Future* framework introduced a new operating model for the Men's and Women's World Cups – a model that sought to enhance revenue generation, decrease operating expenses, and optimize operational efficiencies. Thus, the selection of the United 2026 bid – one that does not require major event-specific construction – enabled FIFA to not only decrease the costs associated with hosting FMWC26, but signal a move away from linkages to *global placemaking*, ending a historical conjuncture where FIFA prioritized event legacies based on the spectacular construction of MWC spaces and towards the (re-)imagining and (re-)organization of urban space. Instead, United 2026 was a timely, cost-certain, and risk-averse proposal for hosting the 2026 FMWC that could use a large selection of stadiums and infrastructure spanning the entire North American continent to deliver unprecedented economic certainty in a broader effort towards rehabilitating the public image of FIFA. In other words, the economic certainty of FMWC26 is a practical means to FIFA's strategic ends.

Economic Impact – An Unprecedented Commercial Opportunity

Although the promise of political unity and the magnitude of economic certainty are certainly important aspects of FMWC26, the event's signature feature is the possibility of the largest economic impact in MWC history. The 2026 tournament is expected to demolish MWC attendance records – which peaked at 3.6 million when it was held in the United States in 1994 – based on both an increase in the total number of games played and the growth of football's popularity in North America. Indeed, FMWC26 offers FIFA an unprecedented *commercial opportunity* to "open the veins" of football commercialism, consumption, and spectatorship throughout North America's nascent football market(s). According to estimates, FMWC26 projects a staggering $11 billion profit for FIFA; more than double that of any previous MWC in history. The revenue projections include more than $5 billion in television rights fees; $3.6 billion for sponsorship and licensing; and at least $2.1 billion in ticket revenue (Bradsher & Panja, 2018). An economic impact study for FMWC26, commissioned by the Boston Consulting Group (BCG), suggests the event will have a cumulative $5 billion in short-term economic activity, including the creation of 40,000 jobs and more than $1 billion in incremental worker earnings from the candidate host cities, for an overall net benefit of $3–4 billion (*GRI Referenced Report*, 2018). The BCG study further estimated that individual host cities could expect to see approximately $160–620 million in incremental activity, translating to a net benefit of approximately $90–480 million per city after accounting for estimated public costs (*United 2026 Bid Book*, 2018). Carlos Cordeiro, then-U.S. Soccer Federation President, proudly proclaimed, "a profit of this magnitude is unprecedented in any single-sport event in the world … In terms of value, it could mean $50 million more per association" (quoted in Bradsher & Panja, 2018, para. 10).

Much of the optimism surrounding FMWC26 economic opportunity is linked to countless opportunities for fans, broadcasters, and commercial partners across North America. Accordingly, FMWC26 will allow FIFA to *extract maximum value* from an unprecedented and untapped market of football tourist-consumers as well as an opportunity to restore and enhance *capital networks and flows* with the North American corporate sector. First, North America has experienced seismic participation and fan growth over the past three decades. Mexico's first division Liga MX ranks fifth in the world in attendance, and football in Canada is growing, particularly following the success of the Canadian Women's Soccer team which won gold at the 2020 Summer Olympic Games (Thompson, 2021). Youth football participation in the United States has doubled since the previous MWC in 1994 and is now played by 4.1 million youth annually, making it the most played youth sport in the country (*United 2026 Bid Book*, 2018). At present, FIFA estimates there are approximately 250 million football fans in the three host countries and anticipates 5.8 million tickets will be sold for the tournament for revenues in excess of $2 billion and a 150% increase in corporate hospitality sales relative to the most recent FMWC (*United 2026 Bid Book*, 2018). The expected global television audience, which is used as a benchmark for predicting both media and marketing revenues, is expected to increase by around 9% in comparison to the baseline audience of the 2014 FIFA Men's World Cup (*FIFA Bid Evaluation Report*, 2018). In summation, North America is "the most lucrative region in the world for football", and staging the competition here will allow FIFA to expand into new commercial fronts and increase economic possibilities by deepening commercial connections to existing football enthusiasts.

Secondly, FMWC26 allows FIFA the opportunity to restore and strengthen commercial and nonprofit partnerships with media partners and financial institutions and to create "a culture of innovation for the benefit of FIFA" (*United 2026 Bid Book*, 2018, p. 10). As United 2026 bid documents point out, North America is already the biggest sports sponsorship market in the world, with companies headquartered in the region contributing over 25% of all worldwide sports sponsorship spending, not including an estimated $40 billion per annum on media advertising for sports programmes and other sport-oriented content (*United 2026 Bid Book,* 2018). FMWC26 offers integrated partnerships with advanced technology companies in Silicon Valley, biotechnical industries in Canada, and petrochemical companies in Mexico to recover from the scandal-induced financial losses. To these ends, and from the outset, FMWC26 is positioned in ways that harmonize with FIFA's desires to restore and expand its relationships with its US global multinational partners and sponsors (specifically, Visa, McDonalds, Coca-Cola, Budweiser, and Johnson-Johnson), and aid in securing more lucrative media rights and commercial partnerships. Thus, the commercial opportunities were at once a mechanism for preserving capital flows and market growth for FIFA and its corporate partners.

Despite this impressive trajectory for football on the continent, the sport is understood to have plenty of room to grow in popularity in North America, particularly the United States. A second MWC hosted in the US, and the momentous commercial revenue generation by FIFA and host nation football federations, have been heralded as the "spark" and "catalyst to generating hundreds of millions of dollars that can be invested into making football in the United States more affordable" (*United 2026 Bid Book*, 2018, pp. 7–8). As I have written with Geoff Kohe (2021), however, the event legacies related to FMWC26 are almost entirely focused on capital accumulation and wealth extraction by FIFA, with a few nominal "trickle-down" investments in soccer-related infrastructure throughout the North American continent that truly lack any clear plan or coordination. More critically, such trickle-down sporting investment is balanced by promises of an inspirational sport participation legacy effect that, while socially palatable, rehearses regurgitated moral axioms that obfuscate corporate opportunism towards new generations of football consumers. In other words, by opening more facilities, getting more people to play football, and growing further interest in the game, this process cultivates future consumers that can be monetized for the primary benefit of FIFA and its member associations. So, while opportunity with the FMWC26 could be tied to growing sports participation and social inclusion among young participants, it is largely focused on the commercial growth and capital accumulation which can grow FIFA's bottom line. And where opportunities for growing sport participation are acknowledged, they are rather directly linked to cultivating the next generation of football consumers.

Conclusion: North America, FMWC26, and the Geopolitical Economy of Sport

> 2026 will be much, much bigger (than 1994). I think this part of the world doesn't realize what will happen here in 2026. The world will be invading Canada, Mexico and the United States.
>
> FIFA President Gianni Infantino (quoted in Stejskal, 2022, para. 1)

In this chapter, I have drawn on my previous research to explore the ways in which the geographic, political, and economic formations of FMWC26 are constituted by, and constitutive of, the contemporary geopolitical conjuncture. More specifically, I have detailed how the conjunctural politics of FMWC26, including the United 26 bid and United as One strategic hosting vision, are characterized by the politics of political unity, a magnitude of economic uncertainty, and unprecedented commercial opportunity. These three interrelated features of FMWC26 are made particularly relevant given FIFA's recent history that involves major scandals, significant public criticisms, and recent reform efforts to rebrand and consolidate its global football empire. Thus, a critical examination of FMWC26 contributes to a contextually specific and empirically grounded understanding of the increasingly interdependent and mutually constitutive relationship between FMWC26 and FIFA.

More broadly, FMWC26 is uniquely situated within/against the contexts and conditions of a "new era of play" for contemporary sport culture in which global-local events, bodies, spaces, and practices "will be shaped by economic and geopolitical interests much more than in the past" (Chadwick and Widdop, 2021, para. 29). The twin dynamics of globalization and digitalization have contributed to a global sport assemblage in which "geography, politics, and economics are interacting with one another giv[ing] rise to the need for a new way of conceiving sport" (Chadwick, 2022, para. 14). Given recent shifts in global economic and political power, with Asian and Middle Eastern nations becoming increasingly influential in sport, FMWC26 represents the ways in which western liberal democracies have joined forces and responded to shifting economic and cultural conditions in order to preserve and extend their sphere of geopolitical influence. The three host nations of FMWC26 have symbolically and materially aligned themselves to leverage North America's strongest features to "open the veins" of one of football's last remaining untapped markets: corporate multinational enterprises, commercially saturated consumer markets, robust spectator-tourist industry, and a spectacular array of built infrastructure (e.g., stadiums, training facilities, infrastructure). Accordingly, broad appeals to political unity and continental cooperation are the rather opaque frames through which the logics of corporate capitalism, conspicuous consumption, and capitalist state ideology underpin FMWC26. In so doing, FMWC26 is an opportunity for western liberal democracies (and their corporate backers) to counteract their waning political and economic sport interests and combat the growing sporting influence(s) of Asian and the Middle Eastern nations. Thus, FMWC26 serves as a pivotal moment in the ideological contestation for global dominance and influence in the contemporary geopolitical economy of sport.

Reference List

Allison, L., & Tomlinson, A. (2017). *Understanding international sport organisations: Principles, power and possibilities.* Routledge, London. ISBN: 9781315743875.

Beissel, A.S., & Andrews, D.L., 2020. Art of the deal: Donald Trump, soft power, and winning the 2026 FIFA Men's World Cup bid. In B. Clift & A. Tomlinson (Eds.), *Populism and the Sport and Leisure Spectacle.* Routledge, London, pp. 234–253. ISBN: 9780367356385.

Beissel, A.S., & Kohe, G., 2020. United as one: The 2026 FIFA Men's World Cup hosting vision and the symbolic politics of legacy. *Managing Sport Leisure. Vol. ahead-of-print No. ahead-of-print.* DOI: 10.1080/23750472.2020.1846138.

Beissel, A.S., & Ternes, N., (2022). The empire strikes back: FIFA 2.0, global peacemaking, and the 2026 FIFA Men's World Cup United Bid. *Journal of Global Sport Management. September.* pp. 1–23. DOI: https://doi.org/10.1080/24704067.2022.2116589.

Black, D., 2007. The symbolic politics of sport mega-events: 2010 in comparative perspective. *Politikon, 34*(3), 261–276.

Bradsher, K., & Panja, T., 2018, 9 June. North American World Cup bid projects US$11 billion profit for FIFA. *The New York Times.* https://www.nytimes.com/2018/05/08/sports/2026-world-cup.html

Chadwick, S., 2022, 21 January. How 2022 will epitomize sport's burgeoning geopolitical economy. *GeoSport.* Available at: https://www.iris-france.org/164078-how-2022-will-epitomise-sports-burgeoning-geopolitical-economy/

Chadwick, S. & Widdop, P., 2021, 13 January. The geopolitical economy of sport – A new era in play. *Asia & The Pacific Policy Society – Policy Forum.* Available at: https://www.policyforum.net/the-geopolitical-economy-of-sport/

Das, A., 2018a, 8 May. North American World Cup bid projects $11 billion profit for FIFA. *The New York Times.* Available at: https://www.nytimes.com/2018/05/08/sports/2026-world-cup.html

Das, A., 2018, 13 June. How 3 letters from Trump might help bring the 2026 World Cup to the U.S. *The New York Times.* Available at: https://www.nytimes.com/2018/06/12/sports/trump-letters-world-cup.html (accessed 13 June 2018).

FIFA Bid Evaluation Report, 2018. Bid evaluation report: 2026 FIFA World Cup. *FIFA.com.* Available at: https://resources.fifa.com/image/upload/2026-fifa-world-cup-bid-evaluation-report.pdf?cloudid=yx76lnat3oingsmnlvzf

Goff, S., 2021, 19 September. D.C. makes its 2026 World Cup pitch to FIFA officials: 'Washington is where you want to be'. *The Washington Post.* Available at: https://www.washingtonpost.com/sports/2021/09/19/washington-dc-2026-world-cup-inspection/

Goff, S., 2022, 16 June. 2026 World Cup host cities are unveiled, but D.C. and Baltimore miss out. *The Washington Post.* Available at: https://www.washingtonpost.com/sports/2022/06/16/2026-world-cup-host-cities/

GRI Referenced Report, 2018. Prepared in accordance with Global Reporting Initiative (GRI) Guidelines by United Bid 2026 Committee. *FIFA.com.* Available at: https://resources.fifa.com/image/upload/gri-referenced-report-united-bid.pdf?cloudid=msbdtfolv8bozcnvxlda

Hall, M., 2018. Are cities starting to see World Cup hosting duties as a poisoned chalice? *The Guardian.* https://www.theguardian.com/football/2018/mar/19/are-cities-starting-to-see-world-cup-hosting-duties-as-a-poisoned-chalice

Horne, J., 2017. Sports mega-events – Three sites of contemporary political contestation. *Sport in Society, 20*(3), 328–340.

Javers, E. [@EamonJavers], 2020, 21 January. FIFA president Gianni Infantino to President Trump in Davos: "I have to inform you that the U.S. is on the verge of becoming the soccer power of the world." [Tweet]. *Twitter.com.* Available at: https://twitter.com/eamonjavers/status/1219680016809779201

Luce, E., 2018, 21 June. The rise of a new generation of anti-Americans. *The Financial Times.* https://www.ft.com/content/ae6d2aca-7530-11e8-b6ad-3823e4384287

Murray, C., 2015, 11 August. Is the US ready – Or even willing – To host the 2026 World Cup? *The Guardian*. http://www.theguardian.com/football/blog/2015/aug/10/is-the-us-ready-or-even-willing-to-host-the-2026-world-cup

Stejskal, S. [@samstejskal], 2022, 16 June. FIFA president Gianni Infantino: "2026 will be much, much bigger (than 1994). I think this part of the world doesn't realize what will happen here in 2026. ... The world will be invading Canada, Mexico and the United States." [Tweet]. *Twitter.com*. Available at: https://twitter.com/samstejskal/status/1537567610488991752

Thompson, S., 2021, 6 August. Olympic success could be a boost to women's, girls' soccer across Canada. *Globalnews.CA*. Available at: https://globalnews.ca/news/8092111/olympic-gold-inspiring-girls-womens-soccer/

United 2026 Bid Book, 2018. Canada, Mexico, and the United States Bid to Host the 2026 FIFA World Cup. *FIFA.com*. Available at: https://img.fifa.com/image/upload/w3yjeu7dadt5erw26wmu.pdf

24

THE ATTEMPTED RESHAPING OF THE TURKISH FOOTBALL LANDSCAPE UNDER THE AK PARTY

A Transaction Cost Economics Explanation

Steven H. Seggie

On 5 May 1996, a goal in the 82nd minute by Fenerbahce's Aykut Kocaman was enough to give Fenerbahce a 2–1 victory in Trabzonspor's Huseyin Avni Aker Stadium. Trabzonspor had led the Turkish Super League for more than half of the season, but with this result they dropped back to second and, although there were still two weeks of the season left, they finished two points shy of Fenerbahce in first (*Turkey Super Lig, 1995/1996 Table*). For the 13th time, Fenerbahce were Super League Champions with Trabzonspor in second and Besiktas in third. Had results gone differently this would have been Trabzonspor's first league championship since 1983–84, but it was not to be. Yet again, one of the big three Istanbul clubs (Besiktas, Fenerbahce, and Galatasaray) were champions, and this was not much of a surprise as in the history of the Turkish Super League only six clubs have been champions with the big three Istanbul clubs dominating (Ambille, 2021). It would not be until the 2021–22 season that Trabzonspor would finally become champions again.

Much has changed in Turkey from the mid-1990s until the present day, and one area where we have observed massive upheaval is in politics. The 1990s were not a particularly fruitful period in Turkish politics with a succession of weak coalition governments, runaway inflation, and terrorism dominating the headlines (Sozen, 2006). On 24 December 1995, national elections were held which resulted in five political parties entering Parliament, with no one party having a majority. It was a particularly traumatic election for the secular elite in Turkey (Burak, 2011) as the Islamist Welfare Party (RP), led by Necmettin Erbakan, got the highest number of votes of all the parties, getting just over 21% of all votes. The other four parties that were able to enter Parliament were Mesut Yilmaz's right-wing secular Motherland Party (ANAP) with nearly 20% of the vote, Tansu Ciller's right-wing secular True Path Party (DYP) with 19% of the vote, the left-wing secular Democratic Left Party (DSP) of Bulent Ecevit

DOI: 10.4324/9781003348238-29

with nearly 15%, and the left-wing secular People's Republic Party (CHP) led by Deniz Baykal with almost 11% (Secor, 2001). This victory for the Welfare Party came just two and a half years after they had won the elections for mayor of Istanbul (Recep Tayyip Erdogan) and Ankara (Melih Gokcek).

If we fast-forward to 2022, only one of these political parties, the CHP, and only one of these politicians, Recep Tayyip Erdogan, can be considered a major force in politics. Although to state that Erdogan is a major force would be to do him a disservice as he has been the dominant force in Turkish politics for the past 20 years. During his time in power, one of his main projects has been the founding of a New Turkey (Keyman, 2014), a Turkey where citizens are more conservative, more openly pious, and less secular. As part of this project, Erdogan has turned his gaze towards sport, and in particular football, and attempted to reshape it in line with New Turkey values. It is well documented that Erdogan was a promising young footballer, and it is even speculated that he could have become a professional player but for his father not considering it to be an appropriate career for him (Ege, 2021). Furthermore, football is by far and away the most popular sport in Turkey, and internationally, football clubs are one of the most common ways for foreigners, particularly Europeans, to engage with Turkey as a result of Turkish teams competing in the UEFA competitions. Therefore, in the same way that the Soviet Union used sporting success for propaganda purposes (Mertin, 2010), Erdogan can use any sporting success on the football pitch as a proxy for the success of his regime. Erdogan is no stranger to doing this domestically, regularly meeting with footballers such as Mesut Ozil, Arda Turan, Ilkay Gundogan, Emre Belozoglu, and others as a way to associate their success with his. Also, his government is no stranger to using football in the international arena, previously using it as part of the Turkey–Armenian reconciliation process in October 2009. As part of this ultimately unsuccessful reconciliation process, then Turkish President Abdullah Gül and then Armenian President Serzh Sarkisian attended both the home and away leg of World Cup qualifying matches between the two countries (Freizer, 2009).

Governance

Once the decision was made to attempt to change football in line with the values of New Turkey, the big question facing Erdogan and his party, the AK Party, was one of governance. How exactly should the AK Party govern any relationship between themselves and football clubs to achieve the objective of having successful clubs aligning with the values of New Turkey? As with any interorganizational governance decision, the choices are on a continuum from market-based governance to bilateral governance to vertical integration (Williamson, 1973; Williamson, 1985). These can be thought of as degrees of closeness or integration between the AK Party and the football club. Broadly speaking, a market-based governance solution would be to wait for the clubs (particularly the big three) to adapt to the values of New Turkey or find ways to incentivize such an evolution.

A bilateral governance solution would involve actively pairing up with some of the leading clubs through some form of joint management or ownership[1] structure. This could take the form of leading AK Party-affiliated businesspeople becoming directors of the big three Istanbul clubs. Finally, the vertical integration solution would be for the AK Party to set up its own football club.

Transaction cost economics (TCE) (Williamson, 1973, 1985) talks to how organizations should govern these relationships given the type and levels of investment required and levels of uncertainty (Rindfleisch and Heide, 1997). TCE outlines three governance problems: the safeguarding problem, the adaptation problem, and the performance evaluation problem. I do not have the space to go into each of these problems in detail here, but suffice to say that in this context the AK Party was faced with both an adaptation problem and a performance evaluation problem. An adaptation problem that existed because of high levels of unpredictability in the environment. This unpredictability stems from not knowing how a team will perform, to not knowing how fans will respond, etc. While a performance evaluation problem exists because it is difficult for the AK Party to assess the performance of the football club it intends to partner with, particularly given the ownership and membership structure of these clubs and the fact that members for the most part may not support the AK Party and its vision of a New Turkey. Proponents of TCE state that when there are adaptation problems and performance evaluation problems then the solution is vertical integration (e.g., Anderson, 1985; Williamson, 1998).

Erdogan's Attempts Pre-2013: A Market-Based Governance Solution

Erdogan's initial attempts centred around the big three Istanbul clubs that were already dominant. He made various attempts to align with these clubs and control them through a series of different measures. His AK Party government passed a bill in 2011 (Law No. 6222) that brought in harsh penalties for crowd violence, and most importantly put match fixing into the realm of public prosecutors (Irak, 2020). This allowed for the public prosecutor to open a match fixing case in July 2011 directed against the major clubs and which led to the arrest and jailing of then Fenerbahce Chairman, Aziz Yildirim. This court case collapsed partly due to pressure and the protests of Fenerbahce fans and partly due to the falling out between the Gulen Movement and the AK Party (ibid.).[2] That said, it left a bitter taste in Fenerbahce fans' mouths towards the government. Furthermore, in May 2013, Besiktas fans fought with the police and tensions were rising. Finally, on 27 May 2013, the Gezi Park protests began, growing from an environmental protest in a fairly nondescript park in central Istanbul to a nationwide protest against the government. Many groups were involved in the protests (McGarry et al., 2019), but some of the most active were football fans, including the Ultras of Besiktas, Fenerbahce, and Galatasaray. In particular, a leading role was played by the Besiktas Ultras group, Carsi, partly down to the fact they were "battle hardened" when it came to confronting the police and also down to their roots as an organization that wanted to combat injustice (Turan and Ozcetin, 2019). The actions of the ultras at Gezi Park were likely the final nail in the coffin of any attempt by the AK Party and Tayyip Erdogan to leave the governance to the market. It was clear that any attempt to incentivize the clubs to adapt to the values of New Turkey was futile and the market-based governance solution had failed. This is no surprise, given that TCE predicts that high levels of uncertainty require high levels of control that were not afforded by the AK Party and Erdogan's actions pre-2013.

Erdogan's Attempts Post-2013: A Vertical Integration Governance Solution

The failure to get the big three Istanbul clubs on board led Erdogan in search of a Plan B, and he found it in the name of Istanbul Buyuksehir Belediyesi. This club was founded in 1990 by the then Social Democratic mayor of Istanbul, Nurettin Sozen. The club, for the most part, played in the second tier of Turkish football but had some success on being promoted to the top tier. In 2014 the club was sold to a group of businessmen close to the AK Party and Recep Tayyip Erdogan (Wilks, 2019). These businessmen included Goksel Gumusdag (AK Party Istanbul city councillor and the son-in-law of Erdogan's wife's brother) and Ahmet Ketenci (brother of one of Erdogan's son's wives). The club changed its name to Basaksehir Football Club and from that season onward showed a remarkable consistency of high-level performance, finishing fourth in 2014–15 and 2015–16, third in 2017–18, second in 2016–17 and 2018–19, and winning the title in 2019–20. In that time, the club was able to purchase players such as Emmanuel Adebayor, Demba Ba, Emre Belozoglu, Gael Clichy, and other top names. The money for these signings did not come from tickets sold as the club at best averages just over 5,000 spectators per game (Irak, 2020) and instead likely came from sponsorship from companies that are close to the government (Wilks, 2019). While it is difficult to know exactly how the club is being financed, it is clear that the club is an AK Party or, more specifically, a Tayyip Erdogan project. As Tayyip Erdogan himself said in an interview on the national broadcaster TRT in 2019 in response to how well Basaksehir were doing, "I'm very proud of Basaksehir because Basaksehir is the club I founded."

So, did this vertically integrated solution create the football club of New Turkey? It is a difficult question to answer. On the one hand, it is impossible to argue with the success the club has had on the pitch. When we consider that this AK Party project really only began in 2014, to become champion within six years and to be in the top four every year before becoming champion is an incredible feat. However, this success on the pitch has not been replicated off the pitch. It is still the big three clubs that have the huge fan bases and crowds at their games. It is still the big three Istanbul clubs that are known throughout Europe.

The Attempted Reshaping of the Turkish Football **207**

Besiktas, Fenerbahce, and Galatasaray may no longer have a monopoly on success, but they still represent Turkish football, and they still do not represent the values of New Turkey.

2021–22 and the Future

This then brings us up to 2021–22, where yet again the big Istanbul clubs have failed to win the league and have had an atrocious season for the most part. It was a particularly bad season for Galatasaray, who finished 16th, and Besiktas, who finished 6th. Fenerbahce managed to finish 2nd and Basaksehir once again finished 4th. The champion? Finally, after all these years, Trabzonspor became champion. Trabzonspor is the team from Trabzon, an AK Party and Tayyip Erdogan stronghold known for its nationalism and religious conservatism (Bozok, 2012), two of the values underlying Tayyip Erdogan's idea of New Turkey. Tayyip Erdogan's family moved to Istanbul from Rize, a town only one hour by car from Trabzon. Furthermore, one of Trabzonspor's best known supporters is Berat Albayrak (Idil, 2020), ex-Minister of Finance and Treasury for the AK Party government and son-in-law of Tayyip Erdogan. Maybe a bilateral governance involving Trabzonspor would have been the most fruitful avenue for the AK Party and Tayyip Erdogan to follow.

Conclusion

As part of his project to develop a New Turkey, Tayyip Erdogan also wanted to transform the footballing landscape. Given the uncertainty in the market and the behavioural uncertainty regarding football teams and their supporters, the theoretical predictions of transaction cost economics tell us that the best way to do this would be for the AK Party to have their own football team. Initially Erdogan and the AK Party tried a market governance solution, but by 2013 it was clear that this was not working. In 2014, they moved on to a vertically integrated solution that involved businessmen close to Erdogan and his party buying Basaksehir and using creative funding from sponsors and elsewhere to build a team capable of winning the Super League in 2019–20. However, it seems that this project was only partially successful and did not have the desired effect off the pitch of changing the Turkish football culture. However, with the victory of Trabzonspor in 2021–22 and the closeness of Erdogan's son-in-law to the club we may be observing a third way. Not a market solution, not a vertically integrated solution, but some sort of bilateral governance solution whereby there is an alliance between Erdogan's family and Trabzonspor. Trabzonspor could be the football club that symbolizes Erdogan's New Turkey.

If Trabzonspor is to be the flagship football club symbolizing a New Turkey, then to be useful to Erdogan and the AK Party it must be able to symbolize this both domestically and internationally. Domestically, this seems possible as it is a club capable of high performance on the field coupled with a strong

208 Steven H. Seggie

football culture off the field. Since Trabzon is in Anatolia, Trabzonspor can position itself as the club of the Anatolian people rather than of the Istanbul elites. However, internationally it is a bit more difficult as the sine qua non is for Trabzonspor to be successful in European competition, which has eluded them thus far. In fact, this season (2022–23) they were unable to reach the group stages of the Champions League, having been knocked out by FC Copenhagen in the qualifying round and dropping down to the Europa League. Without success on the European stage, Trabzonspor will not be able to play its required role of demonstrating the strength of New Turkey through success in the international sporting arena. Erdogan's attempts to use football as a tool of international propaganda for New Turkey have so far fallen short, and given that he is up for re-election in 2023, it is possible that time is running out and in this project he has ultimately failed.

Notes

1 Besiktas, Fenerbahce, and Galatasaray are run as associations with one member one vote and different ways for individuals to become members. The members then elect the directors of the club. As such, directors of the club are not owners in the sense that they would be in the UK for example. A detailed description of the structures and the challenges can be found in Guney (2017).
2 Please see Yavuz (2018) and Martin (2022) for a detailed discussion of the relationship between the Gulen Movement and the AK Party. Both of these authors explain in some detail how they become first allies and then bitter enemies.

References

Ambille, I., 2021. 'Turkish super lig champions' *Interesting Football*, 10 May. Available at: https://interestingfootball.com/turkish-super-lig-champions-list-of-turkish-league -winners-history/ (accessed 18 June 2022).
Anderson, E., 1985. The salesperson as outside agent or employee: A transaction cost analysis. *Marketing Science*, *4*(3), pp. 234–254.
Bozok, M., 2012. *Constructing local masculinities: A case study from Trabzon, Turkey*, Unpublished Doctoral Dissertation, Institute of Social Sciences, Middle East Technical University, Ankara, Turkey.
Burak, B., 2011. The role of the military in Turkish politics: To guard whom and from what?. *European Journal of Economic and Political Studies*, *4*(1), pp. 143–169.
Ege, 2021. 'Erdogan: Babam onumu kesmese futbolcu olacaktim' *A3Haber*, 28 November. Available at: https://www.a3haber.com/2021/11/28/erdogan-babam-onumu -kesmese-futbolcu-olacaktim/ (accessed 4 June 2022).
Freizer, S., 2009. 'Football diplomacy' *International Crisis Group*, 15 October. Available at: https://www.crisisgroup.org/europe-central-asia/western-europemediterranean/ turkey/football-diplomacy (accessed 27 September 2022).
Güney, E., 2017. Supporter ownership in Turkish football. In *Football and supporter activism in Europe* (pp. 257–276). Cham: Palgrave Macmillan.
Idil, N., 2020. 'Politics in stadiums: Fenerbahce fans urge minister Albayrak to keep hands off football' *Duvar English*, 10 February. Available at: https://www.duvarenglish.com

/sport/2020/02/10/politics-in-stadiums-fenerbahce-fans-urge-minister-albayrak-to-keep-hands-off-football (accessed 18 June 2022).

Irak, D., 2020. Football in Turkey during the Erdoğan regime. *Soccer & Society*, *21*(6), pp. 680–691.

Keyman, E., 2014. The AK party: Dominant party, new Turkey and polarization. *Insight Turkey*, *16*(2), pp. 19–31.

Martin, N., 2022. Allies and enemies: The Gülen movement and the AKP. *Cambridge Review of International Affairs*, *35*(1), pp. 110–127.

McGarry, A., Jenzen, O., Eslen-Ziya, H., Erhart, I. and Korkut, U., 2019. Beyond the iconic protest images: The performance of 'everyday life' on social media during Gezi Park. *Social Movement Studies*, *18*(3), pp. 284–304.

Mertin, E., 2010. Participation is not enough. The Soviet Union in the Olympic Movement. *Cahiers de l'INSEP*, *46*(1), pp. 225–233.

Rindfleisch, A. and Heide, J.B., 1997. Transaction cost analysis: Past, present, and future applications. *Journal of Marketing*, *61*(4), pp. 30–54.

Secor, A.J., 2001. Ideologies in crisis: Political cleavages and electoral politics in Turkey in the 1990s. *Political Geography*, *20*(5), pp. 539–560.

Sozen, A., 2006. Terrorism and the politics of anti-terrorism in Turkey. *Nato Security through Science Series E Human and Societal Dynamics*, *14*, p. 131.

Turan, Ö. and Özçetin, B., 2019. Football fans and contentious politics: The role of Çarşı in the Gezi Park protests. *International Review for the Sociology of Sport*, *54*(2), pp. 199–217.

Turkey. Super Lig 1995/1996 Table. Available at: https://tribuna.com/en/league/tr-super-lig/table/1995-1996/ (accessed 15 June 2022).

Wilks, A., 2019. 'How a small Istanbul team with government links rose to challenge Turkey's football elite' *The National*, 13 March. Available at: https://www.thenationalnews.com/world/mena/how-a-small-istanbul-team-with-government-links-rose-to-challenge-turkey-s-football-elite-1.836402 (accessed 1 June 2022).

Williamson, O.E., 1973. Markets and hierarchies: Some elementary considerations. *The American Economic Review*, *63*(2), pp. 316–325.

Williamson, O.E., 1985. *The Economic Institutions of Capitalism: Firms, Markets, Relational Contracting*. New York: The Free Press.

Williamson, O.E., 1998. The institutions of governance. *The American Economic Review*, *88*(2), pp. 75–79.

Yavuz, M.H., 2018. A framework for understanding the intra-Islamist conflict between the AK party and the Gülen movement. *Politics, Religion & Ideology*, *19*(1), pp. 11–32.

25

FOOTBALL AND THE CITY

A Sports Place Branding Perspective of Barcelona and Manchester

Xavier Ginesta and Carles Viñas

Introduction

The link between sport and city brands goes back a long way. In Europe, football clubs have become actors in global corporate diplomacy that helps to position their home towns in the competitive international market of tourists, talent, and investors. The aim of this chapter is to analyze the city brand positioning of Barcelona and Manchester since they share a vector that unites them and forces them to constantly compare: their passion for football; and they host three of the top ten clubs in terms of market value in 2021, according to *Forbes*: the first, FC Barcelona ($4.76B); the fourth, Manchester United ($4.2B); and the sixth, Manchester City ($4B). For the past 16 years, Manchester United have been top of the list 11 times (Ozanian, 2021). In 2021, they were also three of the five highest-income clubs in post-COVID-19 Europe: Manchester City with €644.9M, FC Barcelona with €582.1M, and Manchester United with €558M (Jones et al., 2022).

Conceptual Bases of Place Branding

In today's world, cities need to position themselves internationally. That is why studies on place branding, cutting across the disciplines of geography, political science, and communication (Govers and Go, 2009; Anholt, 2010), help us to understand the global impact of clubs. Place brands are defined based on the influence they exert on people's perceptions. Obtaining a unique identity expressed through a brand offers recognition and differentiation to specific geographical areas, providing them with a positioning that is decisive in the choice preferences of users. In this context, cities yield the projection of their identity to

DOI: 10.4324/9781003348238-30

a new symbolic background that is managed, in part, through the transformation of places into brands (San Eugenio, 2011).

Places, in this global environment, have a growing need to establish their identities not only for economic needs (tourism, market doctrine, etc.) but also due to a new demand to strengthen identities in a global society. Some research (Govers and Go, 2009; Anholt, 2010; San Eugenio, 2011) shows that the logic of implementing place brands has followed, in most cases, processes that are practically identical to the creation of commercial brands, adopting as their own the marketing and communication techniques associated with it (San Eugenio, 2011, p. 732). However, the creation of place brands at every geographical scale (country, city, nation, region, destination, among others) must necessarily include elements that differ from those deployed in the corporate sphere due to two main reasons. First, the necessary reading of the brand creation process from a regional and environmentally sensitive perspective, that is, valuing the tangible and intangible assets of the place. And, second, the public interest that lies behind such initiatives, which clearly associates the creation of place brands with the political needs of the area (Rein and Shields, 2007).

Barcelona: Football after the Olympics

The City of Barcelona is still living from its 1992 Olympic success, which led to an unprecedented transformation: there were significant urbanistic changes that reshape the city, such as the two Ring Roads or the transformation of the maritime seafront that has been a key element to improve the Catalan tourist industry since 1992. At the economic level, in 2020 it was ranked, in the world, the seventh city in terms of foreign investment, the twentieth city in Europe in terms of tourists (7.1 million), and as one of the ten most creative and cultural cities of Europe. The socio-economic impact of hosting the Mobile World Congress (MWC) since 2006 should also be highlighted. And with regard to sports, between 2012 and 2020 it was always among the top ten most valued cities to host sporting events (Udina et al., 2020).

However, Barcelona today has transformed from being an "Olympic city" to a great "capital of football" as a result of the international success of FC Barcelona (between 2006 and 2015 the club won four European Cups) (Kuper, 2021). In 2006, in addition to securing its second Champions League title, it signed the first major global sponsorship agreement with UNICEF, an agreement that ended in 2022 when the club partnered with UNHCR. With its connection to the United Nations, FC Barcelona linked the main motto of its narrative ("More than a club") to the globalization of its football brand ("More than a club in the world"). Previously, in 2005, it also signed an agreement with the Catalan regional Government, to contribute to the international promotion of the brand "Catalonia". The agreement, which was last renewed in September 2021, associates the joint actions of the Catalan Agency of Tourism and the club with the following illustrative slogan: "If you love FC Barcelona, your destination is Catalonia".

The FC Barcelona Experience Tour competes head-to-head with the Dali Theatre-Museum in Figueres to be the most visited museum of Catalonia. Six percent of tourists who arrive in Barcelona admit to being mainly attracted by the international projection achieved by the club (Ginesta, 2022). According to data from the Barcelona City Council, in the five years prior to the COVID-19 pandemic, Camp Nou was the third most visited facility in the city (1,661,156 visitors), only surpassed by the Sagrada Família (4,717,796 visitors) and Park Güell (3,154,349 visitors), the great works of the modernist architect Antoni Gaudí. In economic terms, the activity of FC Barcelona represents 1.46% of the city's GDP and provides 19,451 jobs; in addition, the club's activities generate 1.4 million overnight stays a year and represent 19% of the direct added value of the city's accommodation, food, and drink, according to data from PricewaterhouseCoopers (PwC) (FC Barcelona, 2020; Ginesta, 2022).

Given how the city actively participates in international tourist circuits, the rise of sports tourism, and the impact of the capital of Catalonia as a *smart city*, in 2018 FC Barcelona and the World Tourism Organisation (UNWTO) presented the first edition of the UNWTO Sports Tourism Start-up Competition, an initiative designed to identify innovative projects with the potential to transform and revolutionize the sports tourism sector, which is supported by the Qatar National Tourism Council (QNTC). Furthermore, Leo Messi was appointed Ambassador for Responsible Tourism of the UNWTO. However, these are the only two actions that have resulted from this agreement between the club and the UNWTO.

All this explains how football is creating a "new geography" (Nogué and Romero, 2012); this is to say that football shapes how people conceptualize their symbolic appropriation of the territory. Football is a key element to define people's "sense of place" (Ginesta and San Eugenio, 2022). On the one hand, FC Barcelona opened its doors to the Emirate of Qatar in 2010 with the first sponsorship agreement with Qatar Sports Investments (QSI). And on the other, RCD Espanyol, the second football club in Barcelona, has become associated with the Chinese capital. When Rastar Group sought assets to invest in European football in 2016, Espanyol caught Chen Yansheng's attention for two reasons: it was located in a cosmopolitan city with an international reputation for tourists and investors; and because it was the direct rival of FC Barcelona. The brand "Barcelona" was key for the story that the new Chinese owners had to sell internationally (Ginesta, Sellas, and Canals, 2019).

In the case of Espanyol, the location of its stadium on the outskirts of the Catalan Capital – one of the largest tourist and airport hubs in Europe – has also enabled it to have the longest-term sponsorship contract (of all LaLiga) for a men's first team shirt: Riviera Maya, one of the world's largest sun and beach tourist destinations, has been part of the club's pool of sponsors since 2011, and the current contract runs until 2023.

Manchester: Football and Place Identity

Manchester, the cradle of the Industrial Revolution, is an example of how the intangibles surrounding sport can conceptualize the narrative of a city (Rein and Shields, 2007). This past of Manchester has been relegated, in international tourist circuits, by a discourse that identifies the city with, apart from music, the origin, evolution, commercialization, and mystique of football (James, 2019).

As reported by the *Manchester Evening News* (2018), the city's tourist circuits have three mandatory stops: the National Football Museum and the two stadiums of the Premier League: Old Trafford (located outside the city, in Greater Manchester) and the Etihad Stadium (located east of Manchester city centre). In 2018, Old Trafford and the National Football Museum were among the five most visited facilities per day. Compared to the previous year, tourists grew by 10% (from 1,191,000 to 1,319,000), while their expenditure contributed £670 million to the city (Cox and Ottewell, 2018). "Manchester is synonymous with football; it's written in our DNA", is openly displayed on the City Council's tourism website.

On the one hand, in the city centre the National Football Museum enables us to understand, from the codification of football at the end of the 19th century, the keys to the construction of the main British stadiums thanks to the ingenuity of the architect Archibald Leitch (1865–1939) at the beginning of the 20th century (with venues like White Hart Lane and Old Trafford), the phenomenon of hooliganism, and the impact of the Premier League. And because of their popularity, the major clubs are valuable assets not only for the campaigns of *city marketing* but also in geopolitics. Studies on public diplomacy must consider sport an object of study of the utmost importance (Chadwick, 2022). In this regard, the image of the Chinese leader Xi Jinping with the then Prime Minister David Cameron at the entrance of the National Football Museum of Manchester is fairly representative of the future of football business.

On the other hand, a visit to the stadiums of the two clubs helps us understand why the city can boast of being a first-class sports tourism destination. First of all, the route through Old Trafford enthrones the romanticism of this sport and its epic nature. Culturally, since its inception, the Newton Heath LYR (as Manchester United was originally called)

> represents a typical example of the way in which accelerating urbanisation and industrialisation processes contributed to the physical, spatial and temporal disciplining of the workers' leisure time at the end of the 1800s. There was thus a close connection between Manchester United, industrialisation and the working classes.
>
> *(Frank, 2013, p. 13)*

In a sporting context, the trainer Matt Busby revolutionized British football by making the *Busby Babes* the great football reference point of the time, while the

214 Xavier Ginesta and Carles Viñas

Munich Air Disaster of 1958 forged the founding myth of the glory of Manchester United (Andrews, 2004; Skinner, 2016). Secondly, the Etihad Stadium represents the opposite: the *disneyization* of football (Ginesta, 2022) through a fully experiential visit. To this must be added the evolution of British football towards the positional play system that Josep Guardiola made famous when he led FC Barcelona. After achieving a series of successes in domestic competitions since the Catalan manager signed for the *skyblue* team (2016), the club launched the slogan "We play beautiful football" as a new axis of positioning and corporate identity.

The case of Manchester City represents perfectly the transformation of a local club into an entertainment multinational. Anna Connell, the daughter of St. Mark's church vicar, founded a working men's club to keep West Gorton workers away from alcohol and violence. However, as James (2019, p. 110) explains, her influence on the club's sporting transformation has not been proven. What James (2019, p. 113) does acknowledge is that

> the growth of regular footballing activities in Gorton appears to have diverted attention from scuttling for some of the local population, demonstrating, perhaps for the first time in the region, how association football could be positive influence on the city's youths.

The club, founded around St. Mark's Church, is currently part of the City Football Group (CFG) holding company, which is owned by Abu Dhabi United Group (78%), China Media Capital (12%), and Silver Lake (10%), and in 2021 became the highest-grossing football club in the world (€644.9 million) (Jones et al., 2022, p. 10).

Final Remarks

The cities of Barcelona and Manchester are a good example of how football has become an element that inextricably shapes its city brand. Over time, their clubs have become an attraction for both visitors and investors. At the same time, they have become an economic driver for these cities, which have clearly benefitted from their activity, especially those that have repeatedly participated in European competitions.

Another factor to consider is how the ownership model of these clubs can end up strengthening the city brand. Although the study of the ownership models of FC Barcelona, RCD Espanyol, and the two Manchester clubs are not the subject of this study, we can question whether this might become a determining factor in this club–city relationship. In our case, while RCD Espanyol and the two Manchester clubs have the advantage of acting as business corporations (the first based in China, another in the United States, and the last one in Abu Dhabi), at FC Barcelona it is the members who have the final say in the club's strategic decision-making: for example, the endorsement of the agreement with

UNICEF mentioned above, the signing of new sponsors for the front of the shirt, the extension of Camp Nou, and its title rights. Therefore, as Ginesta and San Eugenio (2022) analyzed in a previous research having Girona FC as a study object – the club belongs to City Football Group – when a new corporation buys a football club, it needs to deeply understand how fans structure their sense of place in order to engage with local communities.

Finally, and as an element of future analysis, we believe it is of interest to reflect on how geography affects the impact of a city brand (Nogué and Romero, 2012). Following Marshall (2021) and his idea of how geography conditions the development of societies, we cannot ignore the fact that its geographical enclave has given Barcelona a natural competitive advantage that its rivals do not possess, and that the city began to successfully exploit from the 1992 Olympic Games onwards, which coincided with FC Barcelona winning its first European Cup. The construction of the Barcelona brand has been able to use this privileged location in the Mediterranean to position itself as one of the European cities with a greater international focus and projection (with tourists, congresses, trade fairs, and investment), which has allowed it not to depend exclusively on football to give international muscle to its brand, as occurs in Manchester where the local narrative has mythologized it.

References

Andrews, D.L. (ed.) (2004) *Manchester United. A thematic study.* London: Sage.
Anholt, S. (2010) *Places. Identity, image and reputation.* Hampshire: Palgrave-Macmillan.
Chadwick, S. (2022) 'From utilitarianism and neoclassical sport management to a new geopolitical economy of sport', *European Sport Management Quarterly.* First online publication. doi: 10.1080/16184742.2022.2032251
Cox, C. and Ottewell, D. (2018) 'More and more tourists are discovering how brilliant Manchester is with overseas visitors up by 10 per cent', *Manchester Evening News*, 25 July. Available at: https://www.manchestereveningnews.co.uk/news/greater-manchester -news/more-more-tourists-discovering-how-14948125 (Accessed: 17 April 2022).
FC Barcelona. (2020) *Impacte econòmic del Futbol Club Barcelona. Temporada 2018–2019.* Barcelona: FC Barcelona.
Frank, S. (2013) *Standing on the shoulders of giants. A cultural analysis of Manchester United.* London: Bloomsbury.
Ginesta, X., Sellas, T. and Canals, M. (2019) 'Chinese investments in Spanish Football: A case study of RCD Espanyol new management trends after rastar purchase', *Communication & Sport*, 7(6), pp. 752–770.
Ginesta, X. and San Eugenio, J. de. (2022) 'Football fans as place ambassadors: Analysing the interactions between Girona FC and its fan clubs after its purchase by city football group (CFG)', *Soccer & Society.* doi: 10.1080/14660970.2022.2069752
Ginesta, X. (2022). *Las multinacionales del entretenimiento. Fútbol, diplomacia, identidad y tecnología.* Barcelona: Editorial UOC.
Govers, R. and Go, F.M. (2009) *Place branding: Glocal, virtual and physical identities, constructed, imagined and experienced.* Hampshire: Palgrave Macmillan.
James, G. (2019) *The emerging of footballing cultures. Manchester, 1840–1919.* Manchester: Manchester University Press.

Jones, D., et al. (2022) *Restart*. Football Money League. Manchester: Deloitte.

Kuper, S. (2021) *Barça. The inside story of the world's greatest football club*. London: Octopus books.

Marshall, T. (2021). *The power of geography: Ten maps that reveals the future of our world*. London: Elliott & Thompson Limited.

Nogué, J. and Romero, J. (eds.) (2012) *Las otras geografías*. València: Tirant Humanidades.

Ozanian, M. (2021) 'The world's most valuable soccer teams: Barcelona edges real madrid to land at no.1 for first tim', *Forbes*, 12 April. Available at: https://www.forbes.com/sites/mikeozanian/2021/04/12/the-worlds-most-valuable-soccer-teams-barcelona-on-top-at-48-billion/?sh=d3ae67416ac5 (Accessed: 23 April 2022).

Rein, I. and Shields, B. (2007) 'Place branding sports: Strategies for differentiating emerging, transitional, negatively viewed and newly industrialised nations', *Place Branding and Public Diplomacy*, 3(1), pp. 73–85.

San Eugenio, J. (2011) *La transformació de territoris en marques: El reconeixement i la diferenciació d'identitats espacials en temps postmoderns. Un estat de la qüestió*. PhD thesis. Universitat Pompeu Fabra.

Skinner, R. (2016) *The Busby Babes*. Romsey: Urbane Publications.

Udina, T., et al. (2020) *Observatori Barcelona 2020*. Barcelona: Ajuntament de Barcelona, Cambra de Comerç de Barcelona.

26

THE EUROPEAN SUPER LEAGUE AND FOOTBALL'S PRIVATIZATION

Alexey Kirichek

In April 2021, the football world was shocked by a large-scale scandal. Twelve of the most titled and honoured European football clubs announced that they would be quitting the UEFA competition system and decided to create an elite tournament for 20 teams, named European Super League. They believed privatization would bring them more money than being part of the UEFA Champions League. At the same time, they hoped to play in the Super League while remaining within the system of domestic championships regulated by National Football Federations. The clubs that remained onboard were promised uncapped solidarity payments of €10 billion for 23 years, which, in their opinion, was much more than the regular revenues from UEFA. However, within days some of the clubs withdrew from the Super League, and many questions still remain unanswered (Brannagan et al., 2021; Wagner et al., 2021).

Privatization of Professional Sports in the World

The entertainment world is ruled by giant media corporations that create amazing spectacles to satisfy audiences. OTT companies (like Amazon Prime, Netflix, HBO, Disney) are gradually becoming global media corporations. In search of new content and social media, these companies began acquiring the rights to sports spectacles. For example, in 2018, Facebook bought some of the Asian broadcasting rights to the Spanish La Liga tournament, and the rights to broadcast matches of the English Premier League in Cambodia, Vietnam, and Thailand for $66 million per year (Tran, 2018). In addition, Amazon acquired the broadcasting rights to some of the English Premier League matches for Amazon Prime subscribers. Beyond broadcast rights, Netflix produced sports documentaries such as "Formula 1: Drive to Survive", "First Team: Juventus", and "Sunderland 'Til I Die". From 2005 to 2007, FC Real Madrid participated in filming Disney's

DOI: 10.4324/9781003348238-31

"The Goal" series. The next step in creating content for streaming platform audiences is the exclusive broadcast of significant sports events. Until now these platforms broadcast such events as part of consortiums or purchased only a part of the packages. The desire to acquire exclusive rights and not share them with anyone else will influence the price setting in the sports broadcast market. The amount of cash on the balance sheets of companies engaged in the streaming business is substantial. For example, Apple has over $48 billion at the end of June 2022, and Amazon has over $60 billion at the end of June 2022. Many of these companies are based in the United States and have been involved in the subscription broadcast of U.S. sports. For example, starting from the 2022/2023 season, the National Football League (NFL) will earn more than $10 billion per season (80% more than the cost of the current contract) or €38 million per game (Belson et al. 2021). Amazon agreed to pay an additional $1 billion to get exclusive access to the part of the NFL match package in 2021 (Smith, 2022).

The privatization of sports by media corporations is not new. Since the late 1980s, global international media rights to the Olympic Games have been acquired by U.S. media corporations. These companies became significant partners when the President of the International Olympic Committee (IOC), Juan Antonio Samaranch, recognized substantial financial prospects from cooperation with U.S. media companies and completely changed the selling of IOC TV rights. The income of the IOC was $5.7 billion in the Olympic cycle of 2013–2016 and was dependent (by 40%) on a media contract with the NBC Universal company (IOC, 2022). These figures don't include the regional media rights that are acquired by the branches of U.S. media corporations. For example, the European broadcast rights belong to Eurosport (part of U.S. Discovery Communications). It should also be noted that half of the sponsors that provide the IOC with another 18% of income (or $1 billion) are U.S. companies (IOC, 2022). The IOC distributes 90% of its total income to the development of the Olympic Movement (IOC, 2022), and a significant part, 38% or almost $2 billion, is sent to the international federations and national Olympic committees. For example, 15 of the 28 international federations from The Association of Summer Olympic International Federations (ASOIF) have massive income from the IOC – about 35–96% of their budgets (Weinreich, 2020). Therefore, some of these international organizations are almost under complete control of the IOC via money from U.S. broadcasting corporations.

UEFA Champions League is a significant football competition's crown jewel of European sports. UEFA is responsible for organizing the Champions League and selling TV and sponsorship contracts. It distributes more than €2.0 billion (UEFA, 2021) between football clubs participating in the group stage through the current sporting model. However, this model has "reached its ceiling" if we compare the audience and their desire to pay for the product with U.S. money for NFL. Furthermore, sales of the group stage matches could no longer provide a high income since the groups' results and the playoff list can be predictable after the toss-up of groups. As a result, the gap between the teams ranked second and third in each group of the UEFA Champions League has significantly widened recently. The growth of the sport's imbalance between so-called rich clubs and the UEFA affected their ability to generate more income. "Rich" clubs had to play with teams from Azerbaijan, Kazakhstan, Belarus, Hungary, and other countries periodically. Teams from these countries couldn't provide the "rich" clubs with extra bonuses in the form of audiences, media, and money; they received only UEFA money for winning the games with teams from these "poor" countries. At the same time, Europe's biggest football teams are becoming trendy in the United States and are desirable for U.S. sports and media companies. Many of Europe's ageing stars have moved to the Major League Soccer (MLS) recently and significantly impacted MLS business. The U.S. sports market needs new content.

All of these issues were signs of a pre-revolutionary situation in European football, as it was still under the control of independent UEFA with relatively low income for main stars.

European Football: A Bastion of Solidarity and Oligarchic Competition

In the twenty-first century, football has taken tremendous steps towards commercialization and enrichment. The background for its rapid development was laid at the end of the twentieth century, when the UEFA, under pressure from "big clubs", completely changed the Champions League from a cup format to the current structure with a group stage. This was done with a bit of help from the President of AC Milan, Silvio Berlusconi, who, in the late 1980s, announced that he would organize other competitions if his club played only two matches in the European competitions in a season. Another factor that influenced European football was big money from TV contracts. It started with the English Premier League signing the first big contract with Sky TV. In 1992–1997, under the first contract, the League received only 0.6 million GBP from Sky for each match. But in 2016–2019, the amount was way more significant – 10.2 million GBP per match (Gibson, 2015). For the last 20 years, the elite championships of all European countries have constantly been growing by 8% annually until 2020. They started with €4.8 billion in 1999 and reached an astronomical €22.5–23 billion in 2019, over 10% of which is due to the UEFA competitions. However, there was also a significant stratification between "rich" and "poor" European football countries. Between 2009 and 2018, the share of the Big 5 countries in the total income increased from 69% to 75%, while the percentage of the 45 countries outside the Big 10 decreased from 16% to 12% (UEFA, 2019, 2020). European football remains one of the few global and popular sports managed by an international sports federation, not by the clubs themselves, as in the U.S. organizational sports model.

The football "ship" managed by the UEFA had to deal with icebergs periodically but bypassed them. For example, in 2000, "big clubs" attempted to destabilize the European competition system and quit it by organizing the G-14 group. This group was led by the President of Real Madrid, Florentino Perez, and planned to establish their own competitions. Finally, the reconciliation pact was signed between the G-14 and the UEFA. The result was the creation of the European Club Association (ECA), which became the labour union for all football clubs that represented their interests in negotiations with the UEFA. The ECA sought to balance UEFA, the big clubs, and the need to demonstrate solidarity among all European clubs by involving "small clubs" in decision-making. UEFA constantly looked for compromises for the benefit of the "rich" clubs but not the disadvantage of the "poor" ones. The Financial Fair Play rules in 2010 aimed to provide a sustainable balance for football development. Meanwhile, the "middle" and "poor" clubs were trying to live following these rules and control their costs, but the "rich" ones were looking for opportunities to bend the rules, including using financial injections made by the owners. As a result, the attempts of the UEFA to control their budgets failed and mainly led to fines and not more severe sanctions (e.g., ban from participation in the UEFA competitions). As a result, UEFA aimed to balance the growing demands of "rich" clubs and the necessity to ensure the long-term competitive development of European football and preserve solidarity with minors. However, "rich" clubs became giant corporations with turnovers of hundreds of millions of euros (the biggest is up to €1 billion), and they need more money. The current format of the Champions League has increasingly failed to satisfy the growing appetites of the "big clubs", from both the sports point of view and the media side. This is in spite of the founding clubs of the new Super League receiving more than €830 million (over 42% of the €1.98 billion in the 2018/2019 season of the Champions League) (UEFA, 2019). Their motivation can be interpreted as: UEFA, thank you very much for organizing the great competition, but we want further to privatize our media and global success in our favour, and we know how to earn more money.

In the last decade football clubs began to think not as digital companies, and the CEO of Real Madrid Jose Angel Sanchez has even said, "We a content producer" (Marcotti, 2015). Leading European clubs started to earn money outside home markets by offering their services and content worldwide – by opening offices in China, the United States, etc. In addition, they created their social media networks to connect with the audiences. Their desire to create content required investments in new football players, new media, and new projects outside the football field. All of this required new sources of income or investors. As the most popular sport on the planet, European football also didn't stand aside from the inflow of foreign investments. One of the first investors was the Russian businessman Roman Abramovich, who purchased FC Chelsea. There were no restrictions on foreign investments in the top five European football countries. Investments were welcomed. Gradually, many leading England and European clubs became the property of foreign investors from the United States, China, Thailand, etc. For example, Boris Johnson, who sharply opposed the creation of the Super League, seemed to ignore the fact that the top clubs in the Premier League are no longer English. However, further growth required new drivers.

"Poor" clubs received solidarity payments from participating in the preliminary rounds of European competitions or through various UEFA development programs. For nearly half of the elite divisions of the UEFA countries, a quarter of their revenue is generated by the earnings from the UEFA. For example, in 2019, the budget of all clubs in the Estonian Premier League was €9 million, 30% of which were connected with the UEFA. For the UEFA, solidarity is the foundation for a long-term and sustainable development of a system within which "small clubs" are given the role of suppliers of football talent and sparring partners for "big clubs" in exchange for loyalty, rewards, and the small chance to play in the Champions League. Every year "rich" clubs, like any big corporations, became more prosperous and looked for new sources to increase profit for their shareholders. However, at a particular development stage for any big business (and football is significant), the primary source of wealth is power and the ability to manage it in your own interests. Therefore, only the control from the "big clubs" over the selling system for commercial and TV rights of the UEFA Competitions could create new sources of income. The work for the new UEFA cycle starting from the 2024/2025 season began in 2019/2020 when UEFA began reforming its competition system. It opened its media contract and sales ledgers to the ECA elite clubs. Their representatives were allowed to work in various UEFA committees responsible for managing the competition system. However, the principle of solidarity and unity, which is fundamental in the UEFA value system, didn't imply betrayal.

Super League: The Revolution without Getting One's Hands Dirty

The Presidents of Real Madrid, Juventus, and their associates played a two-way game. On the one hand, through UEFA and ECA committees they advocated for reforms to the system of European competitions and the distribution of money within one football family. "Rich" clubs get more money, the "poor" ones get less money, and everybody is happy. On the other hand, they were seduced by the model that U.S.-based JP Morgan Chase invested in, with a one-time payment of €350 million to each club for participation in the Super League, and tried to create a new union of 12 apostles to get even more money for the exclusive content (Bassam, 2021). Events related to the Super League developed very rapidly. On Friday, 16 April 2020, the negotiations with the UEFA were over, but the Super League initiators didn't get what they required. So, on 18 April, the leaders of these 12 clubs announced the creation of the European Super League for 20 teams, posted relevant advertisements on their websites, and created a landing webpage.

These 12 apostles of the new faith, who decided to break the system, had a loyal audience; the number of their subscribers on social networks was comparable to the population of our planet. They could reach new sponsors who would have nothing to do with either FIFA or UEFA and whose primary business was most likely connected with the U.S., Asian, and Middle Eastern markets. They could sell their product to American viewers, who were willing to pay significant money compared to European ones for both quality streaming content and superstars. The only thing left for them was to solve the issue related to playing football weekly since their suspension was probable from national championships. The UEFA and FIFA would ban them from their competitions. The question also involved football players. Which of them would play, what would they require, etc.?

To succeed with the Super League project, these clubs needed to fully capture the global media agenda with their project and attract the audience's attention by offering a new football world order with benefits for all participants. However, the further actions of the "revolutionaries" didn't correspond to the precepts of Russian revolutionary Vladimir Lenin. He formulated perhaps one of the vital revolution principles, "War must be waged for real, or it must not be waged at all; there must be no something in between".

The Super League clubs didn't produce any content with their superstars to support their idea. Club managers didn't visit the TV to promote and negotiate TV contracts. None of the sponsors or broadcasters announced their cooperation with the Super League. The lawyers representing the revolutionaries didn't provide any legal comments on statements made by the UEFA, FIFA, and politicians about the inadmissibility of threats following the laws of the European Union. Most importantly, the clubs didn't offer a transparent solidarity system for more than 200 European clubs participating in the UEFA competitions yearly. They had only promised the amount of over €10 billion for 23 years for solidarity. UEFA currently distributes €237.5 million as solidarity payments to clubs (UEFA, 2021), understandably and transparently guaranteed, and for almost half of the UEFA countries, this money is nearly 25% of their total income. This revolution was also not supported by the masses. Football fans showed their solidarity with the current system, especially in England, and strongly opposed the idea of the Super League. Thus, as the revolutionary classicist Vladimir Lenin also wrote, the entire Super League "revolution was carried out in white gloves" (no one wanted to get their hands dirty), which means it was destined to fail from the beginning. In fact, the product called the Super League turned out to be a rebellion without a clear plan of actions.

Having received no support in Europe (media, fans, politicians, etc.) or from overseas, these 12 clubs didn't correctly assess the enemy represented by the UEFA. They seemed to forget the primary principle of the "poker theorem" formulated by David Sklansky and Mason Malmuth. "Every time you play a hand differently from the way you would have played it if you could see all your opponents' cards, they gain; and every time you play your hand the same way you would have played it if you could see all their cards, they lose" (Holodny, 2014). It is however possible that the Super League was motivated by the desire to reach a new level of relations with the UEFA. Immediately after the Super League was terminated, the UEFA announced changes to the format of European club competitions.

To Be Continued ...

It would seem that football, which is part of European culture, cut off the second attempt since the G-14 to privatize such an excellent game in the interests of capital. The UEFA punished the perpetrators with a required €15 million each investment in the grassroots game and 5% of their European revenues in the 2023/2024 season. It also includes a penalty of €100 million if they violate the agreement on non-participation in the competitions without approval by the UEFA (Grez, 2021).

The Super League exposed the edges of fair income distribution between the "rich" and the "poor" ones and revealed issues of social equality and unity within the UEFA football family. The attempt to transform the football industry in Europe will likely occur again because European football is a ready-made product (competitions, superstars, audience) for any media corporation. However, this product remains the last bastion managed by the international federation under solidarity principles. And currently, it's not under the control of politicians and global media corporations. The question of the privatization of European football in favour of the "rich" clubs and/or countries is a question of the price the capitalists are willing to pay. Therefore, the management of sports competitions in team sports will be carried out not by the international federations but in favour of media corporations, like in Formula 1, or by the clubs, like in the American Big Four leagues. Hence, the privatization of sports and football will continue.

References

Bassam, T. (2021), European Soccer Week | Part four: How likely is a breakaway super league? Available from: https://smartseries.sportspromedia.com/features/european-football-super-league-barcelona-jp-morgan-fifa [accessed 25 September 2022].

Belson, K. and Draper, K. (2021), N.F.L. signs media deals worth over $100 billion. Available from: https://www.nytimes.com/2021/03/18/sports/football/nfl-tv-contracts.html [accessed 25 September 2022].

Brannagan, P.M., Scelles, N., Valenti, M., Inoue, Y., Grix, J. and Perkin, S.J. (2021), The 2021 European Super League attempt: Motivation, outcome, and the future of football. *International Journal of Sport Policy and Politics*, 14, pp. 169–176. Available from: Taylor & Francis Online [accessed 25 March 2022].

Gibson, O. (2015), Sky and BT retain Premier League TV rights for record £5.14bn. Available from: https://www.theguardian.com/football/2015/feb/10/premier-league-tv-rights-sky-bt/ [accessed 25 September 2022].

Grez, M. (2021), UEFA forced to drop disciplinary proceedings against remaining Super League clubs. Available from: https://edition.cnn.com/2021/09/28/football/uefa

-drops-super-league-disciplinary-case-spt-intl/index.html [accessed 25 September 2022].

Holodny, E. (2014), This man dropped out of Wharton to become the world's authority on gambling. Available from: https://www.businessinsider.com/wharton-dropout -became-a-poker-star-2014-7 [accessed 25 September 2022].

International Olympic Committee. (2022), *Olympic marketing fact 2022 edition*. Lausanne: International Olympic Committee.

Marcotti, G. (2015), Will Real Madrid stop their showbiz approach to get team back on track? Available from: https://www.espn.com.sg/soccer/club/real-madrid/86/ blog/post/2448605/read-madrid-face-decision-on-carlo-ancelotti-stars [accessed 4 October 2022].

Smith, G. and Shaw, L. (2022), Amazon breaches TV's last stronghold with $13 billion bet on NFL. Available from: https://www.bnnbloomberg.ca/amazon-breaches-tv -s-last-stronghold-with-13-billion-bet-on-nfl-1.1816122 [accessed 25 September 2022].

Tran, K. (2018), Facebook just secured Premier League rights for the next four years. Available from: https://www.businessinsider.com/facebook-wins-premier-league -streaming-rights-2018-7 [accessed 25 September 2022].

Union of European Football Associations. (2021), Distribution to clubs from the 2021/22 UEFA Champions League. Nyon: Union of European Football Associations.

Union of European Football Associations. (2020), 2019 UEFA club licensing benchmarking report. Nyon: Union of European Football Associations.

Union of European Football Associations. (2019a), 2017 UEFA club licensing benchmarking report. Nyon: Union of European Football Associations.

Union of European Football Associations. (2019b), UEFA Champions League: Distribution to clubs 2018/19. Nyon: Union of European Football Associations.

Wagner, U., Storm, R. and Cortsen, K. (2021), Commercialization, governance problems and the future of European Football – Or why the European Super League is not a solution to the challenges facing football. *International Journal of Sport Communication*, 14 (3), pp. 321–333. Available from: https://ntnuopen.ntnu.no/ntnu-xmlui/bitstream /handle/11250/2825286/Wagner.pdf?sequence=4 [accessed 25 September 2022].

Weinreich, J. (2020), How dependent federations are on the revenues of the Olympic Games. Available from: https://www.jensweinreich.de/2020/04/03/exclusive-how -dependent-federations-are-on-the-revenues-of-the-olympic-games/ [accessed 25 September 2022].

PART VI

Motorsport

27

SPORT GOVERNANCE, GEOPOLITICAL CHANGE, AND ORGANIZATIONAL RESILIENCE

The Case of *Fédération Internationale de l'Automobile* (FIA)

Hans Erik Næss

Fédération Internationale de l'Automobile (FIA), the governing body of world motorsport, has since its organizational reshuffle in the early 1990s acquired a position in the global "zones of prestige" (Maguire, 2011) where sport, business, and politics mix (Næss, 2020). This position enables them to influence matters far beyond the racetrack. Organizationally, however, the FIA still has some challenges when it comes to integrating social responsibility commitments with its structural design. Unlike FIFA and the International Olympic Committee (IOC), which have established independent organs to advise on human rights policy, the FIA has embedded its social responsibility policy into its existing organizational chart. At the same time, being loyal to its neutral position as defined by FIA itself, politically sensitive situations have been dealt with on an ad hoc basis (Næss, 2020).

After the Russian invasion of Ukraine, there are many reasons to believe that such a strategy is no longer sustainable. Even though FIA – in contrast to most other sport governing bodies – allowed Russian athletes and teams to compete in motorsport under neutral colours, the long-term consequences of "breaking up with neutrality" are doomed to have a more profound impact than what can be justified with a continued ad hoc approach (Lindholm, 2022). Whereas some of this can be solved by granting greater responsibilities to the FIA Foundation, an independent entity created in 2001 in order to be the social conscience of the automotive world, it nevertheless solves only half of today's challenges because it does not influence the key stakeholders in *motorsport*. Apart from affecting competitors, races, and teams in World Rally Championship (WRC) and Formula 1 with ties to Russia, the FIA as a sport governing body must consider revising its organizational design to act credibly on political issues in the future.

In order to achieve this, "organizational resilience" is by many deemed as necessary, here defined as "the ability of an organization to anticipate, prepare

DOI: 10.4324/9781003348238-33

for, respond and adapt to incremental change and sudden disruptions in order to survive and prosper" (Denyer, 2017, p. 4). Hence, scenario thinking for leaders and organizations that experience "environmental jolts" (Meyer, 1982; Linnenluecke, 2017) is advocated as a relevant tool to improve this ability, according to Hillmann et al. (2018)

> In order to promote an organization's resilience, managers must be able to detect changes in the environment, deal with uncertainty and complexity, critically reflect on existing practices, think in alternative futures, and foster collective problem solving.
>
> *(p. 462)*

This chapter therefore uses the theoretical construct of "scenario praxis" (Ison, Grant, and Bawden, 2014). It refers to a theory-informed practice of "scenarioing" or the scenario planning process. To flesh out this construct this chapter will discuss two situations which FIA may find itself in where the degree of organizational resilience can be crucial to the result. Whereas not everything can be planned for, the aim of this chapter is nevertheless to provide input to the FIA on how to reduce maladaptive responses to governance challenges related to geopolitical shifts and politically sensitive situations, such as war.

Theoretical Framework

The concept of organizational resilience, defined in the introduction, is relevant in scenarioing the FIA's geopolitical role for three reasons. The first reason is the FIA's complex network of stakeholders. As the FIA has been evolving in terms of members, mandate, and responsibilities since the end of World War II, it is the level of stakeholder complexity that defines the FIA's response to issues related to them. The second reason is that organizations must innovate structurally to keep up with changing circumstances and internal desires for change. For SGBs like the FIA, this regards decision-making procedures at the General Assembly to the role of independent units like the Grand Prix Drivers Association (GPDA) or partnerships with the United Nations (UN). The third reason is unexpected situations affecting the FIA's role in geopolitical strides. Although the focus recently has been on the Formula 1 Grand Prix in Saudi Arabia and the Russian invasion of Ukraine, FIA has been involved in at least one geopolitical storm each decade since the FIA's restart as an organization in 1945 (Næss, 2020).

Being prepared for these situations, instead of treating them on a case-by-case basis, has the benefit of keeping the organizational momentum at times when the conditions normally force it to slow down. To address these issues before they become real, it is relevant to explore the notion of "scenario praxis", which is "regarded as a way of not trying to get the future right but avoiding getting it wrong" (Ison, Grant, and Bawden, 2014, p. 627). Scenarioing is basically a management exercise in how to frame a situation as "framing failure is a precursor to maladaptive responses because 'frames' are used by humans to negotiate the complexity of the world by determining what requires attention and what can be ignored" (Ison, Grant, and Bawden, 2014, p. 624). Consequently, the process of engaging in scenarioing is thus subject to "a complex set of framing conditions, and more-or-less conducive institutional settings may exist" (Ison, Grant, and Bawden, 2014, p. 629). Scenarioing therefore needs to be coupled with organizational characteristic and institutional context. As a non-governmental, member-based, non-profit organization, the FIA cannot draw upon the logic of a corporation or a humanitarian organization to face new geopolitical episodes. Scenarioing within the FIA must consider its own position in the institutional landscape.

Whereas I will return to two different scenarios below, there are in the literature on organizational resilience many bids on how to prepare for environmental jolts to the organization in general. One example is the conceptual integrative model of organizational resilience by Hillmann and Guenther (2021), which can be used as a point of departure for assessing the level and quality of organizational resilience in various fields. Their model refers to certain situations that jolt organizations, to which an interpretation of it is set in motion, resources are used, and capabilities assessed, before a response is implemented. Learning outcomes from this process are then used to improve the organization (Hillmann and Guenther, 2021, p. 32). In line with scenario thinking, and the literature on organizational resilience and crisis management, this process is possible to envision before it happens and then "test" various organizational setups to assess the most likely option to avoid getting it wrong. In what follows, this will be operationalized in by two brief scenarios constituting different kinds of potential "jolts" to the FIA.

Scenario 1: Internal Entrepreneurship

Many organizations change from within, and for sport it is notable that athlete activism has been on the rise since the early 2010s (Magrath, 2022), not just in terms of individual engagement, but also in the form of increasing collectivization and mobilization of athletes in "unions". Within the FIA this engagement has so far been mild-mannered and compliant with the mother ship. The exception is the work of seven-time world F1 champion (Sir) Lewis Hamilton, who has actively addressed the social responsibilities of motorsport (The Hamilton Commission, 2021). There is a likely chance that Hamilton expands his engagement against racial discrimination, leading to a demand for radical changes to the FIA's current structure and practice on diversity and inclusion issues as a whole. In this scenario the first question for the FIA, thinking along the lines of the model above, is: how should they respond?

For the sake of simplicity, we can imagine that FIA leaders would meet Hamilton's requests a) with a grand cheer, b) try to solve it diplomatically (by a sit-down with the President), c) leave it to the General Assembly, or d) simply

230 Hans Erik Næss

turn it down. The second aspect, thus, following Hillmann and Guenther (2021), would be what type of resources do they have, or want to use, for the chosen response. By keeping everything as is the FIA must adapt to the situation with the structural means at hand. Currently, there are few structural options within the FIA that Hamilton could exploit to rally his wish to make motorsport a more diverse community. There is no commission or procedure designed to cater to this kind of initiative within the FIA.

By having in place an apparatus to facilitate "institutional entrepreneurship", on the other hand, the FIA would cater to those who want to create a better fit between the organization's commitments and its institutional design and still "own" the process. According to Battilana, Leca, and Boxebaum (2009, p. 68), there are two relational conditions that must be in place for institutional entrepreneurs to arise: field characteristics and actors' social position. The former influence what is possible and the latter how it can be done. An actor who knows the inner workings of the FIA and understands the ramifications of social change upon the organization is well suited to become an institutional entrepreneur – but only if the FIA allows her to be one. To do so, the FIA could consider the findings from Spedale and Watson's (2014) study of an individual entrepreneur where the interaction between individual, society, and organization is key to understanding where emergence is possible:

> Institutional logics and individual actors' tensions constitute recurring interruptions in the stream of ongoing action that is society at large and, at an intermediate level, the business field (i.e. the distinctive field of dealmaking with resource-dependent constituencies).
>
> *(p. 771)*

The alternative to integrating possibilities for institutional entrepreneurship is to see Hamilton's campaign as a bump in the road for a car that is too low rather than developing a robust chassis, to speak in motorsport metaphors. Existing research on organizational response to social and political issues (Greening and Gray, 1994) however points to some paradoxical explanations of why organizations choose this path, where more resources are allocated to management but without structural change that potentially would reduce the need for resource transfer in the first place. The FIA hence need to consider that some managers also have an inadequate understanding of the causes of the situation or what it takes to innovate or prefer impression management techniques to communicate that change is not necessary.

Scenario 2: External Demands

In organizational research it is said that "the less vulnerable an organization think it is, the fewer crises it prepares for; as a result, the more vulnerable it becomes" (Mitroff et al., 1987, p. 285; cited in Greening and Gray, 1994, p. 489). This is crucial to acknowledge for SGBs. Due to cases of corruption and malpractice, the formerly unanimous support for the autonomy of SGBs is characterized by a drift towards a need for them to earn it more explicitly (Næss, 2020). For the FIA, which in contrast to most other global SGBs located in France, not Switzerland, the political and legal aspects of this claim can be exemplified in several ways. External factors which may affect FIA's vulnerability as an autonomous organization include the Duty of Vigilance Law from 2017 which marks the convergence between compliance and respect for human rights. Currently the law only regards organizations with more than 5000 employees, but it can also affect partners of smaller organizations (see Lavite, 2020). Consistent with scenario thinking, one can therefore address the contemporary role of the FIA in geopolitical strife by imagining the following situation: The French law on the contract of association of 1 July 1901, which governs French sport clubs, federations, and their decentralized bodies, is merged with the Duty of Vigilance Law. According to the law, FIA can be held responsible if "inappropriate or maintaining excessive risk created by the organization" occurs.

Combined with the increasing pressure by the actors mentioned above, autonomy and legitimacy as sport governing body may require the FIA to not only take on more responsibilities far beyond the racetrack but also redress its organizational capacity to do so. For example, the European Commission's Expert Group on sporting events underlined in 2016 that:

> it has to be recognised that the autonomy of sports bodies is only justified as long as it is combined with taking due responsibilities especially in relation with good governance and in particular democracy, human rights and labour law in their interaction with the public domain (such as most bidding entities).
>
> *(Expert Group on Good Governance, 2016, p. 4)*

So far, the FIA's response to this has been to include stakeholders on macro, meso, and local levels while addressing four pillars in its commitment to the future: Health and Safety; Environment; Diversity and Inclusion; and Community Development. Launched as the "Purpose Driven" campaign (FIA, 2021, https://purposedriven.fia.com/), stakeholder deliberation and activities include the UN, International Federation of Red Cross and Red Crescent Societies (IFRC), and the use of motorsport events to ease political tension. One example is the European Rally Championship Cyprus Rally in 2017. It was promoted by the FIA as an event bringing communities together through sport, as it crossed a UN-controlled buffer zone and afterwards hailed by the UN as "the most successful measure in the building of trust between the communities [of Nicosia] since 1974" (FIA, 2017).

On the one hand, FIA's engagement is laudable. The conflict between Turkish-occupied Northern Cyprus and the Greek Cypriots in the south, following the Turkish invasion in 1974, has become so vehement that the European

Union's strategy for peace talks has been dubbed "state avoidance" due to its fear of provoking each side (Kyris, 2020). Yet, the perils of engaging in issues like Northern Cyprus–Turkey conflict and promoting values that by no standard are universal – such as democracy, gender equality, and sustainable development goals – is that it ties the FIA to the mast. Similar to debates in humanitarian organizations on neutrality and complicity (see Næss, 2022), the FIA may face a situation where external demands for engagement in return for legitimacy can outstrip its own assessment of what they are willing to do because it has engaged in certain political issues. Said differently: if FIA engages in the Cyprus conflict, why not elsewhere? With increasing political tension related to events in terms of sport-washing, soft power strategies by authoritarian regimes, and the global media attention that comes with a Formula 1 Grand Prix, it is not utopian to foresee a stronger incentive by the French government on the FIA's geopolitical role. In fact, as French law "recognizes the promotion and development of sports as being in the public interest, the State and its bodies naturally play a major role in the organization of sports in France" (Verheyden, 2010, p. 25). If the Macron government reinforces a view on sport as a "total social fact" (*Fait social total*) (Pigeassou, 1997), where social justice in principle would overrule any economic incentive of hosting a Grand Prix in a wealthy state with appalling human rights records, the FIA might be left with much greater responsibilities than they origically aimed for.

Conclusion

To meet both scenarios discussed above resiliently requires structural and cultural changes within the FIA organization. The reason is that environmental "jolts" come in forms where it is not the jolts individually that are the challenge, but the organization's lack of basic adaptivity measures. For example, the FIA could consider a scenario where it defines its political engagement differently than on the basis of past neutrality principles. It is obviously possible to remain neutral but, as evidenced by another study (Næss, 2022), SGBs' existing neutrality stance is rather underdeveloped. This is particularly valid for the FIA's engagement in social issues which affect the geopolitical dynamic where motorsport events, projects, and collaborations are part of the picture – like with Russia, Cyprus, or Saudi Arabia.

As the question "resilience to what?" is central to the literature, it is moreover crucial to identify potential threats connected to the organization's own actions in order to develop resilient structures and procedures for coping with social issues. Rather than relying on campaigns alone, this scenario would include an organizational redesign which could be inspired by FIFA's way of carving out specific human rights principles. Its Human Rights Advisory Council, established in 2017, is an independent unit with a clear mandate and has since inception delivered five reports on how FIFA can integrate human rights responsibilities with its sporting and business activities. This Council moreover used a FIFA report by

John G. Ruggie (2020), the lead author of the United Nations Guiding Principles on Business and Human Rights (UNGPs), as a map to orient FIFA's new role in the geopolitical debate where human rights took central stage.

As the FIA operates by a different business model than FIFA and furthermore is unable to adopt the UNGPs "as is" due to FIA's status as a non-governmental and non-profit organization, it could use the lessons from these trends in human rights discourse and the geopolitics of sport to apply the following scenario: to establish on its own an independent body advising the General Assembly on FIA-related matters. This body would serve a particular function. Plans, strategies, and campaigns to improve the environment, reduce gender inequality and racial discrimination, and contribute to peace are in this context not merely add-ons to the FIA – they are, if organizationally embedded, the FIA's evidence of to what degree rhetoric and practice go hand in hand in terms of earning a legitimate "right to rule" on global motorsport and generating trust and accountability as a geopolitical actor.

References

Battilana, J., Leca, B., and Boxenbaum, E. (2009) 'How actors change institutions: Towards a theory of institutional entrepreneurship', *The Academy of Management Annals*, 3(1), pp. 65–107. https://doi.org/10.1080/19416520903053598

Denyer, D. (2017) *Organizational resilience: A summary of academic evidence, business insights and new thinking.* BSI and Cranfield School of Management. Available at https://www.cranfield.ac.uk/som/case-studies/organizational-resilience-a-summary-of-academic-evidence-business-insights-and-new-thinking (accessed: 7 September 2022).

Expert Group on Good Governance (2016) *Guiding principles relating to democracy, human rights and labour rights, in particular in the context of the awarding procedure of major sport events.* European Commission. Available at: https://s3-eu-west-1.amazonaws.com/fs.siteor.com/msport/files/DWM%20files/Grupy%20eksperckie/4__XG_GG_expert-group-major-sport-events_en.pdf?1480411153 (accessed: 7 September 2022).

FIA (2017) 'FIA ERC reaches mid-season at Cyprus Rally', *fia.com*, 12 June. Available at: https://www.fia.com/news/fia-erc-reaches-mid-season-cyprus-rally (accessed: 7 September 2022).

FIA (2021) *Committed to a better future.* Available at: https://www.fia.com/file/158426/download (accessed: 7 September 2022).

Greening, D.W., and Gray, B. (1994) 'Testing a model of organizational response to social and political issues', *Academy of Management Journal*, 37(3), pp. 467–498. https://doi.org/10.2307/256697

Hillmann, J., Duchek, S., Meyr, J., and Guenther, E. (2018) 'Educating future managers for developing resilient organizations: The role of scenario planning', *Journal of Management Education*, 42(4), pp. 461–495. https://doi.org/10.1177/1052562918766350

Hillmann, J., and Guenther, E. (2021) 'Organizational resilience: A valuable construct for management research?' *International Journal of Management Reviews*, 23(1), pp. 7–44. https://doi.org/10.1111/ijmr.12239

Ison, R., Grant, A., and Bawden, R. (2014) 'Scenario praxis for systemic governance: A critical framework', *Environment and Planning C: Government and Policy*, 32(4), pp. 623–640. https://doi.org/10.1068/c11327

Kyris, G. (2020) 'The European Union in Northern Cyprus: Conceptualising the avoidance of contested states', *Geopolitics*, 25(2), pp. 346–361, https://doi.org/10.1080/14650045.2018.1552945

Lavite, C. (2020) 'The French Loi de Vigilance: Prospects and limitations of a pioneer mandatory corporate due diligence', *Verfassungsblog: On Matters Constitutional*, 16 June. Available at https://verfassungsblog.de/the-french-loi-de-vigilance-prospects-and-limitations-of-a-pioneer-mandatory-corporate-due-diligence/ (accessed: 7 September 2022).

Lindholm, J. (2022) 'How Russia's invasion of Ukraine shook sports' foundation', *International Sports Law Journal*. https://doi.org/10.1007/s40318-022-00211-8

Linnenluecke, M.K. (2017) 'Resilience in business and management research: A review of influential publications and a research agenda', *International Journal of Management Reviews*, 19(1), pp. 4–30. https://doi.org/10.1111/ijmr.12076

Magrath, R. (Ed.) (2022) *Athlete activism. Contemporary perspectives*. London: Routledge.

Maguire, J.A. (2011) 'Power and global sport: Zones of prestige, emulation and resistance', *Sport in Society*, 14(7–8), pp. 1010–1026. https://doi.org/10.1080/17430437.2011.603555

Meyer, A.D. (1982) 'Adapting to environmental jolts', *Administrative Science Quarterly*, 27(4), pp. 515–537. https://doi.org/10.2307/2392528

Næss, H.E. (2020) *A history of organizational change. The case of Fédération Internationale de l'Automobile, 1946–2020*. Cham: Palgrave.

Næss, H.E. (2022) *The neutrality paradox in sport. Governance, politics and human rights after Ukraine*. Cham: Palgrave Pivot.

Pigeassou, C. (1997) 'Les éthiques dans le sport: voyage au cœur de l'altérité', *Corps et culture*, 2. https://doi.org/10.4000/corpsetculture.316

Ruggie, J.G. (2020) 'The social construction of the UN guiding principles on business and human rights', in Deva, S. and Birchall, D. (eds.), *Research handbook on human rights and business*. Cheltenham: Edward Elgar, pp. 63–86.

Spedale, S., and Watson, T.J. (2014) 'The emergence of entrepreneurial action: At the crossroads between institutional logics and individual life-orientation', *International Small Business Journal*, 32(7), pp. 759–776. https://doi.org/10.1177/0266242613480376

The Hamilton Commission (2021) *Accelerating change. Improving representation of Black people in UK motorsport*. Available at: https://static1.squarespace.com/static/5f29736c898 2c82f61df71e0/t/60edd33a6f118478735acbbc/1626198854176/THC+-+Accelerating +Change+-+July+2021.pdf (accessed: 7 September 2022).

Verheyden, D. (2010) 'The organization of sports in France', *The International Sports Law Journal*, 3–4, pp. 25–32. https://www.asser.nl/media/2069/islj_2010-1-2.pdf

28

THE GEOPOLITICS OF MONEY VERSUS MORALS

Location, Location, Location of the Formula 1 Race Calendar

Tim Dewhirst

Formula 1 auto-racing began in 1950, and initially it was principally a European series. Among seven races held during its inaugural season, six were situated in Europe, with the exception being one race at the famed Indianapolis speedway in the USA. Formula 1 has evolved, however, to offer broader reach relative to other motor-racing sports properties and thereby appeals to a comparatively international audience. In due course, races would be held in a broader range of countries, including a marked expansion of the racing calendar to four Gulf states as well as Asia. As discussed in this chapter, the evolving – and perpetually expanding – race locations of the Formula 1 calendar are apparently driven by a variety of factors, including the sports property's principal sponsors or partners, and new Formula 1 ownership (Liberty Media assumed a controlling interest in Formula 1 during 2017). Formula 1 was once largely European in scope but now represents a global entity. Today's sponsors and partners of Formula 1, consequently, tend to be notable multinational corporate brands, which are predictably global in ambition and those looking to expand internationally into new and emerging markets. Moreover, some key existing sponsorship partners of Formula 1, such as Aramco and Emirates, are state-owned, which is suggestive of "soft power" efforts to build political and marketable influence (Chadwick, Widdop, and Burton, 2022).

Early sponsorship, when the races were principally held in Europe, was largely from automobile manufacturers and related sectors such as engine, fuel, and tyre suppliers. Additional funding was provided by affluent individuals, such as Rob Walker, whose amassed wealth reflected the sales of Johnny Walker whisky (Jenkins, Pasternak, and West, 2016). At the turn of the century, Formula 1's reallocation of race locations was driven in part by establishing sites where activations could persist from tobacco sponsors. By 2000, tobacco companies collectively spent roughly $250 million each year towards Formula 1 teams (Grange,

DOI: 10.4324/9781003348238-34

2001), and accounted for more than 70% of sponsorship earnings among race team budgets (Brown and Williamson, 1999). With tobacco companies contributing most of the sponsorship revenue among racing team budgets – yet tobacco sponsorship becoming no longer allowable for several races held in Europe – Formula 1 sought to appease their key sponsors. Accordingly, new races were established in Bahrain, China, and Turkey, where regulations were less stringent regarding the promotion of tobacco products (Simpson, 2004).

Unsurprisingly, oil companies, functioning as fuel and lubricant suppliers, are also visible and prominent Formula 1 partners. Aramco – a Saudi Arabia-based (and state-owned) energy and chemicals company – serves as a notable example. The company proclaims to produce one in eight barrels of the global oil supply. The Formula 1 season calendar increasingly includes races in regions known for oil production. Saudi Arabia, for example, began hosting a Formula 1 race during the 2021 season, which generated heightened scrutiny (Richards, 2021a). Jamal Khashoggi – the *Washington Post* journalist – was murdered by agents with an apparent connection to Saudi Arabia's Crown Prince Mohammed bin Salman (Rachini, 2021). Canadian musician Justin Bieber performed during the inaugural Saudi Arabian Grand Prix despite advance pleas to reconsider and cancel (Associated Press, 2021; Friend, 2021). Saudi Arabia is the host for the second race of the 2022 and 2023 Formula 1 seasons.

Acknowledged as "sport washing", countries with documented human rights abuses commonly host or support high-profile sports properties to improve their image and reputation. Normally, participants of these sports properties are unlikely to bite the hand that feeds them, as observed with the newly minted LIV Golf, whose principal sponsor is the Public Investment Fund of Saudi Arabia. Nevertheless, the seven-time champion Lewis Hamilton has been outspoken about human rights issues where Formula 1 races are held. He wore a rainbow-adorned helmet for races in Qatar and Saudi Arabia to show support for the LGBTQ+ community while also directing attention to the repressive laws in these countries that make same-sex relations illegal (Richards, 2021b).

Formula 1 is staged as opulent and glamorous – and linked with elitism and excess in some circles (Nichols and Savage, 2017) – so upscale and high-status brands are drawn to strategically building associations with the sports property. Like Aramco, Emirates is identified among Formula 1's global (sponsorship) partners. Emirates, which exemplifies another state-owned company, is headquartered in the United Arab Emirates and positioned as the preferred airline for Formula 1 participants as well as for passengers seeking to attend races as a part of destination travel. Emirates, as an airline global partner, speaks to the shifting sites and regions where Formula 1 races are held. Meanwhile, the race car and uniform of the seven-time Formula 1 world champion Lewis Hamilton includes branding from The Ritz-Carlton. Marketing communication for the exclusive and high-status hotel brand highlights locations in Azerbaijan, Bahrain, Qatar, Saudi Arabia, and the United Arab Emirates, where Formula 1 races are held (e.g., the Doha hotel in Qatar is described as set on a private island, fashioning

The Geopolitics of Money Versus Morals **237**

a rich resort experience, and defining elegance). According to marketing documentation from the tobacco industry, made public from litigation, "Formula One is perceived as very glamorous and very exclusive" (Cleverly, 2001, p. 325003468). Formula 1 is seen as indicative of a "jet-setting lifestyle", wherein a wealthy person travels around the world frequently – from one glamorous and exotic place to another – and engages in activities that are inaccessible to ordinary people (Sturm, 2014).

China made its Formula 1 debut when Shanghai hosted a race in 2004. The Chinese Grand Prix was removed from the Formula 1 race calendar for the 2020, 2021, and 2022 seasons, however, due to the pandemic and China's stringent zero-COVID approach. Still, the Chinese Grand Prix's continuation is anticipated as Formula 1 has extended the contract for the race until 2025 (F1, 2021). Once the race does resume, expect reawakened discourse about geopolitical tensions pertaining to China. When China hosted the 2022 Winter Olympics in Beijing, several nation-states – including the USA, Britain, Canada, Australia, India, and Belgium – exercised a diplomatic boycott (Mather, 2022). While athletes from the respective countries participated, government officials or representatives did not attend. The diplomatic boycott was in response to China's human rights abuses and reflected that China has become increasingly isolated on the world stage. The country's actions towards its Uyghur minority are under scrutiny. Additionally, China's enforcement of national security law in Hong Kong violates a previous agreement with Britain. China has been engaged in a tense border dispute with India in the Himalayas. And China is in a territorial dispute concerning the South China Sea – an important shipping passage – with Australia, among other countries. Moreover, China and Canada had a particularly strained relationship once Huawei executive Meng Wanzhou was arrested in Canada at the request of the USA. Soon thereafter, China detained two Canadians, Michael Kovrig and Michael Spavor, for nearly three years in what was widely considered "hostage diplomacy". Tensions are also apparent regarding Taiwan and consideration of its independence versus a "One China" policy. The U.S. President Joe Biden has indicated that U.S. forces would defend Taiwan if invaded by China (Ni, 2022).

The Russian Grand Prix was added to the Formula 1 calendar in 2014, with the race being held in Sochi, which was the site of the 2014 Winter Olympics. The race was last held in 2021, as the 2022 race was cancelled in response to Russia's invasion of Ukraine. Formula 1's press release stated,

> Formula 1, the FIA [Fédération Internationale de l'Automobile, Formula 1's governing body], and the teams discussed the position of our sport, and the conclusion is, including the view of all relevant stakeholders, that it is impossible to hold the Russian Grand Prix in the current circumstances.

The same publicity statement also indicated, "The FIA Formula 1 World Championship visits countries all over the world with a positive vision to unite

238 Tim Dewhirst

people, bringing nations together". While the Russian Grand Prix was expected to relocate to St. Petersburg beginning in 2023, Formula 1 has terminated its contract with the race's promoter, thus Russia will not be hosting races in the foreseeable future (Edmondson, 2022).

Formula 1's position is largely consistent with sanctions announced in the general sports realm in the wake of Russia's invasion of Ukraine. Several notable Russian partnerships have been terminated. Most Russian sports teams can no longer compete internationally, evident by the country's suspension from qualifying matches for FIFA's 2022 World Cup in Qatar. Russian tennis players – including Daniil Medvedev and Andrey Rublev – were banned from competing at Wimbledon in 2022. Beyond cancellation of the Russian Grand Prix, the FIA also announced that Russian flags and the national anthem are banned from Formula 1. The implications of this position were quickly observable. A principal sponsor of the Haas race team was Uralkali, which is a Russian fertilizer company; despite the Haas race team being based in the USA, their race cars were to be adorned in the colours of the Russian flag. For the 2022 season, however, the Haas racing team was prompted to terminate its sponsorship with Uralkali – rebrand – and replace their Russian driver Nikita Mazepin, whose father owns Uralkali and is considered to have close ties with Vladimir Putin (Associated Press, 2022a).

As aforementioned, seven races were held during the inaugural season of Formula 1, yet the 2022 calendar initially featured an all-time high of 23 races (22 races after the cancellation of the Russian Grand Prix). The Miami Grand Prix debuted during the 2022 season, and the 2023 calendar now includes an additional race in Las Vegas; thus, there will be three races situated in the USA. Netflix has apparently played an important role in Formula 1's growing appeal among a U.S. fan base (Noble, 2021; Schoenfeld, 2022). ESPN's Formula 1 ratings have escalated since *Formula 1: Drive to Survive* debuted on Netflix in 2019. The documentary series produced by Netflix and Formula 1 offers a behind-the-scenes look at the races and drivers each season (Abbruzzese, 2021). Oracle and Red Bull, which struck a one-year sponsorship deal with Walmart in early 2021, exemplify recent Formula 1 partnerships primarily targeted towards the U.S. market (Baldwin, 2021; Yeomans, 2021).

Commercial agreements among the racing teams stipulated that the 2023 season would be capped at 24 races. Announcements about new race sites such as Las Vegas prompted speculation that one of the more established and existing sites might be dropped from the schedule. Markedly, the legendary Monaco and Belgium races entered discussion for discontinuation due to commercial reasons (Associated Press, 2022b; Cooper, 2022). These sites are not offering money that measures up to hosting races elsewhere, such as those recently added to the schedule from the Middle East region. Saudi Arabia, for example, pays $60 million per year as a hosting fee for its race. While the Monaco race has been on the schedule since Formula 1's inception in 1950 – and represents one of the sports property's more storied and glamorous races (Sturm, 2017)

– its hosting fee is minimal (purportedly about $15 million) compared to those races newly added (Smith, 2022). Ultimately, the Monaco and Belgium races still appear on the 2023 schedule, but the French Grand Prix has been dropped. Speculation remains, however, about the Belgium Grand Prix beyond 2023 and whether the race might be placed on a rotation schedule and held every other year (Associated Press, 2022c). Liberty Media purportedly seeks to eventually add a race in Africa too. The 24 races scheduled for the 2023 season represent a record number (Richards, 2022), with the opening race in Bahrain, three races situated in the USA (Austin, Las Vegas, and Miami), and the final race hosted by the United Arab Emirates (Abu Dhabi).

Progressively, race sites have moved from city streets to dedicated racing facilities. With escalating costs to host races, state governments have gradually taken the place of private investors as common promoters of Formula 1 races (Codling, 2017). In an era of mounting authoritarianism globally, Formula 1's expansion into new territories is prompting scrutiny. Moreover, some of Formula 1's recently adopted – yet prominent – sponsorship partners are state-owned and collect sizeable state subsidies. For state-owned companies, sometimes their aims can be largely non-commercial; in instances where said companies pay rights acquisitions that are considered above-market rates, questions will emerge about the intended purposes of sponsoring a sports property (Chadwick, 2022; Chadwick, Widdop, and Burton, 2022). A surge of popularity and interest in Formula 1 has been apparent recently, and an expanding race calendar – with races in added locations – is indicative of organizing bodies being responsive to increasing demand and further growing the sports property. Still, Liberty Media and Formula 1 face a dilemma regarding whether their values are being compromised in pursuit of financial interests. Evidently, determination of the Formula 1 race calendar is highly illustrative of the interplay between geography, politics, and economics.

References

Abbruzzese, J. (2021) Drive to thrive: Netflix's docuseries a boost for Formula 1. *NBC* (June 22). Available at: https://www.nbcnews.com/tech/tech-news/netflix-f1-espn-boost-tv-ratings-espn-rcna1237.

Associated Press (2021) Justin Bieber performs in Saudi Arabia despite calls for boycott over human rights. *CBC News* (December 6). Available at: https://www.cbc.ca/news/entertainment/justin-bieber-saudi-arabia-1.6275983.

Associated Press (2022a) Haas to run rebranded F1 cars and Fittipaldi at Bahrain test. *Sportsnet* (March 6). Available at: https://www.sportsnet.ca/auto-racing/article/haas-to-run-rebranded-f1-cars-and-fittipaldi-at-bahrain-test/.

Associated Press (2022b) Monaco's F1 future under scrutiny, drivers want it to stay. *Sportsnet* (May 28). Available at: https://www.sportsnet.ca/auto-racing/article/monacos-f1-future-under-scrutiny-drivers-want-it-to-stay/.

Associated Press (2022c) Belgian Grand Prix keeps its place on Formula 1's calendar for 2023. *The Globe and Mail* (August 28).

Baldwin, A. (2021) Motor racing-Oracle cloud partnership puts the wind in Red Bull's sails. *Reuters* (March 25). Available at: https://www.reuters.com/article/motor-f1-redbull-oracle-idUSL4N2LM46N.

Brown & Williamson (1999) Formula One sponsorship proposal. Note to the Chief Executive's Committee. Bates no. 323011267-323011282.

Chadwick, S. (2022) From utilitarianism and neoclassical sport management to a new geopolitical economy of sport. *European Sport Management Quarterly*, 22 (5), 685–704.

Chadwick, S., Widdop, P., and Burton, N. (2022) Soft power sports sponsorship – A social network analysis of a new sponsorship form. *Journal of Political Marketing*, 21 (2), 196–217.

Cleverly, S. (2001) 2001 Formula One program: Lucky Strike BAR Honda launch. British American Tobacco documentation. Bates no. 325003466–325003489.

Codling, S. (2017) *Speed read F1: The technology, rules, history and concepts key to the sport.* Beverly, MA: Motorbooks.

Cooper, A. (2022) Leclerc: "F1 without Monaco for me is not F1". *Autosport* (May 26). Available at: https://www.autosport.com/f1/news/leclerc-f1-without-monaco-for-me-is-not-f1/10311040/.

Edmondson, L. (2022) Formula One terminates Russian Grand Prix contract. *ESPN* (March 3). Available at: https://www.espn.com/f1/story/_/id/33411099/formula-one-terminates-russian-grand-prix-contract.

F1 (2021) F1 extends Chinese Grand Prix contract to 2025 [Formula 1 press release] (November 6). Available at: https://www.formula1.com/en/latest/article.f1-extends-chinese-grand-prix-contract-to-2025.3EWPSR02zKJ4ItdLHQtk8u.html.

Friend, D. (2021) Human rights group asks Justin Bieber to cancel Saudi Arabia concert. *CBC News* (November 10). Available at: https://www.cbc.ca/news/entertainment/justin-bieber-saudi-arabia-human-rights-foundation-1.6244845.

Grange, M. (2001) Win on Sunday . . .sell on Monday. *R.O.B. Magazine* (August), pp. 36–40.

Jenkins, M., Pasternak, K., and West, R. (2016) *Performance at the limit: Business lessons from Formula 1 motor racing.* 3rd edn. Cambridge: Cambridge University Press.

Mather, V. (2022) The diplomatic boycott of the Beijing Winter Olympics, explained. *The New York Times* (February 6).

Ni, V. (2022) Joe Biden again says US forces would defend Taiwan from Chinese attack. *The Guardian* (September 19).

Nichols, G., and Savage, M. (2017) A social analysis of an elite constellation: The case of Formula 1. *Theory, Culture & Society*, 34 (5–6), 201–225.

Noble, J. (2021) Why 'fighter jet' F1 is winning a new wave of sponsors. *Autosport* (April 8, 2021). Available at: https://www.motorsport.com/f1/news/fight-jet-new-wave-sponsors/6129935/.

Rachini, M. (2021) Saudi Arabia is using Justin Bieber, F1 event to 'whitewash' its human rights record: Human Rights Watch. *CBC Radio* (December 1).

Richards, G. (2021a) F1 under pressure to speak out against Saudi human right abuses. *The Guardian* (December 1).

Richards, G. (2021b) Lewis Hamilton condemns 'terrifying' LGBTQ+ laws before Saudi Arabian GP. *The Guardian* (December 2).

Richards, G. (2022) F1 hits the limit with record 24-race calendar unveiled for 2023 season. *The Guardian* (September 20).

Schoenfeld, B. (2022) 'Drive to survive' made Americans fall in love with Formula 1. *The New York Times* (July 14).

Simpson, D. (2004) Turkey: F1 keeps on coming. *Tobacco Control*, 13, 217–218.

Smith, L. (2022) The future of a storied race. *The New York Times* (May 27).

Sturm, D. (2014) A glamorous and high-tech global spectacle of speed: Formula One motor racing as mediated, global and corporate spectacle. In Dashper, K., Fletcher, T., and McCullough, N. (eds.) *Sports events, society and culture*. London: Routledge, pp. 68–82.

Sturm, D. (2017) The Monaco Grand Prix and Indianapolis 500: Projecting European glamour and global Americana. In Wenner, L.A., and Billings, A.C. (eds.) *Sport, media and mega-events*. New York: Routledge, pp. 170–184.

Yeomans, G. (2021) Red Bull F1 eyes US market with Walmart deal. *SportsPro* (March 15). Available at: https://www.sportspromedia.com/news/red-bull-f1-walmart-america-2021-formula-one/.

29

THE END OF OIL?

Formula One's Changing Face

Josh Rayman

"I smell burning – is it my car?" Max Verstappen (crash.net, 2022), during free practice for the 2022 Saudi Arabian Grand Prix on 25th March. Thick black smoke was visible from the missile strike at an Aramco oil depot nine miles from the Jeddah Corniche racing circuit with Yemen's Houthi rebels claiming responsibility, and the teams and drivers were uncertain about the safety of continuing the event (bbc.co.uk, 2022).

This controversy came at the end of a five-race sequence across the 2021/2022 seasons in the Middle East, visiting Qatar, Saudi Arabia, the UAE, Bahrain, and a second visit to Saudi Arabia. The Saudi race, new for 2021, had already drawn accusations of sportswashing (amnesty.org.uk, 2022). This was the longest series of geographically clustered races outside of Europe in the history of the Formula One calendar.

Facing calls to adapt to the changing world around it, how did the sport arrive at a point where its dependence on oil seems so entrenched?

Whilst motorsport was primarily associated with the tobacco industry, a relationship which stretches back to 1968 when Gold Leaf sponsored the Lotus F1 team, driver retainers were originally paid by oil companies (Grant-Brabham, 2008).

In 1967, Esso left, and the motorsport organizing body lifted restrictions on commercial sponsorship (Collings, 2001) which allowed more expansive uses of the cars as advertising billboards. At first this wasn't fully liberalized – the BBC insisted on sponsor stickers under 55 square inches, ensuring their cameras did not pick up the logos and broadcast product branding (Grant-Brabham & Britton, 2011).

Throughout the 1980s and 1990s, cigarette sponsorship was not uniform, and host countries worked to different rules – meaning F1 cars changed branding race-to-race.

DOI: 10.4324/9781003348238-35

The End of Oil? **243**

Additionally, drivers were sponsored separately from teams. This could be a cost-effective investment, Alain Prost being paid just $75,000 by Marlboro for personal sponsorship in 1984 (Hamilton, 2015). Sponsored drivers carried prominent branding on their helmets and race suits, meaning that the cigarette logos were ubiquitous in the series, appearing on drivers rather than teams, where the team did not receive sponsorship from a tobacco company.

The peak of the visual presence of tobacco brands was in the mid-1990s, with over 80% of the field carrying primary or secondary sponsorship from a tobacco company in 1996.

In the late 1990s the EU banned cigarette advertising, which was an issue for the sport as 30% of the track advertising and the teams' sponsorship income in 1997 was from a small cohort of tobacco companies (Bower, 2011).

There were carve-outs for Formula One, which persisted until the last major brand ceased visible marketing on the car – Marlboro/Philip Morris with Ferrari in 2007, carrying the Marlboro name only in Bahrain and China (grandprix.com, 2007).

In 2006, Bernie Ecclestone claimed the calendar shift was to appeal to markets that still allowed tobacco advertising:

> There's been this big push to keep races in which we can run with tobacco branding. According to the law in Italy, for example, we can run branded there – so it means that we keep two races. Same in Germany. So we've got races that maybe we wouldn't have had otherwise.
>
> *(Roebuck, 2015)*

This does not seem to square up with the financial reality on the ground, seen by the exodus of cigarette money before this, in accordance with the "International Tobacco Products Marketing Standards" agreement made in 2001 (grandprix.com, 2007). Rothmans left in 1999, following a merger with British American Tobacco; SEITA in 2000, leaving with Prost F1; BAT in 2005, after the sale of BAR to Honda; West and Benson & Hedges in 2005; Japan Tobacco in 2006 – leaving only Philip Morris by 2007 (Grant-Brabham, 2008).

Potentially, an explanation for the changing calendar can be found in the sport chasing hosting fees from far-flung locations. In the late 1990s, the holding company operating the commercial rights of Formula One passed through a series of owners. It started with Morgan Grenfell Private Equity in 1999 (atlasf1 .com, 1999). MGPE would also invest in the Arrows F1 team, holding a stake in the team through to its liquidation in 2002 (Allsop, 2002).

By 2004, a group of banks inherited the shares from an insolvent owner. They sued for greater control over the sport and then sold the interest to CVC (Sylt, 2015). This period coincided with a calendar expansion and escalating hosting fees – with deals being announced for races in UAE, India, Singapore, Korea, and Valencia in the 12 months after the CVC deal was finalized.

244 Josh Rayman

This period was delivering a return at the potential cost of the long-term stability of the sport, *"taking jam today, over the sport's future"* (Richards, 2018), and CVC extracted the greatest return out of any owner of the F1 commercial rights – estimated to be more than Bernie Ecclestone (Sylt, 2015).

This had consequences for the established calendar, with historic circuits considered the backbone of the series struggling with the cost. Silverstone was regularly considered at risk (Benson, 2003), despite hosting nearly continuously since 1950 and the fact that a majority of the competing teams were based close to the circuit.

Formula One has principally been a Europe-centric sport, with between one-third (2013) and two-thirds of the calendar (most of the 1990s) held within the continent. This unsurprisingly aligns with the teams, who are mostly based in the United Kingdom. With the exceptions of Alfa Romeo (Switzerland) and Ferrari and Alpha Tauri (Italy), modern Formula One is operated primarily from the English midlands, despite branding (Alpine) and ownership (Mercedes, Red Bull, Haas) from overseas (Asher, 2022).

However, with cigarette sponsorship bans in the European Union, and later the CVC acquisition, Formula One scrambled for money, expanding its calendar eastwards with a slew of additions – Malaysia (1999), Bahrain and China (2004), Turkey (2005), Singapore (De Cotta, 2007) and Valencia (2008), Korea (2010), and India (2011) pushing the Europe percentage from 68% to just 36% in 2013.

It spurred expensive state-backed projects that did not last long on the international stage. Turkey first exited the calendar in 2011 after six years. It returned, briefly, in the pandemic-affected seasons of 2020/2021 as a late-drafted replacement. Although it harboured hopes for a longer-term contract, it had fallen into disuse during the hiatus and was at one point leased to a car rental company for storage (pitpass.com, 2015).

India and Korea would exit the calendar quicker, only a couple of years after the inauguration – purpose-built new venues promising regeneration to their respective regions.

Indian interest emerged in 2004, and after discussions fell through in other regions, the Buddh International Circuit was announced in 2007. Built for the 2010 season (Spurgeon, 2012) and estimated to cost $400 million, the race was halted by a tax dispute only three years later (Kannan, 2013). The country did not hold another major international motorsport event for ten years, with Formula E scheduled to return in 2023, on a street circuit in Hyderabad (Sharma, 2022).

The Korea Auto Valley Operation signed in 2006 a four-year contract for a circuit based near Mokpo which was completed in 2009. It cost $264 million, was subsidized by public money, and was located on the remote southwestern coast. After Formula One left, the circuit was relegated to hosting mostly local and amateur racing, and no international series has visited since 2013 (Sang-Hun, 2015).

Valencia did not complete its first contract of seven years and paid around €300 million (including €100 million in circuit construction costs) for the five races between 2008 and 2012 (sports.in.msn.com, 2012) that were held at the "street" circuit. The site is tied up in legal battles and now houses a shanty town (Bono, 2021), having been abandoned for nearly a decade (Leslie, 2013).

The Malaysian Grand Prix was sponsored by the oil company Petronas, which had had an interest in Formula One stretching back to 1995 when it backed the Sauber F1 team (sauber-group.com, 2019), and continuing after the race with a visible investment in the dominant Mercedes F1 team, their cars carrying the oil brand during its title run from 2014 to 2021.

The Malaysian tourism board sponsored the Stewart F1 team between 1997 and 1999, in the run-up to its first race at the end of 1999. The circuit was a major infrastructure project under Mahathir Mohamad's government. It lasted longer than other races added in this period, exiting the calendar in 2017 (racingnews365.com, 2022), and continues to hold MotoGP races.

From 2009 onwards, a series of Organization of the Petroleum Exporting Countries (OPEC and OPEC+) countries were added to the calendar joining earlier entrant Bahrain – with UAE (2009), Russia (2014), Azerbaijan (2017), and Qatar and Saudi Arabia (2021).

Bahrain started construction in Sakhir in 2002, backed by the crown prince, costing $150 million to build (Wilkins, 2004). It competed with the UAE, Egypt, and Lebanon to host the race and has hosted every season since 2004, except in 2011 due to political unrest (Spurgeon, 2011).

Bahrain held a veto over further Middle East races having committed to the series early on (Baldwin, 2014), but this appears to have been lost or relinquished by the late 2010s with the addition of Qatar.

Abu Dhabi announced its Formula One race at a festival held in 2007, with its first race in 2009 (Joseph, 2007). In 2021, it signed a ten-year extension, with Etihad Airways as the principal sponsor. The circuit is state-owned and construction began in 2007 as part of a plan to turn Yas Island into a multi-purpose entertainment destination (news24.com, 2007).

The Russian Grand Prix was scheduled to move on from the Sochi circuit in 2023, built in the Winter Olympic Park; however, the ongoing conflict in Ukraine caused Formula One to terminate the contract (Benson, 2022).

In Baku, Formula One arrived in 2016 when the city hosted the European Grand Prix. It was renamed the Azerbaijan Grand Prix in 2017 and is scheduled to continue until at least 2024 on a street circuit that was announced in 2014 (formula1.com, 2014). The costs cited for this circuit ($7.9 million) are much lower than those for other street circuits, and the organizers claim the race is run for under $150 million (Alibayli, 2016).

Qatar, with an existing circuit in Losail built in 2004 for MotoGP had been vying for a race for many years. In 2021, it was added to the COVID-altered lineup, and it returns in 2023 with a ten-year contract. The circuit was built for $58 million and opened in 2004, with GP2 Asia in 2009 being the highest-level car race hosted until the 2021 Grand Prix (Tobin, 2021).

Saudi Arabia also joined the circus in 2021, hosting the race at a temporary street circuit whilst construction of a larger facility takes place, scheduled for 2025 (motorsportweek.com, 2022). The Saudi family's involvement in Formula One stretches back to the 1970s, with a race explored in 1975 (Bower, 2011) and its sponsorship of the Williams team between 1978 and 1984.

The Formula One race was announced in 2019, alongside hosting a round of Formula E in Riyadh and taking over the start of the Dakar Rally. In a brandstorming strategy that tracks its expansion in other sports in recent years, alongside the race, Saudi Aramco also took up a significant investment as a principal sponsor of the series, something that can deliver outsized returns in terms of sponsor perception (Grant-Brabham, 2008), at a cost of $450 million over 10 years (Harris, 2020). Additionally, it sponsors the Aston Martin Cognizant team (Mitchell, 2022) and holds an option to acquire a stake in the team in the future.

In 2016, Liberty Media bought a controlling interest in the Formula One Group. Its approach has been to expand the profile of street circuits in the sport – adding street races in Miami, Las Vegas, and Saudi Arabia; expanding online, esports, and social media presence; the Netflix *Drive to Survive* docuseries (tifosy .com, 2021).

During the pandemic, with Formula One gaining greater prominence due to the Netflix docuseries, Aramco accelerated quickly to a broad presence in the F1 paddock, taking up title sponsorship of three races and having trackside hoardings at most events (Harris, 2020), combined with the Aston Martin sponsorship and race in Jeddah.

As the sporting landscape evolves, starting to embrace electric and lower carbon approaches to moving sporting infrastructure from country to country, Formula One retains its 22-race calendar containing multiple long-haul trips. Changing this is something that is beginning to take traction inside F1 management, which has set itself a 2030 carbon-neutral commitment (Benson, 2019).

Compared to Extreme E, an international racing series which leaves six-week breaks between rounds to accommodate a ship moving the crews and equipment around, Formula One's hectic schedule is much more energy intensive. In the 2022 calendar, there is a single race trip to the USA for Miami (between the Australian and Spanish GPs) and back-to-back weekend racing in Baku and Montreal (5,500 miles apart) (formula1.com, 2022).

Several countries have contracts up for renewal in the next few years – France, Belgium, and Mexico in 2022; Japan, Austria, and the UK in 2024; China, Australia, Italy, the Netherlands, and Brazil in 2025 (Rencken & Janse, 2022) – and Liberty has added a third USA race in Las Vegas for 2023 with a three-year contract. This crowding of the schedule has prompted the idea of grouping races by regions and running different groups year to year, as several European races are geographically clustered together (Mitchell, 2022b).

Formula One expanded big in a period of economic instability. It lost the historically reliable source of income in tobacco advertising during unstable economic cycles. It found itself with the twin challenges of replacing that income, whilst striving to remain relevant in a world starting to reckon with the climate crisis.

Relying on state-backed races, an expensive and resource-intensive sport managed to bridge itself from its previous financial model of customer-facing advertising, using free-to-air television coverage to maximize exposure. The durability of this approach may have its limitations, demonstrated by the quick churn of events in the early 2010s. Escalating costs borne by the promoters and state backers has a finite timeline if the revenue promised does not follow.

Although the deck may have been stacked against promoters who were required to bear large costs without necessarily being able to achieve proportionate returns, it may also be that the economic model simply didn't allow promoters the time to build a receptive audience. This is reflected in a comment from Dr Walter Kafitz, former CEO of the Nurburgring circuit, who says "racing in countries without a motorsport tradition isn't sustainable" (Grant-Brabham, 2008).

References

Alibayli, V. (2016) *Baku's Formula One Race: Image Over Cost*. Available at: https:// eurasianet.org/bakus-formula-one-race-image-over-cost (Accessed: 2022/9/28)

Allsop, D. (2002) Debts push arrows to the edge. Available at: https://www.independent .co.uk/sport/motor-racing/debts-push-arrows-to-the-edge-182943.html (Accessed: 2022/6/30).

amnesty.org.uk (2022) Saudi Arabia: F1 Grand Prix must not be allowed to cover up kingdom's brutal human rights abuses. Available at: https://www.amnesty.org.uk/ press-releases/saudi-arabia-f1-grand-prix-must-not-be-allowed-cover-kingdoms -brutal-human-rights (Accessed: 2022/6/30).

Asher, R. (2022) Where are Formula 1 teams based? Mercedes, Ferrari, Red Bull and more. Available at: https://www.autosport.com/f1/news/where-are-f1-teams-based /10348715/ (Accessed: 2023/1/22)

atlasf1.com (1999) New era of arrows ownership. Available at: http://www.atlasf1.com/ news/1999/1053.htm (Accessed: 2022/6/30).

Baldwin, A. (2014) Bahrain can veto Qatar F1 race, says Ecclestone. Available at: https:// www.reuters.com/article/uk-motor-racing-ecclestone-bahrain-qatar-idUKKBN 0JP2EE20141211 (Accessed: 2022/6/30).

bbc.co.uk (2022) Saudi Arabian Grand Prix will go ahead after missile attack. Available at: https://www.bbc.co.uk/sport/formula1/60880598 (Accessed: 2022/6/30).

Benson, A. (2003) Silverstone row made simple. Available at: http://news.bbc.co.uk/ sport1/hi/motorsport/formula_one/3083233.stm (Accessed: 2022/6/30).

Benson, A. (2019) Formula 1 launches a plan to become carbon neutral by 2030. Available at: https://www.bbc.co.uk/sport/formula1/50382898 (Accessed: 2022/6/30).

Benson, A. (2022) Formula 1 terminates contract with Russian Grand Prix. Available at: https://www.bbc.co.uk/sport/formula1/60601632 (Accessed: 2022/6/30).

Bono, F. (2021) The shanty town on Valencia's abandoned Formula 1 circuit. Available at: https://english.elpais.com/society/2021-08-09/the-shanty-town-on-valencias -abandoned-formula-1-circuit.html (Accessed: 2022/6/30).

Bower, T. (2011) *No angel: The secret life of Bernie Ecclestone.* London: Faber and Faber.

Collings, T. (2001) *The Piranha Club: Power and influence in Formula One.* London: Virgin Books.

crash.net (2022) F1 Saudi Arabian GP: Huge fire breaks out in Jeddah ahead of race. Available at: https://www.crash.net/f1/news/999369/1/i-smell-burning-huge-fire-near-f1-saudi-arabia (Accessed: 2022/6/30).

De Cotta, I. (2007) F1 boss to discuss Singapore Grand Prix with Minister of State. Available at: https://archive.ph/20120729053543/http://www.channelnewsasia.com/stories/singaporelocalnews/view/263852/1/.html (Accessed: 2022/6/30).

formula1.com (2014) Azerbaijan layout unveiled for Baku European Grand Prix in 2016. Available at: https://www.formula1.com/en/latest/headlines/2014/10/Azerbaijan-layout-unveiled-for-Baku-European-Grand-Prix-in-2016.html (Accessed: 2022/9/28)

formula1.com (2022) F1 schedule 2022. Available at: https://www.formula1.com/en/racing/2022.html (Accessed: 2022/6/30).

grandprix.com (2007) Marlboro explains tobacco liveries. Available at: https://www.grandprix.com/ns/ns19038.html (Accessed: 2022/6/30).

Grant-Brabham, B. (2008) *An investigation into motorsport sponsorship: A comparative analysis of two and four wheeled sponsorship.* Bournemouth: University of Bournemouth.

Grant-Brabham, B. and Britton, J. (2011) Motor racing, tobacco company sponsorship, barcodes and alibi marketing. Available at: https://tobaccocontrol.bmj.com/content/21/6/529 (Accessed: 2022/6/30).

Hamilton, M. (2015) *Alain Prost.* London: Blink.

Harris, G. (2020) Aramco deal worth more than $450m to Formula 1. Available at: https://www.motorsportweek.com/2020/04/03/aramco-deal-worth-more-than-450m-to-formula-1/ (Accessed: 2022/6/30).

Joseph, N. (2007) Abu Dhabi event draws big crowd – Bernie wants more. Available at: https://www.autoblog.com/2007/02/06/abu-dhabi-event-draws-big-crowd-bernie-wants-more (Accessed: 2022/6/30).

Kannan, S. (2013) Why India's Formula 1 Grand Prix is under threat. Available at: https://www.bbc.co.uk/news/business-24659690 (Accessed: 2022/6/30).

Leslie, J. (2013) Meet the abandoned F1 track that was once an epic street circuit. Available at: https://www.carthrottle.com/post/meet-the-abandoned-f1-track-that-was-once-an-epic-street-circuit/ (Accessed: 2022/6/30).

Mitchell, S. (2022a) Aramco has option to own part of Aston Martin F1 team. Available at: https://the-race.com/formula-1/aramco-has-option-to-own-part-of-aston-martin-f1-team/ (Accessed: 2022/6/30).

Mitchell, S. (2022b) Which GPs are at risk as Vegas forces F1 calendar rotation? Available at: https://the-race.com/formula-1/which-gps-are-at-risk-as-vegas-forces-f1-calendar-rotation/ (Accessed: 2022/6/30).

motorsportweek.com (2022) Saudi says Qiddiya will have 'no restrictions' on ideas. Available at: https://www.motorsportweek.com/2022/03/22/saudi-says-qiddiya-will-have-no-restrictions-on-ideas/ (Accessed: 2022/6/30).

News24.com (2007) Abu Dhabi circuit under construction. Available at: https://www.news24.com/wheels/abu-dhabi-circuit-under-construction-20070718

pitpass.com (2015) Istanbul circuit to be "used car lot". Available at: https://www.pitpass.com/54537/Istanbul-circuit-to-be-used-car-lot (Accessed: 2022/6/30).

racingnews365.com (2022) Why the Malaysian Grand Prix isn't likely to return. Available at: https://racingnews365.com/sepang-ceo-cool-on-malaysian-gp-return (Accessed: 2022/6/30).

Rencken, D. and Janse, J. (2022) How much each circuit on the calendar pays F1. Available at: https://racingnews365.com/how-much-each-circuit-on-the-calendar-pays-to-formula-1 (Accessed: 2022/6/30).

Richards, G. (2018) CVC ownership of F1 should serve as a warning to Premiership Rugby. Available at: https://www.theguardian.com/sport/blog/2018/sep/10/cvc-ownership-f1-warning-premiership-rugby-union (Accessed: 2022/6/30).

Roebuck, N. (2015) Reflections with Nigel Roebuck. Available at: https://www.motorsportmagazine.com/archive/article/october-2015/17/reflections-nigel-roebuck-6 (Accessed: 2022/9/28)

Sang-Hun, C. (2015) A Korean auto-racing debacle, but hope around the bend. Available at: https://www.nytimes.com/2015/02/16/world/asia/a-korean-auto-racing-debacle-but-hope-around-the-bend.html (Accessed: 2022/6/30).

sauber-group.com (2019) History & heritage – Sauber Group. Available at: https://www.sauber-group.com/corporate/history/ (Accessed: 2022/6/30).

Sharma, Y. (2022) International motorsport makes its return to India as Formula E confirm Hyderabad as race venue. Available at: https://www.financialexpress.com/auto/electric-vehicles/international-motorsport-makes-its-return-to-india-as-formula-e-confirm-hyderabad-as-race-venue/2578358/ (Accessed: 2022/6/30).

sports.in.msn.com (2012) Valencia pays 2012 fee, Spain to alternate from 2013. Available at: https://web.archive.org/web/20140225181958/http://sports.in.msn.com/formulaone/article.aspx?cp-documentid=5913688 (Accessed: 2022/6/30).

Spurgeon, B. (2011) Bahrain Cancels Grand Prix Amid Political Unrest. Available at: https://www.nytimes.com/2011/02/22/sports/autoracing/22iht-PRIX22.html (Accessed 2022/9/28)

Spurgeon, B. (2012) How India made its Grand Prix dream come true. Available at: https://www.nytimes.com/2012/10/27/sports/autoracing/27iht-srf1prix27.html (Accessed: 2022/6/30).

Sylt, C., Morson, L. and Reid, C. (2015) Meet the biggest winner in the history of Formula One: CVC Capital Partners. Available at: https://www.theguardian.com/business/2015/jul/25/cvc-capital-partners-biggest-winner-history-formula-one (Accessed: 2022/6/30).

tifosy.com (2021) Formula 1: Liberated by liberty? Available at: https://www.tifosy.com/insights/formula-1-liberated-by-liberty-3476 (Accessed: 2022/6/30).

Tobin, D. (2021) F1 to hold first Qatar Grand Prix at Losail this November. Available at: https://www.motorsportmagazine.com/articles/single-seaters/f1/f1-to-hold-first-qatar-grand-prix-at-losail-this-november (Accessed: 2022/6/30).

Wilkins, R. (2004) Bahrain wins race against time. Available at: https://www.crash.net/f1/news/48157/1/bahrain-wins-race-against-time (Accessed 2022/6/30).

PART VII

Peace, Diplomacy, and Society

30

SPORT, GEO-POLITICS, AND THE PEACE PROCESS

Grant Jarvie

Sport has an opportunity to advance its case as an influencer of geo-politics and an enabler of peace processes. The scale, reach, and popularity of sport make it a useful contemporary tool in enabling human rights and advancing the common good. In a tense world there is a need for politically smarter ways of deepening commitments to peace processes and more effective cultural relations. This proposition builds upon suggestions made by Bell (2017), Pospisil (2016), and the British Academy (2017) that spaces are desperately needed to open the possibility of dialogue involving the interests of more than one group or one state or one community. In other words, actors are usually at the heart of national, international, and sub-national geo-politics. Such additional spaces could be provided through sport. If one accepts the observation that the international peacekeeping community is at a critical moment and that geo-politics cases are invariably complex and often require long-term approaches, then any resources and tools that can help to forge mutuality and trust should be considered as at least optional if not mandatory. Sport, it is argued here, is one such resource and tool.

In presenting such an argument, this chapter on sport, geo-politics, and the peace process is constructed around the following sub-themes: (i) sport, peace, and fragile contexts; (ii) sport, geo-politics, and fragile states; (iii) sport and human rights; (iv) sport, cultural relations, and peace; (v) sport and the common good before finishing with a set of concluding remarks.

Geo-Politics, Peace, and Fragile Contexts

At the time of writing the contemporary global picture remains a messy one. The international community is tense as a new state of geo-politics and fragility threatens stability, shifting world orders, and peacebuilding (Economy, 2022; Cooley and Nexon, 2022; Marc and Jones, 2021). During the Cold War,

DOI: 10.4324/9781003348238-37

254 Grant Jarvie

superpower competition turned civil wars into proxy wars. The post-Cold War era saw major investments in security, development, and political strategies to end civil wars and foster a relatively stable development – with mixed results, until the reversals of the Arab Spring. As fragility spread across the Middle East, that dynamic has brought in more influential, more capable regional actors such as Turkey, Saudi Arabia, Iran, and the United Arab Emirates. Russia and China have increased their engagement both at the global policy level and in specific fragile states. These countries, and the West, have all adopted different strategies and approaches based on their capabilities and strategic economic and security interests – often, in deep contradiction with one another. In the Indo-Pacific, Japan, Australia, and increasingly India are also playing an active role in fragile states, in part, to try to fence off China's ambitions (Economy, 2022; Marc and Jones, 2021). It would be a tragedy if the system for peacebuilding and the efforts to address the root causes of fragility between and within communities gave ground to a return to a full-throated proxy war (Marc and Jones, 2021).

With each challenge there is often a temptation to simplify matters, find a quick solution, and identify, often wrongly, aggressors, transgressors, and/or victims. But humanity, like power politics, is not that simple. Three recent UN reviews of the contemporary global peace-making architecture have described the current situation as being fractured (UN, 2015a, 2015b; United Nations General Assembly, 2015) and call for greater inclusiveness in the forging of social justice and peace. The issues to be confronted may be imposing in their scale, but they need to be faced with fortitude and with cooperative and collaborative spirit. They also need to acknowledge the full range of tools that peacekeepers and others have at their disposal.

Sport, Geo-Politics, and Fragile States

The real politic of sport in the third decade of the 21st century is that it is an invaluable tool for countries to deliver both sporting and non-sporting outcomes. Rather than complaining about the role of politics in sport, the different worlds of sport must live and work with the opportunities it opens up. The modern sports administrator, CEO, or chair of a governing body need to operate in the world of sport and in the world of geo-politics. The modern diplomat or foreign ambassador needs to fully grasp the capability of sport to deliver not just foreign policy but better cultural relations. Sport delivers on these fronts but rarely gets the credit and funding for doing so. So, this is not a question of keeping politics out of sport, you can't stop the politicization of sport, and why would you want to? What it is is a question of recognizing that the sports tool, the sports administrator, the coach, the sport for development officer need to be equipped to work within and with fragile states and communities to work with different stakeholders in the process of peacebuilding through sport.

Sport has always been political, and in being so, it has done many good things and some not-so-good things. The sports tool has helped to shed a light on many aspects of geo-political tension both between and within communities including, for example, the whereabouts of the Chinese tennis player Peng Shuai and the use of the athlete Catherine Freeman as a symbol of reconciliation between aboriginal and white Australia and a country which had much to forgive. In 2024 it will be 100 years since the Chinese-born Scottish athlete Eric Liddell won Olympic gold at the 1924 Paris Olympics. Another opportunity exists for sport to deliver a message and play its part in helping to forge a common good for a better world. When visiting Scotland in 2017 the then-Chinese Ambassador talked of the spirit and humanity of Eric Liddell, who interned in a concentration camp in Weifang in the 1940s where he continued to support children. The athlete's name and story have lived on, providing a bridge for potential cultural relations building, a sustainable space for countries to talk to one another. As the Ambassador observed, "We are living in a time of mutual learning for common progress". Modern sports leaders need to work with the geo-political spaces just as politicians and diplomats need to respect and recognize what sport does on and off-field. Darnell (2022) argued that what is required is organizations, policies, and leaders within sport to support, advocate for, and directly engage with the political struggle for peace and transitional justice. Sport as an enabler for peace should not transcend or sidestep geo-politics but rather engages fully.

It is not as if the role of sport in the peacekeeping process has not previously been commented upon (Armstrong, 2002; Cardenas, 2013, 2016, 2018; Clarke, Jones and Smith, 2021; Darnell, 2022; Gasser and Levinsen, 2004; Giullanotti, 2011; Laureus, 2021; Serena, 2009; Ubaidulloev, 2018; Woodhouse, 2010). Clarke, Smith, and Jones (2021) review of studies building peace through sport concluded that there is scope for more targeted studies to clarify specific demographics of involvement or an optimal timeframe for involvement. Many of the studies reference the importance of being part of broader initiatives, but the best context in which to utilize sport and how much of an impact is being made on the wider communities has yet to be conclusively determined. Cardenas (2016) drawing upon Galtung's (1996) classical three r's of peacebuilding (reconstruction, reconciliation, and rehabilitation) talks of (i) sports-based interventions supporting rehabilitation and healing through psychosocial support and treatment; (ii) sports interventions facilitating reconstruction and the building of relationships and strengthening inter- and intra-community ties as well as sports programmes aiding the process of reculturation through the establishment of sports tournaments and leagues based on accepted cultural regulations; and (iii) sports have been involved in the process of reconciliation at national, community, and individual levels.

Cardenas (2016) calls for a more inclusive definition of cultural expression, one that remains open to sport. Something that is crucial if cultural relations building through sport is going to be grasped as an intervention that both moves the discussion and practice of sport and peacebuilding beyond discussion of soft power, or sport for development or sports diplomacy or supporting fragile states. While the European National Institutes of Culture, including the British

256 Grant Jarvie

Council (EUNIC, 2021), have recently examined the link between culture and peacebuilding within and between fragile countries and regions they have failed to fully grasp let alone acknowledge the role of sport in enabling the five dimensions of state and inter-state fragility, identified by the OECD (2021), namely economic, environmental, political, security, and societal fragility.

Sport and Human Rights

A recent comprehensive systematic examination of political settlements and peacebuilding processes concluded that the human rights space is important. One that is key to the forging of long-term stability (https://peacerep.org/). The local context in which human rights are negotiated during conflict or peace-making is a vital space. A central problem with the orthodox construction of human rights is that visions of the state during periods of transition were often seen to serve the interests of only one group. The value of an alternative approach that allows for negotiated human rights and a negotiated common good is that it offers the possibility of a much more shared concept of the state and/or community; one that can serve a broader set of interests operating beyond that of the individual and a single-interest group. Long-term approaches to social change are necessary rather than short-term fixes. Post–peace agreement landscapes need to involve sustained movement away from conflict, and the implementation of human rights commitments in peace agreements is critical to holding open political space through which conflict resolution can continue to be negotiated between as wide a range of stakeholders as possible (British Academy, 2017, p. 58).

The value of recognizing an approach to human rights through sport is that it brings together such an approach together with a tool (sport) that has scale, connectivity, reach, flexibility, and resources. Marchesseault's (2016) analysis of the place of the bicycle and the cyclist in post-conflict Rwanda provides but one example of a study that evidences both the role of the cyclist as an active agent and form of agency in the construction of and transition to a more peaceful Rwanda. Thorpe's (2018) call for sporting creativity and support for youth agency in sites of war, conflict, and disaster applies not just to local contexts but multi-national or community contexts. More importantly international peace negotiators might listen to Thorpe's (2021) key message that viewing children and youth as victims tends to overlook unique forms of youth agency, resilience, and resourcefulness. The relatively newly formed Centre for Sport and Human Rights (https://www.sporthumanrights.org/) is supporting international organizations such as the IOC and multi-lateral organizations such as the Commonwealth Secretariat and the International Labour Organization to advance human rights in and through sport. It has an opportunity to support those working with geo-politics and the peace process.

International peace negotiators or interveners need to be prepared to take on a level risk and try new things and should be supported to do so. Should we not use any means at our disposal to strive to make the world a less tense, more just, and

Sport, Geo-Politics, and the Peace Process 257

peaceful place? Should we not argue that an opportunity exists to enable sport to be part of the essential geo-political toolbox for anyone involved in social justice, peace-making, forging effective cultural relations, and/or building capability? Should peacebuilding and development actors, foreign diplomats, ambassadors, civil servants, cultural agencies, NGOs, international aid agencies, and academics not recognize fully the full range of social and political tools at their disposal when navigating the peacebuilding process, fighting for social justice, upholding human rights, and creating influence within and through sport? Thus, the value of using field activities such as sport to support human rights in the forging of any peace process requires that sport, including the right to sport, like human rights is seen as a set of commitments and should be understood as but one mechanism that holds open a space through which social and political construction and transition can be enabled.

Sport, Cultural Relations, and Peace

How then can sport and cultural relations enhance peace and stability? If soft power is the pursuit of influence through attraction, cultural relations are the creation of the conditions for sustainable collaboration between like-minded countries for mutual benefit (British Council, 2020). Both are essential, but they are different. They require different strategies, arrangements, and skill sets. The term cultural relations can generally be taken to mean reciprocal, non-coercive transnational interactions between two or more cultures, encompassing a range of activities that are conducted by both state and non-state actors within the space of culture and civil society (Jarvie, 2021; Rivera, 2015). The overall outcomes of cultural relations are greater connectivity, better mutual understanding, more and deeper relationships, mutually beneficial transactions, and enhanced sustainable dialogue between states, peoples, non-state actors, and cultures. They are a tangible component of geo-politics and the peace process in the sense that they encompass the space in which a wide range of non-state actors engage in the fostering of intercultural dialogue. This is a dialogue that can work for or against states, but the greater the number of stakeholders that are involved in the dialogue the greater the potential of fragile peace agreements being successful and sustainable.

Sport is *not* just a commodity but can be an immensely powerful vector of change, value, principle, solidarity, a symbol, means, and arena through which a plurality of views can be listened to. The challenge is a tough one for it requires cultural gatekeepers to be less aloof about what is seen as culture, diplomats to be less aloof about the contribution sport can make, and countries, communities, and individuals to work across contexts to seek mutuality and forge and extend the common good.

Seen in this way, that is to say sport as a resource and an enabler of cultural relations and the peace process, culture can enhance peace and stability in several ways.

The following observations might be considered.

258 Grant Jarvie

- *Economic fragility*: Sport in cultural relations building can contribute to addressing economic fragility by fostering entrepreneurship in sport areas, which in turn enhances employability and can foster the emergence of micro- and small-sized enterprises.
- *Environmental fragility*: Sport in cultural relations building can contribute to enabling environmental fragility by supporting the inclusion of sport actors and resources in the face of natural disasters and climate change, through funding, technical assistance, and environmental preservation activities; by making cultural (inclusive of sport) organizations and venues more environmentally sustainable and responsible towards the climate emergency; and by supporting creative forms of environmental awareness raising through sport.
- *Political fragility*: Sport in cultural relations building can contribute to addressing political fragility by supporting civil society organizations that are committed to fostering democracy and human rights, recognizing the role of sport in the promotion and defence of human rights and the exploration of political issues, providing "safe spaces" for the discussion of controversial topics and the exercise of freedom of expression, protecting cultural (inclusive of sport) agents at risk, and supporting institution-building in the cultural field (e.g., public bodies and strategies concerned with sport as culture generally, as well as their intersections with other areas of peace, stability, and development).
- *Security fragility*: Sport in cultural relations building can contribute to addressing security fragility by facilitating an interpretation of the cultural dimensions of conflicts, responding to the impact of conflicts on sporting heritage (e.g., through restoration, mapping, management, capacity-building), and strengthening prevention and restitution measures towards the illicit trafficking of sport goods and people. This remains a complex area.
- *Societal fragility*: Sport in cultural relations building can contribute to addressing societal fragility by investing in sporting heritage, provision, and practice as a community-building vector, fostering capacity-building that enhances participation in society, enabling the emergence of alternative narratives about society, communities, and individuals and promoting collaboration and networking between sport actors and with broader civil society.

Thus, sport thought of in this way can contribute to cultural engagement and relations building, inclusive of development, enabling of social cohesion, voice, and agency. In this respect, sport can be seen as a good entry point in contemporary notions of "peace", which are increasingly connected to development and social justice, and which go beyond a simple binary opposition of conflict and peace, aggressors and victims, the ruling party, and opposition forces.

Sport and the Common Good

Sport is often seen as a cost-effective social tool and resource through which conversations can take place and capabilities can be built. In this way sport can

Sport, Geo-Politics, and the Peace Process **259**

position itself in spaces where transitional justice is being forged (Duthie, 2017). Successful peace negotiations, conflict resolution, calls for social justice, and effective cultural relations all involve compromise and seldom evoke a pre-commitment to the common good. They require the common good to be constructed in an ongoing way and spaces where this can happen. Thus, sport enabling the common good is best understood as a project of ongoing political construction, rather than a pre-commitment to any new political order or utopian ideal.

It responds to contemporary calls for sport to serve humanity (Hain and Oddendaal, 2020). There needs to be a better balance between sport as an agent of social good and the privatized pursuit of extreme profit working for the few. Making sports policy, sports investment, sports aid, sports research, sports advocacy, commitment, and sport and civil society work for more people, places, and communities more often. The value of such an approach is that it allows for a negotiated common good, the possibility of a much more shared concept of the state and/or community. One that can serve a broader set of interests operating beyond that of the individual, community, single-interest group, or country. In this way sport can be seen as a valuable enabler in the world of geo-politics. Sport can be a space that enables the construction of a common good while fractured national and international communities and societies move through phases of transitional justice. To talk of sport and the common good in this sense means that sport is part of a set of commitments and practices aimed at using public power to deliver public goods to people, regardless of their personal identity, political affiliation, and/or geographic location.

Concluding Remarks

If we are to reach common ground about ways of doing things differently, then there is a need for reflexive responses to challenges to expertise. There is a need for a better dialogue between practitioners, including peacekeepers, and academics about the challenges of new world contexts. There is also a need for those working with geo-politics and the peace process to fully recognize the range of tools at their disposal and use them to help deliver better outcomes.

Firstly, academics working with sport need to continue to be nuanced about what works where, when, and under what circumstances. They also need to be more nuanced about the growing challenges to expertise, the difficulties of critical friendship, and the unpredictability of states, territories, and/or communities undergoing fast-paced multiple political transitions because of any number of fragile contexts and geo-political tensions and alliances.

Secondly, sport like the struggle for human rights commitments should be understood as but one resource that helps to hold open a space through which social and political construction and transition can take place and as an enabler of new social contracts between as wide a range of stakeholders as possible. Something that may be invariably long-term as opposed to short-term. Short-term fixes to geo-political problems involving elite pacts are not sustainable.

Thirdly, there exists an eerie silence within United Nations peacekeeping reports about the role of sport despite the United Nations having mandated sport as an enabler in delivering the sustainable development goals. At the same time British Council and EUNIC critiques of the sustainable development goals argue that culture is a missing pillar within the United Nations sustainable development goals. They also marginalize the role of sport as culture while championing the role of art and music as key tools to be used in enhancing peace and stability within fragile contexts. Both fail to capture the possibilities of sport as a popular low-entry, high-impact point in the pursuit of sustainable long-term social change. This all must change.

Those working in and through sport are well served by the notion of sport enabling cultural relations and human rights and forging an enlarged common good. Sport is seen as a resource and space which can help with making the art of the possible, possible.

References

Armstrong, G. (2002). Talking up the game: Football and the reconstruction of Liberia, West Africa. *Global Studies in Culture and Power* (9): pp 471–494.

Bell, C. (2017). Peace settlements and human rights: A post-cold war cultural history. *Journal of Human Rights Practice* Volume 9 (3): pp 358–378.

British Academy. (2017). *Navigating inclusion in peace settlements: Human rights and the creation of the common good*. London: Author.

British Council. (2020). *Cultural relations for the 21st century*. London: British Council.

Cardenas, A. (2013). Peace building through sport? An introduction to sport for development and peace. *Journal of Conflictology* Volume 4 (1): pp 24–33.

Cardenas, A. (2016). Sport and peacebuilding in divided societies: A case study on Colombia and Northern Ireland. *Peace and Conflict Studies* 23 (2): article 4.

Cárdenas, A. (2018). Sport and Peacebuilding. In Maguire, J, Falcous, M and Liston, K (Eds) *The Business and Culture of Sports: Society, Politics, Economy, Environment*. Chapter 25 , pp. 371–388 Macmillan: London

Clarke, F., Jones, A., and Smith, L. (2021). Building peace through sports projects: A scoping review. *Sustainability* Volume 13 (2129): pp 4–15.

Cooley, A., and Nexon, D. (2022). The real crisis of global order. *Foreign Affairs* Volume 101 (1): pp 103–118.

Darnell, S. (2022). Sport for peace and politics. The Association of Commonwealth Universities. https://www.acu.ac.uk/the-acu-review/sport-peace-and-politics/. [Retrieved 10 September 2022].

Duthie, R. (2017). Justice mosaics – How context shapes transitional justice in fractured societies. https://www.ictj.org/justice-mosaics [Retrieved 9 September 2022].

Economy, E. (2022). Xi Jinping's new world order: Can China remake the international system. *Foreign Affairs* Volume 101 (1): pp 52–67.

EUNIC. (2021). *Cultural relations – Key approaches in fragile contexts: How cultural relations can enhance peace and stability*. Brussels: EUNIC Global AISBL.

Galtung, J. (1996). *Peace by peaceful means: Peace and conflict, development and civilization*. London: Sage.

Gasser, P., and Levinsen, A. (2004) Breaking post-war ice: Open fun football schools in Bosnia and Herzegovina. *Sport in Society* Volume 7 (3): pp 457–472.

Giulianotti, R. (2011). Sport, transnational peace-making, and global civil society: Exploring the reflective discourses of sport, development, and peace project officials. *Journal of Sport and Social Issues* Volume 35 (1): pp 50–71.

Hain, P., and Odendaal, A. (2020). *Pitch battles: Sport, racism and resistance.* London: Rowan & Littlefield.

Jarvie, G. (2021). Sport, soft power and cultural relations. *Journal of Global Sports Management.* 4 August https://www.tandfonline.com/doi/full/10.1080/24704067.2021.1952093 [Retrieved 16 September 2022].

Lauren's (2021) *Laureus Sport Annula Report 2020.* London: Laureus Sport Foundation.

Marc, A., and Jones, B. (2021). *The new politics of fragility.* Washington: Brookings.

Marchesseault, D. (2016). *The everyday breakaway: Participant perspectives on everyday life within a sport for development and peace program* (PhD thesis). University of Toronto, Toronto, Canada.

Pospisil, J. (2016). UN review process: Politics and international state and peacebuilding. Briefing paper 9. Political settlements research programme. Edinburgh University, Edinburgh, Scotland, UK. https://www.pure.ed.ac.uk/ws/portalfiles/portal/23783135/Briefing_Paper_9_2016_UN_Review_Processes.pdf [Retrieved 9 September 2022].

Rivera, T. (2015). *Distinguishing cultural relations from cultural diplomacy: The British Council's relationship with her majesty's government.* Los Angeles: Figueroa Press.

Serena, O. (2009). The contribution of sport within the process of peace and reconciliation. Unpublished paper. https://www.sportanddev.org/sites/default/files/downloads/dissertation_serena_borsani_february_2009.pdf [Retrieved 10 September 2022].

Thorpe, H. (2018). Look at what we can do with all the broken stuff! Youth agency and sporting creativity in sites of war, conflict and disaster. In Meredith, W., Massey, W., Darnell, S. and Smith, B. (Eds). *Sport in under-resourced, underdeveloped and conflict regions.* London: Routledge: pp 146–162.

Thorpe, H. (2021). Informal sports for youth recovery: Grassroots strategies in conflict and disaster geographies. *Journal of Youth Studies* Volume 24 (6): pp 708–730.

Ubaidulloev, Z. (2018). Sport for peace: A new era of international cooperation and peace through sport. *Asia-Pacific Review* Volume 25 (2): pp 104–126.

United Nations. (30 June 2015a) Challenge of sustaining peace: Report of the advisory group of experts on the review of the peacebuilding architecture, A/69/968. https://www.securitycouncilreport.org/atf/cf/%7B65BFCF9B-6D27-4E9C-8CD3-CF6E4FF96FF9%7D/a_72_19.pdf [Retrieved 20 May 2018].

United Nations. (2015b) Preventing conflict, transforming justice, securing the peace: A global study on the implementation of United Nations Security Council resolution 1325. https://wps.unwomen.org/pdf/en/GlobalStudy_EN_Web.pdf [Retrieved 9 September 2022].

United Nations General Assembly (UNGA). (2015). Transforming our world: The 2030 agenda for sustainable development. https://sdgs.un.org/2030agenda [Retrieved 9 September 2022].

Woodhouse, T. (2010). Peacekeeping, peace culture and conflict resolution. *International Peacekeeping* Volume 17 (4): pp 486–498.

31

SPORTS DIPLOMACY IN THE PACIFIC REGION AND THE SINO-AUSTRALIAN GREAT GAME

Stuart Murray and Tony Yang

Introduction

To understand Chinese foreign policy is to consider three leaders and three respective dictums. After a "century of humiliation" at the hands of western powers, Chairman Mao made a slumbering, poverty-stricken nation "stand up" (Thompson, 2020; Shirk, 2018). Deng Xiaoping, Mao's successor and paramount leader from December 1978 to November 1989, made China "get rich" and made it "glorious" to do so (Shirk, 2018; Sornoza-Parrales et al., 2018). President since 2013, Xi Jinping's mandate is also simple: by fostering nationalism, military expansion, and global projects such as the Belt and Road Initiatives, Xi's job is to make the Middle Kingdom "strong" (Sornoza-Parrales et al., 2018; Thompson, 2020).

The trouble with China's becoming strong, however, is that much of the geopolitical real estate they seek is already occupied. This is particularly true in the Pacific region. After the Pacific War (December 1941 to September 1945), a collection of western liberal democracies have laid claim to the area. For decades, the United States of America, along with Australia and New Zealand, has provided security guarantees for many of the islands, as have France and the United Kingdom. As Chinese power and influence continue to grow in the region, such western primacy in the region is no longer assured.

Much of the discourse on East–West strategic competition in the Pacific focuses on the "New Cold War" (Zhao, 2019), geopolitics (Auslin, 2020), and classical security matters such as the balance of power, various security dilemmas, and economic diplomacy (Ravenhill et al., 2019). Human security analyses tend to focus on the role that development, aid, and soft power play in achieving each of the different player's foreign policy goals (Tow, 2016). One perspective missing so far, however, is the role that sports diplomacy plays in the region.

DOI: 10.4324/9781003348238-38

Using Australia and China's different approaches to the Pacific as case studies, this chapter argues that sports diplomacy is central to creating influence, generating power, and winning the battle for hearts and minds (and bodies, if we are talking about sport). The analysis reveals that China prefers a classical approach, employing sport as part of a broader development strategy, whereas the Australians have adopted a more innovative strategy, encapsulated in their $52 million dollar (AUD) *PacificAus* Sports programme. This chapter describes and reviews each country's unique approach before pondering who is winning the Great Game and the implications of the result for the region.

Australia, Sports Diplomacy, and the Pacific

Sport has connected Australia and Pacific Island Nations (PINs) for decades. In 2006, for example, the Australian government implemented sport for development programmes, such as *Pacific Sports Partnerships*, the *Australia Sports Outreach Program*, and *Team Up*, which use sport to deliver positive outcomes in gender, disability, leadership, knowledge, and governance. While impactful at a grassroots, community, and local level, such programmes did not include the elites – that is, government officials, professional sportspeople, and sports industry leaders and executives. This gap led to a shift in focus – from sport for development to sports diplomacy. In 2015, for example, Australia produced the world's first esoteric sports diplomacy strategy, followed by a second in 2019 – *Sports Diplomacy 2030*.

The latter is a "global strategy with a Pacific Focus", and "recognizes the global reach of the sports industry and the significance of sport, while placing special emphasis on the vital connection between Australian and neighbouring Pacific communities" (DFAT, 2019, p. 9). It seeks to build on the "common passion for sport and strong sporting connections, including a large number of Pacific athletes participating in Australian sporting codes" (DFAT, 2019, p. 9). In other words, and seen through the lens of sports diplomacy, the Australian government is strategically harnessing the power of sport for diplomatic outcomes in the Pacific. Chief among those is to create "low-cost, low-risk, and high-profile" sports diplomacy programmes that "build linkages with our neighbours" (DFAT, 2019, p. 11; Keech & Houlihan, 1999, p. 109).

For some, however, *Sports Diplomacy 2030* has its issues (Murray, 2017). Confusion exists between sports diplomacy and sports for development programmes, outcomes, and participants. Many of the PINs also view sports diplomacy entreaties as little more than neo-colonial talent grabs, that is, rich foreigners plundering local players to ply their trade in far-off leagues in Europe, Australia, and the United States of America (Besnier, 2014). Related, an unhealthy donor-recipient perception prevails rather than one of genuine partnerships between Australia and PINs, which is what *Sports Diplomacy 2030* is attempting to achieve.

PacificAus Sports (PAS) – a new sports diplomacy programme launched in 2019 – was created to tackle such issues. It seeks, for example, to solve the player-drain problem, foster pathways for elite athletes and teams to play in each other's countries, and "strengthen Australia's relationships in the Pacific through sport at the community and diplomatic level" (PacificAus, 2019). PAS is a new type of sports diplomacy strategy. Of note are its ambition, size, and scale. Running from 2019 to 2023, the Australian government has budgeted $52 million dollars (AUD) for the programme, one of its largest "ever public diplomacy investment in its history" (Leary, 2021). The programme had one, simple, high-level objective – to enhance Australia's relationships, brand, and diplomacy in the Pacific via sport.

In terms of sport, PAS focuses on the "Big Four" Aussie sports – rugby league, rugby union, netball, and football. It aims to create pathways for Pacific and Australian teams, athletes, and coaches to participate in each other's various Australian and international sporting competitions. In terms of rugby, for example, four Pacific teams (and their retinues) relocated to Australia during the COVID pandemic to compete in elite competition: The Fijian Drua (Men's Rugby Union), Fijiana Drua (Women's Rugby Union), the Papua New Guinea Hunters (Men's Rugby League), and Kaiviti Silktails (Women's Rugby League). PAS also helped Samoan, Tongan, and Fijian netballers compete in Australian competitions and supported many individual athletes in their preparations for the Tokyo 2022 Summer Olympic Games.

Off the pitch, each sporting exchange was accompanied by strategic communications, old and new media releases, public outreach programmes, speaking tours, community events, and school visits. Australian and PIN ministers, ambassadors, diplomats, and politicians looked on from the stands, forming new informal friendships that will, in time, lead to formal gains around the negotiating table.

Generally, PAS has been a success. On the field, it gave PIN teams, players, coaches, and fans what they had always wanted – their own teams playing in Australian competition,[1] a level playing field, and a genuine chance to compete. Authenticity is vital to any twenty-first-century diplomatic message, and PAS is certainly delivered in this respect. The story of the Fijiana Drua provides a case in point: the team capped off an unbeaten season (their first in the competition) by beating the New South Wales Waratahs 36–32 in a thrilling, emotional Grand Final. The scenes at the final whistle were public diplomacy "gold" – some players wept, others wore disbelieving, euphoric grins, and all joined together in the centre of the pitch to sing the gospel song *We Shall Overcome* – a perfect anthem for a team of wandering, female rugby players. As Sarah Leary, a senior Australian diplomatic and one of the architects of PAS, notes,

> Three years on and the initiative has reached 850 Pacific and Australian players and officials, attracted crowds of over 47,000 people and funded over 120 sports diplomacy events, training camps and matches.
>
> *(Leary, 2021, para. 3)*

The programme has one or two issues that its architects may wish to address. While many PIN athletes, coaches, and industry executives were able to enjoy the Pacific-to-Australia pathway, not many Australian players, teams, and coaches made it to the islands. This was due, however, to the COVID pandemic, during which most PINs closed their doors to travellers, sportspeople included. Confusion continues to exist between sport for development and sports diplomacy strategies, programmes, and facilitators. Further clouding the field of play, other Australian government departments such as the Australian Defence Force and Australian Federal Police also run similar "sport for" programmes in the Pacific, often in the same countries and with little inter-governmental cooperation. And, finally, it could be argued that the programme is a touch one-sided; that is, PAS was made by Australian diplomats, sports "people", and others. Future programmes would benefit by including PIN voices, ideas, and people in all phases of the programme – design, implementation, measurement, and evaluation. Good diplomacy can sometimes be quite easy – Australian diplomats, coaches, players, academics, and a whole host of other Engaged Australians working in the region would do well to "shut up and listen" to Pacific voices, ideas, needs, and fears (Gibert, 2022, para. 4).

China, Sports Diplomacy, and the Pacific

When it comes to sports diplomacy and China, the first aspect to note is stadium diplomacy – the construction of sporting venues especially for developing countries (Murray, 2018). Over the past 40 years, China has adopted this approach when helping the "Third World" and as a key aspect of its foreign aid and development programmes (Dubinsky, 2021). The State Council (2011), the equivalent Chinese version of the western government "cabinet", notes of stadium diplomacy that comes with "equality, mutual benefit and no strings attached".

Historically, most of China's stadium construction occurred in Africa. Fifty-eight out of eighty-four stadiums built abroad were in Africa, while eight were constructed across the Pacific and nine in Latin America (Menary, 2015). In terms of the topic of this chapter, PINs have greatly benefited China's stadium diplomacy. Kiribati (Betio Sports Complex), Papua New Guinea (Wewak Stadium), and the Cook Islands (Telecom Sports Arena) are all good examples of stadiums built on Chinese aid or financing. In 2003, Fiji also benefited from a package of USD 16 million to stage the South Pacific Games (PATARA, 2007).

More recently, China's activities with the Solomon Islands provide a fascinating case study of how its stadium diplomacy has become more strategic, political, and robust. In 2009, and after a period of intense Chinese lobbying, The Solomon Islands switched their diplomatic allegiance from Taiwan to the People's Republic of China (Shi, 2019). Since then, China and the Solomon Islands have secured security, economic, and diplomatic agreements; however, it is their recent sports diplomacy that is causing concern for western nations such as Australia.

In 2023, for example, The Solomon Islands will host the Pacific Games 2023, and China is lending a hand to build facilities. A total of 170 Chinese engineers are involved in the construction of aquatic centre, tennis centre, communal food and beverage centre, multifunctional hall, and hockey field (Chinese Government, 2022). China is investing USD 70 million in the Games, an amount facilitated by the state-owned enterprise China Civil Engineering Construction Corporation Ltd (Courmont & Delhalle, 2022). While visiting the construction site recently, the Chinese Ambassador Li Ming proudly noted to Manasseh Sogavare, the Solomon Island's Prime Minister, that "China keeps the promise to start the project on time despite the pandemic; the project commencement marks a milestone for our relations" (MFA, 2022).

However, China's activity in the Pacific has worried Australia. "This is our backyard, not China's", argued a columnist in *The Australian* newspaper (2021). Sharma (2022) went a step further, using the Cuban Missile Crisis to metaphorically describe China's client-state autocracy around Australia's backyard, with the Solomon Islands being the number one proxy. Sport is but another tool of Chinese propaganda sweeping through the region. Chinese flags, developers' logos, and bilateral friendship signs are all visible around venues. Chinese sports diplomacy, therefore, intentionally amplifies "national culture and values to overseas audiences and governments" (Murray & Price, 2020, p. 9).

Besides stadiums, China employs three other sports diplomacy approaches in the Pacific. First, they invite sports teams to visit China. Chinese delegates invited "football professionals from Guadalcanal to visit Guangdong" and enjoy world-class training facilities (MFA, 2021, para. 5). Second, China sponsors sports events in the Pacific. Samoa enjoyed such treatment when China sponsored World Nines Confederation Cup 2020, an International Rugby League–sanctioned tournament (World Nines, 2020). Third, China establishes training academies for PINs. In 2018, for example, the China Table Tennis College Training Centre was established in Papua New Guinea (FMPRC, 2022; ITTF Oceania, 2022).

There are many positives to China's Pacific sports diplomacy. Building stadiums and other sporting facilities stimulates national and regional economies and compliments other infrastructure and development requirements. Many PINs are in desperate need of hospitals, schools, roads, and sports infrastructure can stimulate related investments in health, education, and human resources (USIP, 2022). The Solomon Islands' project, for example, employs approximately 500 local staff (Chinese Government, 2022). For China, its sports diplomacy creates influence that translates to gains in formal diplomacy. Beneficiaries of Chinese aid do switch sides, so to speak (Harding & Pohle-Anderson, 2022). In 2019, for example, Kiribati followed the Solomon Islands and recognized Beijing over Taipei.

In terms of issues, western suspicion over the true intention of China's sports and stadium diplomacy prevails. China's generous stadium diplomacy is often viewed as aggressive acts that undermine the western rules-based international order. Though Chinese Foreign Minister Wang Yi reiterated otherwise, the

USA and its allies see any Chinese presence in the region as a threat and often respond with military exercise between First and Second Island Chains (Beijing Daily, 2022; Al Jazeera, 2022). Second, China's largesse can create economic pressure for PINs, particularly if China withdraws funding or requests repayment on the loans. The West calls this practice "debt-trap diplomacy" (Hameiri, 2020). Also, "fealty is expected" in return for China's generosity (Murray, 2018). As with western nations and their diplomacy, nothing is ever given for free in international relations.

Conclusion

When commentators, politicians, and others use phrases like "the New Cold War", "battles for hearts and minds", and the "weaponization of sport" to describe East–West strategic competition, they miss the bigger, twenty-first-century picture. Both the new theory and practice of sports diplomacy encourage the observer to step beyond such dated thinking. China, the USA, and their allies are not locked in battle towards some inevitable nuclear war, where to win would be to abuse sport in the way that, say, the East Germany (German Democratic Republic, GDR) did in the 1980s.

Genuine, win–win games for hearts, minds, and bodies is a more suitable dictum for sports diplomacy in the Pacific. Such "games" should generate win–win outcomes, for all concerned, and directly contribute to building the "International Society of Sport" (Murray, 2018, pp. 135–137). States being states, China, Australia, and others will inevitably compete but so long as the competition does not turn violent, this is a good outcome for the PINs. The choice is equally good, as savvy Pacific leaders and diplomats can play rival powers off to exact maximum diplomatic concessions; that is, they can "do" diplomacy to eastern and western nations instead of having it always "done" to them. Sport offers them the power to do so, for PINs produce some of the finest athletes on the planet. Ideally, as well as China and Australia "doing" sports diplomacy to the Pacific, it would be beneficial to research what a Fijian, Tongan, or Papua New Guinea Sports Diplomacy strategy might look like.

When it comes to the Pacific region, sports diplomats from both countries do need to "shut up and listen". The Pacific is not a monolith. Every one of the fifteen countries that make up the "Pacific Islands" has different cultures, histories, philosophies, and so on. They do not speak with one voice and often disagree. Each needs to be engaged and treated as a unique sovereign nation that forms part of a region with limited diplomatic representation, skills, and budget. If engaging in sports diplomacy in the region, it is also important to move beyond "Big" popular team sports. Hard as it may be to believe, not everyone in the Pacific likes rugby, football, and netball. Individual sports and sportspeople would produce similar sports diplomacy dividends. The same might be said for Indigenous, local, or cultural Pacific sports and tournaments that generate equal if not more public diplomacy value.

268 Stuart Murray and Tony Yang

When it comes to the Pacific, and seen from an ideal, sports diplomacy lens, it is not really that important who can build better stadiums, train better coaches, or run a better dialogue between diplomats on the sidelines. In short, and in the tumultuous twenty-first century, the more people playing sport and doing diplomacy, the less people being idle and doing war.

Note

1 It should be noted that the New Zealand Government also assists a team – the Moana Pasifika – which, similarly, was based out of New Zealand and played in the 2021–2022 Super Rugby Pacific Competition.

Bibliography

Al Jazeera. (2022). US aircraft carrier Ronald Reagan arrives for South Korea drills. Al Jazeera. https://www.aljazeera.com/news/2022/9/23/us-aircraft-carrier-ronald-reagan-arrives-for-south-korea-drills

Auslin, M. R. (2020). *Asia's new geopolitics: Essays on reshaping the Indo-Pacific* (Vol. no. 706). Hoover Institution Press, Stanford, California.

Ministry of Foreign Affairs of the People's Republic of China. (2022). Wang Yi Attends and Addresses the General Debate of the 77th Session of the United Nations General Assembly.Ministry of Foreign Affairs. https://www.fmprc.gov.cn/mfa_eng/wjdt_665385/wshd_665389/202209/t20220927_10772443.html

Bergin, A. (2021). *This is our backyard, not China's.* The Australian. https://www.theaustralian.com.au/inquirer/this-is-our-backyard-not-chinas/news-story/2841ced94a3b08401c092a19ae02a414

Besnier, N. (2014). Pacific Island rugby: Histories, mobilities, comparisons. *Asia Pacific Journal of Sport and Social Science, 3*(3), pp. 268–276. http://doi.org/10.1080/21640599.2014.982894

Chinese Embassy in the Solomon Islands. (2022). *Zhang Guangbao, leader of China police liaison team to Solomon Islands interviewed by the Solomon star.* http://sb.china-embassy.gov.cn/eng/sgxw_3/202203/t20220304_10647941.htm

Chinese Government. (2022). *China-aided projects help the Solomon Islands to organize the hosting of the Pacific Games 2023.* The Central People's Government of the People's Republic of China. http://www.gov.cn/xinwen/2022-05/26/content_5692444.htm

Courmont, B., & Delhalle, H. (2022). *A China's Soft Power in The Pacific: The Example of the Solomon Islands.*

DFAT. (2019). *Sports diplomacy 2030.* Australian Government. https://www.dfat.gov.au/sites/default/files/sports-diplomacy-2030.pdf

Dubinsky, I. (2021). China's stadium diplomacy in Africa. *Journal of Global Sport Management,* pp. 1–19. https://doi.org/10.1080/24704067.2021.1885101

FMPRC. (2022). *Fact sheet: Cooperation between China and Pacific Island countries.* Ministry of Foreign Affairs, the People's Republic of China. https://www.fmprc.gov.cn/mfa_eng/wjdt_665385/2649_665393/202205/t20220524_10691917.html

Gibert, A. (2022). *Resetting Australia's relationship with the Pacific – Three ideas.* The Interpreter. https://www.lowyinstitute.org/the-interpreter/resetting-australia-s-relationship-pacific-three-ideas

Hameiri, S. (2020). *Debunking the myth of China's "debt-trap diplomacy"*. Lowy Institute. https://www.lowyinstitute.org/the-interpreter/debunking-myth-china-s-debt-trap-diplomacy

Harding, B., & Pohle-Anderson, C. (2022). *China's search for a permanent military presence in the Pacific islands: After the Solomon Islands signed a security pact with Beijing in April, Kiribati may be considering a similar deal*. The United States Institute of Peace (USIP). https://www.usip.org/publications/2022/07/chinas-search-permanent-military-presence-pacific-islands

Information Office of the State Council. (2011). *China's foreign aid*. Information Office of the State Council, People's Republic of China. http://www.unicef.org

ITTF Oceania. (2022). *Papua New Guinea Opens China Table Tennis College Training Center at Butuka Academy*. ITTF Oceania. https://ittfoceania.azurewebsites.net/2022/04/14/papua-new-guinea-opens-china-table-tennis-college-training-center-at-butuka-academy/

Keech, M., & Houlihan, B. (1999). Sport and the end of apartheid. *Round Table (London)*, *88*(349), pp. 109–121. https://doi.org/10.1080/003585399108306

Leary, S. (2021). *Stepping up sports diplomacy in the Pacific: An Australian perspective*. USC Center on Public Diplomacy. https://uscpublicdiplomacy.org/blog/stepping-sports-diplomacy-pacific-australian-perspective

Menary, S. (2015). China's programme of stadium diplomacy. *ICSS Journal*, *3*(3), pp. 2–9.

MFA. (2021). *Li Ming, the Chinese Ambassador to the Solomon Islands, attended an online conference for the China – Solomon Islands football exchange program*. https://www.mfa.gov.cn/web/gjhdq_676201/gj_676203/yz_676205/1206_676860/1206x2_676880/202110/t20211012_9546812.shtml

MFA. (2022a). *Li Ming, the Chinese Ambassador to the Solomon Islands, published "Provocation against China's sovereignty and territorial integrity is doomed to fail"*. https://www.fmprc.gov.cn/gytwwtdlc/zwgzs/202208/t20220806_10736356.shtml

MFA. (2022b). *Li Ming, the Chinese Ambassador to the Solomon Islands, introduced China – Solomon Islands relations and bilateral security cooperation*. https://www.mfa.gov.cn/zwbd_673032/wjzs/202204/t20220422_10672061.shtml

MFA. (2022c). *Prime Minister Manasseh Sogavare, accompanied by Chinese Ambassador Li Ming, inspected the China-aided stadium and university dormitory*. https://www.fmprc.gov.cn/zwbd_673032/wshd_673034/202208/t20220801_10731326.shtml

Murray, S. (2017). Sports diplomacy in the Australian context: Theory into strategy. *Politics & Policy*, *45*(5), pp. 841–861. https://doi.org/10.1111/polp.12218

Murray, S. (2018). *Sports diplomacy: Origins, theory and practice*. Abingdon: Routledge.

Murray, S., & Price, G. (2020). *Towards a Welsh sports diplomacy strategy*. British Council Wales. https://wales.britishcouncil.org/sites/default/files/towards_a_welsh_sports_diplomacy_strategy_0.pdf

PacificAus. (2019). PacificAus sports. https://www.pacificaussports.gov.au

PATARA. (2007). *PATARA sponsors South Pacific Games 2003 and provides Information & Communications Technology for a "Smart Games"*. PATARA Communications & Electronics Limited. https://web.archive.org/web/20120804044326/http://www.patarapacific.com/spg2003

Ravenhill, J., Aggarwal, V., Evans, P. M., & Kerr, P. (2019). *Pacific cooperation: Building economic and security regimes in the Asia-Pacific region*. Routledge. https://doi.org/10.4324/9780429300844

Sharma, D. (2022). *Beijing-backed autocracy in our backyard with "Cuba in the Pacific"*. The Australian. https://www.theaustralian.com.au/inquirer/beijingbacked-autocracy

-in-our-backyard-with-cuba-in-the-pacific/news-story/85382be1f9b1038e058c076
9e02a5230

Shi, X. (2019). *The Solomon Islands cabinet held a meeting and decided to sever the diplomatic relations with Taiwan.* Central News Agency. https://www.cna.com.tw/news/firstnews/201909165005.aspx

Shirk, S. L. (2018). The return to personalistic rule. *Journal of Democracy, 29*(2), pp. 22–36. https://doi.org/10.1353/jod.2018.0022

Sornoza-Parrales, G. I., Conforme-Cedeno, G. M., Saltos-Buri, V. del R., Merchán-Nieto, L. C., Muñíz-Jaime, L. P., & Franco-Yoza, J. A. (2018). The case of China's Economic Reform: The Xi Jinping Era, a comparative analysis with Mao Zedong and Deng Xiaoping. *Polo Del Conocimiento, 3*(7), pp. 38–52. https://doi.org/10.23857/pc.v3i7.528

The Embassy of the People's Republic of China in Solomon Islands. (2022). *Prime Minister Manasseh Sogavare, accompanied by Chinese Ambassador Li Ming, inspected the China-aided stadium and university dormitory.* http://sb.china-embassy.gov.cn/chn/sgxw/202206/t20220624_10709209.htm

Thompson, D. (2020). The rise of Xi Jinping and China's new era: Implications for the United States and Taiwan. *Issues and Studies – Institute of International Relations, 56*(1), pp. 2040004–2040025. http://doi.org/10.1142/S1013251120400044

Tow, W. T. (2016). *New approaches to human security in the Asia-Pacific: China, Japan and Australia.* Routledge.

USIP. (2022a). *China's influence on the freely associated states of the Northern Pacific.* The United States Institute of Peace (USIP) China-Freely Associated States Senior Study Group. https://www.usip.org/publications/2022/09/chinas-influence-freely-associated-states-northern-pacific

USIP. (2022b). *China's influence on the freely associated states of the Northern Pacific.* The United States Institute of Peace (USIP) Senior Study Group Report. https://www.usip.org/sites/default/files/2022-09/ssg-china-influence-on-freely-associated-states-of-northern_pacific.pdf

Will, R. (2012). China's stadium diplomacy. *World Policy Journal, 29*(2), pp. 36–43. https://doi.org/10.1177/0740277512451487

World Nines. (2020). *A new international rugby league tournament is coming (Provisional date to be confirmed in accordance with Covid 19 developments).* World Nines. https://worldnines.com

Zhao, M. (2019). Is a new cold war inevitable? Chinese perspectives on US-China strategic competition. *The Chinese Journal of International Politics, 12*(3), pp. 371–394. https://doi.org/10.1093/cjip/poz010

32

SPORTS, RACE, AND COSMOPOLITANISM

J.P. Singh[1]

In July 2021, Italy defeated England to win the European Soccer Championship. Fans across the European Union cheered the underdogs Italy, which scored its first win at the European championship since 1968. While Italy's win against England, post-Brexit, subtly represented European Union pride, the English team was more diverse: a photograph from the Museum of Migration showed that only 3 of the starting 11 players did not have an immigrant parent or grandparent. The English team exuded enthusiasm among England's minorities. Both sides of the story here reveal rising beyond parochialism: minority populations in England cheered for a sport that is often associated with England's white working class, and continental Europeans overlooked their own national identities to cheer for the Italian team. Nevertheless, as this chapter shows this ideal version of sports and cosmopolitanism is problematic and untenable, especially when it comes to questions of race and racism.

The cosmopolitanism often associated with sporting events arises out of liberal thought: successive interactions lead to people getting to know each other and overcoming their prejudices (Deutsch 2015, Norris et al. 2009). A sporting event, easily understood among the viewers through its shared rules and understandings, therefore, embodies the possibilities of cosmopolitanism. The socially integrative role of sports is often acknowledged (Alkemeyer & Bröskamp 1996), and in the United States most star athletes are African-Americans (Anderson 1995). The celebrations around megaevents such as the Olympics or the Football World Cup, despite displays of nationalism, can be viewed from the perspective of cosmopolitan thought. The best person or team wins, and "sportsmanship" entails that all players respect each other and the results.

Despite international and multicultural sports teams and events, cosmopolitanism can be quite thin, and racism is quite culturally entrenched in sports. British soccer fans are frequently racist: for example, 83 per cent of the 2500 anonymous

DOI: 10.4324/9781003348238-39

272 J.P. Singh

responses in a 2011–2012 survey noted that racism was "culturally embedded" in British soccer and 67 per cent of the respondents had personally witnessed it (Cleland & Cashmore 2016). Despite the professed multiculturalism of British soccer teams, black players suffer subtle or overt discrimination through their position assignments and are often stereotyped (Maguire 1988). The minorities that cheered the English soccer team in 2021 were, therefore, more of an exception to its fandom than the rule. Similarly, Northern Europeans cheering on a Mediterranean country is not a regular practice. Racial divisions also work within the same team. *The Economist* tweeted the following after the Euro Cup: "The most striking aspect of Italy's 26-man squad before it took to the pitch was that, alone among the main contenders, it did not include a single player considered as being of colour" (The Economist 2021). The tweet was itself critiqued for racism, with Italians pointing out that they were once treated as people of colour.

The story of race and cosmopolitanism in sports is complicated, but this chapter argues that racism is especially noticeable and controversial in times of rapid cultural change. Eighteen African-Americans players accounted for 14 of the 56 medals the United States won at the 1936 Berlin Olympics (Wang 2016). Athlete Jesse Owens' four gold medals are often heralded in history as the perfect riposte to what has been called "the Nazi Olympics". History repeated itself during the Trump Presidency when American football players "took to the knee" while the national anthem was played as a form of protest against discrimination at the height of the Black Lives Matter (BLM) movement. Trump supporters labelled the players unpatriotic and directed racist vitriol towards them.

Sports comprise a set of cultural rituals that are well understood among practitioners, both fans and players, through times of stability. To understand racism in sports, a study of the cultures of sports with a racial lens is necessary. While sports are cultural events, they perform double duty in culture: not just as symbolic representations (like art) but also being deeply embedded in ways of life.

Cultures are often understood as a repertoire of options or a toolkit (Swidler 1986, Kymlicka 1995). Sociologist Anne Swidler (1986) notes that cultures present "diverse often conflicting symbols, rituals, stories, and guides to action" that are mobilized through times of cultural stability and change (p. 277). Simplifying cultural ideologies that present binary or divisive choices often manifest themselves through instability. Rather than understand the context of the athletes taking the knee, a simplifying ideology might suggest that they are ungrateful and unpatriotic.

Arguably, sports may even present a case of cultural stasis rather than change, especially in matters of race. Sports are often cast as reflective of society's underlying values than changing them. Following Geertz (1973), culture is about public meanings of values and traits that are held among groups of people. Socialization processes embed these public meanings through everyday language (Berger & Luckmann 1966). Further, culture is the "social unconscious" (Eagleton 2016) that represents sedimented traditions passed on through intergenerational transfer as a form of "social lineage" (Patten 2011).

Sports, Race, and Cosmopolitanism **273**

Understanding culture then means tracing the lineage and traditions deposited deep within the unconscious. The public meanings of culture can reveal deep histories and private reservations. Catalans associated Real Madrid with the Franco regime in the past and Spanish nationalism at present. One of the most bitter rivalries in football is, therefore, between Real Madrid and FC Barcelona, popularly known as Barça. The most American of all sports are baseball and American football. Those who do not follow long-standing rituals set themselves up for scorn, even when the ritual being questioned is society's racism.

Racism in sports can take especially virulent forms because deviations from ascribed roles are interpreted as deviations from culture's symbolic and everyday life aspects. Compounding all this are two other dimensions of culture: difference and power. Culture addresses group identities, but it is also about "othering". Even as African-American athletes won at the Berlin Olympics and highlighted the racist underpinnings of Nazism, racism was rampant in the United States society with de facto segregation and lynchings in the US South. Racist attitudes in sports might then mean allowing for a special place for African-Americans or other minorities in sports but otherwise assigning African-Americans an unequal status in society. Racist attitudes in the United States, often abetted through media, ascribe superior athletic abilities to African-American bodies while perceiving them to be intellectually inferior (Anderson 1995). In other places, such as racist jaunts and epithets directed at non-white football players in France, their sports ability itself may play second shrift to deep-seated racism among the fans.

Racism in sports may be widely diffused in times of cultural stability. Therefore, athletes not playing their assigned roles at any time can make fans angry and upset through unravelling the racist codes underlying fandom. During times of cultural instability, this can lead to boycotts and threats of violence as was the case during the BLM protest with athletes taking the knee. For perspective, consider cultural representations (or symbols) where socially ascribed roles may be questioned: theatre is one such space. Judith Butler (1990) notes that since gender is socially constructed and performed with cues, drag queens through their performances can unravel the meanings of what it means to be feminine. One can then understand, even if in the most troubling of ways, how an African-American athlete who, unlike a drag queen, has not been "authorized" to unravel the social meanings of race is then reviled by racist white fans.

Cultural meanings are often backed with powerful institutions. Spectacle sports are especially important for the powerful institutions that back them: national governments, big business, media, and star-studded personalities. The co-editors of this volume have called this the geo-political economy of sport. This chapter provides the racialized underpinnings of this political economy. If racist meanings have been well-ascribed and understood within sports spaces, then questioning them openly may not lead to empathy, understanding, or acceptance. President Trump's frequent lashing out at African-American athletes who did not stand up for the national anthem is an example of the institutional context.

274 J.P. Singh

By the same token, given that sports as spectacle draws great crowds and attention, questioning racism at these events can also carry double value: it can appeal to fans who are already questioning racism, or it can present an alternative perspective to those who are not doing so – especially at a level that is hard to ignore – from athletes that they may admire. The symbolic power of sports and star athletes is important here, but in the opposite direction from the cultural forces of the status quo. The suggestion here is not that athletes are perfectly poised for questioning racism in society but that their ability to do so must also be acknowledged. It is for this reason that the presence of 18 African-American athletes was a powerful symbol at the 1936 Berlin Olympics. African-American athletes who "broke the colour barrier" are remembered and admired for their ability to do so. These include Jackie Robinson's entry into major league baseball in 1947 after 60 years of segregation (the first African-Americans in major league baseball date back to 1879). The reaction of minority fans about the immigrant lineages of the English football team at Euro Cup 2021 must be seen in similar ways.

Sports teams and their backers can also respond powerfully to the underlying progressive trends in society. An example is the renaming of many professional teams in the United States recently. Washington Redskins became the Washington Football Team in 2020 after pressures from activists, and in 2021 Cleveland Indians became the Cleveland Guardians. In 2020, the National Basketball Association took a strong stance on racial justice without harming its ratings. In June 2020, a Pew Research Poll showed that 67 per cent of the Americans supported the Black Lives Matter movement. National Football League (NFL) quarterback Colin Kaepernick, the first athlete to take the knee in 2016, was "fired" though technically he was told his contract would not be renewed. He opted out of doing so and was blackballed out of NFL. Kaepernick went on to be featured in anti-hate campaigns for Nike. Other businesses joined similar campaigns later with minority athletes (Ivry 2020).

This chapter has emphasized the cultural importance of sports for analyzing racism: sports are symbolic forms that speak to ways of life. Although questioning entrenched racist ways of life is not easy, the chapter suggests that athletes as symbols can make a difference. Markovits and Rensmann (2010) reach a similar conclusion about the potential of sports for globalization: they are reflective of globalization, but sports also deepen it. Millward (2011) notes that English football fans can simultaneously exhibit "thin cosmopolitanism", "mild xenophobia", and "cultural racism". For Millward, cosmopolitanism and racism/xenophobia are not in binary opposition to each other. Fans can, for example, accept and promote non-British members on their teams while expressing xenophobic views towards the country of the athletes' origin. Despite these mixed views, the consensus seems to be that sports literatures have often overlooked racism and domination in sports in favour of speaking to multicultural sports teams: "such

Sports, Race, and Cosmopolitanism **275**

accounts tend to overlook the broader issues of power and domination in society, but at a more concrete level, they tend to ignore changes that have or have not taken place at the level of organizational control" (Jarvie 2003, 2).

Racism and cosmopolitanism are both socially understood, and each is "performed" as a ritual within groups who understand its meanings. Some of the most powerful and inspiring stories in sports are those that have questioned both the endurance of racism and the artificiality of cosmopolitanism.

Note

1 My thanks to the editors of this volume for helpful comments. Discussions with my colleague Antonios Anastasopoulos also improved this chapter.

References

Alkemeyer, T. & Bröskamp, B. (1996), 'Strangerhood and racism in sports', *Sport Science Review* **5**(2), 30–52.

Anderson, P. M. (1995), 'Racism in sports: A question of ethics', *Marq. Sports LJ* **6**, 357.

Berger, P. L. & Luckmann, T. (1966), *The social construction of reality: A treatise in the sociology of knowledge*, Doubleday, New York, NY.

Butler, J. (1990), *Gender trouble: Feminism and the subversion of identity*, Routledge, London.

Cleland, J. & Cashmore, E. (2016), 'Football fans' views of racism in British football', *International Review for the Sociology of Sport* **51**(1), 27–43.

Deutsch, K. W. (2015), *Political community and the North American area*, Princetorn, Princeton University Press.

Eagleton, T. (2016), *Culture*, New Haven, Yale University Press.

Geertz, C. (1973), *The interpretation of cultures*, Basic books, New York, NY.

Ivry, B. (2020), 'Taking a knee, once career poison, now seen as good for business', *Bloomberg News*, 2 September. Available at https://www.bloomberg.com/news/features/2020 -09-02/taking-a-knee-once- career-poison-now-seen-as-good-for-business.

Jarvie, G. (2003), *Sport, racism and ethnicity*, London, Routledge.

Kymlicka, W. (1995), *Multicultural citizenship: A liberal theory of minority rights*, Oxford political theory, Oxford University Press, New York.

Maguire, J. A. (1988), 'Race and position assignment in English soccer: A preliminary analysis of ethnicity and sport in Britain', *Sociology of Sport Journal* **5**(3): 257–269.

Markovits, A. S. & Rensmann, L. (2010), *Gaming the world: How sports are reshaping global politics and culture*, Princeton, Princeton University Press.

Millward, P. (2011), The limits to cosmopolitanism': English football fans at Euro 2008, in D. Burdsey, ed., *Race, ethnicity and football: Persisting debates and emergent issues*, Routledge, pp. 163–174.

Norris, P., Inglehart, R., et al. (2009), *Cosmopolitan communications: Cultural diversity in a globalized world*, Cambridge University Press, Cambridge.

Patten, A. (2011), 'Rethinking culture: The social lineage account', *American Political Science Review* **105**(4), 735–749.

Swidler, A. (1986), 'Culture in action: Symbols and strategies', *American Sociological Review* **51**(2), 273–286.

The Economist (2021), 'Twitter post'. 13 July. https://tinyurl.com/4ezym64d.

Wang, H. L. (2016), 'Black U.S. Olympians won in Nazi Germany only to be overlooked at home', *National Public Radio*. Available at: https://www.npr.org/sections/thetorch/2016/08/13/489773389/black-u-s-olympians-won-in-nazi-germany-only-to-be-overlooked-at-home.

33

TRANSGENDER SPORT BANS COME FOR ELITE SPORT

Federations' New Attempt to Define Womanhood

Sydney Bauer

A revolution is coming in the current sports landscape spearheaded by the International Swimming Federation (FINA). According to a majority of countries that make up the international federation, sport will no longer be constrained by the current system of classification of dividing sport into "male" and "female" categories. Instead, in international FINA events the federation will offer an "open" category for transgender and intersex athletes that do not meet their new, strict policy to compete in the "men's" and "women's" categories. Thus, the federation has determined it is allowed to legally define which classes of athletes, based on the puberty that have gone through at a young age, and those with gender-diverse identities or intersex characteristics should be afforded their own category to preserve the fairness of competition.

What exactly is the dividing line for transgender and intersex athletes from their cisgender counterparts? Puberty. FINA defines specific stages in a pre-adolescent's development known as the "Tanner Stages" as to when athletes' gender is solidified for the purpose of competition. The federation noted that competition is different from the legal frameworks countries around the world set for defining gender – likely at the behest of its human rights group that helped draft the policy – and that given the federation's mandate of sanctioning international competitions, it was within its legal rights to do so. Yet, the policies for transmasculine and transfeminine athletes vary wildly. Transmasculine athletes are allowed to compete in the "men's" category even if they have begun hormone replacement therapy with testosterone at any time, solely if they are after to be granted a Therapeutic Use Exemption (TUE) for the banned substance. Should transfeminine or 46XY DSD intersex athletes want to be granted licence to compete in the "women's" category, they need to prove to an independent expert that they began suppressing "male puberty" before Tanner Stage 2 – or before the age of 12 – and are able to suppress their testosterone limits to

DOI: 10.4324/9781003348238-40

below 2.5 nmol/L continuously from that point. Anyone unable to satisfy these requirements will be allowed to compete in the "open" category should they decide not to compete in the category that matches which puberty they underwent, according to the federation.

Details about what this new "open" category should encompass and how it will work in international competition at FINA-sanctioned events were not forthcoming at the time of the vote. FINA (2022) in its announcement of the policy said that it would allow a working group six months to iron out these details and set up the category.

However, despite the lack of framework for its new category, FINA (2022) in the explicit policy released did offer a robust method of enforcement for athletes that seek to participate under its current "men's" and "women's" categories. Transgender or intersex athletes seeking to compete in categories that match their gender identity are required by FINA to be signed off by an independent expert that determines if their medical history meets the requirements for FINA's "men's" or "women's" eligibility. Yet the federation says it "may monitor an athlete's ongoing compliance with the Eligibility Conditions by any appropriate means", including random testing of their testosterone levels for the purpose of eligibility. Athletes will also be required to submit chromosomal tests to FINA before beginning the eligibility assessment.

FINA's gender inclusion policy is the first by an international federation to be released after the International Olympic Committee (IOC) (2021) changed course on its gender inclusion framework for the first time in two decades. As the Olympic sports' umbrella body has moved towards a framework that de-emphasizes medicalization for gender-diverse bodies, FINA has chosen a different tract: a narrow definition of an athlete's sex that is largely immutable without strict, robust medical intervention for those who are not cisgender. Months before the IOC released its guideline, World Rugby (2021) had announced that it had barred transgender women from competing in events sanctioned by the federation, citing injury risk and other factors. Transgender men are allowed to compete without restriction. At the national level, federations have a bit more leeway, with countries like the United States' USA Rugby (2020) allowing transgender women to compete in nationally sanctioned events if they comply with the old IOC transgender inclusion framework. Other countries have similarly followed suit like Rugby Canada (2020), although the International Rugby League, the largest form of rugby not governed by the international federation, barred transgender women from competing at the elite level (Reuters 2022), showing the influence international federations have on the sports they oversee despite only sanctioning elite competition.

How the IOC became at odds with how international federations began to define the categories is at the heart of the current political tension around the world regarding the status of rights enumerated to transgender people by national governments. For its first decades, the IOC resisted the call to allow women to participate en masse at the Olympics, before a rival organization the International

Women's Sports Federation (FSFI) organized its own event in the 1920s solely for women's athletes (Ripa, 2020). Despite the presence of a handful of women athletes at the 1900 Games in Paris, it would not be until the 1928 Olympics in Amsterdam that a women's competition in athletics was permitted to be organized. It would take nearly 100 years until the Paris 2024 Olympics when the Olympics would achieve gender parity according to the IOC's (2021) own metrics.

With the increased participation of women in elite sport and the increased attention on the Olympic Games came the beginnings of policing who deserved to be on the playing field in terms of competition. From the 1930s (Heggie, 2010), until before the Sydney 2000 Olympics (Brooks, 2000), the IOC required female athletes to submit themselves to gender verification tests to prove they deserved to compete in women's categories. At first, like that of Sprinter Stephens at the 1936 Olympics documented by *TIME* magazine, many of the charges of athletes competing under the wrong sex were charged by the media and fellow athletes. In this, the lines between male and female athletes were more blurred, with coaches noting in another *TIME* article from the Berlin Games that it was not uncommon for female athletes to undergo sex changes and begin living life as men. Standardized sex testing did not become the norm in the Olympics until the 1960s, (Heggie, 2010), as the Cold War heated up with the rise of athletes from the USSR and the GDR.

At the 1968 Winter and Summer Olympics, the IOC began using what was known as the Barr Body Test (Ritchie, Reynard, & Lewis, 2008), to determine if an athlete had XX or XY chromosomes. The test searches for a body in the cell's nucleus found when there is an inactive X chromosome – thus theoretically determining the presence of XX chromosomes in the body. However, such tests easily pick up women with "complete androgen insensitivity syndrome", meaning the presence of XY chromosomes despite external sex organs of women and determining that men with Klinefelter's syndrome – possessing XXY chromosomes – can compete as women having possessed the inactive X chromosome (Ritchie, Reynard, & Lewis, 2008). Following the outcry of Spanish sprinter Maria Martinez-Patino, the ineffective Barr Body Test was phased out by the IOC in the 1990s for another test, "which identifies a specific region of code usually found on the Y chromosome and known as the 'sex determining region Y'" (Heggie, 2010). By 2000 this test and all sex testing had gone by the wayside amid continual athlete outcry.

After abolishing sex testing, the IOC began broadening its inclusion by offering a formalized pathway for transgender and gender-diverse athletes to compete in the Olympics. In 2003 its "Stockholm Consensus" (IOC, 2004) created a pathway for athletes who have medically undergone gender confirmation surgery to compete in the Olympics. Those guidelines would be challenged on human rights grounds by cyclist Kristen Worley from Canada (Brown, 2015), leading to a new consensus statement in 2015 from the IOC that pushed for medicalizing athletes in an effort to broaden inclusion in sports. This policy would

280 Sydney Bauer

stay in force for six years, as federations began once again working to claw back control of defining who is allowed to compete in its categories, before the advent of the IOC's 2021 "framework". This new policy was designed to cede control back to the federations but create an overarching standard taking into account human rights concerns. Ultimately, the framework says that it was designed to respect the current elite sport landscape that is organized into "men's" and "women's" categories and is "aimed at ensuring that competition in each of these categories is fair and safe, and that athletes are not excluded solely on the basis of their transgender identity or sex variations". In the nearly 20 years of having a transgender inclusion policy, only one transgender athlete – a transgender woman named Laurel Hubbard – has competed in the Olympic Games.

The IOC's 2021 framework can be interpreted as both a reaction to the human rights concerns of medicalizing athletes to force them to conform to certain athletic categories and the ongoing fight the World Athletes had been fighting over the eligibility of certain female athletes in its middle-distance events. World Athletics has had a long history of sex testing, being the first federation to call for sex tests in 1950 (Dillema, 2008), and being the first federation to ban such testing in 1992 (Simpson, Ljungqvist, de la Chapelle, et al, 1993), seven years before the IOC followed suit. Yet, in 2009 when an 18-year-old South African named Caster Semenya stormed to a world championship in Berlin at the 800 m distance, World Athletics said a gender verification test was necessary because she had only begun winning races at the elite level "in the last month" according to reports at the time (Clarey, 2009). The tests were determined to be necessary in what was deemed an unprecedented situation, with even her fellow finalist Elisa Cusma of Italy telling *The New York Times*, "For me, she's not a woman. She's a man".

Two years later, World Athletics introduced a testosterone limit on female athletes in certain distances, with officials arguing that naturally occurring high levels of testosterone – outside of conditions such as polycystic ovary syndrome – are the main drivers of performance in track and field (Marchant, 2011). Instead of using internal or external genitalia as a determining factor of who is eligible to compete in "women's" categories in sport, World Athletics took it a step further to say that, in order to keep the two classifications intact for sport, limits must be placed on some athletes to give all others a fair shot. Even with the new rules in place, Semenya competed in the 2012 Summer Olympics winning a silver medal – which was upgraded to gold as the winner was found to be part of the systemic Russian state-sponsored doping scheme. Two years later Indian runner Dutee Chand suddenly found herself withdrawn from the 2014 Commonwealth Games due to high natural levels of testosterone, to which she challenged World Athletics' rules at the Court of Arbitration for Sport (Mancur, 2014).

In 2015 CAS ruled that World Athletics had arbitrarily set its limits for natural testosterone and had two years to show evidence for its 2011 policy (Court of Arbitration for Sport, 2015). This interregnum meant that Semenya was cleared to compete without restriction in the 2016 Olympics, where she won a gold medal, her second Olympic gold. The next year she went on to win another World Championships in the 800 m in London. Eventually, the World Athletics (2018) passed a policy requiring athletes seeking to compete in the women's category for middle-distance races – 400 m, 800 m, and 1500 m – must show a natural level of testosterone below 5nmol/L continuously in order to race. Media response focused on the policy as a reaction to Semenya's dominance in the 800 m, but she was far from the only athlete caught in the policy's crossfire. Semenya was forced to stop running her signature race and was unable to qualify for the Tokyo 2020 Olympics in the 200 m, but two Namibian runners Christine Mboma and Beatrice Masilingi were barred from competing in the women's 400 m due to the policy. After the Games, Masilingi told Burke (2021) the experience was "hard to understand" and described the emotional toll of having to change her entire training routine weeks before the Olympics for a different event.

Disproportionately athletes from the Global South have been affected by the World Athletics bans according to Katrina Karkazis and Rebecca Young-Jordan, who argue in a 2018 paper, World Athletics has recognized this and has its own views about why this has happened.

> According to Bermon, women from Africa and Asia are "arriving" at the highest level because of unfair advantage owing to not having been "treated." The repetition of the word "bias" and the explicit reference to cheating indicates that their very presence in competition is unfair.
>
> *(Karkazis and Young-Jordan, 2018)*

World Athletics' use of natural testosterone when determining eligibility is not the only federation policy that could be said to be prioritizing body standards of the Global North in order to define athletes. In FINA's transgender policy, it specifically cites the Tanner Scale as the method for determining when an athlete reaches a part of male puberty that necessitates them to compete in the "open" category or "male" category despite legally being a transgender woman. The Tanner Scale was developed from one longitudinal study of English children from the 1940s to 1970s and has since become the global standard for puberty milestones. However, the study did not examine how many confounding variables such as the psychological state of children led to their development, as well as their overall health and nutrition (Roberts, 2016). Applying such a scale to the growth and development of gender-diverse and intersex athletes for their hypothetical future athletic competition could have stark implications for athletes all over the world.

The IOC does not have the power to compel federations to make certain decisions under its new transgender framework; however, an Associated Press article (2022) did note that it encouraged bodies to move away from using testosterone as a marker for athletic performance. Yet, FINA, World Athletics, and World Rugby have forged ahead with these inclusion policies. This comes

282 Sydney Bauer

at the backdrop while countries like the United States debate whether or not young transgender girls and boys should have access to sports teams affiliated with schools based on their gender identity or what sex a doctor assigns them at birth (Kliegman, 2022). With no explicit guidance for federations like its 2015 consensus, each individual sport worldwide will now have to consult its athlete and scientific working groups to determine which political definitions of people will be allowed to compete in the "men's" and "women's" categories. Those now with "open" categories still are yet to release their plans for how and where these categories will be administered.

Therein lies the key to the inclusion behind these plans. Sport's history with policing sex has ebbed and flowed throughout the history of the Modern Olympics. Currently, through the guise of athlete health, safety, and opportunity, federations are choosing to double down on certain categories of segregation, inherently protecting its preferred class of athlete. Instead of opening pathways for all elite athletes by looking at whether its current classification systems are the best way to organize itself, sport has chosen its priorities over who gets priority and investment. Both World Athletics and World Ruby cited injuries and damage to potential earnings from broader classes of athletes being able to compete, protecting cisgender women athletes. Likewise for Aquatics, a supposed advantage over cisgender women athletes is being remedied by shifting gender-diverse athletes to a new category. Once again, elite sport continues to define who gets the benefit of inclusion and who gets to compete.

References

Associated Press (2022) *FINA effectively bans transgender athletes from competing in women's swimming events* Available at: https://www.usatoday.com/story/sports/olympics /2022/06/19/fina-adopts-new-policy-transgender-athletes-swimming-events /7677611001/

Brooks, J. R. (2000) *Gender testing at Olympics abolished at last* Available at: https:// www.theglobeandmail.com/sports/gender-testing-at-olympics-abolished-at-last/ article25459571/

Brown, A. (2015) *Worley's case to proceed in Human Rights Tribunal* Available at: https:// www.sportsintegrityinitiative.com/worleys-case-to-proceed-in-human-rights -tribunal/

Burke, P. (2021) *Tokyo 2020 silver medalist Mboma admits 400m Olympic ban was "a very bad experience"* Available at: https://www.insidethegames.biz/articles/1113578/mboma -masilingi-tokyo-2020-400m-ban

Clarey, C. (2009) *Gender test after a gold medal finish* Available at: https://www.nytimes .com/2009/08/20/sports/20runner.html

Court of Arbitration for Sport (2015) *Dutee Chand v. Athletics Federation of India (AF) & The International Association of Athletics Federations (IAAF)* Available at: https://web .archive.org/web/20170704221029/http://www.tas-cas.org/fileadmin/user_upload/ award_internet.pdf (Accessed Sept. 6, 2022)

Dillema, F. (2008) *Foekje Dillema* Available at: https://web.archive.org/web /20160422082250/http://www.foekjedillema.nl/ (Accessed Sept. 6, 2022)

FINA (2022) *FINA announces new policy on gender inclusion* Available at: https://www.fina
.org/news/2649715/press-release-fina-announces-new-policy-on-gender-inclusion

FINA (2022) *Gender inclusion policy* Available at: https://resources.fina.org/fina/document
/2022/06/19/525de003-51f4-47d3-8d5a-716dac5f77c7/FINA-INCLUSION
-POLICY-AND-APPENDICES-FINAL-.pdf

Heggie, V. (2010) 'Testing sex and gender in sports; reinventing, reimagining and reconstructing histories.' *Endeavor, 34*(4), pp. 157–163 Available at: https://www
.sciencedirect.com/science/article/pii/S0160932710000670

IOC (2004) *IOC approves consensus with regard to athletes who have changed sex* Available at: https://olympics.com/ioc/news/ioc-approves-consensus-with-regard-to-athletes
-who-have-changed-sex#:~:text=The%20consensus%20is%20based%20on,and
%20vice%20versa)%20in%20sport.

IOC (2015) *IOC consensus meeting on sex reassignment and hyperandrogenism November 2015* Available at: https://stillmed.olympic.org/Documents/Commissions_PDFfiles/
Medical_commission/2015-11_ioc_consensus_meeting_on_sex_reassignment_and
_hyperandrogenism-en.pdf

IOC (2021a) *Gender equality through time: At the Olympic games* Available at: https://
olympics.com/ioc/gender-equality/gender-equality-through-time/at-the-olympic
-games

IOC (2021b) *IOC releases framework on fairness, inclusion and non-discrimination on the basis of gender identity and sex variations* Available at: https://olympics.com/ioc/news/ioc
-releases-framework-on-fairness-inclusion-and-non-discrimination-on-the-basis-of
-gender-identity-and-sex-variations

Karkazis, K., & Jordan-Young, R. (2018). The powers of testosterone: Obscuring race and regional bias in the regulation of women athletes. *Feminist Formations* Available at: https://www.researchgate.net/publication/324756732_The_Powers
_of_Testosterone_Obscuring_Race_and_Regional_Bias_in_the_Regulation_of
_Women_Athletes?showFulltext=1&linkId=5ae097f2a6fdcc91399dbb60

Kliegman, J. (2022) *Understanding the different rules and policies for transgender athletes* Available at: https://www.si.com/more-sports/2022/07/06/transgender-athletes
-bans-policies-ioc-ncaa

Mancur, J. (2014) *Fighting for the body she was born with* Available at: https://www.nytimes
.com/2014/10/07/sports/sprinter-dutee-chand-fights-ban-over-her-testosterone
-level.html

Marchant, J. (2011) 'Women with high male hormone levels face sport ban.' *Nature.* https://doi.org/10.1038/news.2011.237

Reuters (2022) *Rugby league joins clampdown on transgender athletes in women's sports* Available at: https://www.nbcnews.com/nbc-out/out-news/rugby-league-joins-clampdown
-transgender-athletes-womens-sport-rcna34734

Ripa, Y. (2020). *Women and the Olympic games* Available at: https://ehne.fr/en/encyclopedia
/themes/gender-and-europe/gendered-body/women-and-olympic-games

Ritchie, R., Reynard, J., & Lewis, T. (2008). 'Intersex and the Olympic games.' *Journal of the Royal Society of Medicine, 101*(8), 395–399. https://doi.org/10.1258/jrsm.2008
.080086

Roberts, C. (2016) 'Tanner's puberty scale: Exploring the historical entanglements of children, scientific photography and sex.' *Sexualities, 19*(3), pp. 328–346. https://doi
.org/10.1177/1363460715593477.

Rugby Canada (2020) *Rugby Canada provides update on feedback posed transgender rules* Available a: https://rugby.ca/en/news/2020/09/rugby-canada-provides-update-on
-feedback-to-proposed-transgender-guidelines

Simpson, J. L., Ljungqvist, A., de la Chapelle, A., et al. (1993) 'Gender verification in competitive sports.' *Sports Medicine, 16*, 305–315. https://doi.org/10.2165/00007256-199316050-00002

TIME (1936a) *Olympic games* Available at: https://content.time.com/time/subscriber/article/0,33009,756486-4,00.html

TIME (1936b) *Olympic games* Available at: https://content.time.com/time/subscriber/article/0,33009,756542-3,00.html

USA Rugby (2020) *Transgender athletes & participants* Available at: https://www.usa.rugby/transgender-policy/

World Athletics (2018) *IAAF introduces new eligibility regulations for female classification* Available at: https://worldathletics.org/news/press-release/eligibility-regulations-for-female-classifica

World Rugby (2021) *Transgender guidelines* Available at: https://www.world.rugby/the-game/player-welfare/guidelines/transgender

PART VIII
Implications

34

WHAT THE CASES OF GAZPROM, THE NBA, AND QATAR MEAN FOR SPORT INDUSTRY DECISION-MAKERS

Simon Chadwick and Paul Widdop

Introduction

Sport at the end of the first quarter of the twenty-first century is markedly different to what preceded it, which is posing new and distinctive challenges for decision-makers in the sector. This chapter highlights some of the key issues facing them, using a series of case studies to enable this. To begin with, the chapter profiles three ages of contemporary sport, as this helps explain the nature of the sport industry today. This provides the basis for establishing the importance of geopolitical economy for sport, of which an overview is provided here. Thereafter, the chapter uses three case studies to illustrate the relevance of geopolitical economy but also to highlight some of the key issues being posed for decision-makers in sport.

Three Ages of Contemporary Sport

In the late nineteenth and early twentieth centuries, the development and governance of sports were driven by European utilitarian principles (Lanfranchi and Roach, 2017; Vamplew, 2017). This dictated that sport should provide the greatest good for the greatest number because it is a public good. Such principles led to the creation of structures, systems, and organizations that underpinned a European sporting hegemony, features of which still endure. For instance, Switzerland remains an important global sports governance hub. By the mid-twentieth century, the United States had attained prominence in sport that for the remainder of the century and into the first decade of the twenty-first century would dominate. US sport is essentially based upon neoclassical economic principles, which stress the significance of money, markets, and individual gain – sport in these terms is a private good (Bowles, 1991; Henry, 2012). Hence,

DOI: 10.4324/9781003348238-42

the growth of sponsorship and naming rights, a focus on market expansion and overseas growth, and the proliferation of broadcasting and media rights are all synonymous with the neoclassical economic paradigm. Even today, US engagement with and influence on sport remains strong, evidence of which can be found in the growing number of the country's private equity investors acquiring stakes in European football clubs. Over the last three decades, however, there have been a series of giga-changes – specifically globalization (Schulenkorf and Frawley, 2016), digitalization (Rindfleisch, 2019), and issues of energy and the environment (McCullough et al., 2020) – that have resulted in changes to and challenges for both utilitarian and neoclassical notions of sport.

This has necessitated that a new conception of sport is required, which forms the basis for this book – the geopolitical economy of sport. To begin with, this chapter revisits some of its salient features, which more importantly set the context for understanding what the geopolitical economy of sport means for industry decision-makers. To assist in this process, three cases are used: UEFA and Gazprom, the NBA and China, and Qatar and the FIFA World Cup.

Geopolitical Economy of Sport

The geopolitical economy of sport is defined as being the way in which nations, states, and other entities engage in, with, or through sport for geographic and politico-economic reasons in order to build and exert power and secure strategic advantages through the control of resources within and via networks of which sport is a constituent part (Chadwick, 2022a). This signifies sport as being a geopolitical good, rather than being a public or a private one.

A key feature of geopolitical economy is a role that nations and states intersect with and utilize (Chadwick and Widdop, 2021). In the case of Gazprom, this is the Russian government via its ownership of a gas corporation. In engagements with the NBA, the Chinese government has always played a key role in moderating and controlling the basketball organization's commercial activities (Huang, 2013). With Qatar, the way in which the state has engaged in nation-building through sport differentiates this country from others elsewhere in the world (Chadwick, 2022b). However, it is important to note that sport as geopolitical economy is not solely the preserve of emerging nations, Asian countries, or, as some often claim, despotic regimes. For instance, the British government routinely deploys sports as part of its trade missions, as a driver of economic activity, as a channel through which to project soft power, and for the purposes of enhancing international relationships (Chadwick, 2016).

Engagement with sport is partly driven by geographic factors, both physical and human. In the case of Gulf nations, their investments in sport are partly driven by the need to diversify their economies in order to reduce a dependence on oil and gas revenues. As part of the same strategy, sport for the likes of Saudi Arabia and Abu Dhabi contributes to achieving political ends. This includes promotion of nation brands and the cultivation of diplomatic relationships through sport (Rofe, 2016; Koch, 2018). There are also economic dimensions to such countries' approach to policy and strategy, for example by building a national competitive advantage (Porter, 2011). For Saudi Arabia, this has meant bidding for and hosting sport events, as the country seeks to become an important Afro-Eurasian sports hub (Sports Pro, 2021). By contrast, by engaging stadium diplomacy in Africa, China has sought to sustain its economic performance by gifting venues to countries in return for securing access to valuable natural resources (Will, 2012).

In delivering sport as a good for the greatest number of people enforces upon decision-makers the need to account for a distinctive set of criteria, for instance reconciling the sometimes highly disparate needs of stakeholders. Similarly, the neoclassical focus on markets, profit, and private delivery of sport necessitate a different approach to decision-making. How to meet the specific demands of individual consumers whilst delivering a commercial return is significantly removed from the challenges posed by utilitarianism. Framing sport as geopolitical economy in turn suggests other, different challenges facing decision-makers in sport, which the following three case analyses serve to highlight.

Gazprom and UEFA[1]

Russia is one of the world's largest producers of natural gas, a significant proportion of which is extracted, distributed, and sold by state-owned corporation Gazprom. This feature of Russia's physical geography has enabled the country to generate huge revenues, which had helped fund its political and economic activities. It has helped the country lavishly host events such as the 2014 Winter Olympic Games and the 2018 FIFA World Cup, both of which served a soft power purpose for the government in Moscow. At the same time, gas has helped fuel the rise of an oligarch class as well as the Russian middle class in general. Indeed, Gazprom was formed following the acquisition of Sibneft from Roman Abramovich, who had bought the company during the 1990s era of privatization. Yet the Russian government has also strategically deployed Gazprom to foster a dependence upon the country's gas across several European countries, perhaps most notably Germany. With such dependence has come control hence the positive bilateral relationships that several European countries have had with Russia. Against this backdrop, UEFA signed a number of lucrative sponsorships with Gazprom, most notably for the right to associate with the men's Champions League. Most such deals normally involve business-to-consumer sponsorships, whereas in Gazprom's case, it seemed the corporation was a government-to-government sponsorship. Irrespective of whether Gazprom actually sold extra gas as the result of its UEFA deals, some have labelled these sponsorships as being soft power instruments, sportswashing, and even propaganda. Some credence was given to these views when Russia invaded Ukraine, only months before the UEFA Champions League final was scheduled to take place.

Such is the scale and nature of the issues addressed by this and the two other cases presented here that commentary can only be indicative rather than exhaustive. Nevertheless, it is anticipated that there will still be some salient lessons for all decision-makers in sport. When UEFA first signed its deal with Gazprom in 2012, Russia and its president, Vladimir Putin, had not provoked intense scrutiny by global. However, within two years, the annexation of Crimea and downing of a passenger jet in eastern Ukraine had caused many to question the country and its motives. This implies that strategic foresight needs to play a more prominent role in sport, especially when significant financial decisions are being made. In the same vein, when taking sponsorship decisions like those UEFA made, extending pre-contract due diligence to account for geopolitical factors would appear to be of increasing importance. Gazprom appears to have utilized its UEFA sponsorships as a channel through which to build power and influence from inside the governing body of European football. Indeed, the corporation's chairman was able to secure a position on UEFA's executive committee via his presidency of the Russian football club Zenit Saint Petersburg (which is owned by Gazprom). The fitness-for-purpose of the existing governance arrangements therefore needs stress testing when it is clear that, for example, sponsorships are being deployed for geopolitical purposes.

China and the National Basketball Association[2]

Basketball is a very popular sport in China, which is partially a result of more than two decades working in collaboration with the United States' NBA. This collaboration has seen the NBA creating basketball facilities across the world's most populous nation, whilst engaging and training youngsters to play the sport. Arguably the most potent symbol of the relationship is Yao Ming, who played for both Shanghai Sharks and Houston Rockets. The standard of Chinese professional basketball has been greatly enhanced, whilst commercially the NBA has generated hundreds of millions of dollars from its Chinese operations and the United States itself has garnered soft power returns from the NBA's prominence in China. Yet despite the apparent symbiosis, in late 2019 a tweet by Daryl Morey, then general manager at the Houston Rockets, caused a major furore. During the preceding months, there had been widespread democracy protests in Hong Kong. These were the result of changes within the territory introduced by China following its handover from Great Britain in 1997. Morey took to Twitter to express his support for the protestors, something which the Chinese government objected to. In spite of attempts by NBA commissioner Adam Silver to defuse the situation, officials in Beijing decided to remove the broadcasting of NBA games from Chinese television. This lasted for more than a year and coincided with the global pandemic, which meant that after two decades of operating in China, the NBA's local activities were significantly curtailed. Notwithstanding the territorial and political dimensions of this matter as they pertain to Hong Kong, the Morey episode almost embodied a growing power struggle between China and the United States, manifest in geographic, political, and economic terms. At the same time, it juxtaposed a country in which the state is omnipotent with one where individual liberty pervades. All of this was set against the backdrop of globalization and digitalization, not least Morey's tweet.

The NBA is not alone in having sought entry and penetration into the Chinese marketplace over the last two decades. A small number of sport organizations have successfully achieved this, engaged local consumers, and navigated through a complex market. However, many haven't; China is a large, hugely diverse country, making it difficult to make decisions and create strategy. Furthermore, the political system and social conventions can sometimes render the market impenetrable, which many sport organizations appear not to be aware of. Undertaking rigorous market research and analysis is therefore hugely important, as is building a network of partners who intimately understand the practicalities of operating in what is often a very complex environment. One Daryl Morey tweet is evidence of this; what might constitute freedom of speech in the West may be perceived as a threat to political stability and social order elsewhere. Understanding what is permissible and acceptable is important, though some would question why a US citizen could be cancelled for expressing his political opinions. At one level, this exposes some important communications of management issues, though it also shows how important an understanding of social media environments is. At another level, what the Morey episode raised is the imperative for sport decision-makers to reconcile the sometimes highly disparate demands of multiple stakeholders.

Qatar and the FIFA World Cup[3]

Qatar is a small peninsula with only one land border which links it to Saudi Arabia, one of the Gulf region's political and economic powerhouses. Just to the east is Iran, another large and powerful country, whilst to the north is Turkey. Countries such as Yemen, Syria, and Afghanistan are close by; hence, this small nation of three million people is strategically vulnerable. Addressing this challenge is an ongoing strategic priority for the country. At the same time, on a per capita income basis, Qatar is one of the richest countries in the world, due to its vast reserves of liquified natural gas. The human geography of Qatar is distinctive, with only ten percent of its population being Qatari nationals (the remainder being immigrants). Establishing a coherent national identity has therefore been a challenge; equally, building the nation and establishing its brand globally have been a focus for the country's government over the last 50 years – Qatar was a British protectorate until 1971. Since then, a state-led programme of reform has sought to modernize and build the country by diversifying its economy, strengthening its industrial foundations, and promoting enterprise. Sport has been a means through which Qatar has been able to address these multiple challenges, which the staging of 2022's FIFA World Cup has been a foundation of. The country's tournament hosting has helped to embed it within the wider international community, driven

292 Simon Chadwick and Paul Widdop

the construction of civic infrastructure, enabled the projection of soft power, and provided a focal point for building social cohesion within the country. The programme has not been without criticism or problem: Qatar has been embroiled in a FIFA corruption scandal; some commentators have condemned the country as being contrived, inauthentic, undeserving hosts; and there has been condemnation of its treatment of migrant construction workers, women, and minority groups.

As sport continues to globalize, the need to understand diverse territories grows – as it impacts upon the success of entry to new markets and upon the relationships an organization has with fans, other consumers, commercial partners, and governments. Whether one works for a team, governing body, or consultancy, it is also important to note that in countries like Qatar decisions are primarily driven by political factors. Hence, understanding motive, policy, strategy, implementation, and evaluation at the state level must inevitably play a key role in decision-making. Big state orientation in countries like Qatar means that decision-making processes can often be bureaucratic and therefore often slow. Furthermore, the culture of doing business in such territories is often based upon personal political relationships, as well as an understanding of local socio-political conventions. It is worth remembering as well that decision-making in rentier states such as Qatar is also driven by a need to diversify economic and industrial activity, often through investment in overseas assets. Otherwise, as frequent analyses and criticism of Qatar illustrate, sport's geopolitical economy has thrust all manner of issues – from the treatment of migrant workers to the environmental status of events – into the spotlight. Sport can no longer operate solely on the basis of staging competitive contests.

Conclusions

Following 150 years of contemporary sport during which European utilitarian then later US neoclassical notions of sport have been hegemonic, sport in the twenty-first century is now more appropriately and, indeed, more accurately portrayed as a geopolitical economy. This means that sport exists and functions within an environment within which geography, politics, and economics dictate and are shaping decisions being made. In consequence, the growing influence of state actors, the strengthening of conflicting ideological positions, and the rise particularly of nations in Asia are creating a new set of parameters within which those working in sport must make decisions. By employing three case studies, this chapter has highlighted some of the challenges this poses for sport decision-makers. However, this is only an overview and demands further thought and associated analyses. It is nevertheless hoped that the chapter helps prompt such work.

Notes

1 Readers may want to read the following as a background to this short case: Gazprom and its sponsorship of football. From sex without a condom to major strategic threat

https://www.iris-france.org/154279-gazprom-and-its-sponsorship-of-football-from-sex-without-a-condom-to-major-strategic-threat/

2 Readers may want to read the following as a background to this short case: The NBA in China: Who calls the shots? https://www.policyforum.net/the-nba-in-china-who-calls-the-shots/

3 Readers may want to read the following as a background to this short case: Small Nation, Big Games – Qatar Gets Ready for 2022 https://www.iris-france.org/160117-small-nation-big-games-qatar-gets-ready-for-2022/

References

Bowles, S. (1991). What markets can—And cannot—Do. *Challenge, 34*(4), 11–16.

Chadwick, S. (2016). How football is becoming a major player for British soft power. *Newsweek*, 12th February, accessed via https://www.newsweek.com/football-uk-brexit-soft-power-arsenal-premiere-league-527228

Chadwick, S. (2022a). From utilitarianism and neoclassical sport management to a new geopolitical economy of sport. *European Sport Management Quarterly*, 1–20.

Chadwick, S. (2022b). Football, feuding and games in the Gulf. *Insights*, 21st June, accessed via https://mei.nus.edu.sg/wp-content/uploads/2022/06/Insights-279-Simon-Chadwick.pdf

Chadwick, S., & Widdop, P. (2021). The geopolitical economy of sport: A new era at play. *Asia and the Pacific Policy Forum*, 13th January, accessed via https://www.policyforum.net/the-geopolitical-economy-of-sport/

Henry, J. F. (2012). *The making of neoclassical economics*. London: Routledge.

Huang, F. (2013). Glocalisation of sport: The NBA's diffusion in China. *The International Journal of the History of Sport, 30*(3), 267–284.

Koch, N. (2018). The geopolitics of sport beyond soft power: Event ethnography and the 2016 cycling world championships in Qatar. *Sport in Society, 21*(12), 2010–2031.

Lanfranchi, P., & Roach, J. (2017). Exporting football: Notes on the development of football in Europe. In *Game without frontiers* (pp. 22–45). London: Routledge.

McCullough, B. P., Orr, M., & Kellison, T. (2020). Sport ecology: Conceptualizing an emerging subdiscipline within sport management. *Journal of Sport Management, 34*(6), 509–520.

Porter, M. E. (2011). *Competitive advantage of nations: Creating and sustaining superior performance*. New York: Simon and Schuster.

Rindfleisch, A. (2019). The second digital revolution. *Marketing Letters, 31*(1), 1–5.

Rofe, J. S. (2016). Sport and diplomacy: A global diplomacy framework. *Diplomacy & Statecraft, 27*(2), 212–230.

Schulenkorf, N., & Frawley, S. (Eds.). (2016). *Critical issues in global sport management*. London: Taylor & Francis.

Sports Pro (2021). Newcastle United and Saudi Arabia: Understanding a seismic Premier League takeover. *Sport Pro Podcast*, 14th October, accessed via https://www.sportspromedia.com/insights/podcasts/sportspro-podcasts/newcastle-united-saudi-arabia-pif-takeover-premier-league-podcast/

Vamplew, W. (2017). Industrialization and sport. In *The Oxford handbook of sports history*. Oxford: Oxford University Press.

Will, R. (2012). China's stadium diplomacy. *World Policy Journal, 29*(2), 36–44.

INDEX

Page numbers in **bold** denote tables, those in *italic* denote figures.

acquisitions 94, 113, 239; cross-border 96; football 104
activism 129; athletes' 11, 77, 81, 229; human rights 119; social 119
Africa Cup of Nations (AFCON) 101, 170
aid agencies 257
AK Party 204–207
Al Jazeera 128–129
Alegi, P. 165–168
AlKhalifa, H. 139
alternative football 185–189
Amazon Prime 217
ambassadors 129, 257, 264; brand 88
Amnesty International 145–146, 150, 173
annexation of Crimea 13, 20, 34, 44, 50, 290
anti-gay legislature 45
Anzhi 49, 51, 55, 57
Apartheid 32, 81; anti- 166; South African 71
Arab Spring 128–129, 254
Arnold R 44
artistic gymnastics 37; World Cup 9
Asian Games 101, 105, 130–131
Associated Press 281
Association of Summer Olympic International Federations (ASOIF) 23, 218; Assembly of 38, 40
athletes: African 137, 273–274; agency 9, 13–14; Belarusian 11–13, 21, 30, 36, 39, 70, 73; borderless 90; Chinese 86, 88, 90; deprivation of self-identity 39; dissenting 13; effect of sports sanctions 24; elite 9–12, 14, 70, 85, 90, 264, 282; equal rights 39; exclusion of 280; female 87–88, 137, 279–280; foreign-raised 86; freedom of expression 10; gender 277; gender-diverse 279, 281–282; Global 11; improving cognitive skills 80; individuals 37, 264; initiatives 11; intersex 277–278, 281; isolation from global sports community 39; Israeli 75, 77, **79**, 80; Jewish 77–78; minority 274; murder of Israel 75; naturalized 78, 86; neutral 12, 21, 23; Olympic 75, 86; Pacific 263; paralympic 69–70; patriotic 87; public stance against the war 14; Russian 1, 11–14, 21–24, 29–31, 35–37, 39, 43, 70, 73, 227; silent boycotts 77; slave 37; socially conscious 118; status of 30; training abroad 81; transfeminine 277; transgender 277–280; transmasculine 277; Ukrainian 12, 21; US 10, 38, 271; Western 12–14; withdrawing 75; women 120, 136, 279, 282; young 85; *see also* activisim
Athletes' Commission 10; Rule 50 Guidelines 10
Australia Sports Outreach Program 263
authoritarianism 175; domestic 14; mounting 239; supportive of 118

296 Index

Bach, T. 1, 12, 21–24, 36, 38–39, 70
Bale, J. 89
Barr Body Test 279
Basic Universal Principles for the Good
  Governance of the Olympic and Sports
  Movement (PGG) 40
Basketball Africa League (BAL) 173–174,
  176–178
Battilana, J. 230
Bell, C. 253
Belt and Road Initiatives (BRI) 96,
  108–109, 262
best-practice information 131
Bezos, J. 151
black glove salute 10
Black Lives Matter (BLM) 272, 274
blanket ban on Russian and Belarusian
  athletes 11, 13
Blatter, S. 50, 58, 186
Bloomberg 96
Board of Control for Cricket in India
  (BCCI) 156–159
branding 51, 81, 127, 129–130, 236,
  242–244; attempts 80, 129; cultural
  75, 78; export 75, 80; investment in
  130; nation 44, 75, 78, 80–82, 142;
  national 96; place 75, 80–81, 210;
  political 75, 77; potential tool of 129;
  product 242; re- 51, 150, 194; state
  127, 129–130; strategy 109; team 157;
  tobacco 243
Brannagan, P. M. 145–146
Brinch, J. 185
British Academy 253
British Council 260
British Paralympic Association 70
Burke, P. 281
Bush, G. 151
Butler, J. 273

Cardenas, A. 255
Carlos, J. 10
case studies: China and the National
  Basketball Association 290; Gazprom
  and UEFA 289; Qatar and the FIFA
  World Cup 291
Catalan Agency of Tourism 211
Chadwick, S. 4, 93–94, 96, 142
Champions Trophy 156
Chernyshenko, D. 22, 31
Chinese dream 87
Chinese Football Association (CFA)
  109, 113
Chinese Government 72
Chinese Stadium Diplomacy 111

Chinese Super League (CSL) 104, 108,
  110–113
Chtcherbakova, A. 32
cisgender 277–278, 282
Clarke, F. 255
climate: crisis 247; emergency 258
Cold War 34, 38, 71, 253–254, 279; New
  262, 267
colonial: anti- 166; dominance 166;
  era 136, 153, 166; history 135, 139;
  initiation 165; institutions 166; legacy
  165; neo- 263; orientalist 136; rule 149;
  times 156
commercial: activity 193, 288;
  agreements 238; aspects 160; brands
  211; competition 170; connection 157,
  198; growth 199; implications 155;
  influence 50; interests 156; non- 239;
  objectives 160; opportunities 192,
  196–197, 199–200; partners 198–199,
  292; perspective 159; potential 49, 57;
  reasons 238; relations 177, 193, 195;
  return 289; revenues 53, 199; rights
  221, 243–244; shirt sponsor 130;
  sponsorship 242; sport spectacle 192;
  stakeholders 142; success 58, 89, 195;
  tie-ups 116; weight 157
commercialization 49, 155–156, 213, 219;
  of football 168–169, 197
commodification 136, 169
Commonwealth Games Federation 71
Commonwealth of Independent States
  (CIS) 34, 49, 58
Communist Party 94, 110
complete androgen insensitivity
  syndrome 279
Confédération Africaine de Football
  (CAF) 166, 170
Confederation of Independent Football
  Associations (CONIFA) 186–189
conflict 12, 29, 41, 58, 75, 85, 94, 189,
  256; armed 14; binary opposition of
  258; bloody 60; cultural dimensions
  of 258; Cyprus –Turkey 231–232;
  direct 120; of form and content 40;
  impact of 258; international 45; Israeli–
  Palestinian 81; martial 20; military 50;
  paramilitary 36; political 43, 94; post-
  189, 256; resolution 256, 259; Ukraine
  245; Yemeni 145; zones 128–129
corruption 39, 45, 146, 176, 193, 231;
  allegations of 128–129; high-profile
  194; scandals 2, 194, 292
cosmopolitanism 271–272, 274–275
Council of Europe (COE) 187

Index **297**

Court of Arbitration for Sport 22, 37, 280
COVID-19 pandemic 68, 81, 105, 121,
  159, 176, 210, 212, 237, 245, 264–265
cricket 149, 155–157; boards 157–159;
  commercialized 156; ecosystem 158;
  global revenues 156; influential board
  156; international 156; lack of appeal
  117; obsession 156; origins 156; ploy
  to achieve political gains 158; spirit of
  159; sponsorship 158; viewership 156;
  world 155
criticism 78, 87, 89, 103–104, 106,
  145–146, 158, 292; legitimate 177;
  ongoing 77; prospect of 23; public 197,
  200; rejection of 145; right-wing 88;
  vehement 151
cultural: agencies 257–258; background
  136; branding 75, 78; capital 151;
  changes 232, 272; cities 211; conditions
  200; conjecture 192; differences 194;
  dimensions 258; diplomacy 81; driver
  146; ecology 90; engagement 258;
  events 272; expression 255; field 258;
  forces 274; gatekeepers 257; heritage
  81; identities 88; ideologies 272;
  imperialism 149, 153; importance 274;
  influence 141, 146; instability 273; inter-
  89, 257; lives 102; meanings 273; multi-
  88, 271–272, 274; organizations 258;
  politico- 151; power 109, 118; racism
  274; regulations 255; relations 253–255,
  257–260; representations 189, 273; –
  ritual 37, 272; socio- 146, 194; space 60;
  sports 267; stability 272–273; stasis 272

Dakar Youth Olympics (2026) 103
Darby, P. 166, 168–169
Darnell, S. 255
debt 113; accumulation of 113; dependent
  on 110; relationships 109; -trap
  diplomacy 267
Democratic Left Party (DSP) 203
demography 134, 136
Desrosiers, M-E. 175
digitalization 200, 288, 291
diplomacy 4, 67, 98, 103, 111–112, 129,
  141, 173–175, 178, 194, 264–265, 267;
  basketball 178; corporate 210; cultural
  81; debt-trap 267; economic 262;
  financial 96–97; foreign 121; formal
  266; global 194; hostage 237; political
  legacy of 195; public 75, 77, 81–82,
  105, 194, 213, 264, 267; sports 44,
  72, 86, 96, 103, 131, 174–175, 255,
  262–265, 267–268; sport-tech 80–81;

stadium 95, 101, 103, 105–106, 109,
  111, 265–266, 289; wolf warrior 121;
  see also debt
discrimination 13, 272; anti- 10–11;
  ideologically driven 22; overt 272;
  prohibition of 33; racial 229, 233
disempowerment 43–44, 146; soft 42–43,
  46–47, 141, 144–146
Donbas 45, 50, 60, 189
doping scandal 21, 44–46, 70
Dorries, N. 70
dual: citizenship 85; identity 85–86, 88;
  nationality 136
Dubinsky, Y. 80
Duty of Vigilance Law (2017) 231
dysfunction 38; management 36

economic: acquisition 113; activity
  102, 197, 288–289, 292; agreements
  265; assets 144; benefit 105; boycott
  129; certainty 192, 195–197, 200;
  competition 94, 171; conditions 102,
  200; development 51, 90, 108, 175;
  dimension 3, 103, 289; diversification
  146; driver 146, 214; environment 171;
  formations 192, 199; fragility 256, 258;
  gap 168, 171; geography 169; influences
  95, 141; instability 246; interests 93,
  200, 254; level 60, 211; might 93, 97;
  opportunity 198; partnerships 142,
  191; performance 40, 289; politico-
  29, 31, 50, 288; potential 105, 116;
  power 95, 109, 200; sanctions 20, 24,
  29; socio- 150, 211; terms 212, 291;
  transformation 2, 165, 170
The Economist 85, 272
Education Above All 128
EFI Database 110
eligibility 21, 23, 278, 280–281
elite 95, 137, 151, 263; African-schooled
  166; athletes 9–12, 14, 70, 85, 90, 264,
  282; businessmen 138; championships
  219; clubs 221; competition 264, 278;
  disability sport 67, 69, 72; divisions 221;
  European football teams 138; level 77,
  278, 280; pacts 259; politicians 120;
  ruling 139; secular 203; selection 87;
  sport 134, 136–137, 279–280, 282;
  sport development 139; sporting power
  88–89; sportspeople 11; tournament 217
endorsement 87, 214; brands 87
English Premier League 53, 148, 150, 157,
  170, 175, 217, 219
environmental: awareness 258; fragility
  256, 258; jolts 228–229, 232;

298 Index

preservation activities 258; protest 205; sensitive perspective 211; status 292; sustainability 258
Equality, Liberty, Fraternity Trophy 187
EUNIC 260
European Club Association (ECA) 220–221
European National Institutes of Culture 255
European Rally Championship 231
European Super League 217, 221
European Table Tennis Union (ETTU) 37
European Union 20, 222, 243–244, 271; Third Energy Package 55
exclusion 12, 14, 20, 30–31, 37, 75, 77
experience packages 116
Extreme E 246

Fan, Y. 78
FC Barcelona 130, 169, 210–212, 214–215, 273
Fédération Internationale de Football Association (FIFA): bans 11, 29, 35, 222; capital accumulation 199; Club World Cup (2021) 97–186; commercial opportunities 197; -compatible stadiums 195; confederations 185; Congress 128; corruption and collusion within 145, 193; corruption scandal 292; delegation 196; evaluation 196; Fan Fests 193; formation of 185; full tax exemptions 193; Global Transfer Report 169; official languages 36; official partners 130; post-scandal 195; principles 58; public image of 197; rebranding 194; revenue generation 199; scandals within 2; sponsors 104; suspension by 189; U-20 World Cup (1995) 130; visa-free travel for officials 193; wealth extraction 199; World Cup (1934) 135; World Cup (2010) 168; World Cup (2014) 142, 198; World Cup (2018) 44, 50, 95, 97, 289; World Cup (2022) 101, 127, 128, 135, 138, 142, 145, 148, 238, 291; World Cup (2026) 191; Youth World Championships 167
Fédération Internationale de l'Automobile (FIA) 117, 227–233, 237–238
financial: assets 96; -backing 96; clout 160; decisions 290; difficulties 113; diplomacy 96–97; ends 109; Fair Play 56, 57, 220; fair play mechanisms 49; independence 38; injections 220; institutions 102, 198; interests 239;

limited return 171; losses 198; model 247; muscle 157, 159; problems 56, 59, 110, 112–113; prospects 218; reality 243; regulators 96; resources 95, 137, 169; rewards 145; situation 109; windfall 59
Five-Year Plans 108–109
Floyd, G. 3, 10
foreign: diplomats 257; investments 138, 220
Formula 1 2, 29, 138, 142–143, 148, 151, 217, 223, 227–228, 232, 235–239
Formula E 244, 246
Freedom House 175

Geertz, C. 272
gender 263, 273; -based violence 174; cis-277–278, 282; confirmation surgery 279; defining 277; -diverse 277–279, 281–282; empowerment 175; equality 10, 150, 174, 232; identity 278, 282; inclusion 278; inequality 233; parity 279; question 136; solidified 277; trans-277–282; verification 279–280
geopolitical: actor 233; advantages 94; competitors 94; conjuncture 192, 199; contentions 94; crisis 29, 72; debate 70, 136, 233; divides 194; dynamic 232; economy of sport 3–4, 42–44, 47, 50, 93–94, 98, 101, 103, 155, 160, 192, 199–200, 287–289, 292; environment 85; episodes 229; era 141; evolution 144; factors 290; fallout 70; firmament 186; friction 159–160; gain 142; goals 104; good 288; incident 69, 72; influences 95, 144, 200; interests 200; issues 71; logic of balance of power 29; maelstrom 86; motives 142; objective 35, 127, 145, 157; order 194; pinch points 94; players 12; poly 155; position 35, 72, 94; power 97; purposes 290; real estate 262; reality 35, 47; results 93; role 228, 232; settings 70; shifts 228; skirmishes 160; solutions 35; strategies 144; strides 228; strife 231; tensions 10–11, 85, 89, 96, 155, 237; tightrope 178; tool 113, 145
Ginesta, X. 215
global: Athlete 11; consciousness 129; diplomacy 194; economic crisis (2008) 53; football business complex 165, 170–171; media attention 9, 232; North 150–151, 153, 171, 281; South 137, 151, 281; sport governance 67; sporting power elite 88–89; unity 194

globalization 89, 116, 135, 200, 211, 274, 288; of sports 41
Gold, J.R. 68
golf 22, 143, 145, 148, 151, 236
Golubchikov, O. 51
governance 41, 67–69, 204–206, 263; arrangements 290; bilateral 204–205, 207; bodies 96, 98; challenges 228; decision 204; formal 73; formalized 73; global 9, 14; good 40, 175, 231; market-based 204–207; organizations 96–97; over politics 173, 175, 177–178; processes 69; spatial 51; sport 3, 23, 67, 71–72, 95, 98, 287; stature 71; strong 176; structures 40, 194; system 71; technical 175; top-down 70; vertical integration 206; World Sports 37
Grand Prix Drivers Association (GPDA) 228
Gu Ailing 1, 85–90
Guha, R. 156
Gulf Cooperation Council (GCC) 134, 137–139
Gulf Region 134, 143, 146, 148, 291

Hamilton, L. 118, 229–230, 236
Heraskevych, V. 9, 11
Hillmann, J. 228–230
Hinks, P. 176
Hitler, A. 149
Horne, J. 192
hosting rights 105–106, 128, 131, 141, 191, 193
Houston Rockets 118, 177, 290
human rights 106, 118, 145, 178, 231, 233, 253, 256–258, 260, 277, 279–280; abuses 86, 145, 148, 150, 236–237; activism 119; Advisory Council 232; attention to 14; commitments 259; considerations 9; controversies surrounding 96; defence of 258; discourse 233; Foundation 173; fundamental 30; groups 128; initiatives 10; issues 102, 104, 236; mission 10; policy 227; practices 105; principles 232; record 13, 43, 145–146, 149, 232; respect for 231; responsibilities 232; situation 105; Universal Declaration of 30; violations 14, 77, 173
humanitarian; considerations 9; instruments of power 128; organization 229, 232; values 38
hydrocarbon-based economies 138

identity diaspora 90
impact of war on sport 1

imperialism 57; cultural 149, 153
Indian Premier League (IPL) 143, 155–159
Industrial Revolution 213
industry of relationships 177
Intelligym 80
internal entrepreneurship 229
International Aquatic Federation (FINA) 22, 36, 277–278, 281–282
International Basketball Federation (FIBA) 173
International Contact Group 128
International Convention on the Elimination of All Forms of Racial Discrimination (1965) 39
International Cricket Council (ICC) 117, 156–158
International Federation of Red Cross and Red Crescent Societies (IFRC) 231
International Gymnastics Federation 23
International Handball Federation 136
International Judo Federation (IJF) 36
International Labour Organization 256
International Luge Federation (FIL) 37
International Olympic Committee (IOC) 1, 10, 12, 20–24, 29, 33–34, 36–40, 45–46, 67–71, 73, 77–78, 97–98, 103, 120, 135–136, 192, 218, 227, 256, 278–281
International Paralympic Committee (IPC) 12, 22, 67–73
International Rugby League 266, 278
international sports bodies 29–30, 32
International Sports Federation (ISF) 12, 32–33, 36–41, 69, 71, 219
International Women's Sports Federation (FSFI) 278–279
International YMCA Training School 174
internationalization 113, 135
invasion of Ukraine 11, 12, 20–21, 29–30, 43, 45–46, 67, 69, 71, 227–228, 237–238
Iraqi invasion 138
Islamist Welfare Party (RP) 203
Israeli–Arab dispute 75, 77, 80–81
Israeli ice Skating Federation 77

James, G. 214
Jewish Diaspora 78
Joseph, N. 128
Judaism 78, 80

Kaepernic, C. 3, 10, 274
Kagame, P. 175–178
Karkazis, K. 281

300 Index

Kashmir Premier League (KPL) 157, 159
Key Governance Principles and Key
  Indicators (KGP) 40
Keys, B. 72
Koch, N. 138
Kon'kov, A. 59
Kontinental Hockey League (KHL) 35,
  50–51, **52**, 57
Kostyuk. M. 13
Krasner, S.D. 39
Kuliak, I. 9, 13–14, 23
Kuwaiti Olympic Committee 137

Leary, S. 264
Le Guellec, G. 34
Lenin, V. 34, 222
Levitin, I. 32–33
LGBTQ+ community 146, 236

Maccabiah Games 81
Major League Soccer (MLS) **52**, 219
Markovits, A. S. 274
Marshall, T. 215
Matytsin, O. 31
medal: ceremonies 9; rankings 93
media coverage 70, 129–130, 145
mega-events 42, 44, 46, 50, 94, 96, 138,
  153, 192, 194
migrant workers: conditions 128; death 2;
  exploitation 2; treatment of 146, 292
Miller, A. 56, 58
Millward, P. 274
mimetic isomorphism 141, 144
Morey, D. 118–119, 177, 290–291
Morris, D. 37
Motherland Party (ANAP) 203
Munich Air Disaster (1958) 214
Munich Massacre 75, 77
Murray, A. 13
mutually: beneficial transactions 257;
  constitutive relationship 200

Nadal, R. 13
Næss H. E. 23
Nandy, A. 156
nation building 2, 105, 127, 130, 166, 288
National Basketball Association (NBA)
  3, 50, **52**, 53, **117**, 118–120, 153, 157,
  173–178, 274, 288, 290–291
National Football Federations 217
National Football League (NFL) 10, 157,
  218, 274
National Hockey League (NHL) 23,
  50, 53
national identity 75, 78, 89, 291

National Olympic Committee of
  Israel 77
National Olympic Committees 10,
  21, 218
National Paralympic Committee 67–71
nationalism 89, 93, 105, 207, 262, 271
NATO 20, 22, 119, 128
Navratilova, M. 13
Netflix 217, 238, 246
neutrality 11–12, 14, 29, 72, 227, 232
New Federation Board 185, 187
new world order of sport 33–35
New York Times 193, 280
NF Board 185–187
non-governmental organizations (NGOs)
  192, 257
North American Free Trade Agreement
  (NAFTA) 195
Nye, J. 128, 141

Obama, B. 174
Olympic: Charter 10, 22, 33, 36, 68;
  Truce 11–12, 14, 21, 36, 71, 78
online shopping 116
Organization of the Petroleum Exporting
  Countries (OPEC) 245
organizational resilience 227–229
Ovechkin, A. 13, 23
overseas direct investment (ODI) 96,
  108–111, 113

Pacific Games 265–266
Pacific Sports Partnerships 263
PacificAus Sports (PAS) 263
pandemic: control 96–97; depression 97
Pavlyuchenkova, A. 12–13
peace 4, 9, 21, 233, 253, 255, 257–258,
  260; agreements 256–257; -building
  175, 253–257; -keeping 253–255,
  259–260; -making 254, 256–257;
  negotiators 256, 259; political
  struggle for 255; post- 256; pro-
  11–12; processes 253, 256–257, 259;
  promoting 38–39; sport as an enabler
  for 255; talks 232
People's Republic Party (CHP) 204
personal relationships 174, 177–178
Pervy Kanal Figure Skating Cup 31
Poli, R. 169
Polish Football Association 11
political: activity 37; branding 75,
  77; conflicts 43; consequences 2;
  constituents 4; deveopment 51; fragility
  258; ideology 148–149; independence
  38; influence 39, 50; interests 23, 200;

issues 10, 14, 43, 71, 89, 227, 230, 232, 258; messages 9, 119; motives 12; narratives 47, 151; nature 59, 72; principle **59**; project 60; propaganda 10; purposes 2, 9, 50, 153; reality 30; relations 50, 72, 94, 109, 292; segregation 39; significance 3, 44, 137; spheres 45; status 30; tool 23; transformation 2; turbulence 43; visuals 43; weapon 29–30
politicization 14, 22–23, 36, 254
politico-economic 29, 50, 288
politics 2–3, 13–14, 23, 68, 89, 93–94, 96, 173, 176, 185–187, 192, 200, 203–204, 227, 239, 254, 292; American 38; conjunctural 192, 199; external 192; governance over 175, 177–178; internal 192; international 11, 14, 73, 77; power 254; reputational 141; symbolic 193
Pospisil, J. 253
press freedom 96
privatization 217–218, 223, 289
professionalization 109, 112, 135
property ownership 142
Public Investment Fund 2, 148, 151–152, 236
public memory 45, 47
Putin, V 13, 20–24, 29–31, 33–35, 69, 188–189, 238, 290

Qatar: Foundation 129–131; National Tourism Council (QNTC) 212; Sports Investment (QSI) 130, 212

racism 271–275; anti- 10
racist 271; anti- 11; attitudes 273; codes 273; jaunts 273; meanings 273; underpinnings 273; vitriol 272; ways of life 274; white fans 273
Reach Out to Asia 128
real estate sector 109–113
Red Sports International (IRS) 34
Reuters 70
Rogoff, K. S. 110
Rublev, A. 12–13, 238
Rugby Canada 278
Ruggie, J.G. 233
Russian Artistic Gymnastics Federation 37
Russian attack against Kyiv 9
Russian Federation 21, 31–32, 51
Russian Football Union 2, 37, 56, 58

sanctions 20–22, 29, 33, 36, 41, 43, 220, 238; economic 20, 24; governmental 40; implementation of 39; imposition of 41; informal 118; justification 21; sport 20, 23–24; trade 96
Saudi Arabian Public Investment Fund 2, 151
Schweizer, D. 96
security 175, 254; agreements 265; analyses 262; dilemmas 262; fragility 256, 258; guarantees 262; interests 254; matters 262; national 237
segregation 274, 282; de facto 273; ethnic 39; racial 32
semantic ambiguity 37
Shanghai Cooperation Organization (SCO) 31, 34
Sharma, D. 266
Smith, T. 9–10
socialL identity 78; justice 173, 176, 232, 254, 257–259; justice initiatives 10, 174
societal: change 146; fragility 256, 258; issues 174; make-up 134; values 139
society 4, 60, 89, 96, 116, 118, 137, 156, 230, 258, 273–275; civil 40–41, 158, 257–259; global 211; globalized 89; modern 60; racism 273–274; rural 175; underlying values 272
soft disempowerment 42–43, 46–47, 141, 144–146
soft power 2, 4, 42–47, 50–51, 55, 60, 86, 96–97, 102–106, 109, 112–113, 116, 119, 127–129, 134, 139, 141–142, 144–146, 151, 153, 173–175, 178, 232, 235, 255, 257, 262, 288–290, 292
Solidarity Games 22
South African Apartheid 71
Spedale, S. 230
sponsorship 87, 94–96, 108, 113, 116, 142–144, 153, 156, 158–159, 169–170, 197–198, 206, 235, 238, 242–244, 246, 288–290; agreement 143, 212; commercial 242; consumer 289; contract 212, 218; deals 119, 148, 159, 238; decisions 290; earnings 236; global 170, 211, 236; government-to-government 289; income 243; money 158; partners 235, 239; personal 243; portfolio 2, 142–143, 170; programme 38; properties 2; revenues 170, 236; rights 158; secondary 243; soft power 142; state-funded 141; state-owned 142; subsidized 170; title 246; tobacco 236
sport cities 138
Sport Mega-events (SMEs) 42–47, 138, 192
sport washing 43, 104, 106, 130, 143, 145–146, 148–153, 175, 232, 236, 242, 289

302 Index

sporting international non-governmental organizations (SINGOs) 192
sports: betting 116; *Diplomacy 2030* 263; industry 109, 121, 160, 263; investors 95; labour migration 86, 89; Stadium Diplomacy 95
stakeholders 2, 34, 38, 57, 81, 96, 142, 159, 165, 174, 227–228, 231, 237, 254, 256–257, 259, 289, 291
state branding 127, 129–130
Stockholm Consensus (2003) 279
Stoke Mandeville 68
streaming 81, 116, **117**, 119, 156, 218, 222
Sugden, J. P. 165
Summer Olympics 40, 67, 70, 131, 142, 198, 218, 264, 279–280
suppression of minority groups 148
sustainability 109, 112–113, 195
sustainable: development goals (SDGs) 232, 260; dialogue 257
Swidler, A. 272

taking the knee 2, 272–273
Team USA Council on Racial and Social Justice 10
terrorism 75, 81, 138, 203
Therapeutic Use Exemption (TUE) 277
Three Axe Strokes 93–95, 98
TIME 279
Tolstoy, L.N. 39
Tolstykh, N. 58
tourism 75, 80–81, 131, 138, 153, 195, 211–213, 245
transfer system 113
transgender: athletes 277–280, 282; framework 281; girls and boys 282; identity 280; inclusion framework 278; inclusion policy 280; men 278; people 278; policy 281; sport ; women 278, 280–281
True Path Party (DYP) 203
Trump, D. 96, 151, 191, 193–194, 272
trust 177, 231, 233, 253
Twenty20 World Cup 156

Union of European Football Associations (UEFA) 2, 24, 29, 43, 50, 53, **54**, 55–56, *57*, 61, 142, 165, 188, 204, 217–223, 288–290
United 2026 191, 193–197; bid book 193, 195, 198–199; bid organizers 193; bid partnership 192

United as One 191–195, 199
United Nations (UN) 30, 70, 188, 211, 228, 231, 254, 260; -controlled buffer zone 231; General Assembly (UNGA) 39, 178; Guiding Principles on Business and Human rights (UNGPs) 233; peacekeeping reports 260; resolution 21, 38; Security Council 38; sustainable development goals 260
Universal Declaration of Human Rights 30
universalism 11
urbanization 138
USA Rugby 278
USIP 266
USOC 38

violations 33, 77, 173
Vision 2030 130–131
Vondracek, H. 111
VTB United League 50–51, **52**, *57*, 59

Warsaw Pact 35
Waugh, S. 155
Wimbledon 13–14, 23, 238
Winter Olympics 1, 9, 21, 43, 50, 75, 78, **79**, 80–82, 88, 97, 105–106, 120, 158, 237
Winter Paralympics 1, 11, 67–68, **69**, 72, 75, **76**, **79**, 80, 82
Women's Tennis Association 2
World Anti-Doping Agency 70, 98
World Athletics 280–282; bans 281; Championships 130; rules 280
World Nines 266
World Olympians Association (WOA) 36
World Rugby 278, 281
World Tourism Organisation (UNWTO) 212
World War I 20
World War II 20, 68, 72, 228
World Weightlifting 130
World Wrestling Entertainment 143
Worldwide Olympic Partner Intel 80

xenophobia 274
Xue, H. 109

Yanukovic, V. 60

Zorya Luhansk 61